Expert Systems in Construction and Structural Engineering

Expert Systems in Construction and Structural Engineering

Edited by

PROFESSOR HOJJAT ADELI

The Ohio State University

LONDON NEW YORK

Chapman and Hall

First published in 1988 by Chapman and Hall Ltd
11 New Fetter Lane, London EC4P 4EE
Published in the USA by Chapman and Hall
29 West 35th Street, New York NY 10001

© Chapters 1–13, 15 1988 Chapman and Hall
Chapter 14 1988 G. Trimble

Printed in Great Britain by J.W. Arrowsmith Ltd, Bristol

ISBN 0 412 28910 5

British Library Cataloguing in Publication Data

Expert systems in construction and structural engineering.
1. Civil engineering 2. Expert systems
(Computer science)
I. Adeli, Hojjat
624'.028'5633 TA345

ISBN 0 412 28910 5

Library of Congress Cataloging in Publication Data

Expert systems in construction and structural engineering
edited by Hojjat Adeli.
p. cm.
Includes bibliographies and index.
ISBN 0 412 28910 5
1. Civil engineering—Data processing. 2. Structural engineering—
– Data processing. 3. Expert systems (Computer science) I. Adeli,
Hojjat, 1950–
TA345.E97 1988
624.1'128'5633—dc19 87–17192
CIP

*The editorial contribution of
this book is dedicated to
my father, Dr J. Adeli*

Contents

Preface

The early attempts to apply artificial intelligence and expert system technology to civil engineering problems have been mostly in the areas of construction and structural engineering, so that this book has been limited mostly to these areas. Some of the pioneering researchers in this field have contributed to the book.

The first four chapters are intended to introduce the reader to the rich and vast field of artificial intelligence in general, and to expert systems in particular. The reader should refer to the many fundamental and valuable publications given as references. The potential applications of expert system technology in civil engineering are enormous. I hope that this pioneering work will bring the significance of the subject to the attention of civil engineers and encourage more engineers and researchers to pursue this exciting area of technology, which is certain to have a great impact on the practice of civil engineering.

Hojjat Adeli

January, 1987
Columbus, Ohio

About Hojjat Adeli, Editor of *Expert Systems in Construction and Structural Engineering*

Born in 1950, Hojjat Adeli received his PhD from Stanford University in 1976. He taught at Northwestern University, the University of Tehran, and the University of Utah before joining the Ohio State University in July 1983. A contributor to 20 research journals, he has authored over 130 research and technical publications in various fields of structural engineering and mechanics, computer-aided design, software engineering, artificial intelligence, optimization, and earthquake engineering. He is the Editor-in-Chief of the international journal of *Microcomputers in Civil Engineering*. Professor Adeli is the author of the book *Interactive Microcomputer-Aided Structural Steel Design*, Prentice-Hall, 1988, and co-author of the book *Expert Systems for Structural Design – A New Generation*, to be published by Prentice-Hall in late 1988. He is an active member of professional organizations such as the American Association for Artificial Intelligence and the Association for Computing Machinery. He currently serves on fourteen committees of the American Society of Civil Engineers Aerospace, Engineering Mechanics, Materials Engineering, and Structural Engineering Divisions. He has been included in nine biographical listings, including *Who's Who in Frontiers of Science and Technology, 2000 Notable Americans, 5000 Personalities of the World, International Directory of Distinguished Leadership*, and *Who's Who in the World*. He is a 1987 recipient of American Biographical Institute Commemorative Medal of Honor.

Biographies of contributors

JESUS M. DE LA GARZA. Mr De La Garza is currently a PhD candidate in Civil Engineering at the University of Illinois, Urbana–Champaign, with emphasis on Construction Engineering and Management. He has also held research appointments with the US Army Corps of Engineers.

WEI-MIN DONG. Dr Dong received his PhD from Stanford University. He is currently an Acting Associate Professor in the Department of Civil Engineering at Stanford University. His interests include seismic design of buildings, structural reliability, and the application of artificial intelligence techniques to earthquake hazard mitigation and risk assessment.

STEVEN J. FENVES. Professor Fenves received his BS, MS, and PhD degrees from the University of Illinois at Urbana–Champaign, where he was on the faculty from 1961 to 1972. He is currently the Sun Company Professor of Civil Engineering at Carnegie–Mellon University. He was the Head of the Civil Engineering Department at Carnegie–Mellon from 1972 to 1975 and Director of the Design Research Center from 1980 to 1984. He is the author of over 200 publications. His research interests include design databases, representation and processing of design specifications, and knowledge-based expert systems for design, analysis assistance and design process integration.

GAVIN FINN. Mr Finn is an engineer in the Consulting Group at Stone & Webster Engineering Corporation (Boston, MA). He is involved in the development and implementation of AI computer programs, specifically expert systems. His responsibilities include the initiation of new expert system projects, interaction with technical expert in the knowledge-acquisition process, systems testing and verification, and software interface development. He has served as principal knowledge engineer for all of Stone & Webster's expert systems. Mr Finn holds a BA in Civil Engineering from Oklahoma State University, and an MS in Civil Engineering from MIT.

SHUICHI FUKUDA. Dr Fukuda is an Associate Professor at the Welding Research Institute of Osaka University, Japan. He is also a researcher at the Institute of Industrial Science at the University of Tokyo, where he received his doctorate in 1972. He has authored over 60 publications in Japanese and English. His current research interest is the application of artificial intelligence to the design and fabrication of welded structures.

JAMES H. GARRETT, Jr. Dr Garrett attended Carnegie–Mellon University from 1978 until 1986, where he received the degrees of BS, MS, and PhD in the field of Civil Engineering. He is currently an Assistant Professor of Civil Engineering at the University of Illinois, Urbana-Champaign. His research interests have been centred on the application of artificial intelligence techniques to engineering design. He has written several papers on the usage of knowledge-based system techniques for representing and processing design standards.

C. WILLIAM IBBS. Professor Ibbs received his PhD from the University of California, Berkeley in 1980. He is currently an Associate Professor of Civil Engineering at the University of California, Berkeley, and a leader of that school's Construction and Engineering Management Program. Before this appointment, he was a member of the University of Illinois Civil Engineering Dept. He was recently awarded the Presidential Young Investigator Award from the US National Science Foundation. Dr Ibbs is a member of several American Society of Civil Engineers national technical committees related to construction project control and computer applications. He has more than 25 scientific publications in print.

MARY LOU MAHER. Professor Maher is an Assistant Professor in the Department of Civil Engineering at Carnegie–Mellon University. She received her BS in Civil Engineering from Columbia University in 1979 and her MS and PhD in Civil Engineering from Carnegie–Mellon University in 1981 and 1984, respectively. Her PhD dissertation resulted in the widely-cited expert system HI-RISE. Her research interests include the broad spectrum of computer-aided engineering, including the use of expert systems, databases, and graphics in an integrated computer environment.

WANG PEIZHUANG. Professor Peizhuang is the Director of the Applied Mathematics Division, Beijing Normal University. He is also a visiting professor, Vice-President, and the Director of the Research Center on Fuzzy Information and Knowledge Engineering at Guangzhou University. Professor Peizhuang is also Vice-President of the Chinese Fuzzy Mathematics and Fuzzy Systems Association. He is a Co-Principal Editor of the Chinese

Journal of Fuzzy Mathematics and a member of several editorial boards of Chinese journals. He is the author of two books and more than 60 articles on fuzzy mathematics and probability theory.

WILLIAM J. RASDORF. Dr Rasdorf is an Associate Professor of Civil Engineering and Computer Science at North Carolina State University. He received his BS and MS degrees in Architectural Engineering from Pennsylvania State University and practiced as a consulting structural engineer designing commercial buildings. He then received MS and PhD degrees in Civil Engineering from Carnegie–Mellon University. Dr Rasdorf has been awarded a US National Science Foundation Presidential Young Investigator Award. His research interests include management of engineering databases, knowledge-based expert system development, and artificial intelligence applications in problem-solving, analysis, and design.

TIMOTHY J. ROSS. Dr Ross is currently an Associate Professor of Civil Engineering at the University of New Mexico in Albuquerque, New Mexico. Previously, Dr Ross served for 14 years in the US federal government as a Senior Research Engineer and a Program Manager. His research background is in the areas of structural failure, probability, and stochastic processes, assessment of engineering uncertainties, and expert systems. Professor Ross is a graduate of Stanford University (PhD), Rice University (MS), and Washington State University (BS).

HARESH C. SHAH. Professor Shah received his PhD from Stanford University in 1963. He is currently Chairman of the Department of Civil Engineering at Stanford University. He specializes in applying probability and reliability theories to structural and earthquake engineering, including the safety of buildings and dams. Professor Shah is the author of one book and more than 150 technical reports and papers. He has been a consultant to several governments around the world for developing building codes and earthquake design criteria. He has been on the board of directors of the Earthquake Engineering Research Institute and is listed in American Men of Science.

GEOFFREY TRIMBLE. Dr Trimble was appointed Professor of Construction Management at the University of Technology, Loughborough, United Kingdom in 1967. His research includes behavioural studies on the factors that promote success in the application of numerical techniques.

BRUCE R. WATSON. Dr Watson is an engineer with Information Control Technologies, Inc. of Alexandria, UA. He received a BS degree in Mechanical

Engineering from North Carolina State University and practiced as a manufacturing engineer in factory automation before returning to graduate school and receiving an ME in the Integrated Manufacturing Systems Engineering program at NCSU. His interests include factory automation, management of engineering data, expert system design, and the application of artificial intelligence techniques to engineering problems.

FELIX WONG. Dr Wong received his PhD from the California Institute of Technology. He is currently a senior associate of Palo-Alto (USA) based Weidlinger Associates, an engineering consulting firm. Dr Wong has over 15 years of consulting experience in structural dynamics, control and guidance, numerical analysis, earthquake engineering, and marine engineering. His research interests include the development and application of probabilistic and statistical techniques to geotechnical and structural systems, the application of fuzzy sets, and development of expert systems.

LIU XIHUI. Professor Xihui is a Senior Research Engineer of the Institute of Earthquake Engineering, Chinese Academy of Building Research. He is also a visiting professor at Guangzhou University and the Vice-Director of the Institute of Fuzzy Systems and Knowledge Engineering of that university. He has published more than 60 papers on earthquake engineering and fuzzy set theory and its applications. He was a co-organizer of the 1985 International Symposium on Fuzzy Mathematics in Earthquake Research and the co-editor of the two volumes *Fuzzy Mathematics in Earthquake Research.* He received the K.S. Fu Certificate of Appreciation from the North American Fuzzy Information Processing Society in 1985.

JAMES T.P. YAO. Professor Yao received his BSCE, MSCE and PhD from the University of Illinois, Urbana–Champaign in 1957, 1958 and 1961, respectively. From 1961 to 1964 and 1965 to 1971, he taught in the Department of Civil Engineering at the University of New Mexico. During the 1964–1965 academic year, he was a Postdoctoral Preceptor in the Department of Civil Engineering and Engineering Mechanics at Columbia University, New York. Since 1971, he has been a professor of Civil Engineering at Purdue University, West Lafayette, Indiana. Professor Yao has numerous publications in the areas of structures and probabilistic methods. He is currently the President of the North American Fuzzy Information Processing Society.

X.J. ZHANG. Mr Zhang is a graduate of Zhejiang University and is on leave as Lecturer on Civil Engineering. At present, he is a research instructor and doctoral student of Civil Engineering at Purdue University, Lafayette, Indiana.

Glossary

Attribute: A property or a characteristic of an object. The value of an attribute is a quantity or quality of that attribute. For example, the shape of the cross-section and cross-sectional area are two attributes of a steel hot-rolled beam. For an American Standard W27X102, the values of these attributes are W and 30 inch squares.

CAD: Computer-aided design.

CAI: Computer-aided instruction. Application of computers in education.

Certainty factor (CF): A numeric measure of confidence or belief in a fact.

Cognitive modeling: Development of theories and conceptual models for the human mind and its problem-solving abilities.

Confidence factor: Same as 'certainty factor'.

Context: Same as 'working memory'.

Deep knowledge: Knowledge of basic theories and established principles about a domain.

Demon: A hidden or virtual procedure in an expert system.

Domain knowledge: Knowledge of a specific area of application.

Dynamic memory allocation: The allocation of memory during run-time.

ES: Expert system.

Expert system: An 'intelligent' interactive computer program that can play the role of a human expert by using heuristic knowledge or rules of thumb.

Expert system shell: The expert system without the knowledge base, consisting of the inference mechanism and working memory, and perhaps other expert system development facilities.

Explanation facility: Part of the expert system that explains its line of reasoning. It explains how solutions are found and why certain questions are asked.

Frame: A method of knowledge representation consisting of a number of slots in which different characteristics and features of an object or a chunk of information are described. Slots can store values. They may contain default values, pointers to other frames, or procedures.

Global database: same as 'working memory'.

Heuristics: Rules of thumb or informal knowledge to improve the efficiency of search in a solution space.

Inference engine: Same as 'inference mechanism'.

Inference mechanism: Part of an ES that deduces new facts from known facts.

Knowledge acquisition facility: Part of the expert system that facilitates the structuring and development of the knowledge base.

Knowledge-based system: Same as 'expert system'.

Knowledge engineer: A person who is knowledgeable in AI techniques and builds a knowledge-based or ecpert system.

LISP: Short for *LIS*t *P*rocessing, an AI language based on list processing.

Long-term memory: The portion of the human memory that is used to store information that is not currently being used. This may be compared loosely to a computer's disk.

Machine learning: A branch of AI concerned with creating programs that can learn from experience.

Meta-rule: A rule about other rules.

MIPS: Millions of instructions per second.

Natural language processing system: A computer program that lets the user interact with the computer through a natural language such as English.

Object–attribute–value triplets: A special case of semantic network representation in which there are only three types of nodes, i.e. objects, attributes, and values. Objects can be physical or conceptual entities. Attributes are general properties or features of objects.

Parallel architecture: A computer in which several processors operate simultaneously.

Production rules: A method of knowledge representation consisting of a collection of rules with an IF part (or antecedent part) and a THEN part (or consequent part).

PROLOG: Short for *PRO*gramming in *LOG*ic, a symbolic or AI language based on formal logic and first order predicate calculus.

RAM: Random access memory.

Reasoning mechanism: Same as 'inference mechanism'.

Recursion: A function calling itself.

Robotics: A branch of artificial intelligence concerned primarily with developing computer software for controlling robots in a dynamic environment.

Semantic network: A method of knowledge representation consisting of a collection of nodes for representation of concepts, objects, events, etc., and links for connecting the nodes and characterizing their interrelationship.

Semantics: The meaning of an expression.

Shallow knowledge: Heuristic knowledge obtained through experience.

Shell: See 'expert system shell'.

Short-term memory: The portion of the human memory that is used to store information temporarily when one thinks about a subject or problem. This may be loosely compared to a computer's RAM.

Surface knowledge: Same as 'shallow knowledge'.

Syntax: The formal pattern or order of symbols in an expression.

User interface: The part of the computer program that stands between the user and the computer.

Value of an attribute: See 'attribute'.

Working memory: A temporary storage for the current state of a specific problem being solved.

1

Artificial intelligence and expert systems

HOJJAT ADELI

1.1 THE HUMAN MIND AND PROBLEM-SOLVING

The thinking of the human mind is an extremely complicated process. In modeling the information processing of the mind, separate short-term and long-term memories are identified. Data is continuously entered to the brain through the five sensory organs or sensors and stored in the short-term memory temporarily. The human mind filters this data, decides what is important, and stores the important information in the long-term memory in complicated networks of some kind. The information stored in the long-term memory is mostly in symbolic forms and patterns, i.e. objects and relationships among them. Research in human cognition suggests that this information is stored in the brain as clusters of symbols or chunks of information.

The human brain is slow in storing information. It takes approximately seven seconds to store a chunk of information in the long-term memory. This is the reason why it usually takes years to become an expert in a particular domain. On the other hand, the human brain is incredibly efficient in symbolic pattern recognition and retrieving the information stored in the long-term memory. The processing cycle for accessing a chunk of information is estimated at approximately 70 milliseconds (Townsend and Feucht, 1986).

As a very simple example of the pattern recognition and information retrieval capability of the human mind, read the following and then try to remember it:

Dlgnoe tgae gdrbie si a nspsnsuieo rbgdei

Now, do the same thing with the following:

Golden gate bridge is a suspension bridge

Needless to say, storing and retrieving the second piece of information is much faster than the first one.

For the second case, the reader clusters the information into seven chunks and therefore needs to remember only seven chunks of information. In contrast, in the first case he or she must remember 41 chunks of information. Research in human cognition suggests that the human brain can keep from four to seven chunks of information in short-term memory simultaneously. It is this pattern recognition and chunking of information that is used most effectively by an expert in a particular domain. Chess masters can duplicate the chess board by observing a game for a few seconds. They cannot simply memorize the positions of 32 pieces on a given board. Instead, they cluster the pieces into a few recognizable patterns of pieces. While the human mind is weak in numerical processing compared with the most simple calculator it can outperform the largest and fastest computers in symbolic processing and reasoning. Simulating the symbol processing ability of the human brain has been a subject of particular interest to people involved in developing intelligent machines.

1.2 ARTIFICIAL INTELLIGENCE

In 1950, Alan Turing gave the following definition for machine intelligence: a machine can be considered intelligent only if a human being communicating with the machine from a distance through a teletype cannot recognize whether he is communicating with a machine or human being. No computer at present can pass this so-called Turing test.

In a broad sense, artificial intelligence (AI) is a branch of computer science concerned with making computers act more like human beings. When one attempts to establish a more specific definition, however, one is bound to find various definitions partly due to AI being a young discipline. Some of these definitions are

1. AI is a branch of computer science concerned with symbolic reasoning and problem solving.
2. "A subfield of computer science concerned with the concepts and methods of symbolic inference by a computer and the symbolic representation of the knowledge to be used in making inferences. A field pursuing the possibilities that a computer can be made to behave in ways that humans recognize as 'intelligent' behavior in each other" (Feigenbaum and McCorduck, 1983).

Twelve other definitions of AI have been collected by Williamson (1986). Even here there is no universally accepted and coherent definition of intelligence. Over 100 different kinds of intelligence have been identified by psychologists and the well-known IQ tests measure only twelve of them.

AI research may be classified into seven categories as shown in Fig. 1.1. These categories clearly identify separate areas of research but are closely interrelated. For example, expert system developers use AI knowledge representation techniques and problem-solving approaches.

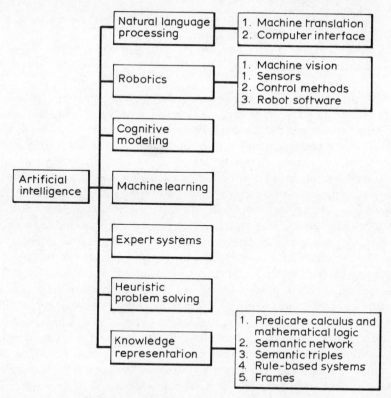

Fig. 1.1 Research in artificial intelligence (AI).

A natural language processing system is a computer program that lets the user interact with the computer through a natural language spoken by people, such as English. Research in natural language processing may be divided into two categories. The first category is concerned with understanding the written language, i.e. the syntax and semantics of the language. This is called natural language understanding. The second category deals with the spoken language by identifying various individual sounds.

A natural language processing system should be able to receive input in the context of the natural language, store knowledge in its domain of application, draw conclusions or inferences from the knowledge base, and generate responses (Harris, 1985). A natural language processing system has the following elements:

1. A lexicon or list of words.
2. A syntax for specifying the order of words in a sentence and rules of grammar.
3. A set of transformation rules for converting the user input into the system output.

4. Semantic analysis for determining the sense of words and sentences by themselves and in relation to others.
5. A parser whose role is to decompose a statement into its lexical items and determine its syntax.

Robotics is primarily concerned with developing computer software for controlling robots in a dynamic environment. The software guides the robot to move and 'see' or 'feel' the changes in its environment. Robots may be classified into fixed and mobile robots. Mobile robots may be wheeled vehicles, robot arms mounted on tracked vehicles such as a small tank, or with legs (two, four, or six legs). Robots have numerous potential applications in construction and manufacturing engineering such as machine loading and unloading, materials handling (e.g. packaging), fabrication (e.g. drilling, grinding, and application of glues, sealers, and caulking materials), spray painting, spot and arc welding, inspection, testing, and assembly line applications (Critchlow, 1985).

Cognitive modeling is concerned with the development of theories and conceptual models for the human mind and its problem-solving abilities. The research on cognitive modeling can lead to new problem-solving methods, diagnosis and treatment of mental diseases, and even new computer architectures. While the present common computer architecture has a serial architecture and is fundamentally different from that of the human brain, there is a renewed interest in exploring new parallel computer architectures that may eventually simulate the human brain. The brain's basic unit is the neuron. The total number of neurons in the human brain is estimated at 10 to 100 billion (Restak, 1984). Neurons communicate with each other through chemical and electrical processes in a highly distributed manner. The highly complex distributed processing of the brain may be imitated in future computer architectures (McClelland and Rumelhart, 1986; Rumelhart and McClelland, 1986).

Can computers learn by themselves or can they be taught to learn? This is the primary focus of researchers involved in the area of machine learning. Automatic learning is identified with true intelligence and thus is a highly desirable feature in intelligent machines or systems. During the early days of AI, there was considerable hope of simulating the learning ability of human beings by machines. The topic was dropped partly due to hardware limitations. But, with the recent development of powerful supercomputers and new parallel architectures, machine learning is again being pursued actively by AI researchers (Forsyth and Rada, 1986).

During the early days of AI in the sixties, AI researchers attempted to model the human thinking process by developing general problem solvers and general-purpose programs for solving broad classes of problem. This effort was not very successful even though it produced some interesting research results. In the seventies, AI researchers focused their attention on representation and search techniques, i.e. how to represent knowledge and to search for a solution in order to solve the problem most efficiently. It was around the mid-seventies that AI researchers started to realize that the problem-solving ability of humans lies basically in their *knowledge of a particular domain and not so much in the inferential mechanism they use.* In other words, it was concluded that a computer program should contain a large domain-specific knowledge base in order to be able to solve complex real word problems and thus become intelligent (Waterman, 1986).

1.3 EXPERT SYSTEMS

Computer programs using AI techniques to assist people in solving difficult problems involving knowledge, heuristics, and decision-making are called expert systems, intelligent systems, or smart systems. An expert system is an 'intelligent' interactive computer program that can play the role of a human expert by using heuristic knowledge or rules of thumb. The heuristics are usually accumulated by a human expert over a number of years. Using heuristics, an expert system can make educated guesses, recognize promising approaches, and avoid blind search; and consequently it can narrow down the search process in a solution space.

Various other interpretations and definitions of expert systems (ES) can be found in the AI literature. For example:

1. "An intelligent computer program that uses knowledge and inference procedure to solve problems that are difficult enough to require significant human expertise for their solution" (Feigenbaum, 1981).
2. "An interactive computer program incorporating judgement, experience, rules of thumb, intuition, and other expertise to provide knowledgeable advice about a variety of tasks" (Gaschnig *et al.*, 1981).
3. "An expert system solves real-world, complex problems using a complex model of expert human reasoning, reaching the same conclusions that the human expert would reach if faced with a comparable problem" (Weiss and Kulikowski, 1984).

Hayward (1985) discusses the difficulties in defining expert systems including the exploratory nature of the ES development techniques. The boundary between conventional data processing and the ES approach is subject to interpretation. While some classic AI expert systems such as DENDRAL (see Section 1.8.1) solve the problem of combinatorial explosion using heuristics, some other early expert systems such as MYCIN (see Section 1.8.2), PROSPECTOR (see Section 1.8.3), and XCON (see Section 1.8.5) do not handle a large search problem but use specialized knowledge in their respective domains. Hayward (1985) suggests that the significance of these systems lies in the translation of the expert's knowledge in a computable form. In Section 1.4 we will try to delineate the differences between the traditional computer programs and expert systems.

There is also a fundamental difference between the current successfully implemented expert systems (see Section 1.8) which are mainly based on heuristic knowledge (called surface knowledge in AI terminology) and the expert systems for most engineering applications. Any significant engineering ES most probably must rely on well-established theories and principles (called deep knowledge in AI terminology) requiring numerical computations in addition to heuristics. Thus, interaction of numerical data processing and AI technologies becomes an imperative consideration for developing expert systems in most engineering domains.

Very few true 'expert systems' exist today. There are only a few systems that have been reported to perform rather close to a human expert (see Section 1.8). Expert system technology is still in its infancy. A more appropriate name for them may be knowledge-based systems or intelligent assistants. In this book, however, we refer to them as expert systems. Aside from being brief, this name also conveys a very important idea behind this technology, i.e. simulating the valuable expertise of human experts. In other words, while today's expert systems may be primitive they are expected to mature in the forthcoming years and approach what should in fact be called expert systems.

Finally, the present prevalent definition of expert systems presented in this section is based on the fundamental premise that the knowledge necessary in the expert system can be obtained from human domain experts or documented materials developed by them. In the opinion of the author, this definition of an expert system should be extended. For the solution of complex engineering problems, the knowledge base of an expert system may contain knowledge obtained via machine intelligence or learning, in addition to heuristic knowledge obtained from human sources. An example of this type of expert system is presented in Section 5.2.5.

1.4 CONVENTIONAL PROGRAMS VERSUS EXPERT SYSTEMS

The following differences may be found between traditional computer programs and expert systems (Adeli, 1986):

1. Expert systems are knowledge-intensive programs.
2. Expert systems use heuristics in a specific domain of knowledge in order to improve the efficiency of search.
3. In an expert system expert knowledge is usually divided into many separate independent rules or entities. The knowledge representation is transparent, i.e. rather easy to read and understand.
4. The knowledge base used in an expert system is usually separated from the

methods for applying the knowledge to the current problem. These methods are referred to as the inference mechanism.

5. Expert systems are usually highly interactive.
6. The output of an expert system can be qualitative rather than quantitative.
7. Expert systems tend to mimic the decision-making and reasoning process of human experts. They can provide advice, answer questions, and justify their conclusions.

1.5 ARCHITECTURE OF AN EXPERT SYSTEM

An ES has three main components (Fig. 1.2):

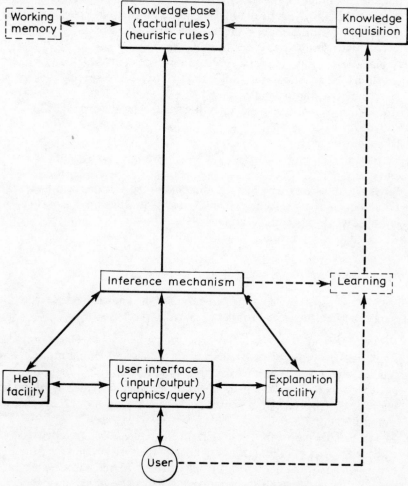

Fig. 1.2 Components of an expert system.

1. Knowledge base. It is the repository of information available in a particular domain. The knowledge base may consist of well-established and documented definitions, facts, and rules, as well as judgemental information, rules of thumb, and heuristics.
2. Inference mechanism (also known as inference engine or reasoning mechanism). It controls the reasoning strategy of the ES by making assertions, hypotheses, and conclusions. In rule-based systems (to be described in Chapter 2), for example, the inference mechanism determines the order in which rules should be invoked and resolves any conflict among the rules when several rules are satisfied.
3. Working memory (also known as context or global database). It is a temporary storage for the current state of specific problem being solved. Its content changes dynamically and includes information provided by the user about the problem and the information derived by the system.
   The other desirable features of an ES are:
4. Explanation facility. It provides answers to questions (e.g. why a certain question is being asked) and justifies answers (e.g. why a specific conclusion or recommendation is made).
5. Knowledge acquisition. It facilitates the structuring and development of the knowledge base.
6. Debugging facility.
7. Help facility. It helps and guides the user how to use the system effectively and easily.
8. Intelligent interfaces. The user interface allows the user to interact with the ES and query the ES. It may include natural language processors, menus, multiple windows, icons or graphics.
9. Knowledge base editors.

1.6 ADVANTAGES OF EXPERT SYSTEMS

Advantages of expert systems and separation of the knowledge base from the inference mechanism are (Andriole, 1985; Adeli, 1986):

1. Knowledge is more explicit, accessible, and expandable. One can find a similarity between expert systems and the human reasoning process. The human mind absorbs new information without disturbing the knowledge already stored in the brain or affecting the way in which it processes information. The same argument applies to modifying information already stored in the brain.
2. The knowledge base can be gradually and incrementally developed over an extended period of time. The modularity of the system allows continuous expansion and refinement of the knowledge base. In rule-based systems, for example, any rule can be deleted or new rules can be added independently and the ES is ready to be used without any other modification.

3. A general system with one inference mechanism can be developed for different types of applications simply by changing the knowledge base.
4. The same knowledge may be used in different problems by possibly employing different inference mechanisms. For example, if a design specification such as the AISC specification (AISC, 1980) for structural steel design is put into such a knowledge base it may be used directly for the design of different types of structures.
5. An ES can explain its behavior through an explanation facility.
6. An ES can check the consistency of its knowledge entities or rules and point out the faulty ones through a debugging facility.
7. An ES is not biased and does not make cursory or irrational decisions. It uses a systematic approach for finding the answer to the problem.

The use of expert systems results in a more effective, accurate, and consistent distribution of expertise. There are also side benefits from developing expert systems and performing research in this area:

1. Understanding the problem-solving ability and the reasoning process of human experts.
2. Accumulation and codification of knowledge in a particular domain.
3. Better articulation, representation, and utilization of knowledge.

1.7 LIMITATIONS OF EXPERT SYSTEMS

At the present stage of technology, the following limitations may be noted for expert systems:

1. They do not learn.
2. They lack common sense and intuition.
3. Their performance degenerates fast near the boundaries of their expertise.
4. Most expert systems today lack a user-friendly natural language interface and are not easy to use by non-experts.
5. Many of them require expensive dedicated AI machines for efficient operation. This limitation is gradually being overcome by the availability of powerful microcomputers (see Chapter 4).
6. Capturing rare expertise remains a problem. This area deserves special attention by engineering researchers and experts.
7. They are suitable for problems involving deduction and not so much for problems involving induction or analogy.

1.8 EXAMPLES OF SUCCESSFUL APPLICATIONS OF EXPERT SYSTEM TECHNOLOGY

In the following sections, we briefly describe several successful applications of expert system technology.

1.8.1 DENDRAL

Developed in the early and mid-1970s at Stanford University, DENDRAL is an ES for identifying the molecular structure of organic compounds from mass spectral and nuclear magnetic response data (Lindsay *et al.*, 1980). DENDRAL uses heuristic rules to prune the very large possibilities for the molecular structure of an unknown compound.

1.8.2 MYCIN

Developed at Stanford University in the mid-1970s, MYCIN is designed to help physicians in the diagnosis and treatment of meningitis (inflammation of the membrane enveloping the brain and spinal cord) and bacteremia infections (involving bacteria in the blood) (Shortliffe, 1976; Buchanan and Shortliffe, 1984). The knowledge base of MYCIN contains about 450 rules. MYCIN is the first major ES to perform at the level of a human expert and to explain to the user its reasoning process. Various evaluations made at Stanford University indicate that MYCIN is as good as most highly skilled specialists of infectious diseases (Harmon and King, 1985). It is of interest to note that MYCIN was developed over a period of five years with an estimated manpower of 50 man-years.

1.8.3 PROSPECTOR

Developed at Stanford Research Institute in the late 1970s, PROSPECTOR is a diagnostic ES for mineral exploration (Duda *et al.*, 1979; Gaschnig, 1982). It imitates the reasoning process of an experienced exploration geologist for finding an ore deposit in a particular region. Geologists primarily use surface geological observations which are usually uncertain and incomplete. PROSPECTOR uses production rules and plausible reasoning. The knowledge base of PROSPECTOR contains about 1600 rules. Bayesian probability is used for treating uncertainties in information and rules on the field evidence and geological data. This ES has revealed a molybdenum deposit in the state of Washington whose value is estimated at millions of dollars (Hayes-Roth *et al.*, 1983).

1.8.4 CADUCEUS (formerly named INTERNIST)

CADUCEUS is an expert system for the diagnosis of diseases of internal medicine (Pople, 1982). It contains more knowledge than a human internist and can diagnose complex test cases which puzzle the human experts. The knowledge base of CADUCEUS includes about 500 diseases, 350 disease manifestations, and 100 000 symptomatic associations. It contains over 15 000 rules and covers some 25% of diseases of internal medicine. The developers of CADUCEUS are still working on this most ambitious ES development project.

1.8.5 XCON

Originally called R1, XCON (short for expert configurer) designs the configuration of VAX-11/780 computer components for the Digital Equipment Corporation (DEC) according to the requests of a customer (Kraft, 1984). Developed in the OPS5 environment, a production system programming language developed at Carnegie–Mellon University (see Section 3.7), XCON includes about 800 rules concerning the properties of some 400 VAX computer components. DEC usually sells one-of-a-kind custom-made computer systems. XCON takes a client's order as input. Its output is a set of diagrams displaying relationship among different components of the computer system. A technician uses these diagrams to assemble the whole system. Compared with conventional programs, this system can incorporate the frequent changes much more efficiently.

REFERENCES

Adeli, H. (1986) Artificial intelligence in structural engineering. *Engineering Analysis*, **3**, No. 3, 154–160.

AISC (1980) *Manual of Steel Construction*, American Institute of Steel Construction, Chicago, Illinois.

Andriole, S.J. (ed.) (1985) *Applications in Artificial Intelligence*, Petrocelli Books, Princeton.

Buchanan, B.G. and Shortliffe, E.H. (1984) *Rule-Based Expert Systems – The MYCIN Experiments of the Stanford Heuristic Programming Project*, Addison-Wesley, Reading, Massachusetts.

Critchlow, A.J. (1985) *Introduction to Robotics*, Macmillan Publishing Company, New York.

Duda, R.O., Hart, P.E., Barrett, P., Gaschnig, J., Konolige, K., Reboh, R. and Slocum, J. (1979) Development of the PROSPECTOR System for Mineral Exploration, Final Report, SRI Projects 5821 and 6415, Stanford Research Institute, Menlo Park, California.

Feigenbaum, E. (1981) Expert Systems in the 80's, in *Machine Intelligence* (ed. A. Bond).

Feigenbaum, E.A. and McCorduck, P. (1983) *The Fifth Generation*, Addison-Wesley, Reading, Massachusetts.

Forsyth, R. and Rada, R. (1986) *Machine Learning: Applications in Expert Systems and Information Retrieval*, Halsted Press, New York.

Gaschnig, J. (1982) PROSPECTOR: an expert system for mineral exploration, in *Introductory Readings in Expert Systems* (ed. D. Mitchie), Gordon and Breach Science Publishers, New York.

Gaschnig, J., Reboh, R. and Reiter, J. (1981) Development of a Knowledge-Based

System for Water Resources Problems, SRI Project 1619, Stanford Research Institute, Menlo Park, California.

Harmon, P. and King, D. (1985) *Artificial Intelligence in Business*, John Wiley, New York.

Harris, M.D. (1985) *Introduction to Natural Language Processing*, Reston, Reston, Virginia.

Hayes-Roth, F., Waterman, D.A. and Lenat, D. (eds) (1983) *Building Expert Systems*, Addison-Wesley, Reading, Massachusetts.

Hayward, S.A. (1985) Is a decision tree an expert system, in *Research and Development in Expert Systems* (ed. M.A. Bramer), Cambridge University Press, Cambridge, UK.

Kraft, A. (1984) XCON: an expert configuration system at Digital Equipment Corporation, in *The AI Business: The Commercial Uses of Artificial Intelligence* (eds P.H. Winston and K.A. Prendergast) The MIT Press, Cambridge, Massachusetts.

Lindsay, R.K., Buchanan, B.G., Feigenbaum, E.A. and Lederberg, J. (1980) *Applications of Artificial Intelligence for Organic Chemistry – The DENDRAL Project*, McGraw-Hill, New York.

McClelland, J.L. and Rumelhart, D.E. (eds) (1986) *Parallel Distributed Processing – Explorations in the Microstructure of Cognition. Volume 2: Psychological and Biological Models*, The MIT Press, Cambridge, Massachusetts.

McCorduck, P. (1979) *Machines Who Think*, W.H. Freeman, New York.

Pople, H.E., Jr., (1982) Heuristic methods for imposing structure on ill-structured problems: the structure of medical diagnosis, in *Artificial Intelligence in Medicine* (ed. P. Szolovits), Westview Press, Boulder, Colorado.

Restak, R.M. (1984) *The Brain*, Bantam Books, New York.

Rumelhart, D.E. and McClelland, J.L. (eds) (1986) *Parallel Distributed Processing – Explorations in the Microstructure of Cognition. Volume 1: Foundations*, The MIT Press, Cambridge, Massachusetts.

Shortliffe, E. (1976) *Computer-Based Medical Consultation*, Elsevier, New York.

Townsend, C. and Feucht, D. (1986) *Designing and Programming Personal Expert Systems*, TAB Books, Blue Ridge Summit, Philadelphia.

Waterman, D.A. (1986) *A Guide to Expert Systems*, Addison-Wesley, Reading, Massachusetts.

Weiss, S.M. and Kulikowski, C.A. (1984) *A Practical Guide to Designing Expert Systems*, Rowman and Allanheld Publishers, Totowa, New Jersey.

Williamson, M. (1986) *Artificial Intelligence for Microcomputers – The Guide for Business Decision Makers*, Brady Communications, New York.

Winston, P.H. (1984) *Artificial Intelligence*, Addison-Wesley, Reading, Massachusetts.

2

AI techniques and the development of expert systems

HOJJAT ADELI

2.1 BASIC STEPS FOR THE DEVELOPMENT OF AN EXPERT SYSTEM

The major steps in development of an expert system are (Harmon and King, 1985):

1. Selection of an expert system programming language, environment or shell
2. Selection of AI techniques for representation and inference mechanism
3. Analysis, acquisition, and conceptualization of the knowledge to be included in the knowledge base
4. Formalization and development of the knowledge base
5. Development of a prototype system using the knowledge base and AI tools
6. Evaluation, review, and expansion of the expert systems
7. Refinement of the user interface
8. Maintenance and updating of the system.

The traditional way of developing an ES assumes that an AI specialist called a knowledge engineer cooperates with one or a group of domain expert(s) knowledgeable about the particular domain (Hayes-Roth *et al.*, 1983). The knowledge engineer must first make himself or herself familiar with the application domain and then try to acquire, compile, organize, and formalize the domain expert's knowledge mostly through interviews.

As more engineers learn about AI tools and techniques the present philosophy does not seem to be the most effective one for development of expert systems in engineering. Familiarity of a conventional knowledge engineer with a particular engineering domain may not be achieved easily. In other words, explaining the knowledge of an engineering domain to a knowledge engineer can be difficult. Thus, it appears that most of the engineering expert systems will be developed by engineers knowledgeable in their domain as well as ES development tools and techniques. These engineers will substantiate and complement the knowledge base of the ES by consulting other highly knowledgeable domain experts.

2.2 KNOWLEDGE REPRESENTATION

There are two fundamentally different approaches to knowledge represent-ation. They are procedural representation and declarative representation. Procedural representation is commonly used in traditional algorithmic programming and has the advantage of being very efficient. In this type of representation, however, knowledge is context dependent and embedded in the code. The result is an opaque knowledge, making it unintelligible and difficult to modify.

In declarative representation, knowledge is encoded as data and is therefore more understandable, easier to modify, and context independent. While semantics in procedural representation are distributed over the code, in declarative representation they are collected in one place. Thus, we can summarize the advantages of declarative knowledge representation as (a) ease of comprehension, (b) ease of modification, (c) context independence, and (d) semantic transparency. These characteristics are essential in expert systems. Thus, expert systems usually use declarative knowledge representation. In engineering applications where substantial numerical computation is invol-ved, a hybrid procedural–declarative knowledge representation appears to be the best solution.

Several approaches for declarative representation of knowledge are avail-able in the AI literature (Brachman and Levesque, 1985; O'Shea and Eisenstadt, 1984; Hayes-Roth *et al.*, 1983). The major ones are

1. Formal methods based on the predicate calculus and mathematical logic
2. Semantic networks
3. Semantic triples (object–attribute–value triplets)
4. Rule-based or production systems, and
5. Frames consisting of generic data structures in predefined information categories called slots.

2.2.1 Semantic networks

Semantic networks consist of a collection of nodes for representation of concepts, objects, events, etc., and links for connecting the nodes and characterizing their interrelationship. An advantage of this representation method is its flexibility which means new nodes and links may be added whenever needed. Another characteristic of semantic networks is inheritance. That is, each node can inherit the characteristics of its connected nodes. A good account of semantic networks is presented in Nilsson (1982). For an example of a semantic network, see Fig. 6.7.

2.2.2 Object–attribute–value triplets

Semantic triples or object–attribute–value (OAV) triplets represent a special case of semantic networks in which there are only three types of nodes, i.e. objects, attributes, and values. Objects can be physical or conceptual entities. Attributes are general properties or features of objects. The value determines the particular character of an attribute in a specified situation. While semantic networks may have complicated links the object–attribute–value triplets use only two simple relationships, i.e. the object–attribute link and the attribute–value link.

Table 2.1 shows an example of OAV triplet (Adeli and Paek, 1988). In this example, the object is W-shape. It has 18 attributes. They are the name (designation) of the object and its various cross-sectional properties.

2.2.3 Production rules

The production system has been the most favorable representation approach for building computer expert systems. A production system is a collection of

Table 2.1 An OAV representation for properties of a W-shape

W-shape	
Attributes	*Value*
Name:	W36X300
Cross sectional area (A):	88.3
Depth (d):	36.74
Web thickness (t_w):	0.945
Flange width (b_f):	16.655
Flange thickness (t_f):	1.68
Distance from outer face of flange to web toe of fillet (k):	2.8125
Radius of gyration of a section comprising the compression flange plus 1/3 of the compression web area, taken about an axis in the plane of the web (r_T):	4.39
d/A_f:	1.31
Moment of inertia about the strong axis (I_x):	20300
Section modulus about the strong axis (S_x):	1110
Radius of gyration about the strong axis (r_x):	15.2
Moment of inertia about the weak axis (I_y):	1300
Section modulus about the weak axis (S_y):	156
Radius of gyration about the weak axis (r_y):	3.83
Torsional constant (J):	64.2
Plastic modulus about the strong axis (Z_x):	1260
Plastic modulus about the weak axis (Z_y):	241

rules which consist of an IF part and a THEN part or antecedent–consequent or situation–action parts (left-hand side and right-hand side parts). The general form for the rules is

Rule N
IF [(antecedent 1)--(antecedent n)]
THEN [(consequent 1 with certainty c_1)---
        (consequent m with certainty c_m)]

The rule number is a unique number for identifying the rule. The value of this number does not specify the order of application of the rule. Each rule represents an independent chunk of knowledge. Antecedents can be considered as patterns and consequents as conclusions or actions to be taken. The antecedent part of a rule is matched with the content of the working memory. When all the conditions in the antecedent part are satisfied the rule is fired. Examples of production rules can be found in Sections 5.2.2, 5.3.4, 5.4.1, and 5.4.3.

Certainty factors will be discussed in Section 2.3.1. Production rules facilitate the generation of explanations because the antecedent–consequent or IF–THEN rules can easily be transformed into questions.

2.2.4 Frames

Frame systems are suitable for more complex and richer representation of knowledge. A frame consists of a number of attributes, called slots, in which different characteristics and features of an object or a chunk of information are described. Slots can store values. They may contain default values, pointers to other frames, or procedures. The procedures may determine the values of slots. In other words, a procedure consists of a set of instructions for determining the value of a slot. This is called procedural attachment. For an example of a frame representation, see Section 11.2.4.

2.2.5 Mathematical logic

The most basic logical system is propositional logic. Each basic element of the system, or proposition, can be either true or false. The propositions can be connected to each other by using the connectives AND, OR, NOT, EQUIVALENT, IMPLIES, etc.

A problem with propositional logic is that it is not possible to reason about the items within the proposition. An extension of propositional logic is predicate calculus in which propositions can contain variables. For examples of logic representation, see Section 11.2.3.

2.3 REPRESENTING UNCERTAINTY IN THE KNOWLEDGE BASE

Various methods have been used to deal with uncertain or incomplete information in the knowledge base. Some of these methods are described briefly in the following sections. Further discussion of representing uncertainty is presented in Section 9.4.2.

2.3.1 Certainty factors

Certainty factors were first used in MYCIN, a medical ES introduced in Section 1.8.2. Certainty factors are attached to rules in rule-based systems. Each rule is assigned a certainty factor usually in the range -1 to 1 (or 0 to 1 or 0 to 100). Certainty factors indicate the level of confidence in a piece of information. They are simply informal measures of confidence and not probabilities. Simple rules are used to combine the uncertainties in various pieces of information. In MYCIN, for example, the following formulae are used (Buchanan and Shortliffe, 1984):

$$CF(X, Y) = \begin{cases} CF(X) + CF(Y) - CF(X)CF(Y) & CF(X) \text{ and } CF(Y) > 0 \\ \dfrac{CF(X) + CF(Y)}{1 - \min[|CF(X)|, |CF(Y)|]} & CF(X) < 0 \text{ } or \text{ } CF(Y) < 0 \\ -CF(-X, -Y) & CF(X) \text{ and } CF(Y) < 0 \end{cases}$$

where $CF(X)$ is the certainty factor for evidence or fact X, $CF(Y)$ is the certainty factor for evidence Y, and $CF(X, Y)$ is the combined certainty factor. Note that the range of certainty factors in the above equations is -1 (for total belief) to -1 (for total disbelief). There is a similarity between the above rule and the probability of joint events in the probability theory. The certainty factor is increased with the number of pieces of evidence.

2.3.2 Bayes theorem

Bayes theorem is well known in statistics and probability literature (Benjamin and Cornell, 1970). It provides a method for calculating the probabilities of an event or fact based on the knowledge of prior probabilities. The difficulty in using Bayes theorem is that in order to obtain the probability of a conclusion the probabilities of observed facts must be independent.

2.3.3 Fuzzy logic

Quite often information available about a problem domain may not be expressed in crisp true or false form. In other words, there may be vagueness or fuzziness in the knowledge. The theory of fuzzy sets originated by Zadeh (1975) can be used to present information with unsharp or 'gray' boundaries. In the crisp set theory, an element is either in the set or not in the set. Thus, it may be said that the membership degree of the element in the set is binary, that is either one or zero. The notion of membership degree is generalized in the theory of fuzzy sets. In this theory, an element may be in a set with a degree of membership between 0 and 1. Therefore, a fuzzy set consists of a number of elements with assigned degrees of membership. The degrees of membership are collectively called the membership function.

Development of proper and reliable membership functions appears to be the primary obstacle for application of the theory of fuzzy sets to practical civil engineering problems at present. Several researchers have attempted to formalize the development of membership functions. Saaty (1986) presents a hierarchical approach to scaling the membership function. Cinvanlar and Trussell (1986) use statistical data to construct membership functions. Application of fuzzy sets in expert systems is presented in Chapters 9–12.

2.4 INFERENCE MECHANISMS

A number of different heuristic problem-solving paradigms are available in the AI literature, for example, the describe-and-match paradigm, the goal-reduction paradigm, generate-and-test systems, means–ends analysis, back-tracking, and rule-based (production) systems (Barr and Feigenbaum, 1981 and 1982; Cohen and Feigenbaum, 1982; Rich, 1983; O'Shea and Eisenstadt, 1984; Winston, 1984; Charniak and McDermott, 1985; Brownston *et al.*, 1985). Some of these approaches overlap or can be used in conjunction with each other.

The majority of knowledge-based expert systems developed so far are based on the production system paradigm. These expert systems generally have the advantages described in Section 1.6. Another advantage of the production system paradigm is its suitability for parallel computations because pieces of a production system can execute independently. A production system consists of three main elements:

1. A set of IF–THEN rules or knowledge base
2. A global database or working memory, and
3. An inference mechanism.

Notwithstanding its simplicity the production system represents a powerful model for human information processing and problem-solving ability. Rule-based deduction systems can explain how and why they perform certain actions and they can evaluate their outcomes and results. They can handle unplanned but helpful interactions. In other words, they can utilize a portion of knowledge whenever suitable or necessary not just whenever the programmer foresees that it may be useful.

How are the rules found from the knowledge base and which rules shall be used? In order to answer this question we need to choose an inference mechanism or a control strategy which is the heart of an expert system. The inference mechanism fires rules according to its built-in reasoning process. The two main inference mechanisms are forward-chaining and backward-chaining.

1. Forward-chaining (aka antecedent reasoning and data-driven control strategy). In this inference mechanism, rules are scanned until one is found whose antecedents (left-hand sides) match the information for the problem entered in the working memory. Then, the rule is applied and the working memory is updated. This process is repeated until the goal state is achieved or no usable rule is found. If the goal state is not known and has to be constructed or the number of possible outcomes is large then the forward-chaining mechanism is often recommended. Complex planning problems can be tackled by this approach.
2. Backward-chaining (aka consequent reasoning and goal-driven strategy). In this inference mechanism, rules are scanned and those whose consequent actions can lead to the goal are found. For each of these rules a check is made whether its antecedents match the information in the working memory. If they all match the rule is applied and the problem is solved. If there exists an unmatched antecedent a new subgoal is defined as 'arrange conditions to match that antecedent'. This process is applied recursively. If the values of goal state are known and their number is small then backward-chaining seems to be quite efficient. Backward-chaining is often employed in diagnostic expert systems.
3. A combination of backward-chaining and forward-chaining (the hybrid approach). This approach can be utilized through the use of the 'blackboard' environment. The blackboard will keep track of the simultaneous application of forward and backward reasoning chains.

The blackboard model of problem solving and the evolution of blackboard architecture are presented in two recent articles by Nii (1986a and b). The blackboard model is a structured type of opportunistic reasoning model in which chunks of knowledge are used backward or forward at the best opportunity. The knowledge necessary for solving the problem is divided into independent groups of rules called knowledge sources. The blackboard, a central global database, plays as a communication vehicle among knowledge sources and keeps track of incremental changes made in the problem state until a solution is found.

The blackboard concept was first implemented in HEARSAY-II, a speech understanding system developed by Reddy *et al.* (1973). More recently, the blackboard architecture has been used in HASP, a knowledge-based system for detecting submarines by interpreting continuous sonar signals passively collected through hydrophone arrays monitoring an ocean (Nii, 1986a).

2.5 KNOWLEDGE ACQUISITION

In an engineering problem, knowledge can be well-established equations, graphs, tables of data, algorithmic analysis procedures, and experiential knowledge. Various types of experiential knowledge may be recognized such as the steps to be followed for solving a problem, use of the right equation or data, and use of the proper application programs. Considering the increasing availability of powerful ES development environments or shells, knowledge acquisition and encoding is appearing as the most time-consuming part of developing an ES.

In developing an ES for an engineering problem, knowledge may be acquired through various means:

1. Technical literature (books, manuals, journal articles, etc.). For example, the knowledge in HI-RISE has been acquired from a textbook (see Chapter 6).
2. Interviews with domain experts. This can be in the form of questions and answers and example problem-solving sessions. The two methods complement each other. In the latter case, the expert will be asked to solve example cases.
3. Questionnaires sent to the experts.
4. Experimentation. Sometimes, the knowledge necessary to solve a problem may be partly obtained through numerical or other types of machine experimentation (Adeli, 1987). Once the necessary knowledge for solving a particular problem is obtained it can be used in a knowledge base for solving similar problems in the future.

The last method of knowledge acquisition has not been used in traditional expert systems where knowledge is basically acquired from domain experts. However, knowledge acquisition through machine experimentation appears to be useful in certain complex domains of engineering such as structural optimisation (see Section 5.2.5). For further discussion of knowledge acquisition, see Chapter 14.

REFERENCES

Adeli, H. (1987) Knowledge acquisition in expert systems for structural design, *Proceedings of the International Symposium on Fuzzy Systems and Knowledge Engineering*, Guangzhou, Guiyang, China.

Adeli, H. and Paek, Y. (1988) Representation of Design Knowledge in a Symbolic Language, to be published.

Barr, A. and Feigenbaum, E.A. (1981) *The Handbook of Artificial Intelligence*, Vol. 1, William Kaufman, Los Altos, California.

Barr, A. and Feigenbaum, E.A. (1982) *The Handbook of Artificial Intelligence*, Vol. 2, William Kaufman, Los Altos, California.

Benjamin, J.R. and Cornell, C.A. (1970) *Probability, Statistics, and Decision for Civil Engineers*, McGraw-Hill, New York.

Brachman, R.J. and Levesque, H.J. (1985) *Readings in Knowledge Representation*, Morgan Kaufman, Los Altos, California.

Brownston, L., Farrell, R., Kant, E. and Martin, N. (1985) *Programming Expert Systems in OPS5 – An Introduction to Rule-Based Programming*, Addison-Wesley, Reading, Massachusetts.

Buchanan, B.G. and Shortliffe, E.H. (eds) (1984) *Rule-Based Expert Systems – The MYCIN Experiments of the Stanford Heuristic Programming Project*, Addison-Wesley, Reading, Massachusetts.

Charniak, E. and McDermott, D. (1985) *Introduction to Artificial Intelligence*, Addison-Wesley, Reading, Massachusetts.

Cinvanlar, M.R. and Trussell, H.J. (1986) Constructing membership functions using statistical data. *Fuzzy Sets and Systems*, **18**, No. 1, 1–14.

Cohen, P.R. and Feigenbaum, E.A. (eds) (1982) *The Handbook of Artificial Intelligence*, Vol. 3, William Kaufman, Los Altos, California.

Harmon, P. and King, D. (1985) *Artificial Intelligence in Business – Expert Systems*, John Wiley, New York.

Hayes-Roth, F., Waterman, D.A. and Lenat, D. (1983) An overview of expert systems, in *Building Expert Systems* (eds F. Hayes-Roth, D.A. Waterman and D.B. Lenat), Addison-Wesley, Reading, Massachusetts.

Nii, H.P. (1986a) Blackboard systems: the blackboard model of problem solving and the evolution of blackboard architecture. *AI Magazine*, **7**, No. 2, 38–53.

Nii, H.P. (1986b) Blackboard application systems, blackboard systems from a knowledge engineering perspective. *AI Magazine*, **7**, No. 3, 82–106.

Nilsson, N. (1982) *Principles of Artificial Intelligence*, Springer-Verlag, Berlin.

O'Shea, T. and Eisenstadt, M. (1984) *Artificial Intelligence – Tools, Techniques, and Applications*, Harper and Row, New York.

Reddy, D.R., Erman, L.D. and Neely, R.B. (1973) The HEARSAY speech understanding system: an example of the recognition process, *Proceedings of the International Joint Conference on Artificial Intelligence*, Tokyo, pp. 185–93.

Rich, E. (1983) *Artificial Intelligence*, McGraw-Hill, New York.

Saaty, T.L. (1986) Scaling the membership function. *European Journal of Operational Research*, **25**, No. 3, 320–9.

Winston, P.H. (1984) *Artificial Intelligence*, 2nd edn, Addison-Wesley, Reading, Massachusetts.

Zadeh, L.A. (1975) Fuzzy logic and approximate reasoning. *Syntheses*, **30**, 407–28.

3

AI languages and programming environments

HOJJAT ADELI

3.1 CLASSIFICATION OF COMPUTER SOFTWARE

Computer software can be classified into six levels as shown in Table 3.1. At the lowest level is the machine language consisting of binary digits 0 and 1. At the next level, an operating system is the software that manages the fundamental operation of the computer and its resources. Most application programs are written in high-level languages such as FORTRAN, BASIC, PASCAL, and LISP.

A programming environment consists of a number of subroutines or modules usually developed in a high-level language and suitable for a particular domain or class of problems. Using these modules an application programmer can develop specific programs in that domain. To further facilitate computer programming, programming tools have been recently developed. Among the popular programming tools are spreadsheets and database management systems (Adeli, 1988). Expert system tools or shells have been developed to facilitate the development of expert systems. They will be reviewed in Chapter 4. Although high-level languages, programming environments, and programming tools have been identified as three different levels in this chapter, the distinction may be subject to interpretation; and they all may be classified as a single tool.

Table 3.1 Various levels of software

1. Machine language
2. Operating system (e.g. MS DOS, UNIX)
3. High-level languages (e.g. FORTRAN, BASIC, PASCAL, C, LISP, PROLOG)
4. Programming environment (e.g. INTERLISP, OPS5)
5. Programming tools (e.g. spreadsheets, database management systems, ES shells)
6. Application programs

There is a fundamental difference between AI languages such as LISP and PROLOG and conventional procedural languages such as FORTRAN. In a procedural language, instructions are given in imperative forms; first do this, then do that, next do that, etc. The step-by-step strategy for solving a problem is explicitly given by the programmer. In contrast, AI languages are declarative languages in which information is presented in a descriptive form. This latter approach appears to be closer to the thinking process of human beings.

3.2 LISP

LISP, an acronym for *LISt Processing*, was invented by McCarthy in 1960 for nonnumeric computations (McCarthy, 1960). Development of LISP is considered a major advancement in AI. LISP is the most widely-used language among AI researchers in the United States (Barstow *et al.*, 1983; Harmon and King, 1985; Berk, 1985; Tucker, 1986; Anderson *et al.*, 1987). The features and advantages of LISP can be summarized as follows (Adeli and Paek, 1986a and 1986b):

1. LISP is very powerful in manipulating symbolic expressions.
2. Data and programs in LISP have the same form and are treated in the same way. Both data and program are represented as lists. Therefore, the LISP programming can be done in the so-called data-directed programming style. That is, LISP programs can treat other LISP programs as data. This feature makes the LISP programs dynamic and very easy to change. A program written in LISP can modify its code as easily as it can change its data.
3. Unlike FORTRAN, due to dynamic creation of variables, LISP functions can recursively call themselves.
4. Memory management in LISP is performed automatically. Lists not in use are erased by the system. Thus, the programmer does not have to worry about the storage assignment. The implicit abandoning of LISP objects is called garbage collection (Gabriel, 1987).
5. LISP programs are easy to debug. LISP functions can be tested independently even though they may call other functions yet to be defined.
6. In LISP, program development and execution are done in a highly interactive environment. This takes place in read–evaluate–print loops.
7. LISP has simple and flexible syntax and is rather easy to read. Both lower and upper case letters can be used in defining variables.
8. LISP is a flexible and dynamic language. It can be extended by the programmer by creating new high-level functions.
9. In contrast to most other programming languages, variables in LISP are not restricted by type and may have any complicated data structure.

10. LISP can be used in both compiled and source-code forms. For an introduction to compiling LISP procedures, see Pumplin (1987).

As a flexible language LISP has not been standardized. Instead a variety of LISP-based programming environments have been developed such as ELISP, MacLISP (Moon, 1974), FranzLISP, Common LISP (Winston and Horn, 1984), and INTERLISP (Teitelman, 1978; Kaisler, 1986). Recently, there have been attempts to standardize LISP, mostly around Common LISP. While Common LISP is considered as *de facto* standard dialect of LISP by many, there is also a sentiment against standardization (Allen, 1987). One important characteristic of LISP is flexibility, and standardization is argued to work against flexibility. A version of Common LISP named Golden Common LISP is now available for use on an IBM personal computer.

3.3 PROLOG

PROLOG, an acronym for *PRO*gramming in *LOG*ic, is based on formal logic and a simplified version of the first order predicate calculus (Clocksin and Mellish, 1981). PROLOG is popular in Europe (especially in the United Kingdom, France, and Hungary) and Japan (Wigan, 1986) and is gaining popularity in the United States. PROLOG has its own inference mechanism.

Allwood *et al.* (1985) report their experience with PROLOG-based ES shells and point out that PROLOG is a versatile language for database-type applications. For ES development, however, they note the limitation in numeric data types, large memory requirement, and slow execution with many implementations of the language.

3.4 TURBO PROLOG

An IBM PC-based PROLOG compiler has recently reached the market by the developer of the Turbo PASCAL, called Turbo PROLOG (Borland, 1986). It does not follow the syntax of PROLOG closely as presented by Clocksin and Melish (1981). Some of the advanced programming techniques of PROLOG are also missing in Turbo PROLOG (Rubin, 1986). However, Turbo PROLOG is intended to provide an easy-to-use environment for programmars with PASCAL and C experience. In the tradition of PASCAL, Turbo PROLOG is a strongly-typed language. Its built-in types are symbol (atom), integer, real, string, character, and file, in addition to user-definable types.

The user interface consists of a horizontal bar menu at the top of the screen and four windows, i.e. the message window, the edit window, the dialogue window for interaction with the running program, and the trace window for displaying the debugging output from using its trace facility. The arrangement size, and color of the four windows can be changed. Turbo PROLOG has fullscreen editing that supports multiple windows. A second file may be viewed and edited in an auxiliary editor window. Content of this window may be copied to the main editor window. Its trace facility can be used for error checking and debugging. The help facility is not context dependent. It allows the programmer only to scroll the content of a help file saved on the disk. Rubin (1986) compares the compile and run-time speed of Turbo PROLOG with two other PROLOG compilers and finds Turbo PROLOG faster than the other two compilers. One has to be cautious, however, in that speed performance can depend on the type of application and the host operating system to a great extent.

3.5 EXPERPROLOG II

PROLOG II is an enhanced version of PROLOG specially designed to be transportable across various computers. One of the most important features of this new version of PROLOG is the inclusion of cyclic data structures or infinite trees (Shafer, 1987). An infinite tree has infinite branches (i.e. branches that do not terminate). Infinite trees have applications in natural language processors. ExperTelligence of Santa Barbara, California, has recently introduced ExperPROLOG II for the Macintosh. ExperPROLOG II appears to be one of the most powerful and flexible microcomputer versions of PROLOG. It takes good advantage of the graphic capabilities of Macintosh including QuickDraw graphics, window control, menus, and the mouse interface.

3.6 INTERLISP

INTERLISP may be classified as a high-level language or a programming environment. INTERLISP seems to be the most highly developed implementation of LISP. INTERLISP has the rich characteristics of the Conversational LISP (CLISP) interpreter, a powerful error correction facility, and extensive library. INTERLISP contains a number of features that facilitate the design of large expert systems (Rich, 1983).

1. In addition to lists, INTERLISP has a collection of other data types such as arrays and bit strings.
2. INTERLISP has a spaghetti stack for storing program contexts. The spaghetti stack is a tree structure in which several parallel contexts can be stored in such a way that control can be transferred backward and forward between them.
3. INTERLISP has a DWIM (for *Do What I Mean*) facility which acts as an interface between the user and the system. It corrects the mistyped words, for example.

3.7 OPS5

OPS5 (for *Official Production System*, Version 5) is a LISP-based ES programming environment developed at Carnegie–Mellon University (Forgy, 1981; Brownston *et al.*, 1985). OPS5 is a popular production system tool and consists of three components:

1. An unordered collection of production rules consisting of left-hand sides of patterns and right-hand sides of actions
2. Working memory elements or data structures
3. An inference engine and a rule interpreter that matches the left-hand sides of the rules to the working memory elements.

The strength of OPS5 lies in the efficient interpreter for the matching process. However, it requires large memory and cannot be easily interfaced to other programs. OPS5 has been used to develop XCON, an ES for configuring the components of VAX-11/780 computers (see Section 1.8.5).

3.8 OPS83

An outgrowth of OPS5, OPS83 (Forgy, 1983) is a proprietary ES programming environment implemented in C for development of rule-based expert systems. It has four basic features. First, it supports algorithmic computations in addition to production rules. An ES developed in OPS83 can consist of rules, functions, and procedures. Functions and procedures are executed sequentially. However, a data-driven strategy is used for firing rules.

Second, it can be interfaced with other application programs rather easily. They are treated as procedures and functions. Third, OPS83 is designed to be portable. It runs on both mainframe computers and microcomputers. Finally, the programming in OPS83 is done in modules; each module is compiled by the OPS83 compiler individually. This results in fast running expert systems.

Neiman and Martin (1986) report firing speed ranging from 8 rules/second for complicated rules with significant right-hand side (consequent) processing to 140 rules/second for very simple rules, in UNIX operating system and on a VAX 11/780 computer. The speed on an IBM PC is about 10% and on an IBM PC AT is about 50–80% of the speed of the VAX implementation. OPS83 is suitable for the development of small to medium size expert systems.

3.9 OBJECT-ORIENTED LANGUAGES

Object-oriented programming languages have been recommended for simulation, graphics, and recently AI programming. There is no agreement on the definition and fundamental principles of an object-oriented programming language (Stefik and Bobrow, 1986). However, the basic idea behind these languages is to program with 'objects'. An object is the primitive element of an object-oriented programming language. Objects combine the properties of procedures and data. In conventional procedure-oriented languages, active procedures act on passive data. In an object-oriented language, objects (data) operate on themselves. Objects send 'messages' to each other. Computations and operations are done through sending messages to objects.

Pascoe (1986) argues that an object-oriented language must support data abstraction, dynamic binding, and hierarchical inheritance. Data abstraction indicates that a calling program should not make any assumption about the data type it uses. The inheritance property of object-oriented languages makes them suitable for knowledge systems using semantic networks or frames. The most popular object-oriented programming language is SMALLTALK which is available on microcomputers (Kaehler and Patterson, 1986). Object-oriented languages for the Apple Macintosh are reviewed by Schmucker (1986).

3.10 PROCEDURAL LANGUAGES

While the majority of expert systems have been developed in symbol manipulation languages such as LISP and PROLOG, a number of expert systems have been developed in procedural languages such as FORTRAN, PASCAL, FORTH, and C. For the development of many engineering expert systems in which considerable numerical algorithmic computation is involved in addition to symbolic manipulation, AI programming languages such as LISP and PROLOG may not be arguably the language of choice. Among the popular algorithmic languages, Pascal and C might be better candidates in these cases. The reader should note that the question of the 'best' language can be the subject of hot debate and philosophical discussion!

PASCAL is named after the French mathematician Blaise Pascal (1623–62) who is known as the inventor of the first digital calculating machine (Baron, 1986). PASCAL has its roots in ALGOL and is an extended and more elegant and lucid version of ALGOL. Among various versions of PASCAL, Turbo PASCAL (Radford and Haigh, 1986), a compiled language with fast execution, enjoys popularity among microcomputer programmers, especially users of MS DOS and CP/M computers.

The following features and advantages may be noted for PASCAL (especially in comparison with FORTRAN and BASIC) (Adeli and Al-Rijleh, 1987):

1. The principles of structured programming are incorporated into the language itself. The primary idea behind the concept of structured programming is to reduce complexity through modular programming and effective communication.

2. Predefined variable types are character, string, boolean (with values of either true or false), integer, real number, and array. In addition, PASCAL allows the programmer to define variable types. Thus, the programmer is not limited to a fixed number of variable types.
3. Pascal supports recursion. That is, a subroutine may call itself.
4. With the use of CASE statement, branching can be accomplished more efficiently in PASCAL than in BASIC or FORTRAN.
5. PASCAL has the variable-type pointer which makes it possible to define logical trees. This feature is particularly useful in AI applications. It can also be used for dynamic storage allocation.
6. Compared with looping statements available in FORTRAN and BASIC, PASCAL has the additional looping statements REPEAT–UNTIL which makes the looping more direct and natural for certain cases.
7. Various types of variables (e.g. strings, boolean variables, and integers) can be stored and lumped together by using the RECORD statement.
8. In PASCAL, all the variables must be defined before any executable statement. This helps the programmer in debugging the program such as finding the typographical errors.
9. Turbo PASCAL has excellent string manipulation capabilities.
10. Turbo PASCAL has powerful graphic capabilities.

It may be noted that recently developed languages such as Modula-2 (Beidler and Jackowitz, 1986) and Ada (Olsen and Whitehill, 1983) that are descendants of PASCAL may finally supercede PASCAL, perhaps in the 1990s.

C is designed to be a portable language. C is a very efficient language and is specially suitable for graphic-based programs. While LISP is memory intensive and requires large processing power, C has limited symbolic manipulation and memory management capabilities. Comparing LISP with C, Barber (1987) argues that because LISP provides a better development and maintenance environment its high hardware cost will eventually be compensated by a decrease in the software maintenance cost, as the hardware cost continues to decline and new powerful processors such as 80386 with execution speeds of 3–4 MIPS (million instructions per second) and virtual memory systems (up to 4 gigabytes physical and 64 terabytes virtual) are built.

REFERENCES

Adeli, H. (1988) Microcomputers in Civil Engineering, in *Encyclopedia of Microcomputers* (eds A. Kent and J.G. Williams), Marcel Dekker, New York.
Adeli, H. and Al-Rijleh, M.M. (1987) Interactive computer-aided design of trusses using Turbo Pascal. *Microcomputers in Civil Engineering*, **2**, No. 5, 101–16.
Adeli, H. and Paek, Y. (1986a) Computer-aided design of structures using LISP. *Journal of Computers and Structures*, **22**, No. 6, 939–56.

Adeli, H. and Paek, Y. (1986b) Computer-aided analysis of structures in INTERLISP environment. *Journal of Computers and Structures*, **23**, No. 3, 393–407.

Allen, J.R. (1987) The death of creativity: is Common LISP a LISP-like language?. *AI Expert*, **2**, No. 2, 48–61.

Allwood, R.J., Stewart, D.J. and Trimble, E.G. (1985) Some experiences from evaluating expert system shell programs and some potential applications, *CIVIL-COMP 85* (*Proceedings of 2nd International Conference on Civil and Structural Engineering Computing*, Vol. 2, CIVIL-COMP Press, Edinburgh, UK, pp. 415–20.

Anderson, J.R., Corbett, A.T. and Reiser, B.J. (1987) *Essential LISP*, Addison-Wesley, Reading, Massachusetts.

Barber, G.R. (1987) LISP vs. C for implementing expert systems. *AI Expert*, **2**, No. 2, 28–31.

Baron, N.S. (1986) *Computer Languages – A Guide for the Perplexed*, Anchor Press, Garden City, New York.

Barstow, D.R., Aiello, N., Duda, R.O., Erman, L.D., Forgy, C.L., Gorlin, D., Greiner, R.D., Lenat, D.B., London, P.E., McDermott, J., Nii, H.P., Politakis, P., Reboh, R., Rosenschein, S., Scott, C., Van Melle, W. and Weiss, S.M. (1983) Languages and tools for knowledge engineering, in *Building Expert Systems* (eds F. Hayes-Roth, D.A. Waterman and D.B. Lenat), Addison-Wesley, Reading, Massachusetts, pp. 283–348.

Beidler, J. and Jackowitz, P. (1986) *Modula-2*, PWS Publishers, Boston, Massachusetts.

Berk, A.A. (1985) *LISP: The Language of Artificial Intelligence*, Van Nostrand Reinhold, New York.

Borland (1986) *Turbo Prolog – Owner's Handbook*, Borland International, Scotts Valley, California.

Brownston, L., Favell, R., Kant, E. and Martin, N. (1985) *Programming Expert Systems in OPS5*, Addison-Wesley, Reading, Massachusetts.

Clocksin, W.F. and Mellish, C.S. (1981) *Programming in Prolog*, Springer-Verlag, New York.

Forgy, C.L. (1981) *OPS5 User's Manual*, Technical Report CMU-CS-81-135, Carnegie–Mellon University.

Forgy, C.L. (1983) *The OPS83 User's Manual and Report*, Production Systems Technology, Pittsburgh, Philadelphia; Gordon and Breach Science Publishers, New York.

Gabriel, R.P. (1987) Memory Management in LISP, *AI Expert*, **2**, No. 2, 32–8.

Harmon, P. and King, D. (1985) *Artificial Intelligence in Business*, John Wiley, New York.

Kaehler, T. and Patterson, D. (1986) *A Taste of Small Talk*, W.W. Norton, New York.

Kaisler, S.H. (1986) *INTERLISP – The Language and Its Usage*, John Wiley, New York.

McCarthy, J. (1960) Recursive functions of symbolic expressions and their computation by machine. *Communications of the ACM*, **3**, No. 4, 184–95.

Moon, D.A. (1974) *MacLISP Reference Manual*, Massachusetts Institute of Technology, Cambridge, Massachusetts.

Neiman, D. and Martin, J. (1986) Rule-based programming in OPS83. *AI Expert* (premier issue), pp. 54–63.

Olsen, E.W. and Whitehill, S.B. (1983) *Ada for Programmers*, Reston Publishing Company, Reston, Virginia.

Pascoe, G.A. (1986) Elements of object-oriented programming. *Byte*, **11**, No. 8, 139–44.

Pumplin, B.A. (1987) Compiling LISP procedures. *AI Expert*, **2**, No. 2, 40–6.

Radford, L.E. and Haigh, R.W. (1986) *Turbo Pascal for the IBM PC*, PWS Publishers, Boston, Massachusetts.

Rich, E. (1983) *Artificial Intelligence*, McGraw-Hill, New York.

Rubin, D. (1986) Turbo PROLOG: a PROLOG compiler for the PC programmer. *AI Expert* (primer issue), pp. 87–97.

Schmucker, K.J. (1986) Object-oriented languages for the Macintosh. *Byte*, **11**, No. 8, 177–85.

Shafer, D. (1987) ExperTelligence's PROLOG for the MAC: ExperPROLOG II. *AI Expert*, **2**, No. 1, 75–8.

Stefik, M. and Bobrow, D.G. (1986) Object-oriented programming: themes and variations. *AI Magazine*, **6**, No. 4, 40–62.

Teitelman, W. (1978) *INTERLISP Reference Manual*, Xerox Palo Alto Research Center, Palo Alto, California.

Tucker, A.B., Jr. (1986) *Programming Languages*, 2nd edn, McGraw-Hill, New York.

Wigan, M.R. (1986) Engineering tools for building knowledge-based systems on microsystems. *Microcomputers in Civil Engineering*, **1**, No. 1, 52–68.

Winston, P.H. and Horn, B.K.P. (1984) *LISP*, 2nd edn, Addison-Wesley, Reading, Massachusetts.

4

Expert system shells

HOJJAT ADELI

4.1 INTRODUCTION

To facilitate the development of knowledge-based expert systems, expert system programming environments or shells have recently been developed. They contain specific representation methods and inference mechanisms. They are easier to use but less flexible than an AI language such as LISP.

Selection of an ES shell for engineering applications should be based on the following considerations:

1. Type of application
2. Type of machine (microcomputers, mainframe computers, or dedicated AI machines) and operating systems
3. Maximum number of rules allowed (in production systems)
4. Response time (in solving problems or answering questions)
5. Type of control strategy and inference mechanism
6. User-interface (graphics, natural language processing, etc.)
7. Availability of complex mathematical routines
8. The ability to interface with other programs written in the language of the shell or foreign languages
9. Programming aids (e.g. editors, debuggers, and a help facility)
10. Portability
11. User support
12. Cost

Few engineering problems can be solved by a purely heuristic approach. Numerical algorithmic routines must usually be combined with heuristics. Thus, an ES shell or programming environment suitable for engineering applications should ideally be able to handle scientific numerical computations within the system.

In this chapter we will briefly describe some of the more popular ES shells. Additional information may be found in Hayes-Roth *et al.* (1983a), Harmon and King (1985), Waterman (1986), Williamson (1986), Wigan (1986), and Adeli (1987). Ludvigsen *et al.* (1986) review seven commercial ES shells popular in the United States in terms of user-friendliness, documentation, and user support. A review of nine ES shells popular in the United Kingdom is given by Allwood *et al.* (1985).

The first two ES shells (EMYCIN and KAS) may be termed research tools. EXPERT, ROSIE, S.1, KEE, ART, and ESE are classified as large systems requiring mainframe computers. The remaining shells are small shells available on microcomputers.

4.2 EARLY RESEARCH TOOLS

4.2.1 EMYCIN

In the late 1970s, the developers of MYCIN realized that by stripping it from its medical knowledge base it could be used to develop other diagnostic expert systems. Thus, the first widely-used ES shell was created and called EMYCIN (for Essential *MYCIN* or Empty *MYCIN*) (Van Melle, 1979). Thus, similarly to MYCIN, EMYCIN is LISP based and uses production rules and object–attribute–value triplets for knowledge representation and backward-chaining as the inference mechanism. The ability to explain its line of reasoning was an important feature of EMYCIN. Subsequently, editing and debugging aids were added to EMYCIN to facilitate ES development. EMYCIN has been used to develop various diagnostic expert systems. It has been used to develop the first experimental ES in the area of structural engineering, i.e. SACON, an ES for the proper application of a general-purpose finite element structural analysis program (see Section 5.2.1).

4.2.2 KAS

As the MYCIN project resulted in the ES shell EMYCIN, PROSPECTOR (see Section 1.8.3) also led to the development of another ES shell for diagnosis and classification problems, called KAS (for *K*nowledge *A*cquisition *S*ystem). KAS uses rule-based representation with a partitioned semantic net for organizing the process of rule matching. Implemented in INTERLISP, KAS uses both backward and forward-chaining and certainty factors, and has explanation, knowledge acquisition, and tracing facilities (Reboh, 1981).

4.3 LARGE SHELLS

4.3.1 EXPERT

Developed at Rutgers University, EXPERT is the only major ES shell implemented in FORTRAN (Weiss and Kulikowski, 1984). It uses a rule-based representation strategy, backward-chaining inference mechanism, and certainty factors similar to EMYCIN. It was originally developed for use in biomedical problems. It has been used for developing a rheumatic disease consultant, a diagnostic and treatment system for patients with ocular herpes complex, and a serum protein electrophoresis interpreter. However, EXPERT may be used for any diagnosis/prescription paradigm. In non-medical applications, it has been used to develop an oil exploration ES by interpreting well log data (Weiss and Kulikowski, 1984) and a spill-management ES for the discovery and containment of hazardous chemical and oil spills (Barstow *et al.*, 1983).

EXPERT has explanation, knowledge acquisition, consistency checking, and trace facilities. The consistency checking facility is based on a database of representative cases with known solutions. When the ES developer adds a new rule EXPERT tests the consistency of the rule with the solutions of the representative cases stored in the database. When there is an inconsistency, EXPERT explains the reason for inconsistency of the rule. The runtime trace facility helps the users in debugging by letting them follow the logic of the ES.

EXPERT has no interactive editor. Although it is implemented in FORTRAN it can handle only standard mathematical operations ($+$, $-$, $/$, $*$, $**$) and cannot be interfaced to other programs (even those written in FORTRAN) (Ludvigsen *et al.*, 1986).

4.3.2 ROSIE

Developed by Rand Corporation in INTERLISP (Fain *et al.*, 1981 and 1982), ROSIE has also been classified as an AI programming environment. It uses a rule-based representation combined with nested procedures (procedures which call other procedures that in turn call other procedures). Each procedure is defined by a set of rules. The combination of rules and procedures adds flexibility to the program but makes the explanation of the ES operation more difficult. ROSIE has an English-like syntax which makes it easily readable. It has editing and debugging facilities (without graphical aids) but no knowledge acquisition facility and a very limited explanation facility. It cannot directly handle complex mathematical operations and cannot be easily interfaced to other programs.

4.3.3 S.1

Developed by Teknowledge Inc. in LISP, S.1 is one of the largest and most expensive commercial ES shells (price range $50 000–$80 000). It is suitable for diagnosis/prescription paradigms. It uses production rules and object–attribute–value triplets for knowledge representation. Similarly to EMYCIN, certainty factors are used for incomplete or inexact information. It has numerous development facilities including menus, graphical displays of the reasoning process, help and explanation facilities, and error analysis and debugging facilities. The explanation facility can answer questions such as why, how, and what. It does not handle complex mathematical operations. Its interface to databases is done by escaping into LISP.

4.3.4 KEE

KEE (*K*nowledge *E*ngineering *E*nvironment) is a large, flexible, and powerful ES shell developed by IntelliCorp in LISP. It has many features and can be extended by the user; and thus may also be classified as an AI programming environment. Since it uses various representations (rules and frames) and inference mechanisms (backward-chaining and forward-chaining) it is also called a hybrid ES in AI terminology. Procedural knowledge written in LISP can be attached to the slots in the frame representation. KEE is interfaced to the user through graphics. It can display the line of reasoning for reaching a conclusion graphically.

KEE has been developed on the methodologies of object-oriented pro-gramming. Frames can be organized hierarchically and slots and their values can inherit from higher level objects. A change made in the slot values will propagate automatically throughout the logical structure of the knowledge base. The LISP machine-based KEE can be used effectively only by experienced knowledge engineers and costs about $60 000. KEE has been used to develop an ES in the area of construction management (see Section 5.3.1).

4.3.5 ART

Developed by Inference Corporation, ART (*A*utomated *R*easoning *T*ool) is a powerful ES tool developed in LISP for use on LISP machines (Clayton, 1985; Williams, 1985). ART consists of four parts: a knowledge language, a compiler for transforming the knowledge language into LISP, an inference mechanism called 'knowledge applier', and a development environment. Knowledge representation in ART includes IF–THEN rules, OAV triplets, 'facts' expressed in a logical–relational notation, and procedural representation of algorithmic knowledge. The inference mechanism or knowledge applier described as the 'opportunistic reasoner' includes both backward-chaining and forward-chaining. ART's development environment includes debugging and trace facilities. The cost of ART is around $60 000.

4.3.6 Expert System Environment (ESE)

Expert System Consultation Environment (IBM, 1986a) and Expert System Development Environment (IBM, 1986b and 1986c) are a pair of complementary programs developed recently by the IBM Corporation for developing and executing expert systems. The first program is used to develop expert systems and, in particular, knowledge bases. The second program provides the facilities for executing them (the interactive execution of the ES is called consultation). The programs have been implemented in Pascal and operate on an IBM System/370 under either VM/SP or MVS systems. The two programs are collectively referred to as the Expert System Environment (ESE). ESE is a powerful ES shell with many features and facilities.

The system supports both backward-chaining and forward-chaining. Further, it allows the knowledge base to be organized into hierarchical structures called Focus Control Blocks (FCB); each FCB can have its own inference mechanism. Selection of the inference mechanism is controlled through a control language. Thus, the ES developer can decompose a large complex problem into smaller and consequently more manageable subproblems and solve each subproblem independently.

The knowledge base of ESE can consist of three types of objects: parameters (domain facts), rules, and FCBs. Parameters are the basic objects that can hold values such as constraints (e.g. to be greater than zero), prompt messages, and properties indicating whether the information for the parameter should come from a default value, the user, an external procedure, or from the processing of the rules. Rules establish the relationships among parameters. The uncertainty can be incorporated into the system by associating each parameter value with a numeric weight between -1.0 and 1.0.

Other very useful features of the system are rerun and 'undo' capabilities. Any interactive session or consultation may be stored and subsequently rerun. Answers to the questions given previously may be changed during the rerun. Also, the user can undo or change a previously given response. The system allows access to external procedures, e.g. for obtaining information from a database.

The Expert System Environment has explanation, debugging, editing, and help facilities. The explanation facility can answer three different types of questions: WHY, WHAT, and HOW. During the interaction with the ES, the user can ask WHY a question is being asked. By asking WHAT a more detailed explanation of the question will be provided to the user. After the system makes a conclusion or recommendation, the user can ask HOW, to receive a logical explanation of the reasoning process.

The debugging facility provides a trace or 'roadmap' through the reasoning process of the system. This trace helps the ES developer to test the knowledge base and make the necessary corrections. The Expert System Development Environment has editors that let the ES builder build the knowledge base and the user use the ES through an English-like syntax. The editors have a built-in automatic error checking that brings any semantic or syntactic error to the attention of the user for correction. For ease of use, the editors divide the screen into three independently scrollable windows. An online help facility is provided in both the development and consultation environments.

The commands FIND and RERUN are also useful for debugging. The FIND command can be used to find certain facts or rules in the knowledge base that satisfy a specific condition quickly and efficiently without scanning many rules and parameters. The RERUN command can be used to rerun the latest consultation session.

ESE has been used to develop an ES for the optimum design of bridge trusses, called BTEXPERT (see Section 5.2.5).

4.4 MICROCOMPUTER-BASED SHELLS

4.4.1 EXPERT-EASE

Developed by Expert Software International in PASCAL, EXPERT-EASE appears to be the first ES shell for a personal computer (Perrone, 1983). The knowledge is created by inputting examples through a matrix of attributes and generic recommendations for a decision-making problem. For this reason, it has also been called a 'decision making spreadsheet' (Harmon and King, 1985). From the examples, EXPERT-EASE generates a procedure for solving the problem and a decision tree representing the procedure. It provides the user with menus but has no explanation facility, cannot handle complex mathematical operations, and cannot be interfaced to other programs.

4.4.2 M.1

Developed by Teknowledge Inc. in 1984, M.1 is an ES shell developed in PROLOG and available on an IBM PC with 128K of RAM. It uses a rule-based representation with attribute–value pairs and a backward-chaining and limited forward-chaining inference mechanisms. It is intended to be used primarily by experienced programmers for exploratory ES development with a knowledge base of generally less than 200 rules. Similarly to EMYCIN, it is suitable for diagnosis/prescription paradigms. An important feature of M.1 is the use of variable rules. Using this feature, the ES developer does not have to enter many similar rules one at a time. A generic rule can be defined for a set of similar rules. Uncertain information is entered by using confidence factors from 0 to 100.

M.1 uses menus and has an explanation facility as well as a tracing facility for debugging. Using tracing windows one can observe what options are available, what rule is being considered, and what conclusions have been made. It has no editor, cannot handle complex mathematical operations, and cannot be directly interfaced to other programs. It costs $5000. M.1 has been used to develop an ES for diagnosing malfunctions in hazardous waste incineration facilities (see Section 5.4.2).

4.4.3 The deciding factor

The deciding factor is a diagnostic microcomputer-based ES shell that uses rules for knowledge representation and depth first backward-chaining (Campbell and Fitzgerrell, 1985). Rules are required to be organized hierarchically. Each rule is assigned a degree of belief ranging from -5 (certainly not true) to $+5$ (certainly true). The default value is zero. It can answer the questions of how a hypothesis is being evaluated and why a particular question is being asked. In addition, similarly to a help facility, explanation screens can be called for additional information or explanation of the questions, using the built-in word processor. It also allows users to backtrack its dialogue with the system and modify their previous responses. This ES shell has been used to develop expert systems in the area of construction management (see Section 5.3.1).

4.4.4 RuleMaster

Developed by Radian Corporation, RuleMaster is a microcomputer-based shell for use on UNIX and MS DOS operating systems. Backward-chaining or forward-chaining or a combination of them may be used. A rather unique feature of this shell is that it is both a rule-based and induction system. In an induction ES shell, the ES is built from examples that describe a particular problem. The induction system transforms these examples into rules for solving the problem.

Induction systems usually use a spreadsheet interface for obtaining the examples in table form from the knowledge-base builder. One advantage of induction systems is ease of use. Also, they eliminate redundant information by analyzing the contents of tables. Induction systems become problematic when there are very few attributes or the addition of new examples contradicts the previous examples. The contradiction among examples must be solved by the knowledge base builder or the domain expert. Induction systems are most useful when a large number of usable data already exist (Thompson and Thompson, 1986 and 1987). Using the examples, RuleMaster automatically induces IF–THEN–ELSE rules in Radial language with a structure similar to PASCAL (Van Horn, 1987).

Expert systems developed by RuleMaster can be compiled into C. The result is faster and more compact programs. RuleMaster uses fuzzy logic to handle two different types of uncertainty, uncertainty in the IF–THEN rules and uncertainty in the input given by the user.

4.4.5 INSIGHT 2 +

Developed by Level Five Research in Pascal (1986), INSIGHT 2 + is presently available on an IBM PC. Its Macintosh version is planned to be released soon.

INSIGHT 2 + uses a rule-based representation with object–attribute (OA) pairs and both backward-chaining and forward-chaining inference mechanisms. Its facilities include a help facility, explanation facility, confidence factor, and mathematical functions such as trigonometric and exponential functions.

Knowledge representation in INSIGHT 2 + is through IF–AND–OR–THEN–ELSE rules in a language called Production Rule Language (PRL). PRL also accepts procedural or action-oriented rules. Fact types available in PRL are simple facts, numeric facts, object–attribute (OA) facts, and string facts.

A simple fact data type is defined as any statement with possible outcomes of true or false. Numeric data types are integer and floating point numbers. The OA data type is a very useful representation scheme for describing objects or elements with common states or conditions. Objects may have multiattributes, each attribute having its own confidence factor. String facts are any combination of ASCII characters with a maximum length of 80 characters. Relational operators such as > (greater than), < (less than), < > (not equal), and = (equal) can be used in the antecedent part of the rules.

INSIGHT 2 + allows chaining of two or more knowledge bases by using the CHAIN function. Facts common in or shared by several knowledge bases can be declared by the SHARED function. Thus, the domain knowledge can be partitioned into smaller knowledge bases and chained together before execution.

An important feature of INSIGHT 2 + is that knowledge bases can be compiled before execution. This means high speed of execution which is very important for the solution of engineering problems. The compiler checks the syntax of the source code. When an error is found the compilation stops and an error message is displayed. The error message provides a good explanation for the cause of the error and indicates the location of the error in the knowledge base.

INSIGHT 2 + provides a modified subset of the Pascal language, called DBPAS. External algorithmic programs written in DBPAS (.PAS files) can be called from a knowledge base. DBPAS also supports dBase II and dBase III data files. INSIGHT 2 + provides a multiwindowing text editor for creating knowledge bases and DBPAS programs. Thus, different files may be simultaneously viewed or edited.

The ACTIVATE facility is intended to allow the user to execute external programs written in languages other than DBPAS directly from INSIGHT 2 +. In this case, however, commands for interpreting the ASCII data coming from INSIGHT 2 + and returning the data in INSIGHT 2 + format must be provided in the external program by a knowledge engineer. The procedure for interfacing Turbo PASCAL programs to a knowledge base is provided by INSIGHT 2 +.

The explanation facility of INSIGHT 2 + is through the 'reports' system.

The user can enter the reports system by pressing the WHY? function key. Four menus are provided for obtaining information about the reasoning process. From the Facts Menu the user can see his or her answers to the questions and conclusions drawn from those answers, review the facts by the fact type, or change the answers and rerun the knowledge base. Using the Rules Menu, the user can review the rules of the knowledge base one rule at a time and trace the line of reasoning. The user can ask INSIGHT 2 + to display all the rules that conclude the same fact. From the Reports Menu, INSIGHT 2 + generates knowledge trees showing the logical sequence of rules fired. Using the Options Menu, the user can save the context of a knowledge base session on a disk for future use or rerun a knowledge base using a new context.

INSIGHT 2 + does not have any built-in graphic facilities, except for a bar chart which is displayed for showing the confidence values. However, graphic routines developed in other languages can be easily linked to INSIGHT 2 + (see Section 5.2.6). The user interface is primarily through menus and function keys. Menu selection is done by positioning the cursor arrow at the desired choice. Error handling in INSIGHT 2 + needs to be improved.

INSIGHT 2 + has been used to develop an ES for selection of waste disposal landfill sites described in Section 5.4.3, and an ES for the design of roof trusses described in Section 5.2.6. The latter ES involves extensive numerical algorithmic computations in addition to symbolic processing of heuristic rules and empirical knowledge. INSIGHT 2 + handles this kind of mixed symbolic/algorithmic processing quite well with one problem. The *first* conclusion of rules in PRL must be either a simple fact or an OA fact and cannot be numeric or string facts. This makes the knowledge base development rather awkward for rules with only one numeric conclusion.

INSIGHT II + can be used on an IBM PC with 256K of RAM. In order to use all of its features, however, a minimum of 512K is required. To summarize, INSIGHT 2 + is easy to use, is reasonably well documented, allows easy integration with algorithmic programs written in Turbo Pascal, its knowledge bases can be compiled, and it has a relatively modest price tag of $495. Within this price range, INSIGHT 2 + appears to be one of the best commercial ES shells available in the market for developing engineering expert systems on microcomputers.

4.4.6 1st-CLASS

1st-CLASS is a combined rule-based and induction (example-based) ES shell implemented in Microsoft Pascal and Macro Assembler (Thomas, 1986). Among its facilities are a help facility and automatic report generation.

Development of a knowledge base by 1st-CLASS is through the use of six menu-based screens called Files, Definitions, Examples, Methods, Rules, and Advisor. The Files screen is used to create, save, get, and print knowledge bases. The Definitions screen lets the user create a knowledge base template similar to a Lotus 1-2-3 spreadsheet. Using the Methods screen, the user can choose one of the four methods for creating rules. One way of creating rules is through examples. 1st-CLASS automatically induces rules from the examples. In doing so, it eliminates factors that have no effect on the results to create an efficient decision tree. The Examples screen allows the user to enter the examples. The Rules screen transforms the definitions and examples into a rule or decision tree which is displayed graphically on the screen. Finally, the interactive consultation with the knowledge base and expert system is carried from the Advisor screen which is in fact a series of screens.

Uncertainty in 1st-CLASS is taken into account through weights (from 0 to 100). These weights are used to calculate various statistical quantities such as the average weight of examples that produces a particular result, the proportion of the active examples that cause a particular result, etc. A special feature of 1st-CLASS is the 'what–if' facility. Using this facility during the interactive advising session, the user can change the answers to some of the questions while keeping the answers to other questions unchanged.

1st-CLASS allows chaining of various knowledge bases through both backward and forward-chaining. It can be interfaced with the Lotus 1-2-3 spreadsheet to exchange numeric and logical data. External application programs in languages such as Pascal, BASIC, and C can be linked to 1st-CLASS but only with rather insignificant programming efforts. 1st-CLASS does not have an automatic explanation facility. Instead, an explanation facility must be tailored and developed by a knowledge engineer according to the topic of the knowledge base/expert system.

In an attempt to make the 1st-CLASS instruction manual very easy to use, very little technical information about the architecture of the system is provided in the manual. While this approach may be considered adequate for somebody who wants to develop a financial or stock market advisor it is certainly not very informative for engineers and scientists interested in developing significant expert system applications. 1st-CLASS has been used to develop expert systems for diagnosis problems and economic analysis. 1st-CLASS can be used on an IBM PC with a minimum of 256K RAM and has a price tag of $495.

4.5 THE FUTURE OF EXPERT SYSTEM SHELLS

In the future, ES shells will perhaps be developed for a class of problems, e.g. diagnosis, interpretation, etc. It is important to note that ES shells developed so far are most suitable for the solution of diagnosis problems. They cannot be used directly for the solution of planning or design problems. Shells can be appropriately developed only for a particular class of design problems.

REFERENCES

Adeli, H. (1987) Software review: INSIGHT 2 +. *Microcomputers in Civil Engineering*, **2**, No. 2, 173–4.

Allwood, R.J., Stewart, D.J., and Trimble, E.G. (1985) Some experiences from evaluating expert system shell programs and some potential applications, *Proceeding of the Second International Conference on Civil and Structural Engineering Computing*, Vol. 2, Civil-Comp. Press, London, pp. 415–20.

Barstow, D.R., Aiello, N., Duda, R.O., Erman, L.D., Forgy, C.L., Gorlin, D., Greiner, R.D., Lenat, D.B., London, P.E., McDermott, J., Nii, H.P., Politakis, P., Reboh, R., Rosenschein, S., Scott, C., Van Melle, W. and Weiss, S.M. (1983) Languages and tools for knowledge engineering, in *Building Expert Systems* (eds F. Hayes-Roth, D.A. Waterman and D.B. Lenat), Addison-Wesley, Reading, Mass., pp. 283–348.

Campbell, A.N. and Fitzgerrell, S. (1985) *The Deciding Factor User's Manual*, Power Up Software, San Mateo, California.

Clayton, B.D. (1985) *ART – Programming Tutorial*, Vols 1–3, Inference Corporation, Los Angeles, California.

Fain, J. *et al.* (1981) *The ROSIE Language Reference Manual*, Report N-1647-ARPA, Rand Corporation.

Fain, J. *et al.* (1982) *Programming in ROSIE: An Introduction by Means of Examples*, Report N-1646-ARPA, Rand Corporation.

Harmon, P. and King, D. (1985) *Artificial Intelligence in Business*, John Wiley, New York.

Hayes-Roth, F., Waterman, D.A. and Lenat, D. (eds) (1983a) *Building Expert Systems*, Addison-Wesley, Reading, Mass.

Hayes-Roth, F., Waterman, D.A. and Lenat, D. (1983b) An overview of expert systems, in *Building Expert Systems* (eds F. Hayes-Roth, D.A. Waterman and D. Lenat), Addison-Wesley, Reading, Mass.

IBM (1986a) *Expert System Consultation Environment User Guide*, SH20-9606-1, IBM Corporation, Cary, North Carolina.

IBM (1986b) *Expert System Development Environment User Guide*, SH20-9608-1, IBM Corporation, Cary, North Carolina.

IBM (1986c) *Expert System Consultation Environment and Expert System Development Environment Reference Manual*, SH20-9609-1, IBM Corporation, Cary, North Carolina.

Level Five Research (1986) *INSIGHT 2 + Reference Manual*, Version 1.0, Level Five Research, Indialantic, Florida.

Ludvigsen, P.J., Grenney, W.J., Dyreson, D. and Ferrara, J.M. (1986) Expert System Tools for Civil Engineering Applications, in *Expert Systems in Civil Engineering* (eds C.N. Kostem and M.L. Maher), American Society of Civil Engineers, pp. 18–29.

Perrone, J. (1983) *Expert Systems Get Personal: Modeling Expertise with the IBM PC*, Jeffery Perrone and Associates, San Francisco.

Reboh, R. (1981) *Knowledge Engineering Techniques and Tools in the PROSPECTOR Environment*, SRI Technical Note 243, Stanford Research Institute, Menlo Park, California.

Thomas, W. (1986) *1st-CLASS Instruction Manual*, Programs in Motion, Wayland, Massachusetts.

Thompson, B. and Thompson, B. (1986) Finding rules in data. *Byte*, **11**, No. 11.

Thompson, B. and Thompson, B. (1987) Creating expert systems from examples. *AI Expert*, **2**, No. 1, 21–6.

Van Horn, M. (1987) RuleMaster – an expert system software package for MS–DOS machines. *Byte*, **12**, No. 1, 341–2.

VanMelle, W. (1979) A domain-dependent production rule system for consultation programs, *Proceedings 6th International Joint Conference on Artificial Intelligence, Tokyo, Japan*, pp. 923–5.

Waterman, D.A. (1986) *A Guide to Expert Systems*, Addison-Wesley, Reading, Massachusetts.

Weiss, S.M. and Kulikowski, C.A. (1984) *A Practical Guide to Designing Expert Systems*, Rowman and Allanheld Publishers, Totowa, New Jersey.

Wigan, M.R. (1986) Engineering tools for building knowledge-based systems on microsystems. *Microcomputers in Civil Engineering*, **1**, No. 1, 52–68.

Williams, C. (1985) *ART – The Automated Reasoning Tool: Conceptual Overview*, Inference Corporation, Los Angles, California.

Williamson, M. (1986) *Artificial Intelligence for Microcomputers – The Guide for Business Decision Makers*, Brady Communications, New York.

5

An overview of expert systems in civil engineering

HOJJAT ADELI

5.1 POTENTIAL APPLICATIONS OF EXPERT SYSTEMS IN CIVIL ENGINEERING

An overview of expert systems in civil engineering, excluding those described in other chapters of the book, is presented in this chapter. At present, expert systems are most effective in areas where judgement and experience plays an important role and there is no underlying theory or the theory is inadequate for a satisfactory solution to the problem.

1. Diagnosis (e.g. operational problems in a wastewater treatment plant)
2. Fault detection (e.g. maintenance of construction equipments)
3. Prediction (e.g. prediction of earthquake hazard at a particular site)
4. Interpretation
5. Monitoring
6. Instruction
7. Planning
8. Design

5.2 STRUCTURAL ENGINEERING

The application of AI in the computer-aided design of structures is a recent development (Adeli, 1986). Elias (1983) reviews the possibilities of using AI techniques in the design of aerospace structures. Dixon and Simmons (1983) explore application of expert systems in mechanical design. MacCallum (1982) discusses the development of an expert system for the design of ships. Brown and Chandrasekaran (1984) present a general approach to the creation of computer-based expert consultants for design problems. They formulated a framework in which knowledge is decomposed into substructures and each substructure is in turn divided into a hierarchy of conceptual specialists. They applied this methodology to develop an ES for mechanical design with design refinement as the central problem-solving activity.

Potential applications of AI in structural engineering design and detailing were first proposed by Fenves and Norabhoompipat (1978). Rooney and Smith (1983) proposed an expanded model of the design process by introducing a feedback mechanism consisting of three steps: acquisition of experience, application of experience, and database management. They applied this model to a very simple structure, i.e. a single-span simply-supported steel wide-flange beam.

Expert systems for structural design are presented in detail in Chapter 6. Other expert systems in the area of structural engineering reported in the literature are described in the following sections. It should be noted that development of expert systems for solution of practical problems in the area of structural engineering is a substantial undertaking that should not be underestimated. Most expert systems developed so far are basically experimental systems. They show the present status of affairs and potential applications, or present conceptual frameworks.

5.2.1 SACON and other expert systems for structural analysis

Developed by Bennett and Engelmore (1979) using the ES shell EMYCIN (see Section 4.2.1), SACON interacts with the user for proper application of the MARC finite element structural analysis program. It consists of 170 production rules and 140 consultation parameters such as types of materials, loadings, and load components. It uses backward-chaining as inference mechanism. SACON is intended to help less experienced engineers to use a large general-purpose structural analysis software, i.e. MARC. A similar experimental ES has been developed by Fjellheim and Syversen (1983).

Rivlin *et al.* (1980) also attempted to develop a knowledge-based consultation system and to establish a finite element structural analysis knowledge base for the use of the MARC finite element program in FORTRAN. They employed the backward-chaining inference mechanism. Their finite element structural analysis knowledge base includes information about the three stages of the structural analysis problem, i.e. pre-analysis, analysis, and post-analysis.

1. Pre-analysis stage. In this stage the type of analysis is defined. Using the knowledge of geometrical configuration, loading environment, material behavior, and expected response of the structure, an appropriate type of analysis such as static, dynamic, linear elastic, elastoplastic, small-displacement, and large-displacement is recommended by the consultation system.
2. Analysis stage. It includes input data of the structural problem to be analyzed and the response of the structure subjected to a given loading

condition. The consultation system requires only necessary input from the user. It makes the required decisions for complying with the MARC program input requirements. Thus, the user is relieved from the large quantity of numerical data and various input formats.

3. Post-analysis stage. Nodal and element quantities obtained such as nodal displacements, velocities, and accelerations, and element stresses, strains, and temperatures are examined for adequacy of the analysis and recommendations are made for additional analysis if necessary.

Expert systems reviewed in this section are front-end systems intended to help the user in the selection of solution methods. They do not assist the user in modeling the physical problem or structure. Expert systems for finite element modeling should be able to recognize the prominent features of the real world physical problem and translate them into suitable representations.

5.2.2 SSPG

Developed by Adeli and Peak (1986), SSPG is a small experimental knowledge-based system for the design of stiffened steel plate girders. It is written in ELISP which is an implementation of Rutgers/UCI LISP for DEC-20 systems. The design of a stiffened steel plate girder does not involve a lot of common sense knowledge. To start the design, however, the human designer selects a number for the ratio of the depth of the web, h, and the length of the span, L, based on his or her previous experience. The choice of ratio h/L depends on a number of parameters including the span length, yield stress of steel, F_y, and the loading (e.g. intensity of the distributed load, w). The authors had two objectives in developing SSPG. First, to investigate the practicality of LISP for computer-aided detail design of structures. In such designs not only are heuristics important but also substantial numerical calculations are involved. To the authors' knowledge this was the first program written in LISP for detailed structural design.

The second objective was to explore a new approach to computer-aided structural design. The present approaches to structural design may be divided into four categories. By design here is meant the final detailed design that will produce a practical solution ready to be built or manufactured.

1. Manual design in which the computer is used for analysis of the structure but the actual design is performed with the help of manuals, charts, etc.
2. Interactive computer-aided design in which the computer is used for numerical calculations not only for analysis but also for design, for graphical display of input and output, for error checking, etc. A good interactive program may even show some sort of psuedo-intelligence through effective interaction with the user, presenting various options, providing numerous error messages, preventing the user from entering data

in violation of standard design specifications, suggesting practical ranges of design parameters, etc. (see Adeli and Fiedorek, 1986a and b, for example).

3. Optimum design based on mathematical nonlinear programming (NLP) techniques. While there are many optimization algorithms for the preliminary design of structures, application of mathematical programming techniques to the detailed design of structures has been quite limited. The high nonlinearity and discontinuity existent in the detailed design of structures can baffle many optimization algorithms or make them prohibitively expensive for the design of actual structures.

4. Knowledge-based systems for structural design. While this approach may appear a totally new approach to structural design a closer look makes it an extension of the interactive computer-aided design. The main problem in the development of a large interactive CAD system is the *creation and effective use of a knowledge base*, and this is where AI techniques can play a useful role. Additional discussion of the similarity between interactive and expert systems may be found in Fayegh and Russell (1986).

The detailed optimization of a welded stiffened plate girder on the basis of the AISC (AISC, 1980) specification is a nontrivial problem. Due to the highly nonlinear and implicit nature of design constraints as well as to the existence of discontinuities, the optimization of stiffened plate girders is computationally expensive and cannot be easily achieved by most available mathematical programming techniques (Adeli, 1984). Douty (1976) studied the problem of the optimum design of welded plate girders by sequential linear programming in an iterative manner. He observed that the solution could oscillate between 'large flange–shallow web' values and 'small flange–deep web' values. While various schemes have been proposed in the optimization literature to cope with such behavior they seem to work only for certain cases and ranges of design variables and their reliability and effectiveness are questionable. Recently, Abuyounes and Adeli (1986) presented a practical procedure for the minimum weight design of stiffened steel plate girders subjected to arbitrary loading using the general geometric programming technique. While the algorithm is robust it produces theoretical sizes for flange and web plates and stiffeners.

Using an interactive BASIC program for the design of stiffened steel plate girders, the optimum h/L ratios or 'practical' minimum weight design of the plate girder were found in terms of the span length, yield stress of steel, and the intensity of the distributed load on the girder. This information was then fed into SSPG as 300 IF–THEN or production rules. SSPG designs the web plate, flange plates, bearing stiffeners, and intermediate stiffeners using actual steel plates with thicknesses available in the market.

The production rules in SSPG are for four different types of steel commonly used in steel structures, i.e. A36 with yield stress of 36 ksi, A529 with yield stress of 42 ksi, A441 with yield stress of 50 ksi, and A572 with yield stress of 60 ksi.

The rules were found for four different load intensities of 3 kips/ft, 4 kips/ft, 5 kips/ft, and 6 kips/ft and eighteen different span lengths ranging from 50 to 500 ft (Fig. 5.1). These rules are used in the following form:

IF   the type of steel is A36   AND
          the load intensity is 6 kips/ft   AND
          the length of the span is 200 ft
THEN   the ratio of the span length to the depth of the web should be selected
          around 14.

Of course, design by SSPG is not limited to the aforementioned combinations. If a plate girder must be designed, say, for a span of 345 ft and a load intensity of 5.6 kips/ft, then SSPG generates several candidate h/L ratios from the production rules using a breadth-first search technique and designs the plate girder using these ratios. SSPG gives a number of designs around the 'practical' minimum weight design.

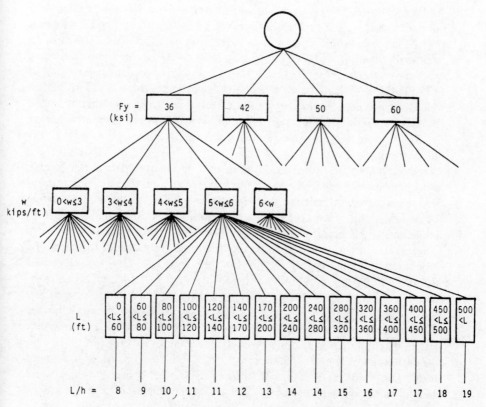

Fig. 5.1 Decision tree for optimum values of span-to-web depth ratio in SSPG.

In the design of stiffened steel plate girders other heuristic rules may determine:

1. What type of steel to use
2. Whether to use single-sided or double-sided stiffeners
3. Whether to use continuous or intermittent welds to connect the web plate to the flange plates and the stiffeners to the web plate.

SSPG is a knowledge-based system for the following reasons:

1. It attempts to design the plate girder the way an experienced human designer would design it.
2. It uses explicitly represented heuristic knowledge for finding a practical minimum weight design. The heuristic knowledge is used to reduce the extremely large space of design for finding the minimum weight design.

5.2.3 Expert systems for the design of composite structures

An ES for the design of a sandwich panel made of a honeycomb or foam core bonded to metallic or composite facesheets has been developed by Pecora *et al.* (1985) called the Composites Design Assistant (CDA). CDA consists of a backward-chaining ES shell written in PROLOG, a relational database manager written in FORTRAN, a laminate analysis program also written in FORTRAN, and a rule-based knowledge base. Honeycomb core material as well as various metallic and composite material properties are obtained from the relational database manager. The analysis program can take into account the hygrothermal effects, mechanical loading, viscoelasticity, and various failure modes.

They state that an 'automatic designer' or a 'design optimizer' is not feasible at the present state of technology. CDA is hence an interactive CAD program or expert assistant intended to guide the designer by asking the user to provide the design conditions (panel boundary conditions, external loads, deflection limitation, safety factor, skin material, approximate skin thickness, and core material and orientation), calculate the unknown design variables, check the design requirements (safety factors for skin and core, face wrinkling and intracell dimpling, compatibility of core with skin, plate effects, and environment effects), and advise the designer on the acceptability of the design. The knowledge base in CDA has been acquired from two composites handbooks. CDA interacts with the user iteratively in order to produce a satisfactory design. The interaction is done through a sequence of menus.

Zumsteg and Flaggs (1985) describe a proof-in-concept system to be used during the preliminary design of stiffened cylindrical composite panels and shells. The knowledge base of this ES, called the Buckling Expert, contains knowledge of various analysis methods, when and how to use them, and how to interpret the results. The knowledge in the system has been acquired from a journal article that summarizes the experience of an expert in the field. Buckling Expert uses an ES shell called the Lockheed Expert System (LES) written in PL/1 in which knowledge can be represented as IF–THEN rules applied in a backward-chaining manner, WHEN–THEN rules applied in a forward-chaining manner, and facts in the attribute database manipulated by the rules. The system is interfaced to application programs for stress, buckling, and vibration analysis written in FORTRAN, using standard command language and database management utilities.

5.2.4 GEPSE

Chehayeb *et al.* (1985) report the development of GEPSE, a *General Engineering Problem Solving Environment*, in C. The choice of language C was based on its transportability and efficient numerical processing. The inference mechanism in GEPSE is forward-chaining. Engineering knowledge is divided into 'static' and 'active' knowledge. Static knowledge includes the physical description of an engineering system. Active knowledge is defined as scientific laws and heuristic rules that must be satisfied in a particular domain. C's data structures and pointers are used to represent the static knowledge. Active knowledge is represented by procedures and IF–THEN rules using a syntax similar to LISP's syntax. Meta-rules are employed to control the overall problem-solving process. The user interface includes menus and multiple-window input/output. Different windows are used to display and modify the static knowledge, display and modify rules, communicate with the system, and display the trace of the inference mechanism. GEPSE has been used for the description and verification of a simply-supported reinforced concrete beam subjected to a uniformly-distributed load. Longitudinal and cross-sections of the beam are displayed using the graphics command of the C language.

5.2.5 BTEXPERT – an expert system for the optimum design of bridge trusses

Optimum design of a structure is usually achieved through the use of mathematical programming techniques without including any knowledge of the structural design in the optimization process. The application of AI in structural optimization was proposed by Adeli (1984). Arora and Baenziger (1985) also discuss the potential applications of AI in design optimization and present the basic concepts for developing an expert system for design optimization. This system, however, does not take advantage of any specific design domain. Expert systems are developed most effectively for solving problems in a particular domain.

Rogers and Barthelemy (1985) describe a prototype ES for helping the users of the general-purpose optimization FORTRAN program Automated Design Synthesis (ADS) developed by Vanderplaats (1985), called EXADS. In choosing a proper optimization approach, users of ADS must make a decision at three levels. First, they must choose one of the eight strategies available such as sequential unconstrained minimization using the exterior penalty function method, augmented lagrange multiplier method, etc. Next, they must choose one of the five optimizers such as the method of feasible directions for constrained minimization. Finally they must select one of the eight one-dimensional search techniques. Thus, users must choose from about 100 combinations. EXADS is intended to help the user in selecting the right combination. It uses a backward-chaining inference mechanism and a knowledge base with approximately 200 rules. The rules were developed on the basis of guidelines given in the ADS manual (Vanderplaats, 1985), discussion with optimization experts, and a literature search. It has been implemented in Franz LISP on the DEC-VAX and IQ-LISP on the IBM PC/XT computers. It should be noted that EXADS does not aid users in solving a particular class of optimization problem. Users must first formulate the optimization problem using their knowledge of the particular domain.

Gero and Balachandran (1986) discuss the potential of using expert systems for Pareto (multicriteria) optimization. Conflicting criteria must be satisfied in a multicriteria design optimization. The two main problems in multicriteria optimization are generation of the Pareto optimal set and selection of an approximate solution algorithm. They have developed a prototype system using production rules for knowledge representation in a combination of LISP, PROLOG, and C languages on a SUN microsystem workstation. The rule-based knowledge base and the inference mechanism are implemented in LISP, the pattern-matching knowledge used to recognize variables and their relationships is implemented in PROLOG, and optimization algorithms are implemented in C. A high-level controller implemented in LISP lets the three components communicate with each other. The system has been applied to simultaneous maximization of two linear functions of eight variables subjected to eight linear inequality constraints.

The process of detailed design of a large structure made of a large number of components is quite involved. Intuition, judgement, and previous experience have to be used for selecting the right values for the design parameters. Further, since design is an open-ended problem, i.e. in general there is a large number of design alternatives satisfying all the specified constraints, the selection of the optimum design becomes an extremely challenging problem. The most common criterion for selecting the optimum design is minimizing the weight or cost of the structure. The experience of an experienced designer is not usually sufficient to produce the minimum weight/cost structure, especially when the structure is large and has many components. Thus, there is a need to introduce mathematical optimization in the design process.

The fundamental method of knowledge acquisition recommended in practically all the recent books on expert systems is to find one or several human experts in the problem domain and use their knowledge in the expert system (see references at the end of Chapter 1). In fact, this is how the most celebrated expert systems in the fields of medical diagnosis, mineral exploration, and computer configuration have been developed (see Section 1.8).

Adeli and Balasubramanyam (1988) present and expert system for optimum design of bridges trusses, called BTEXPERT (for *Bridge Truss EXPERT*). The scope of BTEXPERT is at present limited to the optimum design of three types of bridge trusses, i.e. Pratt, Parker, and K-Truss for a span range of 100– 520 ft. Design constraints and the moving loads acting on the bridge are based on the American Association of State Highway and Transportation Officials (AASHTO) specifications (AASHTO, 1983).

BTEXPERT is fundamentally different from the structural design expert systems developed so far in two respects. First, mathematical optimization is introduced in the expert system. Second, the machine (computer) is used to obtain parts of the knowledge necessary in the expert system. They are thus extending the current prevalent concept of expert systems by incorporating machine intelligence into the expert system.

Bridges are to be designed for combined dead and live loads. Live loads are usually specified by design specifications. AASHTO live loads are used in BTEXPERT. These loads can be classified into three categories: two-axle truck (H 15 and H 20), two-axle truck plus one-axle semitrailer (HS 15 and HS 20), and uniform lane loadings consisting of a distributed load of uniform intensity but variable length and a single moving concentrated load (Fig. 5.2).

The process of finding the maximum axial forces due to live loads acting on the bridge truss is not straightforward due to the complexity of AASHTO live loads. Adeli and Balasubramanyam (1987a) developed a heuristic approach for finding the maximum compressive and tensile forces in the members of a bridge truss based on the classification of the shape of the influence line diagrams (ILDs) and the type of AASHTO live loads. The procedure uses information about the shape of ILDs for the bridge truss type under consideration. For statically indeterminate trusses, this information is obtained through machine experimentation for any given type of truss. The ILDs for member axial forces of a bridge truss are classified according to their shapes. Decision trees and heuristic rules have been developed for finding the maximum compressive and tensile forces in the members of a given type of truss. This heuristic procedure results in substantial savings in structural analysis computations.

BTEXPERT has been developed using the Expert System Development Environment (ESDE) and the Expert System Consultation Environment (ESCE), described in Section 4.3.6. The two programs are collectively referred

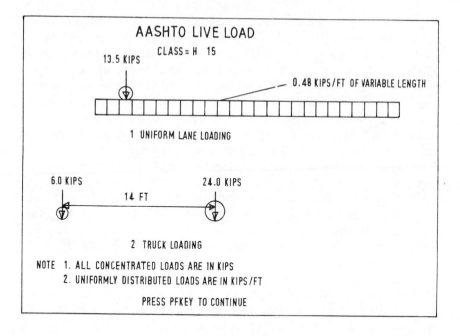

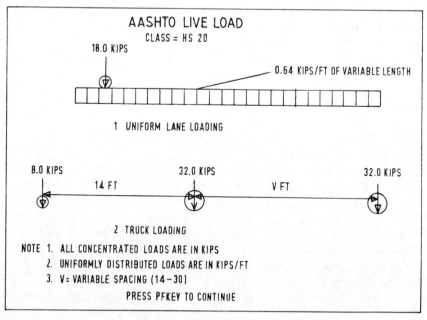

Fig. 5.2 AASHTO live loads plotted by BTEXPERT.

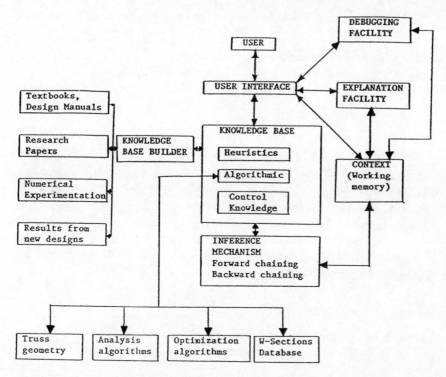

Fig. 5.3 Architecture of BTEXPERT.

to as the Expert System Environment (ESE). The analysis and optimization algorithms have been coded in FORTRAN 77. A graphics interface has been developed using the Graphical Data Display Manager (GDDM) (IBM, 1984).

A schematic representation of the architecture of BTEXPERT is shown in Fig. 5.3. The various components of BTEXPERT are briefly described in the following sections.

(a) *Knowledge base*

The knowledge base of BTEXPERT consists of the domain-specific knowledge and the control knowledge. The domain specific knowledge consists of rules and algorithmic procedures. The control knowledge consists of control commands for solving a problem. Knowledge representation in BTEXPERT consists of facts or parameters, rules, and focus control blocks (FCBs).

A fact or a parameter has a name, type (number, string, boolean, or bitstring), single or multiple value, and other properties. As an example

Slab_continuous_over_3_or_more_stringer_beams

is a boolean parameter and has a value of 'yes' or 'no'.

Rules are concerned with domain facts. Each rule represents an independent piece of knowledge. Rules are classified into the following three categories:

1. Inference rules: The default type of any rule is the inference rule. These rules are processed either by forward or backward-chaining.
2. Single fire monitors: Single fire monitors function independently without any reference to inference rules. Once a parameter in the IF part of a rule gets a value, the single fire monitor is processed.
3. Multiple fire monitors: They are processed exactly like a single fire monitor except that they may be executed many times.

FCBs are the main building blocks in the ESE. The control knowledge needed for solving a problem is developed in FCBs. An FCB represents a certain task to be completed during the problem solving. FCBs can have a hierarchical organization. The decision regarding the assignment of parameters and rules to various FCBs is made by the knowledge base builder. The control knowledge needed for solving a problem can be represented by means of control commands.

(b) *Inference mechanism*

The ESE has both backward-chaining and forward-chaining mechanisms. For an explanation of various inference mechanisms, see Section 2.4.

(c) *User interface*

User interface is provided in the form of visual edit screens and menus in which the user has to type in the values of the required parameters at the appropriate field. Further, a graphic interface has been developed for displaying the truss configuration with joint or member numbering (see Fig. 5.4, for example), the design AASHTO live loads (Fig. 5.2), and ILDs for various member axial forces.

(d) *Explanation facility*

The explanation facility helps the user to examine the reasoning process. The explanation consists of both the RULE text and RULE comments coded by the knowledge base builder. The explanation facility commands are:

1. EXHIBIT: It displays the current value(s) of a specific parameter.
2. HOW: It displays an explanation of how the system determined a value for a parameter.
3. WHY: It displays an explanation of why the system is asking a given question.

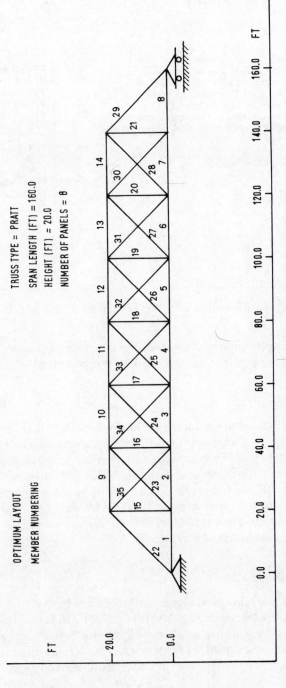

Fig. 5.4 A sample Pratt truss plotted by BTEXPERT.

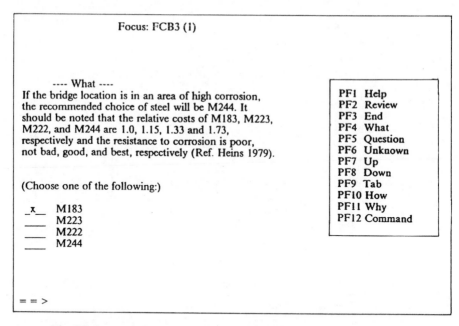

Fig. 5.5 A sample explanation by WHAT command from BTEXPERT.

4. WHAT: It displays more information about a given parameter. Figure 5.5 shows a sample explanation generated by this command.

(e) *Debugging facility*

The ESDE knowledge acquisition editors check each parameter, rule, and FCB for syntax errors whenever they are typed into the system. However, it is the responsibility of the knowledge base builder to make sure that the knowledge base is consistent and complete, since ESE does not check for inconsistencies either between individual rules or in various parts of a rule. The knowledge base builder can use the TRACE facility to debug errors detected in the results. The knowledge base builder can visualize the important steps and the rules fired by the system.

(f) *Knowledge acquisition*

In BTEXPERT, domain knowledge is partly obtained from textbooks, design manuals, design specifications (e.g. AASHTO, 1983), and research papers and journal articles. In addition to these sources, to bridge the gaps in the knowledge base, a detailed numerical machine experimentation in the problem domain was undertaken in order to obtain optimum values of primary design parameters. Knowledge acquisition through machine experimentation was first used by Adeli and Paek in a small knowledge-based system for the design of simply-supported stiffened steel plate girders, called SSPG (Adeli and Paek, 1986) (see Section 5.2.2).

In order to conduct machine experimentation, a software for layout optimization of trusses was developed in FORTRAN 77, called IOTRUSS (Adeli and Balasubramanyam, 1987b). The layout optimization in IOTRUSS is based on changing certain key dimension(s) of the truss and performing optimization for each layout by taking advantage of the interactive environment of the computers with graphic facilities. In contrast to formal shape optimization procedures that are computationally expensive and may produce non-practical designs, the synergic man–machine approach used in IOTRUSS is an effective method for the practical layout optimization of trusses.

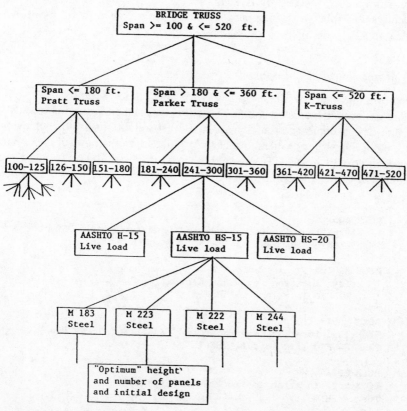

Fig. 5.6 Decision tree for optimum values of height, number of panels, and initial cross-sectional areas (BTEXPERT).

The software IOTRUSS was used to find the optimum values for the height, number of panels, and initial cross-sectional areas of truss members for various span lengths, AASHTO live loads, and grades of steel (Fig. 5.6). The information obtained through machine experimentation was subsequently used in the knowledge base of BTEXPERT.

(g) *Knowledge base development*

The rules and procedures used in BTEXPERT are classified into a number of FCBs. As discussed earlier, each FCB contains rules and procedures for a specific task. The main idea of using FCBs is to classify all the rules and procedures required in an expert system according to their intended use and sequence of application. As an example, one FCB contains the rules for selecting the right type of design live loads for the bridge under consideration, as shown in Fig. 5.7. Another FCB contains the rules for obtaining the yield stress and the relative cost of the steel used in the truss bridge. Another FCB calculates the thickness of the deck slab, and so on. For more on FCBs, see Adeli and Balasubramanyam (1988).

(h) *Mathematical optimization*

The optimum design of a bridge truss consists of selecting the right combination of the cross-sectional areas of the truss members so as to satisfy all the design constraints and produce a least-weight truss. For achieving this, an optimization problem has been formulated on the basis of the design constraints of the AASHTO specifications (Adeli and Balasubramanyam, 1988). The allowable compressive stresses and the slenderness limitations

```
RULE R0011
If Bridge_location is ´State—Road´ and Traffic is ´Light´
Then AASHTO_live_load is ´H—15´

RULE R0012
If Bridge_location is ´Trunk—Highway´
Then AASHTO_live_load is ´HS—15´

RULE R0013
If Bridge_location is ´State—Road´ and Traffic is ´Heavy´
Then AASHTO_live_load is ´HS—15´

RULE R0014
If Bridge_location is ´Interstate—Highway´
Then AASHTO_live_load is ´HS—20´
```

Fig. 5.7 Sample rules for selecting the right type of design live loads.

provided by the AASHTO specification involve the minimum radius of gyration of the cross-section.

Treating the minimum radii of gyration of the cross-sections as additional design variables will double the number of design variables and therefore is not computationally efficient. For all practical purposes, it may be assumed that there exists a relationship between the area of the cross-section and the minimum radius of gyration. At present, the cross-sectional type of the bridge truss members used in BTEXPERT is limited to standard W-shapes given in the AISC manual (AISC, 1980). After a study of the relationship between the cross-sectional area and minimum radius of gyration for W-shapes tabulated in the AISC manual, this relationship was approximated through the use of a piecewise linear regression fit for W-shapes of a given nominal depth (say W12). For finding the solution to the nonlinear programming problem, the method of feasible directions (Vanderplaats, 1984) has been implemented.

It should be noted that the initial layout optimization by BTEXPERT is based on the knowledge learned through machine experimentation. BTEXPERT, however, performs mathematical optimization for finding the optimum cross-sectional areas. Using these optimum areas and heuristic rules, wide flange sections are selected for truss members from a database containing the W-sections given in the AISC manual (AISC, 1980).

To summarize, the approach used in developing BTEXPERT is not based merely on heuristics and experiential knowledge. It uses sophisticated mathematical optimization techniques and knowledge obtained via machine learning. BTEXPERT may be considered as a prototype for a new generation of expert systems for structural design. The approach used in BTEXPERT is not limited to the design of a particular class of structures and can be applied to other types of structures. This new generation of expert systems embracing various advanced technologies such as artificial (machine) intelligence, numerical optimization techniques, and interactive computer graphics will have enormous practical implications.

(i) *Further extensions*

BTEXPERT is currently being extended to the optimum overall design of steel truss and plate girder bridges. In this case, a single optimization algorithm is not the most prudent strategy; and therefore a multialgorithm approach will be used. For optimum design of steel plate girders, the algorithm developed by Abuyounes and Adeli (1986 and 1987) for optimization of simply-supported homogeneous and hybrid plate girders and recently extended by Adeli and Chompooming (1987a and b) for optimization of continuous prismatic and nonprismatic plate girders will be employed.

Heuristic rules and procedures are being developed to improve the efficiency, robustness, and accuracy of the optimization process. For example, heuristic rules are currently being developed for the choice of the right optimization algorithm and appropriate control parameters via machine experimentation. Other heuristic rules are being developed for the classification of constraints into inactive, partially active, active, and violated constraints. The inactive constraints will not be included in the optimization process through a constraint deletion process.

A heuristic procedure is being developed for capturing the trend information of design variables during the optimization process. Based on the results obtained during the optimization cycle, the design variables are classified into fixed, increasing, decreasing, and oscillating variables. Extrapolation procedures can be developed for increasing or decreasing design variables. Finally, heuristic rules are being developed for performing exact reanalysis at selected intervals and selection of approximate reanalysis techniques based on the maximum change in the design variables in a particular design.

5.2.6 RTEXPERT – an expert system for the design of roof trusses

Adeli and Al-Rijleh (1987) present an ES for the design of steel roof trusses, called RTEXPERT (for *Roof Truss EXPERT*). RTEXPERT has been developed in Turbo Pascal, using the ES shell INSIGHT 2 + (see section 4.4.5). The scope of RTEXPERT at present is limited to the design of three types of roof trusses, i.e. flat Pratt trusses, pitched Pratt trusses, and Fink trusses.

```
                    Dead Weight of Coverings
       Please select your choice of shingles. (Ref. ANSI,1982)

           SHINGLES                 WEIGHT (lbs./ft.^2)
           ~~~~~~~~~~~~~~~~~~~~~~~~~~~~~~~~~~~~~~~~~~~~~~

      ──── Asbestos cement shingles............. 4

           Asphalt shingles..................... 2

           Cement tile.......................... 16

           Clay tile............................ Varies

           Wood shingles........................ 3

           Copper or tin........................ 1

           Slate , three sixteenth of an inch... 7

           Slate , one fourth of an inch........ 10


        2 UNKN  3 STRT  6 WHY?          8 MENU  9 HELP  10 EXIT
```

Fig. 5.8 Types of shingles displayed by RTEXPERT.

```
                  Dead Weight of Coverings
Please select your choice of deck. (Ref. ANSI, 1982)

    DECK                    WEIGHT (lbs./ft^2)
~~~~~~~~~~~~~~~~~~~~~~~~~~~~~~~~~~~~~~~~~~~~~~~~~~~~~

---- Metal , 20 gage...................... 2.5

     Metal , 18 gage...................... 3

     2 inch wood.......................... 5

     3 inch wood.......................... 8

     Back to the composition menu




     2 UNKN  3 STRT  6 WHY?            8 MENU  9 HELP  10 EXIT
```

Fig. 5.9 Types of decks displayed by RTEXPERT.

```
                  Dead Weight of Coverings
Please select your choice of insulation. (Ref. ANSI, 1982)

    INSULATION              WEIGHT (lbs./ft.^2/in.)
~~~~~~~~~~~~~~~~~~~~~~~~~~~~~~~~~~~~~~~~~~~~~~~~~~~~~

---- Cellular glass........................ 0.7

     Fibrous glass......................... 1.1

     Fiberboard............................ 1.5

     Perlite............................... 0.8

     Polystyrene foam...................... 0.2

     Urethane foam with skin............... 0.5

     Back to the deck menu




     2 UNKN  3 STRT  6 WHY?            8 MENU  9 HELP  10 EXIT
```

Fig. 5.10 Types of insulation displayed by RTEXPERT.

```
                    Dead Weight of Coverings
      Please select your choice of waterproofing membrance. (Ref. ANSI, 1982)

         WATERPROOFING         WEIGHT (lbs./ft.^2)
      ~~~~~~~~~~~~~~~~~~~~~~~~~~~~~~~~~~~~~~~~~~~~~~~

      ——— Bituminous , graval coverd........... 5.5

          Bituminous , smooth surface.......... 1.5

          Liquid applied....................... 1

          Single ply sheet..................... 0.7

          Back to the insulation menu




         2 UNKN   3 STRT           6 WHY?            8 MENU   9 HELP   10 EXIT
```

Fig. 5.11 Types of waterproofing displayed by RTEXPERT.

```
                              RTEXPERT

      The following is a list of all the steel types in the AISC Manual for Steel
      Construction(1980). If the steel type you are going to use is different from
      the ones shown below, set the arrow on 'None of the above' and press return.

      Please select the steel type you wish to use in the design

      ——— Carbon

          High strength low alloy

          Corrosion resistant high strength low alloy

          None of the above




         2 UNKN  3 STRT           6 WHY?            8 MENU   9 HELP   10 EXIT
```

Fig. 5.12 Types of steel displayed by RTEXPERT.

```
                              RTEXPERT
     Please select the corrosion-resistant high-strength low-alloy steel
     you wish to use.
     NOTE 1 : The first number in the brackets is the yield stress,
              and the second number is the ultimate strength, in ksi.
     NOTE 2 : For more explanation press function key 5 EXPL.
                 (Ref. AISC, 'Manual of Steel Construction', 1980)

───  A242 (42 , 63)

     A242 (46 , 67)

     A242 (50 , 70)

     A588 (42 , 63)

     A588 (46 , 67)

     A588 (50 , 70)

     Change steel type



        2 UNKN   3 STRT          5 EXPL   6 WHY?           8 MENU   9 HELP   10 EXIT
```

Fig. 5.13 Types of corrosion-resistant high-strength steel displayed by RTEXPERT.

```
                         Explanatory Information


  ┌──────────────────────────────────────────────────────────────────┐
  │                                                                    │
  │          CORROSION-RESISTANT HIGH-STRENGTH LOW-ALLOY STEEL         │
  │          ~~~~~~~~~~~~~~~~~~~~~~~~~~~~~~~~~~~~~~~~~~~~~~~~~~~         │
  │     A242 and A588 corrosion-resistant high-strength low-alloy  is  │
  │     the  most  expensive   steel. However,  this disadvantage may  │
  │     be offset when the steel is going  to  be used uncoated. This  │
  │     steel type form a tightly adherent  oxide on its surface when  │
  │     it is exposed  to  atmosphere.  Therefore, it  requires  less  │
  │     maintenance.                                                   │
  │     When coated, this steel provides longer coating life than the  │
  │     other structural steel types.                                  │
  │                                                                    │
  │     Ref. AISC, 'Manual of Steel Construction' , 1980               │
  │                                                                    │
  └──────────────────────────────────────────────────────────────────┘
Press function key 8 BACK to continue



           3 STRT                          7 PRNT   8 BACK   9 HELP   10 EXIT
```

Fig. 5.14 Explanatory information and advice about corrosion-resistant high-strength steel provided by RTEXPERT.

RTEXPERT employs previously-acquired knowledge for selecting the appropriate type of truss, designing the layout of the truss (i.e. selecting the appropriate pitch and number of panels), preliminary design, and utilizes heuristic rules for finding the controlling members for truss design. The heuristic rules reduce the amount of computations needed for the design of members. RTEXPERT presents the final detailed design including computer-generated graphics for truss configuration and cross-sections.

The basis of the detailed design is the American Institute of Steel Construction Specification (AISC, 1980). Dead, live, snow, and wind loads are based on the American National Standard Institute (ANSI) Specification (ANSI, 1982). In present computer-aided design programs, the user must calculate and input the forces acting on the structure due to various loads such as dead, live, snow, and wind loads. RTEXPERT relieves the user of this tedious chore. Instead, the user needs only to select the type of roof

```
                         RTEXPERT

  For the span of      96.00 ft I suggest using pitched pratt truss

  (Ref. Jack C. McCormac,'Structural Steel Design',Third Edition)

  Select the truss you want to use please


 ──── Flat pratt

     Flat pratt top chord inclined

     pitched pratt

     Fink




      2 UNKN   3 STRT          6 WHY?           8 MENU   9 HELP   10 EXIT
```

Fig. 5.15 Sample advice provided by RTEXPERT for selecting the right type of truss.

```
  ┌────────────────────────────────────────────────┐
  │            ** RESOLUTION MENU **                 │
  │            ~~~~~~~~~~~~~~~~~~~~~~~~~              │
  │                                                  │
  │   1 -  HIGH RESOLUTION    (640 x 200)            │
  │   2 -  MEDIUM RESOLUTION (320 x 200)             │
  │                                                  │
  └────────────────────────────────────────────────┘

        ENTER YOUR CHOICE PLEASE ==>> ?
```

Fig. 5.16 Resolution menu in RTEXPERT.

material or coverings (shingles, insulation, waterproofing, etc.). RTEXPERT provides the user with a list of materials commonly used in the United States for roof coverings, as shown in Figs 5.8–5.11. RTEXPERT then automatically calculates all the nodal forces acting on the truss due to dead loads.

For snow and wind loads, the user needs only to identify the name of the location (city and state) of the structure. RTEXPERT automatically computes all the nodal forces due to snow and wind loads. RTEXPERT has a database for snow loads and basic wind velocities in major cities of the United States. For small cities, the user must provide the necessary information. The database can easily be extended to include all the cities in the United States.

RTEXPERT guides the user in the design decision-making process through providing various menus and explanations. Figure 5.12 shows the three basic

```
        ** HIGH RESOLUTION COLORS MENU **
        ~~~~~~~~~~~~~~~~~~~~~~~~~~~~~~~~~~~~

   1  -   BLACK                2  -   BLUE
   3  -   GREEN                4  -   CYAN
   5  -   RED                  6  -   MAGENTA
   7  -   BROWN                8  -   LIGHT-GRAY
   9  -   DARK-GRAY           10  -   LIGHT-BLUE
  11  -   LIGHT-GREEN         12  -   LIGHT-CYAN
  13  -   LIGHT-RED           14  -   LIGHT-MAGENTA
  15  -   YELLOW              16  -   WHITE
```

ENTER YOUR CHOICE PLEASE ==>> ?

Fig. 5.17 High resolution colors menu in RTEXPERT.

```
            ** GRAPHICS MENU **
            ~~~~~~~~~~~~~~~~~~~~~

   1  -   INITIALIZE GRAPHICS
   2  -   RESOLUTIONS AND COLORS MENUS
   3  -   TRUSS CONFIGURATION
   4  -   TRUSS WITH JOINT NUMBERS
   5  -   TRUSS WITH MEMBER NUMBERS
   6  -   TRUSS WITH JOINT AND MEMBER NUMBERS
   7  -   TRUSS WITH LOADS
   8  -   LOADS WITH JOINT NUMBERS
   9  -   LOADS WITH MEMBER NUMBERS
  10  -   LOADS WITH JOINT AND MEMBER NUMBERS
  11  -   CROSS SECTION TYPE NUMBERS
  12  -   GRPHIC MANIPULATION MENU
  13  -   MAIN MENU
```

ENTER YOUR CHOICE PLEASE ==>> ?

Fig. 5.18 Graphics menu in RTEXPERT.

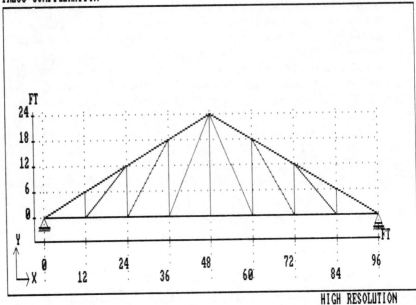

Fig. 5.19 Sample truss configuration with coordinate axes.

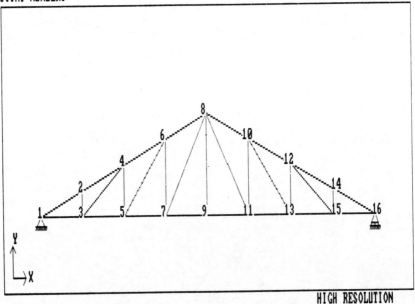

Fig. 5.20 Sample truss with joint numbers.

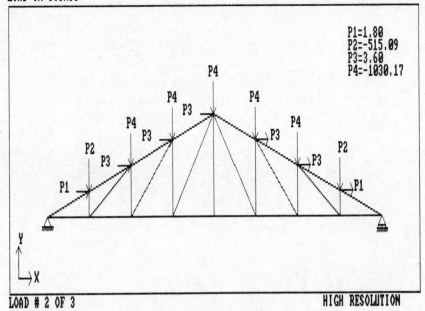

Fig. 5.21 Sample truss with loads.

GRAPH MANIPULATION

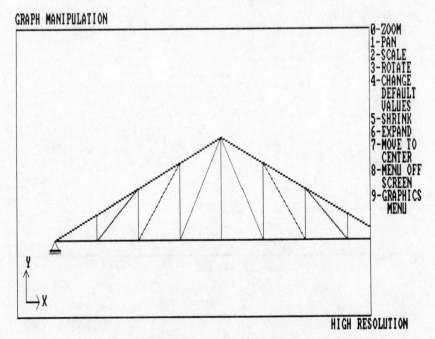

Fig. 5.22 Graphics manipulation menu.

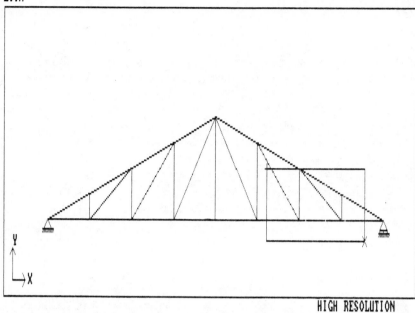

Fig. 5.23 A rectangular part identified for zooming.

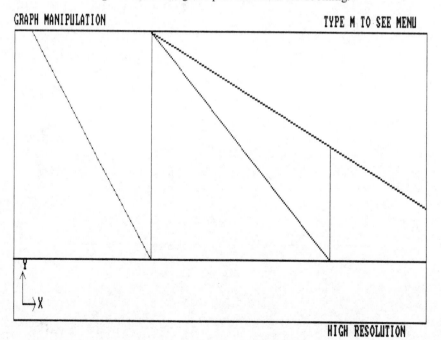

Fig. 5.24 Zooming of the rectangular part shown in Fig. 5.23.

steel types commonly used in steel trusses. If users select corrosion-resistant high-strength steel, then they will be provided with the menu shown in Fig. 5.13. By using the explanation facility of the system, the user can obtain information and advice about the usage of various steel types. An example of this type of explanation is presented in Fig. 5.14. An example of advice given by RTEXPERT for selecting the right type of truss is given in Fig. 5.15.

RTEXPERT has extensive graphic capabilities. The system has been implemented on an IBM Personal Computer. For displaying various truss graphics, the user can choose between the high resolution and medium resolution from the resolution menu of Fig. 5.16. He or she can also choose the display colors after selecting the screen resolution from two colors menus. Figure 5.17 shows the high resolution color menu.

Figure 5.18 shows the main graphics menu. RTEXPERT can display the truss configuration (Fig. 5.19), truss with joint numbers (Fig. 5.20), truss with member numbers, truss with joint and member numbers, truss with loads (Fig. 5.21), loads with joint numbers, loads with member numbers, loads with joint and member numbers, truss with cross-section type numbers, and the cross-section of various members. RTEXPERT has a myriad of graphics manipulation capabilities, including zooming, panning, scaling, rotating, shrinking, and expanding (Fig. 5.22). As an example of zooming, part of a

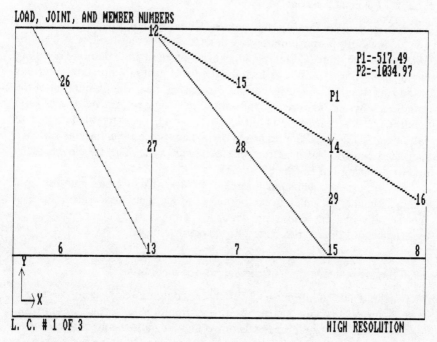

Fig. 5.25 Zooming of the rectangular part shown in Fig. 5.23 with joint, member, and load numbers.

truss identified by a rectangle through cursor movement in Fig. 5.23 has been zoomed in Fig. 5.24. Zoomed displays can also include joint, member, and load numbers (Fig. 5.25).

5.3 CONSTRUCTION ENGINEERING AND MANAGEMENT

5.3.1 Howsafe

To evaluate the safety-related aspect of a construction contractor's organization and operating procedures, Levitt (1986) has developed an ES called Howsafe, using the microcomputer-based ES shell The Deciding Factor (see Section 4.4.3). Construction safety research has been documented in various technical reports and journals. Howsafe is intended to be an electronic means for disseminating the knowledge of construction safety. Using Howsafe, a field construction manager can evaluate a project's or company's safety practices. A similar ES is being developed by Levitt and Kunz (1985) for selecting the type of contract for a planned construction project, using the ES shell KEE (see Section 4.3.4).

5.3.2 ES for plant selection

An experimental ES for selecting materials handling equipment for construction of concrete frame buildings is described by Wijesundera and Harris (1985). The ES suggests suitable categories of plant for materials handling based on a variety of factors including type of ground and soil conditions at the site, whether open excavations are present near the foundation of the structure, physical features of the structure (shape, size, height, etc.), and conditions of site access and obstruction. Using an external database of equipment data, the ES presents more specific recommendations on each suggested category such as the type of tower crane. The system has been developed using the ES shell SAVOIR.

They report problems encountered in knowledge representation and coding. Weights for different factors may not be easily established. Some of the decision-making knowledge depends on the particular expert's past experience and thus varies from one expert to another.

5.3.3 Expert systems for construction project monitoring

McGartland and Hendrickson (1985) discuss potential applications of expert systems in the area of construction project monitoring. Project monitoring involves checking, regulating, and controlling the performance and execution of a construction project. Two areas of project monitoring are discussed as good candidates for ES development: cost and time control, and purchasing and inventory control.

An ES for the cost and time control aspects of project monitoring can analyze and verify the weekly input to a database of activity schedules and estimates, recognize cost overruns or time slippage problems and diagnose potential causes, suggest remedies for the diagnosed problems, suggest possible changes in activities duration or cost, and revise the project schedule for efficient allocation of resources and minimizing the overall time and cost.

An ES for purchasing and inventory control can be developed with the goal of minimizing the overall materials cost. The system can help a project manager for determining the most economical inventory levels by comparing the cost of storing the materials in inventory with the cost of unavailability when they are needed. McGartland and Hendrickson (1985) suggest forward-chaining as the suitable inference mechanism for project monitoring expert systems. They also present sample heuristic rules in scheduling and inventory control.

5.3.4 DURCON

Being developed by Clifton *et al.* (1985), DURCON (for *DU*Rable *CON*crete) is a prototype ES for selecting the constituents of concrete exposed to aggressive environments. It addresses the deterioration of concrete due to four factors, i.e. freeze–thaw, sulfate attack, corrosion of reinforcing steel, and cement–aggregate reactions. The knowledge base in DURCON consists of specification rules from the American Concrete Institute Guide to Durable Concrete (ACI, 1977) and heuristic knowledge obtained from human experts on the durability of concrete. DURCON is a rule-based system developed in PASCAL on an IBM PC using the forward-chaining mechanism. An example of the rules used in DURCON is

IF	severe freeze–thaw conditions are anticipated	AND
	the nominal size of aggregate is 3/8 in. (9.5 mm)	
THEN	the percentage of entrained air should be 7.5	

5.3.5 Other potential applications

Some potential applications of expert systems in construction engineering and management are briefly described in this section. Some of these have already been initiated by ES developers and researchers. Additional examples of expert systems in construction engineering are presented in Chapter 7.

1. ES for finding the cause of moisture penetration in buildings (Allwood *et al.*, 1985).
2. ES for helping to interpret building regulations.

3. ES for selecting the appropriate type of mechanical (heating, air-conditioning, etc.) or electrical facilities for a building.
4. A building security ES for monitoring and evaluating the input obtained from sensors located at various locations in the building, and informing the security personnel when the building is at risk.

5.4 ENVIRONMENTAL ENGINEERING

5.4.1 Expert systems for hazardous waste management

Expert systems are being developed in the area of hazardous waste management. There are numerous inactive hazardous waste sites in the United States. The development of expert systems for characterizing a site in terms of safety, ecological, and environmental risks should prove a valuable tool for evaluating the environmental risk and prioritizing the remedial measures. A waste management system requires expertise in various disciplines such as chemistry, geology, engineering, and toxicology. Law *et al.* (1986) report initial steps taken for the development of a hazardous waste management ES by implementing a prototype ES for determining the permeability (hydraulic conductivity) of the soil and the ground-water flow direction and gradient in OPS5. These items are essential in a hazardous waste site investigation.

The knowledge base of the prototype ES includes rules and facts documented in handbooks as well as rules of thumb obtained from the domain experts. They use the US Environmental Protection Agency (EPA) Hazard Ranking System (HRS) developed by MITRE Corporation (MITRE, 1982) for scoring or ranking the site for its potential to cause health, ecological, or environmental problems. Information presented in the HRS system can be written as production rules. For example,

IF	the depth of the aquifer is shallow (< 20 ft)	AND
	the net precipitation is high (> 15 in.)	AND
	permeability is high (> 0.001 cm/sec)	AND
	the hazardous substance is liquid, sludge, or gas	
THEN	a ground-water release is virtually certain.	

In the HRS scoring system, the assessment of the ground-water migration is divided into four groups: route characteristics, containment, waste characteristics, and the site environment. Law *et al.* concentrate on the first group, i.e. ground-water routing and in particular the determination of the permeability level and ground-water flow direction and gradient. For the determination of the permeability level, for example, they use heuristic rules of the following type:

IF	soil stratification is observed	AND
	there exists a less permeable layer above the soil	
	layer containing the water table	

THEN   the permeability level should be determined from the
         less permeable layer because vertical flow governs.

Their final product is expected to classify an inactive hazardous waste site in terms of the level of ground-water contamination, surface-water pollution, and air pollution. One difficulty they are trying to overcome is the resolution of conflicts among various data sources.

5.4.2 An expert system for fault diagnosis of hazardous waste incineration facilities

Huang *et al.* (1986) describe an ES for diagnosing malfunction in hazardous waste incineration facilities, using the microcomputer-based ES shell M.1 (see Section 4.4.2). It is intended to analyze possible failure modes in the incineration systems and provide countermeasures for dealing with sources of failure. Through an operability study of the incineration facility, failure modes of the system are represented diagrammatically by a hierarchical fault tree. The fault tree is then transformed into a collection of production rules. To represent the imprecise nature of the knowledge of failure, they use fuzzy probabilities. However, uncertainty in M.1 is represented through certainty factors (see Section 2.3.1). In order to apply fuzzy probabilities, they ignore the certainty factor in M.1 and introduce additional production rules for manipulating fuzzy probabilities.

5.4.3 Expert systems for selection of waste disposal landfill sites

In order to select an appropriate site for a waste disposal landfill, biogeo-chemical and hydrologic characteristics of various sites must be extensively studied. The landfill operation includes depositing, compacting, and covering the wastes. The decision-making process of site selection is dependent on heuristic and empirical rules and expert opinion. Rouhani and Kangari (1987) present a prototype ES for the selection of waste disposal landfill, using the INSIGHT 2 + ES shell (see Section 4.4.5. The knowledge base is based on the rules from the US Environmental Protection Agency manual for ranking of uncontrolled hazardous waste sites.

Factors affecting the site selection process are divided into four categories: ground-water route characteristics (seasonal rainfall, permeability of the vadose zone, etc.), waste characteristics (toxicity and quantity of waste), containment facility characteristics, and targets at risk (nearby population, production wells in the vicinity, and use of aquifer). An example rule from the last category is

IF   the distance to the nearest production well is between 1 and 2 miles
AND   the population is between 101 and 1000
OR   the distance to the nearest poduction well is between 2 and 3 miles

AND   the population is between 1001 and 3000
THEN   the condition is relatively safe with an assigned value of 12

A score is assigned to each factor. For ranking the site, an overall score is computed by multiplying the scores for the four factors involved.

Wilson *et al.* (1986) also describe an ES for the evaluation of hazardous sites.

5.4.4 An expert system for analysis of acid rain data

Evaluation of the acidification of aquatic systems such as lakes requires a study of the complicated interaction among aquatic chemistry (water quality), hydrology, atmospheric precipitation, and soil sensitivity data. Swayne and Fraser (1986) describe the development of an intelligent interface and expert system for regional analysis of acid rain data on an IBM PC AT, called RAISON-Micro (*R*egional *A*cidification Analysis by *I*ntelligent *S*ystems *O*n a *Micro*computer). The software is primarily written in C, using the Lattice C compiler and Halo graphics library. It uses a hierarchical map-oriented query language based on a pictorial representation of the region to be analyzed. A custom-developed spreadsheet model is used for the analysis of data. Information from various databases (water chemistry, watershed data etc.) can be accessed simultaneously in spreadsheet form. The program is interfaced to the user through a pull-down menu.

5.4.5 An expert system for assessing groundwater contamination potential by organic chemicals

By combining expert knowledge with a chemical transport and degradation model and using the M. 1 ES shell (see Section 4.4.2), Ludvigsen *et al.* (1986) present a demonstration ES for assessing the ground-water contamination potentials due to organic chemicals. The system uses the ratio of the travel time for a pollutant to pass through the region under consideration and the pollutant's degradation life and confidence factors to rank the organic soil pollutants. At the top level of decision-making, the ranking process is based on three factors: soil characteristics (soil texture, moisture, porosity, permeability, etc.), site conditions (area of containment, recharge rate, etc.), and the characteristics of organic constituents which are presently limited to polynuclear aromatic compounds.

5.5 WATER RESOURCES ENGINEERING

5.5.1 FLOOD ADVISER

An estimation of design flood (the maximum flood) is essential in the design of various structures such as dams, culverts, storm sewers, and bridges. It is common to specify the design flood by its return period which may vary from a few years to 200 years. Various methods are available for estimating the design flood and the selection of the most appropriate method depends on a variety of factors including the importance of the project, the availability of data, and so forth. Fayegh and Russell (1986) outline FLOOD ADVISOR, an experimental ES developed in C for giving advice on the selection of the most suitable method for flood design estimation by classifying the problem into five categories:

1. The stream flow data has been recorded in a station within the basin for a long period of time.
2. The stream flow data has been recorded in a station within the basin for a short period of time.
3. Regional stream flow data is available.
4. Precipitation data is available.
5. No stream flow or precipitation data is available.

The ES also provides information on how to use the recommended method, runs the appropriate flood estimation programs written in FORTRAN and C, and provides an explanation for interpreting the output.

5.5.2 An ES for selecting simulation models in urban storm sewer design

Ahmad *et al.* (1985) describe an ES for selecting the correct simulation model, inputting the correct data, and interpreting the results in urban storm sewer analysis and design. The system is implemented in PROLOG using a rule-based PROLOG shell. It is intended to be used as an intelligent advisor for using a large storm sewer analysis and design package. Knowledge in the system is represented in rules such as

```
IF (NO SURFACE FLOODING) AND (NO SURCHARGING)
AND (AREA IS UNIMPORTANT TO PROBLEM)
THEN (USE SEWERED-SUB-AREA MODEL)
```

5.6 GEOTECHNICAL ENGINEERING

5.6.1 An expert system for geotechnical site characterization

The process of geotechnical site characterization involves finding the properties (such as density, stiffness, and strength) and geometry (such as location, depth, and extent of geologic strata) of soil deposits and locating ground-water tables and piezometric pressures at the construction site of a facility. Geotechnical engineers and geologists try to present a picture of the subsurface conditions using selected field and laboratory test data and heuristic knowledge based on their previous experience with sites similar in geology and geomorphology. Three basic steps can be identified in the site characterization process: field exploration, laboratory testing, and interpretation.

Rehak *et al.* (1985) present a framework for developing an ES for the interpretation of geotechnical site characterization data leading to a probable geometry of deposits and engineering properties of subgrade soils, called SITECHAR. Knowledge types included in the knowledge base of initial SITECHAR are knowledge of geometry and trends, matching soils by description, geomorphology, geology, searching for marker beds, and proximity (such as 'near', 'above', 'adjacent', etc.). They present examples of rules for each category of knowledge. The problem-solving approach is based on the blackboard model in which the overall problem solution is controlled through a single coordinating knowledge-based supervisor. The architecture of the proposed blackboard model, however, works mainly in parallel. This is in contrast to most current blackboard models that are hierarchical.

5.6.2 An expert system for the interpretation of cone penetrometer data

Mullarkey *et al.* (1985 and 1986) describe the development of an ES for interpretation of geotechnical characterization data from cone penetrometer logs, called CONE. CONE is intended (1) to check the validity of the raw data, (2) to classify the soil types, (3) to profile the soil strata, and (4) to infer the geotechnical design parameters such as the friction angle (or angle of shearing resistance) of sands and undrained shear strength of clays. As the cone penetrometer is driven down the soil layers raw data about the cone tip resistance, soil friction, and excess pore pressures (in the case of the piezocone penetrometer) is collected. CONE uses this data to infer the type and geotechnical characteristics of soil layers.

The knowledge base in CONE includes numeric and linguistic or descriptive data such as friction angle or site location, numeric and descriptive inferred data such as shear strength and soil type, and descriptive judgemental information such as appropriateness and accuracy. Fuzzy logic is used to represent the uncertainty in the empirical interpretation of data because the uncertainty is mostly due to vagueness and impreciseness rather than randomness. CONE has been implemented in OPS5 (see Section 3.7) using LISP functions to represent the fuzzy uncertainty. They interestingly note that a typical run of CONE may take up to 1.5 hours on a DEC-20 computer.

5.6.3 An expert system for the design of retaining walls

An ES for selecting and sizing earth retaining walls is described in Gero and Coyne (1986). The knowledge base of the system contains knowledge of various prototypical retaining wall cross-sections and how to select among them. This knowledge is not well documented in the literature; it was obtained through a survey of experts. The selection of the most appropriate type of retaining wall is based on the type of application, soil and topographical conditions, and designer preferences. The ES has been implemented in Quintus PROLOG and C on a SUN 2 Microsystem. User interface is through multiple window and graphics. The inference mechanism is implemented in PROLOG and the graphics in C. Various types of retaining wall cross-section as well as the final design including all the necessary dimensions are presented graphically.

5.6.4 An expert system for retaining wall failure diagnosis

Various factors can cause the failure of a retaining wall. Examples are, the addition of backfill loading such as new roads and buildings close to the wall, natural weathering of the wall, rusting of the reinforcement bars due to corrosive elements in the water, expansion damage during the freeze–thaw cycles, poor construction workmanship, inadequate investigation of the subsoil condition, etc. Chahine and Janson (1987) describe the implementation of an ES in TOPSI for the preliminary diagnosis of the failure of retaining walls, called WADI. TOPSI is a rule-based ES environment similar to OPS5 (see Section 3.7) implemented in Turbo Pascal. WADI is applicable to two types of retaining walls: cantilever reinforced concrete walls and gravity concrete or rubble walls. Domain expertise in WADI was mostly obtained from books and journal articles.

WADI obtains the description and characteristics of the retaining wall, the characteristics of the backfill and bearing soils, and data describing the failure symptoms from an inspection database which includes information collected during field inspection. Using this information and performing some preliminary calculations, WADI first generates all the potential general problems which are classified into the footing problem, the drainage problem, the construction problem, and weak bearing soil. In the next step, a stability analysis is performed and factors of safety against overturning, sliding, and settlement are computed and compared with the allowable values. Final conclusions include an explanation of the potential causes of retaining wall failure and prioritized recommendations for remedial action.

5.7 EXPERT SYSTEMS IN CIVIL ENGINEERING EDUCATION

Expert systems should find very useful applications in civil engineering education, but little has been explored in this direction. A few initial attempts have been reported in the literature. Starfield *et al.* (1983) employed the ES concept in teaching a senior-level mining engineering course. Students were asked to develop conceptually an ES for choosing the appropriate rock blasting method (e.g. smooth blasting or presplitting) for producing a rather smooth and controlled rock surface at the boundaries of an excavation. Students compiled the questions that the ES should ask the user, and the IF–THEN rules that the system would use as its knowledge base. Starfield *et al.* (1983) conclude that experience of developing such conceptual expert systems by students is similar to gaining practical experience.

Slater (1986) presents preliminary work for developing an intelligent computer-aided instruction system for qualitative prediction of deflections and moments in continuous beams. The system is intended to help students in sketching deflected shapes and bending moment diagrams. The rule-based tutoring system should be able to provide explanation and error diagnosis for students.

REFERENCES

AASHTO (1983) *Standard Specifications for Highway Bridges*, 13th edn, American Association of State Highway and Transportation Officials, Washington.

Abuyounes, S. and Adeli, H. (1986) Optimization of steel plate girders via general geometric programming, *Journal of Structural Mechanics*, **14**, No. 4, 501–24.

Abuyounes, S. and Adeli, H. (1987) Optimization of hybrid steel plate girders. *Computers and Structures*, to be published.

ACI (1977) Guide to durable concrete – ACI 201.2R-77. *Journal of the American Concrete Institute*, December.

Adeli, H. (1984) Artificial intelligence in computer-aided design of structures, in *Engineering Mechanics in Civil Engineering* (eds A.P. Boresi and K.P Chong), American Society of Civil Engineers, New York, pp. 320–3.

Adeli, H. (1986) Artificial intelligence in structural engineering. *Engineering Analysis*, **3**, No. 3, 154–60.

Adeli, H. and Al-Rijleh, M.M. (1987) An expert system for design of roof trusses. *Microcomputers in Civil Engineering*, **2**, No. 3.

Adeli, H. and Balasubramanyam, K.V. (1987a) A heuristic approach for interactive analysis of bridge trusses under moving loads. *Microcomputers in Civil Engineering*, **2**, No. 1, 1–18.

Adeli, H. and Balasubramanyam, K.V. (1987b) Interactive layout optimization of trusses. *Journal of Computing in Civil Engineering*, **1**, No. 3, 183–96.

Adeli, H. and Balasubramanyam, K.V. (1988) A knowledge-based system for design of bridge trusses. *Journal of Computing in Civil Engineering*, **2**, No. 1.

Adeli, H. and Chompooming, K. (1987a) Optimization of multispan plate girders, to be published.

Adeli, H. and Chompooming, K. (1987b) Interactive optimization of nonprismatic girders, to be published.

Adeli, H. and Fiedorek, J. (1986a) A MICROCAD system for design of steel connections – program structure and graphic algorithms. *Computers and Structures* **24**, No. 2, 281–94.

Adeli, H. and Fiedorek, J. (1986b) Microcomputer-aided design and drafting of moment-resisting connections in steel buildings. *Microcomputers in Civil Engineering*, **1**, No. 1, 32–44.

Adeli, H. and Paek, Y. (1986) Computer-aided design of structures using LISP. *Journal of Computers and Structures*, **22**, No. 6, 939–56.

Ahmad, K., Langdon, A.J., Moss, W.D. and Price, R.K. (1985) Implementation issues of hydrological expert systems – a civil engineering case study, *CIVIL-COMP 85, Proceedings 2nd International Conference on Civil and Structural Engineering Computing*, Vol. 2, CIVIL-COMP Press, Edinburgh, UK, pp. 407–14.

AISC (1980) *Manual of Steel Construction*, 8th edn, American Institute of Steel Construction, Chicago.

Allwood, R.J., Stewart, D.J. and Trimble, E.G. (1985) Some experiences from evaluating expert system shell programs and some potential applications, *CIVIL-COMP 85, Proceedings 2nd International Conference on Civil and Structural Engineering Computing*, Vol. 2, CIVIL-COMP Press, Edinburgh, UK, pp. 415–20.

ANSI (1982) *Minimum Design Loads for Buildings and Other Structures*, ANSI A58.1-1982, American National Standards Institute, New York.

Arora, J.S. and Baenziger, G. (1985) Use of AI in design optimization, *Proceedings 26th AIAA/ASME/ASCE/AHS Structures, Structural Dynamics, and Materials Conference, Orlando, April 1985*.

Bennett, J.S. and Engelmore, R.S. (1979) SACON: a knowledge-based consultant for structural analysis, *Proceedings 6th International Joint Conference on Artificial Intelligence, Tokyo*, pp. 47–9.

Brown, D.C. and Chandrasekaran, B. (1984) Expert systems for a class of mechanical design activity, *Proceedings of the International Federation for Information Processing WG5.2 Working Conference on Knowledge Engineering in Computer-Aided Design, Budapest, Hungary, 11–14 September*.

Chahine, J.R. and Janson, B.N. (1987) Interfacing databases with expert systems: a retaining wall management application. *Microcomputers in Civil Engineering*, **2**, No. 1, 19–38.

Chehayeb, F.S., Connor, J.J. and Slater, J.H. (1985) An environment for building engineering knowledge based systems, in *Applications of Knowledge-Based Systems to Engineering Analysis and Design* (ed. C.L. Dym), AD-10, American Society of Mechanical Engineers, New York, pp. 9–28.

Clifton, J.R., Oltiker, B.C. and Johnson, S.K. (1985) *Development of DURCAN, an Expert System for Durable Concrete: Part I*, Report NBS IR 85-3186, National Bureau of Standards, US Department of Commerce, Gaithersburg, Maryland.

Dixon, J.R. and Simmons, M.K. (1983) Computers that design: expert systems for mechanical engineers. *Computers in Mechanical Engineering*, November, pp. 10–18.

Douty, R.T. (1976) Structural design by conversational solution to the nonlinear programming problem. *Computers and Structures*, **6**, 325–31.

Elias, A.L. (1983) Computer-aided engineering: the AI connection. *Astronautics and Aeronautics*, American Institute of Aeronautics and Astronautics, July–August, pp. 48–54.

Fayegh, D. and Russell, S.O. (1986) An expert system for flood estimation, in *Expert Systems in Civil Engineering* (eds C.N. Kostem and M.L. Maher), American Society of Civil Engineers, New York, pp. 174–81.

Fenves, S.J. and Norabhoompipat, T. (1978) Potentials for artificial intelligence applications in structuring design and detailing, in *Artificial Intelligence and Pattern Recognition in Computer-Aided Design* (ed. J.C. Latombe), North-Holland, Amsterdam.

Fjellheim, R. and Syversen, P. (1983) *An Expert System for Sesam-69 Structural Analysis Program Selection*, Technical Report CP-83-6010, Division for Data Technology, Computas, Norway.

Gero, J.S. and Balachandran, M. (1986) Knowledge and design decision processes, in *Applications of Artificial Intelligence in Engineering Problems: Proceedings 1st International Conference, Southampton University, UK* (eds D. Sriram and R. Adey), Vol. 1, Springer-Verlag, New York, pp. 343–52.

Gero, J.S. and Coyne, R.D. (1986) Developments in expert systems for design synthesis, in *Expert Systems in Civil Engineering* (eds C.N. Kostem and M.L. Maher), American Society of Civil Engineers, New York, pp. 193–203.

Huang, Y.W., Shenoi, S., Mathews, A.P., Lai, F.S. and Fan, L.T. (1986) Fault diagnosis of hazardous waste incineration facilities using a fuzzy expert system, in *Expert Systems in Civil Engineering* (eds C.N. Kostem and M.L. Maher), American Society of Civil Engineers, New York, pp. 145–58.

IBM (1984) *Graphical Data Display Manager: Application Programming Guide*, Program 5748-XX H, release 4, 3rd edn, IBM Corporation, Cary, North Carolina.

Law, K.H., Zimmie, T.F. and Chapman, D.R., (1986) An expert system for inactive hazardous waste site characterization, in *Expert Systems in Civil Engineering* (eds C.N. Kostem and M.L. Maher), American Society of Civil Engineers, New York, pp. 159–73.

Levitt, R.E. (1986) Howsafe: a microcomputer-based expert system to evaluate the safety of a construction firm, in *Expert Systems in Civil Engineering* (eds C.N. Kostem and M.L. Maher), American Society of Civil Engineers, New York, pp. 55–66.

Levitt, R.E. and Kunz, J.C. (1985) A knowledge-based system for updating engineering project schedules, in *Applications of Knowledge-Based Systems to Engineering Analysis and Design* (ed. C.L. Dym), AD-10, American Society of Mechanical Engineers, New York, pp. 47–65.

Ludvigsen, P.J., Sims, R.C. and Grenney, W.J. (1986) A demonstration expert system to aid in assessing groundwater contamination potential by organic chemicals, *Proceedings 4th Conference on Computing in Civil Engineering*, American Society of Civil Engineers, New York, 1986.

MacCallum, K.J. (1982) Creative ship design by computer, in *Computer Applications in the Automation of Shipyard Design IV* (eds D.F. Rogers, B.C. Nehrling and C. Kuo), North-Holland, Amsterdam.

McGartland, M.R. and Hendrickson, C.T. (1985) Expert systems for construction project monitoring. *Journal of Construction Engineering and Management*, American Society of Civil Engineers, **111**, No. 3, 293–307.

MITRE (1982) *Uncontrolled Hazardous Waste Ranking System – A User's Manual*, MITRE Corporation, FR Vol. 47, No. 137.

Mullarkey, P.W., Fenves, S.J. and Sangrey, D.A. (1985) *CONE: An Expert System for Interpretation of Geotechnical Characterization Data from Cone Penetrometers*, Report R-85-147, Department of Civil Engineering, Carnegie–Mellon University.

Mullarkey, P.W. (1986) A geotechnical KBS using fuzzy logic, in *Applications of Artificial Intelligence in Engineering Problems: Proceedings 1st International Confer-*

ence Southampton University, UK (eds D. Sriram and R. Adey), Vol. 2, Springer-Verlag, New York, pp. 847–9.

Pecora, D., Zumsteg, J.R. and Crossman, F.W. (1985) An application of expert systems to composite structural design and analysis, in *Applications of Knowledge-Based Systems to Engineering Analysis and Design* (ed. C.L. Dym), AD-10, American Society of Mechanical Engineers, New York, pp. 135–47.

Rehak, D.R., Christiano, P.P. and Norkin, D.D. (1985) SITECHAR: an expert system component of a geotechnical site characterization workbench, in *Applications of Knowledge-Based Systems to Engineering Analysis and Design* (ed. C.L. Dym), AD-10, American Society of Mechanical Engineers, New York, pp. 117–133.

Rivlin, J.M., Hsu, M.B. and Marcal, P.V. (1980) *Knowledge Based Consultation for Finite Element Structural Analysis*, Report AFWAL-TR-80-3069, US Air Force Flight Dynamics Laboratory, Wright–Patterson Air Force Base, Ohio.

Rogers, J.L., Jr. and Barthelemy, J.-F.M. (1985) *An Expert System for Choosing the Best Combination of Options in a General-Purpose Program for Automated Design Synthesis*, NASA Technical Memorandum 86329, US National Aeronautics and Space Administration, Langely Research Center, Hampton, Virginia.

Rooney, M. and Smith, S.E. (1983) Artificial intelligence in engineering design. *Computers and Structures*, **16**, 279–88.

Rouhani, S. and Kangari, R. (1987) Landfill site selection: a microcomputer expert system. *Microcomputers in Civil Engineering*, **2**, No. 1, 47–53.

Slater, J.H. (1986) Qualitative physics and the prediction of structural behavior, in *Expert Systems in Civil Engineering* (eds C.N. Kostem and M.L. Maher), American Society of Civil Engineers, New York, pp. 239–48.

Starfield, A.M., Butala, K.L., England, M.M. and Smith, K.A. (1983), Mastering engineering concepts by building an expert system. *Engineering Education*, November, pp. 104–7.

Swayne, D.A. and Fraser, A.S. (1986) Development of an expert system/intelligent interface for acid rain analysis. *Microcomputers in Civil Engineering*, **1**, No. 3, 181–5.

Vanderplaats, G.N. (1984) *Numerical Optimization Techniques for Engineering Design with Applications*, McGraw-Hill, New York.

Vanderplaats, G.N. (1985) *ADS – A FORTRAN Program for Automated Design Synthesis – Version 1.1*, NASA Contractor Report 177985, US National Aeronautics and Space Administration, Langely Research Center, Hampton, Virginia.

Wijesundera, D.A. and Harris, F.C. (1985) The integration of an expert system into the construction process, *CIVIL-COMP 85, Proceedings 2nd International Conference on Civil and Structural Engineering Computing*, Vol. 2, CIVIL-COMP Press, Edinburgh, UK, pp. 399–405.

Wilson, J.L., Mikroudis, G.K. and Fang, H.Y. (1986) GEOTEX: a knowledge-based system for hazardous site evaluation, in *Applications of Artificial Intelligence in Engineering Problems: Proceedings 1st International Conference Southampton University, UK* (eds D. Sriram and R. Adey), Vol. 2, Springer-Verlag, New York, pp. 661–71.

Zumsteg, J.R. and Flaggs, D.L. (1985) Knowledge-based analysis and design systems for aerospace structures, in *Applications of Knowledge-Based Systems to Engineering Analysis and Design*, (ed. C.L. Dym), AD-10, American Society of Mechanical Engineers.

6

Expert systems for structural design

M.L. MAHER, S.J. FENVES and J.H. GARRETT

6.1 INTRODUCTION

The use of computers in structural design to date has been extensive, but limited to algorithmic analysis, proportioning, and graphical presentation of results. The engineer is now able to apply very complex analysis procedures and as a result is able to design more complex structures. However, many of the problems the engineer must address are peripheral to the algorithmic analysis phase of the design; for example, the specification of the initial design configuration and the development of the mathematical model of the design. These problems are not amenable to purely algorithmic solutions; they are often ill structured and the experienced engineer deals with them using his or her judgement and experience. The use of expert system techniques provides a means for using the computer to assist in the solution of these ill-structured problem areas.

This chapter begins with an overview of the structural design process. This is followed by a discussion of expert system methodologies and their relevance to the structural design process. Expert system applications to structural design are presented, including applications to preliminary design, analysis, detailed design, and integrated design.

6.2 OVERVIEW OF THE STRUCTURAL DESIGN PROCESS

The structural design process starts with the definition of a need to transmit loads in space to a support or foundation, subject to constraints on cost, geometry, or other criteria. The final product of the design process is the detailed specification of a structural configuration capable of transmitting these loads with the appropriate levels of safety and serviceability. The design process may be viewed as a sequence of three stages, as described below.

1. *Preliminary design* (conceptual design) involves the synthesis of potential configurations satisfying a few key constraints. Important aspects of this

stage are: synthesizing feasible structural configurations from subsystems applicable to the particular design at hand; formulating and evaluating specific constraints applicable to the configuration(s) chosen (this step may require an approximate analysis to estimate the response of the structure); and choosing one or at most a few of these configurations.

2. *Analysis* is the process of modeling the selected structural configuration and determining its response to external effects. Important aspects of this stage are: transforming a real structure into a mathematical model; selecting and using an analysis procedure; and interpreting the results of the analysis in terms of the actual physical structure.

3. *Detailed design* is the selection and proportioning of the structural components such that all applicable constraints are satisfied. Important aspects of this stage are: detailing the main structural components (beams, columns, etc.) and their subcomponents (connections, reinforcement, etc.); using some controlling constraints (e.g. load-carrying capacity or buckling) followed by the evaluation of secondary constraints (e.g. local buckling or crippling).

There may be significant deviations between the properties of components assumed at the analysis stage and those determined at the detailed design stage, which would necessitate a reanalysis. Other major and minor cycles of redesign may also occur. The process continues until a satisfactory (or optimal) design is obtained. The *conceptualize–analyze–detail* cycle is typical of many design paradigms.

6.3 EXPERT SYSTEM METHODOLOGIES FOR ENGINEERING DESIGN

Expert systems are interactive programs that provide advice on problems that require experience in a particular domain. Many expert systems have been developed and documented in the area of diagnostics, most notably in the medical field (see Section 1.8). In contrast, few expert systems have been developed for design applications (see Chapter 5). As will be illustrated in this section, the considerations in developing an expert system for a design problem are different from those for a diagnostic problem. This section describes some problem-solving strategies that can be implemented for design problems using expert system techniques.

There are many problem-solving strategies that can be implemented using expert system tools and techniques. However, there are basically two approaches to problem solving currently used in expert systems: the derivation approach and the formation approach. The derivation approach involves deriving a solution that is most appropriate for the problem at hand from a list of predefined solutions stored in the knowledge base of the expert system. The formation approach involves forming a solution from the eligible solution components stored in the knowledge base. Depending on the complexity of the problem being solved, an expert system may use one or both of the approaches described above.

Problem solving involves the search for a solution. The search begins at an initial state of known facts and conditions and ends at a goal state. The solution path consists of all states that lead from the initial state to the goal state. In a formation approach to problem solving the known facts and conditions are combined to form a goal state. In a derivation approach, the known facts and conditions are used to derive the most appropriate goal state.

Domain-independent problem-solving strategies are commonly referred to as weak methods and may lead to combinatorial explosions due to a potential lack of focus. Expert systems can be considered strong problem solvers since they employ domain knowledge in the solution strategy. In this section a number of problem-solving strategies currently used in expert systems are briefly presented and discussed in the light of their potential for implementing a formation or derivation approach. More detailed descriptions of a number of problem-solving strategies can be found in Nillson (1980) and a review of problem-solving strategies appropriate for engineering design in Maher (1984).

The strategies appropriate for the implementation of a derivation approach are: forward-chaining, backward-chaining, and mixed initiative (see Chapter 2). These strategies require that the goal states represent the potential solutions and the initial states represent the input data. The use of these strategies requires the development of an inference network representing the connections between initial states and goal states, as illustrated in Fig. 6.1. The

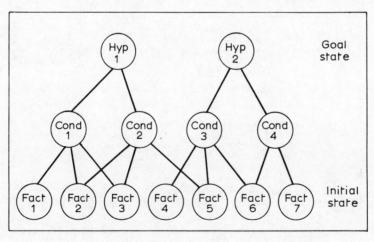

Fig. 6.1 Inference network for a derivation problem.

advantage of using one of these strategies is that they are currently implemented in a variety of expert system tools so that the development process involves defining, testing, and revising an inference network.

The problem-solving strategies appropriate for implementing a formation approach are: problem reduction, plan–generate–test, and agenda control. These strategies may be supplemented with the concepts of hierarchical planning and least commitment, backtracking, and constraint-handling techniques. The development of an expert system using one of these strategies requires the definition of the components of the solution and a description of how the components can be combined. An illustration of the unconnected graph of components is shown in Fig. 6.2. The solution is not completely defined by a goal state, but requires that the solution path be known also. The disadvantage of using one of these strategies is the lack of a standard implementation or expert system tool that employs a strategy appropriate for the formation approach. These strategies are typically implemented using a lower level language such as LISP or a knowledge representation language such as KEE.

The solution to an engineering design problem is shaped by the constraints that must be satisfied. An important aspect of any design application is the representation and use of constraints. Constraint satisfaction techniques involve the determination of problem states that satisfy a given set of constraints. Stefik (1980) proposes three operations on constraints:

1. *Constraint formulation* is the operation of adding new constraints representing restrictions on variable bindings. Typically, the constraints contain increasing detail as the solution progresses.
2. *Constraint propagation* is the operation of combining old constraints to

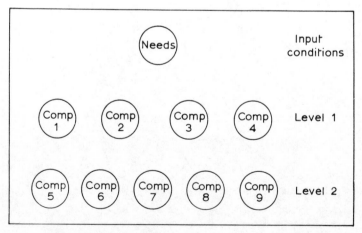

Fig. 6.2 Unconnected graph for a formation problem.

form new constraints. This operation handles interactions between subproblems through the reformulation of constraints from different subproblems.

3. *Constraint satisfaction* is the operation of finding values for variables so that the constraints on these variables are satisfied.

There are a few prototype expert systems for structural design, illustrating the potential for expert systems to aid the design process. This chapter does not include a list of all applications; four specific applications were selected as representative of the authors' work in these areas. Each application is described by presenting the problem it addresses and the organization and implementation of the expert system.

6.4 PRELIMINARY DESIGN: HI-RISE

The preliminary structural design of buildings is based on the designer's experience as well as his or her understanding of the behavior of structural systems. Configuring a structural system for a given building requires a combination of structural system knowledge, experience, and creativity. In practice, only a single or a few alternative configurations may be considered for a given building due to the time required to determine the structural feasibility and efficiency of each alternative. The use of an expert system consultant during the preliminary stages of building design serves two purposes:

1. Several alternative configurations can be considered, modified, and optimized.
2. The experience of senior structural designers can be available to the junior designers in a firm.

HI-RISE is an expert system that configures and evaluates several alternative structural systems for a given three-dimensional grid. The expertise in HI-RISE is derived primarily from a recent book on preliminary structural design (Lin and Stotesburg, 1981) containing approximate analysis techniques and applicable design heuristics.

HI-RISE addresses the preliminary structural design stage by generating feasible structural configurations satisfying a few key constraints. Classes of generic structural subsystems are used as a basis for the generation of feasible systems. Some examples of structural subsystems are: rigidly connected frames, cores, trussed tubes, and braced frames. The generic structural subsystems are expanded and combined to fit the conditions of the particular building. Expansion involves preliminary analysis and proportioning of the components of each configuration to determine its physical feasibility. Constraints applicable to preliminary structural design range from subjective constraints imposed by the architect to functional constraints imposed by the laws of nature. The preliminary structural design of a building requires decisions as to which constraints are applicable and when these constraints are to be considered.

6.4.1 Scope of HI-RISE

The scope of HI-RISE is best clarified by describing the input to the system and the output the user of the system can expect. The input to HI-RISE assumes that space planning has been completed and that any further revision of the spatial layout is done manually by the user. This allows HI-RISE to be concerned only with the structural aspects of the design. The output presented to the user by HI-RISE is a description of the feasible structural systems, detailed to the level necessary for selection and for further modeling and analysis of a selected alternative using formal analysis techniques. The input and output are handled by a graphics-based user interface (Barnes, 1984).

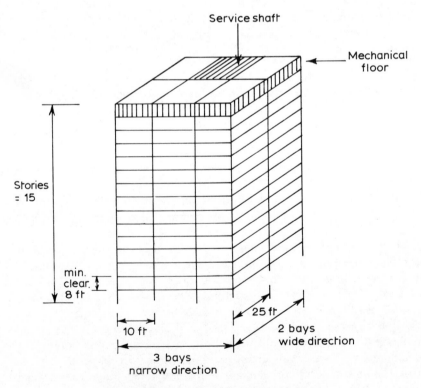

Fig. 6.3 Graphical representation of input.

(a) *Input*

The input to HI-RISE is a three-dimensional grid. The representation of the input grid is illustrated in Fig. 6.3. The input grid specifies to HI-RISE the spatial constraints the building must satisfy. The topology of the grid is defined by the number of stories and the number of bays in each direction, where the directions are referenced by *narrow* and *wide*. The narrow direction is parallel to the face of the grid with the smaller total dimension, and the wide direction is parallel to the face of the grid with the larger total dimension. The geometry is defined by the dimensions of the bays and the minimum required clearance for a typical story. Other spatial constraints, such as the location of vertical service shafts or internal spaces, are specified in terms of their location on the input grid. Other input information required by HI-RISE is the intended occupancy of the building, and the wind and live load.

(b) *Output*

Once the input has been specified, the interaction between the user and HI-RISE is graphical. The context representing the feasible structural alternatives is displayed in tree form as it is generated by HI-RISE. This provides a mechanism by which the user may monitor the activities of HI-RISE. Currently, the user cannot gracefully interrupt HI-RISE, as all interaction is initiated by HI-RISE. In addition, HI-RISE evaluates each alternative according to its relative cost and other features. The user is presented with HI-RISE's calculation of relative cost and evaluation of all feasible alternatives.

The user participates in the selection of a structural alternative from the set of feasible alternatives generated by HI-RISE. Each feasible alternative can be presented to the user graphically, using the original grid and indicating the type and location of the feasible system under consideration. Information about the building components of any feasible alternative may be requested. This information includes the dimensions and designations of the components that make up the structural systems. The user then has the option of choosing a feasible system for further consideration or letting HI-RISE choose on the basis of its own evaluation.

6.4.2 Organization of design knowledge in HI-RISE

The design knowledge that is used by HI-RISE can be considered in two categories: process knowledge and structural knowledge. The process knowledge is a representation of the structural design process formalized by the implementation of HI-RISE. The structural knowledge is a representation of the structural systems and heuristics that HI-RISE considers. These two categories of knowledge are further described below.

(a) *Process knowledge*

Within HI-RISE, the preliminary design process is divided into two major tasks; each task addresses the design of a functional system. The functional systems are designed in a fixed order: first the lateral load resisting system is designed, followed by the design of the gravity load resisting system. The design of a new functional system is not started until the previous functional system design is completed. This convention has the advantage of confident access to information generated in a previous task and the disadvantage of needing information from a task not yet started. In the above task order, results from the design of the gravity system, namely, the type, depth and weight of the floor system, are needed for the design of the lateral system. This information is estimated within the lateral system design task with heuristics using the input information of occupancy and bay span. The task order enumerated above was chosen because the design of high-rise buildings is usually governed by the design of the lateral load-resisting system.

Each of the two major tasks are decomposed into a set of similar subtasks. The subtasks have the same goals for each functional system; however, the details of reaching these goals differ. The general goals of the subtasks are described below.

(i) Synthesis. The first subtask is to synthesize a set of alternatives for the functional system under consideration. The synthesis is performed by combining the appropriate generic subsystems stored in the knowledge base. The search space is pruned using heuristic elimination rules.

(ii) Analysis. The purpose of the analysis subtask is to evaluate the feasibility of an alternative and to define its component groups. Feasibility is evaluated by the formulation and evaluation of one or more feasibility constraints. Analysis provides one set of ingredients of the constraints, namely, the required load capacity of the system components. Component groups are defined so that preliminary sizing proportioning is performed only for one component in a group.

(iii) Parameter selection. The parameters of the system are initially selected using heuristics. These initial parameters are used to evaluate the feasibility constraints. If a constraint is violated, some heuristic recovery rules are applied to revise the parameters. Once satisfactory parameters are selected, i.e. all applicable constraints are satisfied, the alternative is considered feasible.

(iv) Evaluation. Evaluation of a structural design may be based on many diverse features of the design. Evaluation is usually done by designers in an abstract form. Some of the features that may be considered are aesthetics, economics, efficiency, and structural integrity. HI-RISE evaluates alternatives with a linear evaluation function. There is a distinct evaluation function for each of the functional tasks. The variables in the function are features of the system that may be quantified.

(v) System selection. HI-RISE presents all structurally feasible systems to the user indicating which system has been determined to be the 'best', selected as the system with the minimum value assigned by the evaluation function. The user may either accept the recommended design or override the decision of HI-RISE and choose one of the other structurally feasible systems.

(b) *Structural knowledge*

The structural knowledge is organized into three major levels: the global level, the functional level, and the physical level. The physical level is further subdivided into the subsystem level and the component level. The organization of these levels is illustrated in Fig. 6.4.

(i) Global level. The global level contains information global to the entire building design. In HI-RISE, this includes information such as the intended occupancy of the building, the topology and geometry of the three-dimensional grid, and the location of vertical service shafts. This information is

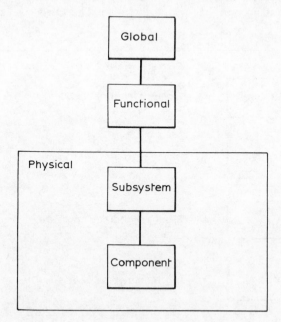

Fig. 6.4 Overall organization of design information.

divided into two sublevels: building information and grid information. HI-RISE does not generate any global information; this information is specified by the user to define a particular design problem

(ii) Functional level. The functional level separates the design information according to function. In HI-RISE, the design information is grouped into two functions, the lateral load-resisting system and the gravity load-resisting system. The lateral load-resisting system defines the structural systems, subsystems, and components that are responsible for resisting lateral loads such as wind or seismic forces. The gravity load system defines the floor system and components responsible for transmitting the gravity loads to the foundation.

(iii) Physical level. The physical level is the hierarchical representation of the structural system alternatives and is composed of the subsystem and component levels. The subsystem level represents the structural subsystems generated during the synthesis task to configure alternative functional systems. The details of these levels differ for the two functional systems.

A lateral load-resisting system is configured from four hierarchical levels of information, as shown in Fig. 6.5. The first level is the representation of alternative three-dimensional subsystems, such as core or orthogonal 2D systems. The second level is the representation of alternative two-dimensional vertical subsystems, such as a braced frame. The third level contains the

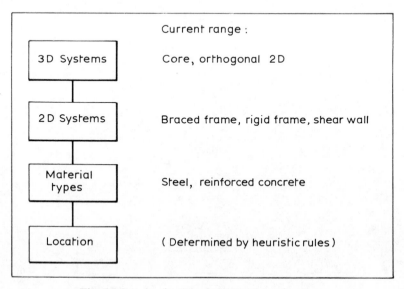

Fig. 6.5 Levels of synthesis for the lateral system.

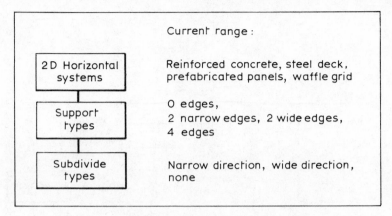

Fig. 6.6 Levels of synthesis for the gravity system.

alternative materials, such as steel. The fourth level includes the alternative locations of the lateral load-resisting system.

The gravity load system is configured by the selection of a two-dimensional horizontal subsystem, such as a reinforced concrete slab or a concrete-topped steel deck. This level is similar to the second and third levels of the lateral system. The second and third levels of the gravity system determine how the slab will be supported and whether intermediate beams will be needed. The levels of synthesis for gravity systems are shown in Fig. 6.6.

(iv) Component level. The component level is the representation of the information associated with the components in each subsystem. Components include beams, columns, diagonals, walls, and slabs. Beams and columns are divided into groups containing components with similar design requirements and are represented in two levels: the first level contains information about all the beams or columns in a subsystem, the second about a typical beam or column in a group.

The result of applying the process knowledge to the structural knowledge is a set of alternative design solutions. These design solutions are illustrated in Fig. 6.7 in the form of a tree. The nodes in the tree represent design selections and the links represent the relationships between the selections. There are three different relationships between the nodes in the tree: *is-alt, part-of, uses*. The is-alt relationship indicates the descendents of the node form alternative configurations; for example, the is-alt relationship between a steel node and a location node indicates that there may be alternative locations for a structural system composed of steel frames. The part-of relationship indicates that the descendents of a node are all part of a single configuration; for example, there are specific beams, columns, and diagonals that are part of a steel braced frame

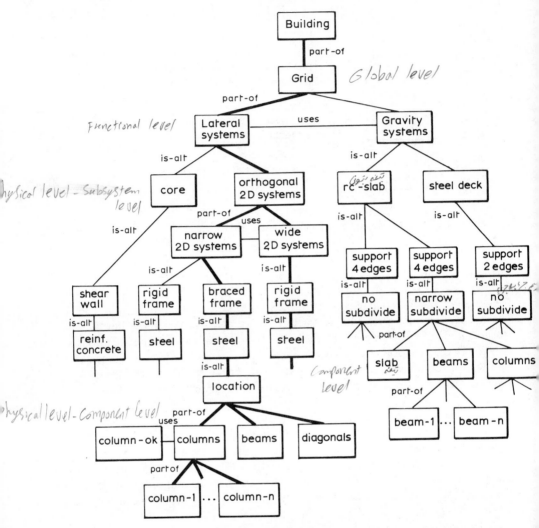

Fig. 6.7 Example of a solution tree.

at a specific location. The uses relationship is a lateral link used, for example, to connect a constraint and the subsystem or component it constrains.

A partial solution is highlighted in Fig. 6.7. This partial solution represents one alternative; other paths through the solution tree represent the other alternative solutions. The highlighted path indicates that steel braced frames in the narrow direction and steel rigid frames in the wide direction represent an alternative configuration for the lateral load resisting system.

6.4.3 Implementation of HI-RISE

The preliminary design process in HI-RISE is formalized and stored in the knowledge base in the form of production rules and LISP functions. This knowledge base contains heuristics, or surface knowledge, in the form of rules; for example, rules are used to represent the elimination heuristics checked during synthesis. The knowledge closer to basic principles, or deep knowledge, is typically represented in LISP functions; for example, LISP functions are used to represent HI-RISE's understanding of the behavior of certain structural systems.

HI-RISE is implemented in PSRL, a frame-based production system language developed at Carnegie–Mellon University (Rychener, 1984). PSRL combines the production system approach with the features of SRL, the Schema Representation Language. (Wright and Fox, 1983). SRL is a LISP-based declarative formalism for representing structured objects and their interrelations. Rules in PSRL are expressed in an extension of Forgy's OPS5 (see Section 3.7) language syntax so that the running environment is similar to that of OPS5. Since rules are translated into schemata, and operate with respect to schemata, the PSRL environment also includes the full set of SRL commands and utilities. Rules are partitioned into small packets that are stored in schemata, organized using SRL relations, and triggered by SRL demons. The development of HI-RISE makes use of these three features of PSRL: rule sets, schemas, and demons.

(a) *Rule sets*

A rule set is defined as a small production system that has its own control strategy. Rule sets are used in HI-RISE to control the order of tasks, to synthesize structural systems, to group elimination rules into classes, and to proportion components. An example of a rule set is a group of elimination heuristics considered after the selection of a 2D lateral system. One rule included in the group is:

IF number of stores > 40
  AND 2D lateral system is rigid frame
THEN alternative is eliminated

(b) *Schemas*

A schema is similar to a frame in other representation languages. A schema may have any number of slots and slot values. A slot may simply be an attribute or may be a relation. Slot values may be attribute values or other schemata. This representation allows the definition of a tangled hierarchy with inheritance most often occurring from parent to descendent. Schemata are used in HI-RISE to define the templates used for the instantiation of the solution tree. An example of a schema is one that represents the lateral system in the narrow direction:

```
{2D-lateral
      direction: narrow
      part-of: 3D-lateral
      description: rigid frame}
```

(c) *Demons*

A demon is a function to be evaluated when a certain condition exists. A demon may be associated with any slot in a schema. Demons are used in HI-RISE to trigger the execution of a rule set or to evaluate a LISP function. The ability to evaluate LISP functions provides a means for representing analysis procedures that may be difficult to represent in pure if-then rule form.

6.5 ANALYSIS ASSISTANCE

Analysis is the process of determining the response of a fully specified structure to its environment. The response quantities of interest are the stresses and stress resultants (forces and moments) in various regions or components and the deflections of various points. The environment describes the loads acting on the structure, including equivalent loads produced by thermal effects, material changes such as shrinkage and creep, or differential displacements. A fully specified structure is one whose topology, material properties, and boundary conditions have all been previously described.

The most highly developed area of analysis is the finite element method (FEM). The high level of maturity of the FEM methodology is evidenced by the large number of available commercial programs and the even larger number of textbooks, journals, short courses and other dissemination mechanisms devoted to the subject. Essentially, FEM has become the standard method for modeling and evaluating the physical performance of structural and mechanical systems in the aerospace, nuclear, marine, civil and mechanical disciplines. In all these fields, there is a need for modeling an increasingly wider range of physical performance phenomena in all stages of system design, from the earliest conceptual studies to the most detailed component performance evaluations.

6.5.1 Need for modeling and interpretation assistance

With the availability of literally hundreds of general-purpose FEM programs coupled with their broad range of capabilities, the role of the finite element analyst has drastically changed. Increasingly, the primary functions of the analyst are those of (1) *modeling*, i.e. translating a physical problem into an appropriate computational mechanics model, and (2) *interpreting* the results obtained from the mathematical model in terms of physical performance. However, there is a major mismatch between the needs for more extensive and realistic use of FEM and the capability of analysts to respond to these needs.

On the one hand, it may take an analyst a year or more to learn to effectively and efficiently use the common options and capabilities of a large FEM program. The total set of capabilities of a comprehensive FEM program is not likely to be exercised by any single user during his or her entire professional career. The novice analyst, and even an experienced analyst confronting a new class of problems, is even less well prepared to make modeling and interpretation decisions in terms of defining the aspects of the problem pertinent to the mathematical model, selecting the appropriate options for modeling these aspects, evaluating the resulting response, and revising the model as warranted.

On the other hand, there is a very small number of experienced finite element modelers, who can confidently and reliably model physical problems for finite element analysis and interpret the results in terms of the key design objectives and constraints. Furthermore, their expertise is likely to be confined to a particular class of problems (e.g. thick-walled vessels) and to the capabilities and limitations of one (or a very few) FEM programs.

The major professional need, then, is to accumulate, organize and thereby facilitate the transfer of the expertise of experienced modelers to other, less experienced analysts for the same class of problems and same FEM programs and, eventually, 'aggregate' such expertise over many different classes of problems and many different FEM programs.

6.5.2 Role of expert systems

Knowledge-based expert systems (ES) show the promise of providing a methodology for such FEM modeling aids. FEM modeling and analysis assistant ESs, rather than being separate, *stand-alone* expert system applications, may be termed *intelligent pre- and post-processors*, in the sense that they act as knowledge-based front ends or interfaces to algorithmic programs. Architecturally, they are closely related to classification or diagnostic systems, in that they are data-driven (by either input data or analysis results) and their task is to select the appropriate analysis model or the correct interpretation of the analysis results (including selecting calibration and refinement steps, if appropriate). In both modeling and interpretation, the ES selects from a class of known models, processes, etc., represented in its knowledge base, rather than plans or designs a set of actions known only by the applicable constraints.

Several hybrid ESs have been developed which incorporate two forms of knowledge representation: *declarative knowledge*, representing either purely empirical knowledge or the expert's compiled causal knowledge, i.e. the shortcuts they have acquired from experience so that they don't always have to reason from first principles (Chandrasekaran and Mittal, 1985); and *procedural knowledge*, representing those components of the domain knowledge in which the problem-solving strategy is well established and can be implemented as an algorithm. In these ESs, linkages are provided from the declarative knowledge to procedural components, typically in the form of 'procedural attachments', so that the appropriate algorithms can be 'called' as part of the overall problem-solving strategy (Smith and Young, 1983).

In a useful FEM modeling and analysis assistant, the FEM program cannot be viewed as a single 'procedural attachment' to be called once when the model has been generated. Rather, an intimate, two-way, closed-loop linkage must be provided. Through this linkage, the ES has to assist the analyst to prepare components of the model, possibly execute portions of the analysis, and build up the model incrementally. Similarly, the ES needs to assist in the incremental evaluation and interpretation of a model and in the calibration and refinement of a sequence of models.

6.5.3 Precedents

Two early precursors of analyst assistant ES were HYDRO and SACON. HYDRO (Gasching *et al.*, 1981) is a knowledge-based expert system developed using the PROSPECTOR (see Section 1.8.3) framework to aid a hydrologist in generating numerical parameter values required as input to the Hydrocomp HSPF watershed hydrology simulation program. The knowledge base of HYDRO consists of a large number of small inference networks that represent the expert's knowledge for generating the individual input parameter values.

An early expert system addressing some aspects of an automated consultant to advise nonexpert engineers in the use of a FEM program was SACON (see Section 5.2.1). The structural mechanics knowledge base of SACON consists of: (1) rules for inferring analysis strategies, consisting of the identification of the most appropriate analysis class to be performed and associated analysis recommendations; (2) rules for inferring the controlling stress, deflection, and nonlinear behavior of substructures; and (3) mathematical models, in the form of procedural attachments, for estimating non-dimensional stress and deflection bounds for each substructure, based on its boundary conditions and loading. SACON was never intended for production use. Its sole purpose was to evaluate the EMYCIN environment for diagnostic applications other than the original domain of the medical diagnostic system MYCIN. Expert systems such as HYDRO and SACON provided the first practical mechanisms for using expert advice in the modeling (pre-processing) and interpretation (post-processing) of physical models.

Two knowledge-based analysis and design systems that can serve as direct prototypes of the FEM modeling and interpretation assistant sketched here have been developed at Lockheed Palo Alto Research Laboratory: the Composites Design Assistant (CDA) and the Buckling Expert, as described in Section 5.2.3.

The development strategy of the Lockheed research group for building and evaluating knowledge-based systems is worth reproducing here (Zumsteg and Flaggs, 1985):

1. Develop rules incorporating experts' knowledge of structural behavior, which analysis code to use, and whether the expert system can solve the problem.
2. Develop rules incorporating experts' knowledge of which options in a given analysis code should be used.
3. Develop rules incorporating experts' knowledge of how to set up input for analysis code (which will require that the user provide the structural geometry, material properties, loading conditions and modeling constraints).
4. Interface the analysis code(s) to the expert system (the manner in which this is accomplished depends on the component operating systems) so the expert system can run the analysis code(s).
5. Develop rules incorporating the capability to run the analysis code, using the input constructed by the rules from step 3.
6. Interface the analysis code(s) to the expert system so that the expert system can extract results from the analysis code(s) output.
7. Develop rules incorporating the experts' knowledge of how to use the results of the analysis to determine the behavior of the structure.
8. Develop rules incorporating the experts' knowledge of how to determine the adequacy of the structure, and how to modify the structure to improve its behavior.

The last item in the list, the 'experts' knowledge of... how to modify the structure to improve its behavior', expands the context from analysis proper to the broader issue of design, a promising area of ES application addressed earlier in this chapter.

6.5.4 A framework

The challenge in developing an ES environment for finite element modeling and analysis assistance lies in the fact that it must simultaneously serve two different purposes. On the one hand, the environment must provide a maximum level of independence to user organizations, so that they can 'customize' the ES to reflect their own expertise. On the other hand, the environment should support the aspiration of eventually providing a repository of pooled knowledge that can serve as a 'community memory' of the discipline. The development of a 'general-purpose' FEM modeling and analysis assistant thus poses two sets of significant issues.

First, the development of a modeling and analysis assistant for the full range of physical problem types encountered in FEM work and applicable to a wide range of FEM programs is clearly an effort of the order of twenty or more man-years, requiring the cooperative effort of many domain experts and a large group of knowledge engineers. There seems to be no clear incentive for unilateral development of such a system by any one FEM program vendor or any one user organization.

A conceptual framework for the FEM analysis and interpretation assistant is based on the blackboard architecture, consisting of a number of domain knowledge sources that communicate through a global data structure, the blackboard, controlled by an inference mechanism (Hayes-Roth, 1985; Rehak and Howard, 1985). The knowledge sources have access to resources to aid them in their task. Finally, the inference mechanism makes use of a number of strategist knowledge sources that guide the solution strategy. The principal components of the system are described in detail below.

(a) Blackboard

The blackboard consists of information generated by the knowledge sources (KS) during the problem-solving process. The blackboard is hierarchically organized into levels representing the abstraction hierarchy of the problem. Normally, the knowledge sources are specific to certain levels in the blackboard, i.e. their activation depends on information posted at one level and their actions post or modify information at some other level.

For the FEM analysis and interpretation assistant, the blackboard levels, proceeding from the most abstract to the most detailed, are:

- *Abstract model*, the highest-level global description of problem to be analyzed and the goals of the analysis and modeling task
- *Behavior model*, defining the significant modes of behavior and likely failure modes and limit states to consider
- *Analysis model*, identifying the analysis models and options appropriate to the task
- *Geometry model*, representing the geometric aspects to include in the model
- *Discrete model*, including the idealizations at the substructure and element group levels
- *Mapped model*, the problem mapped to a neutral file or to the input to a specific FEM program, and
- *Response model*, resulting from the execution of the FEM program.

Typically, the action of the KS is to elaborate from the abstract to the detailed representation; however, when the geometry of the structure is given first, the role of the KS is to extract the higher levels from the geometric model.

In addition to the vertical abstraction hierarchy sketched above, the blackboard can have a horizontal dimension as well. In most blackboard systems, the horizontal dimension represents alternate plausible hypotheses or partial design solutions. While segments of the blackboard may deal with alternative hypotheses (e.g. alternative behaviors, analysis options, or discretizations), the main use of this dimension will be to 'track' the evolution of the model.

(b) *Knowledge sources*

The knowledge sources are independent chunks of knowledge. They do not communicate directly, but participate in the problem-solving process by acting on entries in the blackboard. Each KS consists of a condition part and an action part; the KS becomes a candidate to be executed when the condition part is satisfied in the blackboard; execution triggers the action part which makes additional entries on the blackboard.

One set of KS serve to elaborate the model from one level of abstraction to the next lower one. Their function is implicit in the definition of the blackboard levels. These KS are:

- *Abstraction modeler*
- *Behavior modeler*
- *Analysis model generator*
- *Geometry builder*
- *Mapper*
- *Response extractor.*

In addition, as indicated earlier, there is a need for a *geometry extractor* KS which extracts from a given FEM model geometry the pertinent analysis, behavior and abstract models. Finally, there is a *response evaluator* KS which takes the existence of a response model as its condition and evaluates the response with respect to the high level models at the abstract, behavior and analysis levels.

(c) *Resources*

The knowledge sources are augmented and assisted by analytical knowledge and reference information collectively called *resources*. Three principal types of resources are identified:

1. *Physical class taxonomies* represent an extended taxonomy or semantic network of the various classes of physical problems amenable to FEM modeling. Their purpose is to provide pattern matching capabilities to the

abstraction modeler, behavior modeler and analysis model generator so that the definition of problem class and key problem parameters can be used by the modelers in their tasks at each level of abstraction. The major design objective in developing these taxonomies will be to avoid exhaustive enumeration of individual problems to be encountered, but rather to build a multi-level classification of problem types based on their functionality, behavior, failure modes, analysis strategies and spatial decompositions. It is also expected that a large part of knowledge acquisition can be isolated into modifying these taxonomies either by specialization (customization to individual organizations) or generalization (merging or pooling knowledge of separate organizations).

2. *Program capability taxonomies* represent, in a manner similar to the above, the capabilities, advantages and limitations of FEM programs. The taxonomy must be rich enough so that the mapper KS can make recommendations on the appropriate program(s) to use based on the high level abstractions generated by the other KS, or, if a particular program is not available in the integrated system, make recommendations on alternative modeling strategies so that the available program(s) can be effectively and efficiently used. As the previous taxonomy, the program capability taxonomy needs to be designed so that knowledge acquisition about additional programs can be largely isolated to expansion of the taxonomy data base.

3. *FEM programs per se*, including translators to and from neutral files, are isolated in the design to serve only as resources operating on the mapped model to produce the response model. The issues in this interconnection are largely implementational, and deal with the question of intimately integrating algorithmic programs, likely to be written in FORTRAN, with the knowledge-based components. It is expected that advances in operating systems and versatile workstations will greatly simplify the run-time linkages needed.

(d) *Strategist knowledge sources*

The overall problem-solving strategy of the system is guided or focused by a number of strategist knowledge sources. In contrast to the domain KS, the strategist KSs don't deal with FEM modeling and interpretation knowledge, but with the process knowledge (goals, subgoals, pre-conditions of domain tasks) needed to accomplish tasks.

Five distinct strategists are foreseen:

1. The *model generator strategist* is expected to be most frequently used. Its role is to guide the modeling process in a top-down or backward-chaining fashion from the most basic definition of a problem through recursive

expansions in the abstraction hierarchy to execution to the completed model.

2. The *model extractor strategist* guides the process when the problem geometry is already available, e.g. from a CAD system description. It needs to 'drive' some of the KS in a bottom-up or forward-chaining strategy to infer behavior and controlling modes and analysis options.

3. The *calibration/refinement strategist* guides the process after an initial model has been generated and analyzed, suggesting refinements at the discrete and mapped model levels so as to improve the realism and 'ruggedness' of the model and the responses it generates. It is possible that this strategist will need some additional domain KS, not previously listed, dealing with sensitivity analyses and response post-processing (e.g. code conformance checking).

4. The *evolution strategist* guides the process, including the previous three strategists, to assist in the dynamic evolution of a FEM analysis task from the simplest, approximate model to models of increasing complexity, realism and reliability. The first version may use a depth-first strategy, forcing the generation of an early, approximate model, to be successively refined and expanded at the behavior, analysis and geometry levels. Eventually, this strategist will need to contain a cost estimation KS, so that effective tradeoffs between model complexity and modeling costs can be made.

5. The *training/education strategist* would be user-, rather than problem-oriented. It would use the rest of the system to provide training and education to users to assist not just absolute novices, but to analysts switching to different physical classes or different programs.

(e) *Summary*

The conceptual framework presented responds to the dual need of providing simultaneously for specialization by individual organizations and for potential generalization by the discipline at large. The framework addresses the issue by including in the knowledge sources only general, commonly agreed upon modeling knowledge and relying on the resources for much of the specialized, individual knowledge. To cite some trivial illustrations, few analysts would disagree with 'rules' such as:

IF fatigue is an important behavior mode
THEN make provisions for fatigue analysis

or

IF sharp gradients in stresses
THEN consider mesh refinement

Where analysts legitimately differ is in the premises leading to the above conditions (when is fatigue an important behavior mode or what constitutes sharp gradients?) and in the implications of the above conclusions (how to make appropriate fatigue analysis provisions or mesh refinements). Furthermore, the analysts' expertise and knowledge is likely to be based on experience with specific classes of problems (e.g. bridges versus pressures vessels) so that the problem class designation can directly 'trigger' many of the details needed. This separation of knowledge types is the guiding motivation for the separation of knowledge sources and resources presented. Similarly, the separation of strategist knowledge sources from the domain knowledge sources is predicated on the use of the rich literature on problem-solving strategies in AI and expert systems for the design of the domain-independent strategists.

6.6 DETAILED DESIGN: SPEX

Detailed design is the determination of the properties of *all* structural components subject to the satisfaction of structural integrity and functionality constraints. Functionality constraints ensure that the structure performs its intended function. For example, a functionality constraint might limit the column spacing in a parking garage to be no less than 30 ft in order to ensure that enough open space exists for cars to enter and exit the garage. Structural integrity constraints ensure that the structure is safe and serviceable and that the behavior of each structural component does not exceed any of its behavior limitations. A *behavior limitation* is a specific limit state for a component in a specific stress state; a *limit state* is a unique mode in which a component fails to perform its intended function, such as yielding or buckling. Most structural integrity constraints are derived from the requirements of a governing structural design standard; the requirements of a design standard are mathematical and logical representations of behaviour limitations of a component.

The determination of component properties is not solely performed in detailed design, but in preliminary design as well. However, only the properties of *key* components are determined during preliminary design, while those of *all* components are determined during detailed design. Not only is the number of components designed influenced by the *design stage* (either preliminary or detailed), but so is the detail to which each component is designed. The stage of design can be viewed as an indication of the accuracy of the predicted force distribution in a structure. At a preliminary stage of design, the predicted force distribution is inaccurate and hence component design should only be approximate, while at a detailed stage of design, the force distribution is much more accurate and so should be the component design.

6.6.1 Preliminary component design

During preliminary design stages, the structural response to external loads, determined by structural analysis, may vary greatly from one iteration to the next. Because of the variance in force distribution during preliminary design, designers do not design a component so that *all* of its behavior limitations are satisfied. As the force distribution changes, the component becomes over- or under-conservative and must be redesigned. Satisfying all of the behavior limitations of a component is time consuming and cannot be performed every time the force distribution is altered. Thus, designers use their design experience to select a few key component behavior limitations and only consider those limitations during preliminary design stages.

In addition to only satisfying a few key behavior limitations during preliminary design, designers also only determine values for a few key component properties. For example, common key properties for the preliminary design of steel beams are the section modulus and the cross-sectional area. The consideration of only key component properties in preliminary stages of design is called *sizing*; the key component properties are called *sizing attributes*. During sizing, only the relationships between the sizing attributes and the key behavior limitations are considered; the relationships between the sizing attributes and the detailed component properties are not considered. The effect of sizing is to remove unnecessary component details from consideration during the task of satisfying the key behavior limitations.

6.6.2 Detailed component design

During detailed design, the predicted force distribution within the structure is much more accurate. The designer must now ensure that all applicable behavior limitations for all components are satisfied. However, designers do not attempt to satisfy all behavior limitations simultaneously. Instead, they use their design experience, the same experience used in selecting key behavior limitations in preliminary design, to select a set of behavior limitations to explicitly satisfy. However, unlike preliminary design stages, the unselected behavior limitations are checked after the component is designed. If any behavior limitation is violated, the component is redesigned to satisfy that behavior limitation in addition to those originally selected.

At detailed design stages, the designer must determine *all* component properties. The determination of all component properties, and not just key component properties, is called *proportioning*. In addition to the relationships considered during sizing, proportioning considers the relationships involving detailed component properties, such as the relationship between section modulus and the flange and web dimensions.

The results from sizing (i.e. the values of the sizing attributes) can directly or indirectly influence proportioning. When the sizing attributes are forced to maintain their values during proportioning, sizing directly influences proportioning. When the sizing results are used only as a starting point for the proportioning process, sizing indirectly influences proportioning. The values of the sizing attributes found during sizing may be changed during proportioning in order to satisfy relationships not considered during sizing.

6.6.3 Formal model

The following steps compose a formal model of the component design process that is consistent with the definitions of preliminary component design, detailed component design, sizing and proportioning.

1. Define the design task by providing: the component type, certain component properties (e.g. length), the governing design standard, any external constraints to be satisfied, the forces on the component, the design stage (detailed or preliminary), sizing attributes, etc.
2. If the design stage is preliminary, no requirements are checked after the component is designed and hence, none need to be identified for checking.
3. If the design stage is detailed, retrieve all requirements within the design standard that could possibly govern the design of the specified component and that should therefore be checked for conformance.
4. Using design experience, select a set of behavior limitations that should be explicitly satisfied during the design process, and translate the behavior limitations into specific design standard requirements. The requirements resulting from the translation behavior limitations are called *design requirements.*
5. From the set of design requirements, build a set of *design constraints* that, when satisfied, guarantee the satisfaction of the design requirements. Sizing attributes will affect the generation of design constraints, in that certain constraints will be suppressed by the presence of sizing attributes. If no sizing attributes are declared, then all component properties are determined, i.e. proportioning is performed.
6. To the set of design constraints, add any external constraints, which may be functionality constraints or additional structural integrity constraints.
7. Find a set of component data item values that satisfies all of the design and external constraints. The satisfaction of the constraint set involves some form of search, which can be in the form of a mathematical programming problem or a database lookup.
8. If the set of constraints is found to be unsatisfiable, some of the requirements might be inapplicable and must be *replaced* with other requirements.
9. If the design stage is preliminary and the set of design constraints is satisfied, no conformance checking is performed. All requirements not considered as design requirements are assumed to be satisfied. At this point, the component design process is complete.
10. If the design stage is detailed and the set of design constraints is satisfied, check the rest of the requirements that were not selected as design requirements.

11. If the design stage is detailed and no violated requirements are found, the set of design requirements is clearly a *superset* of the set of governing requirements and a component design has been found that conforms to the governing design standard. At this point, the component design process is complete.
12. If the design stage is detailed and a requirement is found to be violated, the violated requirement is *added* to the design requirements, the constraint set is modified, and then the constraint set is re-satisfied starting with the set of variable values from the previous solution.

6.6.4 Implementation of SPEX

A knowledge-based structural component design system, SPEX, implements the model of component design described above. SPEX is classified as a *knowledge-based* system because:

1. It applies explicitly represented heuristic (shallow) knowledge to specific subproblems in the design process, such as hypothesis generation and backtracking control; and
2. It treats the design standard to which its results must conform as explicitly represented causal (deep) knowledge and uses this knowledge to design a structural component.

SPEX is implemented as a *blackboard* system because the component design process uses both knowledge-based and algorithmic subprocesses and the blackboard architecture facilitates the integration of diverse knowledge sources. The architecture of SPEX is shown in Fig. 6.8 and a HEARSAY-II-like (Erman, *et al.*, 1980) presentation of the interaction between the knowledge sources and the levels of abstraction in the blackboard is shown in Fig. 6.9. The arrows represent the refinement of component design information from one level of abstraction to another.

(a) *Blackboard*

The blackboard is divided into five levels of abstraction: task specification, design focus hypothesis, standard requirements, constraints and solution. The levels of abstraction in the blackboard provide a medium for top-down translation of a high-level task description into a low-level description of the properties of the component.

(b) *Knowledge base*

The knowledge base in SPEX is divided into two parts: the design process modules and design knowledge. The design process modules are described as

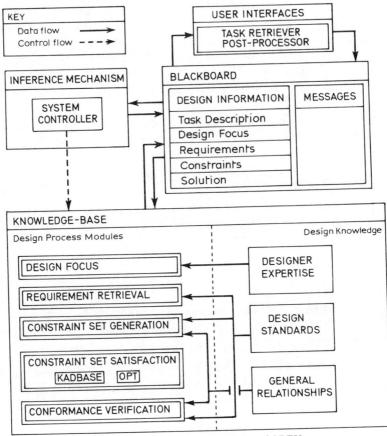

Fig. 6.8 The functional modules of SPEX.

follows.

1. The design focus module generates, or completes, a design focus hypothesis (a set of behavior limitations to satisfy during design) using a set of expert rules for choosing the proper focus of the design process.
2. The requirement retrieval module generates two lists of requirements: a list of requirements that must be checked and found to be satisfied and a list of requirements that are translations of the behavior limitations within the design focus hypothesis, called design requirements.
3. The constraint set generation module generates a set of constraints from the design requirements. If the constraint set is unsatisfiable, this module must determine if the problem lies in its construction of constraints or in the design focus hypothesis. For the first case, the constraint set will be modified in an attempt to make the constraint set satisfiable, but the design focus hypothesis will remain unchanged. For the second case, the constraint

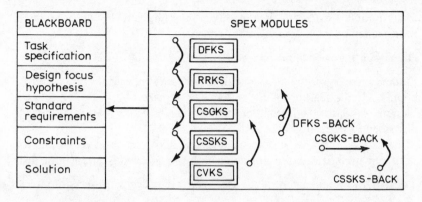

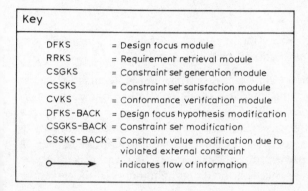

Fig. 6.9 Interaction between blackboard and knowledge-base modules.

set will be modified to reflect any changes in the design focus hypothesis made by the design focus module. The two alterations to the constraint set described are *backtracking* strategies.

4. The constraint set satisfaction module determines the optimal component design within the solution space defined by the constraint set. The optimal design is found by using either a nonlinear constraint satisfaction routine, OPT (Beigler and Cuthrell, 1985), or a knowledge-based database interface, KADBASE (Howard, 1986). Obviously, the database lookup can only be performed if a database of component designs exists. If no database exists, the constraints must be satisfied using mathematical optimization techniques. The sequential quadratic programming (SQP) algorithm is used by OPT to find component properties that satisfy the set of constraints and give an optimal value for a given objective function.

5. The conformance verification module checks the resulting component design not only for conformance with the design requirements, but for conformance with *all* applicable standard requirements. If violated requirements are found, another backtracking situation occurs and the design

focus module must be invoked to alter its hypothesis such that the violated requirements become design requirements.

The design knowledge in the knowledge base consists of:

1. Designer expertise: designer-specific expertise for the generation, completion, and modification of design focus hypotheses
2. Design standards: a formal model of the governing design standard, described in Garrett (1986); and
3. General relationships: structural, material and geometric definitions of data items referenced, but not defined, in the governing design standard.

The design knowledge sources are used by various design process modules.

(c) *User interfaces*

In addition to the design process modules of the knowledge base, the following user interfaces use and post entries on the blackboard.

1. The task specification user interface assists the user in defining the type of component, the governing standard, the design method, the design stage, any complete or partial design focus, etc.
2. The postprocessor provides the user with commands for displaying information about the component design, such as a description of the task, the component properties, the constraint set that was generated, the requirements that were checked, the design requirements, the governing requirements, etc.

(d) *Control*

The modules in the knowledge-base are invoked by the *system controller* based on the current state of the design.[1] The current state of design is represented by messages on the *message blackboard* and design information on the *design information blackboard*. The system controller uses a set of control rules that specify modules to invoke based on information present on the message and design information blackboards.

6.6.5 Illustrative example

The example is a *detailed* design of a singly-reinforced rectangular concrete beam that must conform to the ACI 318–77 Specification (ACI, 1977). The beam is designed for two behavior limitations: yielding of the tension

---

[1] The user interfaces are not invoked by the system controller, but are automatically invoked at the beginning and end of a SPEX execution.

reinforcement and crushing of the concrete, both due to flexure. The moment on the beam is given as 2400 in-kips. The objective is to minimize the sum of the concrete area and twice the steel area; multiplying the steel area by a factor of 2 is an approximation of the difference in unit cost between steel and concrete. In addition, an external constraint is specified: the beam depth must equal twice the beam width.

The solution of this problem begins with the task specification shown below:

SPEX > **standard aci77**
[load aci77.1]   ; SPEX loads the model of the spec,
[load concrete-defs.1]   ; general concrete relationships

SPEX > **component type (concrete rectangular singly-reinforced beam)**
SPEX > **component properties x-unbraced-length 120 y-unbraced-length 0**

                                                  ; The component is fully braced in
                                                  ; direction of the weak (y) axis

SPEX > **designer d1**
SPEX > **task design**
SPEX > **stage detailed**

SPEX > **external constraint (d = 2*b)**
SPEX > **objective function (MIN b*d + 2.0*As)**

                                                  ; A depth limitation is declared and
                                                  ; the objective function is a
                                                  ; function of concrete and steel
                                                  ; areas

SPEX > **loading condition moment 2400**

                                                  ; The maximum moment on the beam Mu
                                                  ; is 2400 in-kips

SPEX > **material props yield-strength 80 compressive-strength 4**

                                                  ; The steel yield strength, Fy, is
                                                  ; 80 ksi and the concrete compressive
                                                  ; strength, fc, is 4 ksi

SPEX > **focus**

    (and
        (stress-state flexure moment tension
            (limit state strength yield elastic reinforcement〈 COMPLETE 〉))
        (stress-state flexure moment compression
            (limit-state strength crushing 〈COMPLETE 〉)))

                                                  ; The design focus hypothesis is

; given as the combination of
; yielding of the rebars and the
; crushing of the concrete, both
; due to flexure

SPEX > **q**

; Task specification is complete

After the task has been specified, the requirement retrieval module is invoked to build two lists of requirements: those for checking and those for design. The requirements retrieved for checking[2] are:

aci-beam-flexure-yielding-reinforcement
aci-beam-flexure-cracking
aci-beam-flexure-crushing

The design requirements are found by locating the requirements associated with the behavior limitations identified in the design focus hypothesis. The design requirements are:

aci-beam-flexure-crushing
aci-beam-flexure-yielding-reinforcement

The concrete requirements, represented as decision tables,[3] are as follows.

Requirement = aci-beam-flexure-yielding-reinforcement

$\dfrac{b}{d} \leqslant 1.0$	T	T	F	I
$\dfrac{b}{d} \geqslant 0.25$	T	T	I	F
$Mu \leqslant Md$	T	F	I	I
satisfied	X			
violated		X		
not-applicable			X	X

[2] Many more requirements would normally be retrieved for checking. However, the portion of the ACI Specification that was modeled only addressed these requirements.

[3] A decision table is a formal way of representing the logic involved in making a decision. It consists of three parts: conditions, actions, and rules. Within the rules of a decision table, the 'T' represents that the condition must be true, the 'F' represents that the condition must be false, and the 'I' represents that the condition value is immaterial.

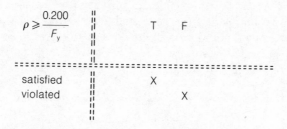

Requirement = aci-beam-flexure-cracking

$$\rho \geqslant \frac{0.200}{F_y}$$

	T	F
satisfied	X	
violated		X

Requirement = aci-beam-flexure-crushing

$$\rho \leqslant 0.75\rho_b$$

	T	F
satisfied	X	
violated		X

After the checking and design requirements have been retrieved, the constraint set generation module is invoked to build a set of constraints from the design requirements. The constraint expressions generated from the design requirements and the general concrete relationships for Md, β_1, A_s, ρ and ρ_b are:

$$d = 2b$$

$$Md = 0.9\rho bd^2 (80.0)\left(1 - 0.59\rho\left(\frac{80.0}{4.0}\right)\right)$$

$$\frac{b}{d} \geqslant 0.25$$

$$2400.0 \leqslant Md$$

$$\frac{b}{d} \leqslant 1.0$$

$$\beta_1 = 0.85$$

$$\rho_b = 0.85\beta_1 \left(\frac{4.0}{80.0}\right)\left(\frac{87.0}{87.0 + 80.0}\right)$$

$$\rho = \frac{A_s}{bd}$$

$$\rho \leqslant 0.75\rho_b$$

After the constraints have been generated, the constraint set satisfaction module is invoked to find a set of design variables (the variables appearing in the constraints) that satisfy the generated constraints. The constraints are satisfied either by optimization techniques or database lookup. In this example, the optimization routine, OPT (Biegler and Cuthrell, 1985), is used to satisfy the constraints. The resulting values for the design variables are:

$$A_s = 2.243268887243628$$
$$b = 8.914350754582612$$
$$d = 17.828701509016522$$
$$Md = 2399.999999999997$$
$$\beta_1 = 0.85$$
$$\rho_b = 0.01881961077844311$$
$$\rho = 0.01411470808372217$$

After the constraints have been satisfied, all requirements on the check list are checked. In this example, all three requirements are satisfied. Hence, the resulting concrete beam has a width, b, of 8.9 in., a distance between the compression face and the centroid of the reinforcement steel, d, of 17.82 in. and an area of reinforcement steel, A_s, of 2.24 in. The bending resistance of such a beam, Md, is computed to be 2400 in-kips.

Summary

The component design system described above basically selects requirements, generates constraints, and then satisfies those constraints to find a set of values for the properties of the component. The system is knowledge based because designer expertise is used to select behavior limitations on which to focus the design process, which the system then translates into design standard requirements. The designer expertise can be used to select key behavior limitations for either preliminary or detailed design, the difference being that in detailed design, the unselected behavior limitations are checked after the component is designed.

6.7 INTEGRATED DESIGN

In the previous sections, applications of expert systems in the three stages of structural design were presented. In the design of complex structures these three stages may be performed by different experts. For example, architects, space planners, and structural engineers are normally jointly responsible for the preliminary design, while the detailed design is accomplished by teams of structural engineers, detailers, and draftsmen. Furthermore, each of these tasks is divided into a number of subtasks; dividing the design task itself demands considerable experience. Hence the design task requires a good deal of coordination among different experts. Based on these considerations, a *conceptual* view, consistent with (Sriram, 1986), of an integrated design system that utilizes the concept of cooperation of different experts is proposed. The overall organization of the system is similar to that referred to as a blackboard, as introduced in Section 5. The organization of the knowledge base, the blackboard and the inference mechanism are described below.

6.7.1 Knowledge base

The knowledge base consists of a number of knowledge modules (KMs). Some KMs incorporate both textbook and heuristic (surface) knowledge, while other KMs comprise fairly deep knowledge (surface knowledge is usually represented as production rules encoding empirical associations based on experience, while fairly deep knowledge is typically comprised of algorithmic procedures). These KMs form a hierarchy of four levels: the *strategy, activation, specialist,* and *resource levels*. The knowledge levels are briefly described below.

1. Strategy level KMs analyze the current solution state to determine the appropriate next action. This level supplies the knowledge required for *focusing attention* on a certain part of the solution. Knowledge from this KM is used by the blackboard monitor to fire the appropriate activator. For example, a strategy KM would be responsible for recognizing when a preliminary design solution should be subjected to a formal analysis.
2. Activation level KMs know when to use the specialist KMs. The task of KMs at this level is to invoke the appropriate specialists for a given strategy. The system may incorporate two activators – the event driver and the goal driver. The event driver invokes appropriate specialists based on a certain event or group of events. The goal driver acts on those KMs which are responsible for putting a potential design alternative in the blackboard. For example, the event driver would invoke the KM for analyzing the structure if all the required input data is available, while the goal driver would set up the task of analysis as a goal and would try to obtain the input data from the user or other KMs. Essentially, the event and goal drivers are used to control the sequence of execution of the knowledge modules (KMs). This type of knowledge is called *process control knowledge*.
3. Specialist KMs are used to assess the current state of the design. Some KMs are comprised of pure production rules, while other KMs invoke analytical models of knowledge from the resource plane. The KMs at this level are comprised of smaller independent modules which are called knowledge sources (KSs). There are two types of KSs: KSs unique to a certain KM and KSs common to several KMs. These KSs are activated by appropriate KMs. Each KM at the specialist level will be specified in four

parts: (i) conditions under which it is to be activated; (ii) kinds of changes it makes to the blackboard; (iii) conditions under which KMs at the resource level are activated; and (iv) conditions under which KSs are activated. An example of a specialist KM is HI-RISE or SPEX.

4. Resource level KMs contain the knowledge required for analysis and design. Typical KMs at this level are: analyzers, geometric modelers, codes, catalogs of available components, database management systems, costing procedures, etc.

6.7.2 Blackboard

The blackboard contains the information about the current state of the design solution. The current state can be represented by a solution tree, similar to the one generated by HI-RISE, and by a record of the tasks that have been completed or are currently active. The main units in the blackboard are hypotheses or guesses. For example, a possible 3D hypotheses such as a *core* or *tube-in-tube* may exist in the blackboard. The hypotheses are guesses about particular aspects of the problem and may be related through structural links. For example, the gravity load functional level can have many alternative configurations which are linked through an is-alt (is an alternative) link. The hypothesis structure formed from the most up-to-date information is known as the current best design (CBD).

6.7.3 Inference mechanism

The inference mechanism consists of two main components: the agenda and the monitor. The agenda keeps track of all the events in the blackboard and calculates the priority of execution of tasks that are generated as a result of activation of the KMs. The activation and interaction between various levels is accomplished by the blackboard monitor. In the proposed system, the agenda is implemented as a queue and the priority of execution may be set by the user; the user will have considerable control over the agenda. The monitor performs the following tasks: (1) check the blackboard for appropriate KMs to fire and (2) take the activity with the highest priority from the agenda and execute it.

The activation of a certain KM depends on the result of actions of other KMs. For example, the KM for detailed design stage would be activated after the analysis is complete. This can be cast into the following production rule:

IF   The analysis of structure is complete, AND
        detailed design is required
THEN   Activate the knowledge module for detailed design.

Similar production rules can be used to provide an alternative solution to the problem of interaction of multidisciplinary design databases.

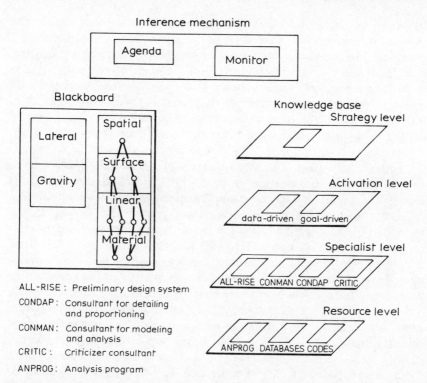

Fig. 6.10 A conceptual view of an integrated structural design and analysis system.

The integrated structural design system is illustrated in Fig. 6.10. The decomposition of the design problem, as described above and illustrated in the figure, represents a conceptual design of an integrated system. It is likely that as the integrated structural design system is further explored and developed many of the details of the system will change. However, the use of a blackboard architecture and a decomposition of the knowledge base into knowledge modules appears to be an effective way of dealing with multiple sources of knowledge.

6.8 SUMMARY AND CONCLUSIONS

The use of expert system techniques for structural design problems promises to extend the capabilities of human designers and to improve structural designs. A discussion of the relevant techniques and some prototype applications are included in this chapter. From the description of the applications it is apparent that, in addition to the promise these techniques hold for improved structural design, there is much work to be done.

One interesting observation from the application of expert systems to structural design is introduced in Section 6.4.3 on detailed design: the experience of a detailed designer is useful and applicable to preliminary component design. The experience in using the design codes for detailing can be applied to the component sizing problem. This observation can be extended to the analysis expert. The experience of the analysis modeler is not only applicable when a structure is completely defined, but also when the structure is being configured and checked for structural feasibility. If the experience of the analysis modeler and detailed designer can be properly represented, it can be accessed and applied during the preliminary design stage.

Another observation is that the blackboard architecture appears to be broadly useful in structural design problems. This architecture provides a formalism for multiple experts, or knowledge modules, to communicate and cooperate on a design problem. One aspect of this cooperation that is important to the integrated use of multiple experts is that of constructive criticism or design evaluation. HI-RISE addresses design evaluation using limited knowledge. Given an integrated design environment, design evaluation can be drawn from all levels of design experience; for example, the preliminary design could be evaluated by a detailer or a construction expert.

As more expert system applications to structural design problems reach the prototype or development stage, we will have a better understanding of the role and implications of such systems. Based on the work described in this chapter, the use of expert systems to represent design knowledge can help us expand and improve our current understanding of design problems and their solutions.

REFERENCES

ACI, (1977) *Building Code Requirements for Reinforced Concrete*, American Concrete Institute, ACI Committee 318, Detroit, Michigan.

Barnes, S. (1984) *DICE Design Interface for Civil Engineering*, Master's thesis, Carnegie–Mellon University.

Biegler, L.T. and Cuthrell, J.E. (1985) Improved infeasible path optimization for sequential modular simulators: the optimization algorithm. *Computers and Chemical Engineering* **9**, No. 1, 257–67.

Chandrasekaran, B. and Mittal, S. (1985) Deep versus compiled knowledge approaches to diagnostic problem-solving. *International Journal of Man–Machine Studies*, **19**, 425–36.

Erman, L.D., Hayes-Roth, F., Lesser, V.R. and Reddy, D.R. (1980) The Hearsay-II speech understanding system: integrating knowledge to resolve uncertainty. *Computing Surveys*, **12**, No. 2, 213–53.

Garrett, Jr., J.H. (1986) *SPEX–A Knowledge-Based Standard Processor for Structural Component Design*, PhD thesis, Carnegie–Mellon University.

Gaschnig, J., Reboh, R. and Reiter, J. (1981) *Development of Knowledge-Based System for Water Resources Problems*, Technical Report SRI Project 1619, Stanford Research Institute International, Stanford.

Hayes-Roth, B. (1985) A Blackboard Architecture for Control. *Artificial Intelligence*, **26**, No. 3, 251–321.

Howard, H.C. (1986) *Interfacing Databases and Knowledge Based Systems for Structural Engineering Applications*, PhD thesis, Carnegie–Mellon University.

Lin T.Y. and Stotesbury, S.D. (1981) *Structural Concepts and Systems for Architects and Engineers*, John Wiley, New York.

Maher, Mary Lou (1984) *HI-RISE: A Knowledge-Based Expert System for the Preliminary Structural Design of High Rise Buildings*, PhD thesis, Department of Civil Engineering, Carnegie–Mellon University.

Maher, M. L. (1986) Problem solving using expert system techniques, in *Expert Systems In Civil Engineering* (eds. C.N. Kostem and M. L. Maher), American Society of Civil Engineering, New York, pp.7–17.

Nillson, N.J. (1980) *Principles of Artificial Intelligence*, Tioga Publishing Company, Palo Alto, California.

Rehak, D.R. and Howard, H.C. (1985) Interfacing expert systems with design databases in integrated CAD systems. *Computer-Aided Design*, November.

Rychener, M.D. (1984) PSRL: An SRL-Based Production-Rule System, *Reference Manual* Carnegie–Mellon University, Pittsburgh.

Smith, R.G. and Young, R.L. (1983) The dipmeter advisor system, in *Proceedings of the 7th International Joint Conference on Artificial Intelligence, Vancouver*, pp. 122–9.

Sriram, D. (1986) *Knowledge-Based Approaches For Structural Design*, PhD thesis, Carnegie–Mellon University.

Stefik, M. (1980) *Planning With Constraints*, Technical Report STAN-CS-80-784, Computer Science Department, Stanford University.

Wright, J.M. and Fox, M.S. (1983) *SRL/1.5 User Manual*, Technical Report, CMU Robotics Institute Pittsburgh.

Zumsteg, J.R. and Flaggs, D.L. (1985) Knowledge-based analysis and design for aerospace structures, in *Applications of Knowledge-Based Systems to Engineering Analysis and Design*, American Society of Mechanical Engineers, New York, pp. 67–80.

7

Expert systems applications in construction engineering

GAVIN A. FINN

7.1 INTRODUCTION

Although much has been said of the potential role of expert systems in construction and engineering, the majority of work in this area has been academic in nature. A common, although unfounded, belief that this technology is too immature for practical implementation has proliferated through the industry. There are significant potential applications within the capabilities of current technology, however, that could represent improvements in technologies, performance levels, and product reliability.

The advantages of expert systems techniques are numerous. There are a number of problems that exist in the construction engineering environments that simply cannot be solved by procedural, algorithmic computer techniques. In addition, some existing approaches using the conventional methods are inadequate. This type of problem is typically complex in nature, requiring the knowledge and experience of a recognized expert who has developed expertise through years of experience.

7.2. DEVELOPMENT AND DISTRIBUTION ISSUES

7.2.1 Languages and tools

In academic research, expert systems have mostly been developed in LISP, although the Japanese and Europeans tend to favor PROLOG. Relatively few programmers outside the research environment are proficient in these languages, however. While LISP and PROLOG offer advantages over procedural languages in their ability to perform symbolic reasoning, it is not necessarily expedient to use these languages in the industrial environment. Neither LISP nor PROLOG are easily interfaced with other languages, so that existing programs, written in FORTRAN or BASIC, would most likely have to be rewritten if they are to be used in conjunction with the expert systems. If expert systems are to be used in the construction or engineering environments, however, it is extremely important to be able to exploit the existence of this base of programs. (This consideration may not be important in other disciplines, where there may not be an existing program base.)

The alternative to using an AI language is to use a commercial expert system shell. The major difference between using such a development tool as opposed to the use of a language is that shells usually contain both an inference mechanism and a knowledge acquisition module, and these do not have to be programmed by the developers. Of course, using a shell limits the structure of the system to its particular inference techniques and representation method, and as such, there is a certain loss of flexibility that is inherent in the bottom-up (language level) approach. In the construction engineering environments, the ability of the expert system to interface with other software is highly significant. In order to provide a useful and complete solution, it may be necessary to use analysis routines, graphics, or data-base management systems. Consideration of such requirements is necessary when selecting appropriate expert system software. Many commercially available shells allow for these interfaces, but some are stand-alone systems, and it is important to recognize the need for an integrated solution before a particular tool is selected.

Another factor in the selection of a development tool is the cost of the tool itself, or the cost of development of the tool. The cost of commercially available shells varies widely. A sometimes overlooked cost, however, is the distribution cost for the inference mechanism, which can be prohibitively high. If the application is to be distributed to a large number of users, then it is desirable to use a tool that does not require purchase of a full development system for each run-time copy.

The development environment should be as easy to use as possible, keeping in mind the fact that many of the domain experts will not be experts in the use of computers. A complex, highly sophisticated shell may be too complicated for the developers, and this may lead to an inefficient development process, or may even preclude the successful development of the expert system application. Additionally, the shell should allow for easy end-user interaction. The ultimate user of the expert system application is often forgotten, but should be of primary importance when considering software tools. The system should be easy to use and easy to understand, and, as in the case of the developer, the end-user should not have to contend with complicated interfaces or terminology that is too sophisticated.

The software environment decision should depend primarily on the application. If a shell is available such that the solution requirements of the problem can be adequately represented, it could be expedient to use the existing program. If the application requirements and constraints are such that none of the available shells provide an adequate environment for solution, then it may be necessary to implement a language-level solution. It is vitally important that these decisions be made on an application-by-application basis, however, because every problem has its own unique set of constraints. The use of a tool simply because it is inexpensive (or for any other single reason) could be too limiting a compromise, and will adversely affect the nature of the system.

7.2.2 Hardware requirements

Many expert system development efforts have been centered around specialized AI computers, such as LISP machines. Other expert system applications have been developed using conventional hardware, such as personal computers, minicomputers, engineering workstations, and mainframes. As in the case of the software environment, the hardware should be chosen with both the developers and the end-users in mind. The ease of use of the hardware/operating system could significantly affect both the efficiency of the development process, and the ability of the end-users to use the application successfully.

Availability of the computers is also a key factor in selection of hardware tools. If the application is intended to be a stand-alone system, then it may be feasible to invest in a specialized computer for this purpose. If the system is intended to be used by a variety of end-users, then an existing multi-user system, or a personal-computer environment may be more desirable.

The availability of personal computers on construction sites and in engineering offices suggests that this may be a good environment for distribution of expert systems applications (Finn and Reinschmidt, 1986). End-users are familiar with the hardware; software for performing algorithmic and data-base functions is widely available for personal computers (and in use on sites); and there are a variety of very useful expert system shells available for personal computers (see Chapter 4).

In addition, the in-core memory and program and data storage capabilities of today's personal computers are sufficiently large for most construction engineering expert systems applications. Experience has shown that initial expectations by industry analysts and AI researchers that personal computers could not be used for real-world expert systems, were incorrect. In fact, it is far more likely that an expert system development project that focuses on an application suited to a personal computer will succeed than an overly ambitious project, that requires a great deal of storage and computing power.

7.3 APPLICATIONS

Because of the level of detail and understanding required in most construction and engineering problems, it is far easier and less expensive to develop applications that address specific, narrowly-defined problems, than it is to develop general problem-solving systems. This is due primarily to the fact that the amount of knowledge required to solve even a small expert system problem is most often far greater than originally estimated. The consequences of attempting to build expert systems for a problem without a reasonably accurate measure of the extent of knowledge required for the solution could include an incomplete system, major development cost and time overruns, project abandonment, and even disillusionment with the entire field. Because there are no guidelines or standards for assessing the knowledge requirements of typical problems, it is far better to begin with a narrowly-defined scope. Experience has shown that, inevitably, the problem's complexity and scope grows during development.

7.3.1 Applications in welded construction

Expert systems for a variety of problems in the area of welded construction have been developed by Stone & Webster (Hathaway and Finn, 1986), and have actually been implemented in the field.

(a) *Welding procedure selection expert system*

In today's construction projects, elaborate designs, exotic materials, new welding technologies, and complicated codes necessitate increased numbers of welding procedures. Selection of appropriate welding procedures has proved to be a major challenge not only for the construction supervisor or field engineer, but even for the welding engineers/specialists. Several methods have been devised by a number of construction companies to alleviate this problem. One method is to pre-identify the weld procedures on the drawings adjacent to the field weld; another is to develop a matrix or weld map on a separate document. Maintenance of these schemes has proved to be time consuming, difficult, and expensive. Construction delays and problems in the field have not been eliminated because the correct weld procedure has not always been made available, and incorrect procedures are still used.

Recognizing the need for a better system for pre-identifying and selecting weld procedures, an expert system for performing this task has been developed. There were two basic requirements of the system. First, it should be capable of determining what weld procedures would be required based on the design documents. This would allow adequate time to qualify new procedures, when required, to support the construction schedule. Second, the expert system had to be easy enough to operate so that construction supervisors and field engineers (with a minimum amount of computer experience) could select the most efficient procedure. Microcomputers were selected as the appropriate hardware, because of their ease of use and their availability on construction sites. A simple rule processing system was selected as the inference shell because of its extensive user-interface, its straightforward knowledge representation method, and its available links to databases. This shell was also used in all of the other welding expert systems, described later. It should be noted that an earlier procedure selection system, developed within a commercial spreadsheet program, was used as the starting point for the development of the expert system. The limitations imposed by the spreadsheet approach strongly suggested the need for a more flexible method, one which would allow for a more natural representation of the knowledge. (Because of the existence of tables which reference material codes to properties, these tables, created by the spreadsheet, were used by the expert system directly.) Thus, users need only identify material types, and the expert system automatically searches the tables for the appropriate properties.

The expert system was developed by the company's welding specialist, who designed it such that it incorporates the same type of reasoning strategy that he would use if asked to select a welding procedure. With limited interaction from a knowledge engineer, the specialist directly interfaced with the shell, in development mode, and personally built the knowledge base. Rules were derived from the procedures manuals and code books, in conjunction with the expert's judgement and experience. The knowledge base contains over two hundred rules, and incorporates four database/table lookup procedures. The system operates by asking the user some basic questions about the welding operation, such as the fabrication code, the materials to be welded, thicknesses of the materials, welding processes, etc. By forward-chaining through a rule base, the system then identifies possible candidate solutions. Using a backward-chaining procedure, the system then determines whether the requirements for each candidate procedure would be met, and based on the user's process preference, either a single procedure is identified as the only appropriate procedure for the proposed welding operation, or a set of procedures is recommended. Users in the field obtain a print-out directly, and they use this at the welding site.

(b) *Welder qualification test selection expert system*

As with the selection of welding procedures, selection of the qualification tests required for welders on current construction projects involves a complex interpretation of codes and standards. Unlike the welding procedures, the qualification tests are based on performance essential variables as well as materials. For instance, if welders are to be welding in all positions, they would take a test in the 6G position (ASME IX code, meaning 45 degrees from the horizontal). Other variables include the thickness of the material, the type of process, etc. All of these variables combined can lead to the need for several tests. Studies conducted by construction industry researchers have indicated that a single qualification test for a welder can cost up to $1000 per test.

Maximizing the welder's range is, therefore, a significant consideration when determining the tests that a welder would be required to take. Most engineering/construction companies have developed standard qualification tests which identify thickness, positions, diameter, and other variables for which a welder would be qualified. However, determining which set of tests is appropriate for a given job often requires a specialist, and is therefore an ideal application for an expert system.

Again, the mode of operation of the system is similar to the type of conversation that the weld supervisor might have with the specialist. In this case, the system asks specific questions about the welding job, and then the rules are processed in order to identify those tests that would appropriately qualify a welder. As in the case of the procedure selection system, material property tables are used to facilitate the user interface and amount of data that users are required to input. Conclusions are drawn as to the required tests, and they are identified for the user.

A rule, taken directly from the system, reads as follows:

IF   The qualification code is ASME IX
and   You will not weld pipe

THEN   The configuration type is plate
and   The minimum diameter parameters are not required

NOTE: Essential variables for diameters for pipe are not required when welding on plate only.

Another rule taken from this system which illustrates the actual selection of a test, follows:

IF   The qualification code is ASME IX
and   The process combination is SMAW
and   The configuration is pipe
and   The filler metal is an F-34 electrode
and   The root pass conditions will not apply
and   Multiple process conditions are satisfied

THEN   Select Welder Qualification Test   #071

Notice that some of the conditions can be asked of the user directly, while others are derived by the expert system itself.

This expert system has made selection of welder qualification tests a simple process – helping to eliminate unqualified field welding. Consistent expert judgement is now available in the field whenever it is required. Users of this system have reported an increased confidence in test selection, and a drastic decrease in the incidence of incorrect testing, as a result of using the expert system.

(c) *Weld estimating expert system*

Estimating the quantity of weld filler material required for a particular application is a necessary but often difficult task for the construction supervisor. Depending on the type of material and quality requirements, some weld material can have a lead time to purchase of up to eight weeks. If the material is not ordered on time, or is ordered in insufficient quantities, schedules could become severely impacted. Because of the high cost of some of the materials, such as a nickel alloy, overbuying is not always a feasible solution – a precise estimate of materials is essential. In addition to material quantities, the construction supervisor must also determine the required man-hours for the welding process.

Based on the requirements of these tasks, an expert system for performing welding estimates of both man-hours and materials seemed to be a natural solution, and such a system has been developed. The expert system considers all of the variables associated with field welding, such as the weld joint design, weld process, material deposition efficiency, waste, available working hours per day, etc., and considers each variable's impact on the estimate both independently, and in conjunction with other variables.

The ability to obtain accurate man-hour estimates for individual jobs has allowed management to more clearly view the welding effort, regardless of the support craft and unit rates of the estimate. By using this expert system, accurate estimates are obtained consistently by supervisors, helping to prevent material shortages and excesses, and thus helping to improve the conformity of the actual job to the proposed schedule.

(d) *Weld defect diagnostic expert system*

Welding defects are extremely common on most construction sites. These defects can drastically impair construction schedules, and can escalate project costs. The industry has improved the methods by which welds are scrutinized, to help identify weld defects more consistently. Unfortunately, the identification of the defects has not significantly reduced their frequency of occurrence. As the inspection methods change, and as codes and procedures change, construction supervisors have had to become experts in repairing weld defects. Studies have shown that weld repairs are extremely expensive, and in some cases can have more adverse effects than the defect itself. For example, a root repair on a typical pipe weld can cost as much as the original weld, and may have to be repaired several times before it is brought into conformance.

With the view that the prevention of recurrences of defects was probably the best approach to reducing weld defects, an expert system has been developed to identify the causes of the defects, and to recommend procedures for ensuring that a similar problem does not occur again.

Most welded defects can be minimized, if not eliminated, when the welding operation has been thoroughly analyzed to identify areas where the probability of weld defects would be greatest. The weld defect diagnostic expert system not only takes into account equipment and process variables, but also uses knowledge about welding techniques and environmental conditions to help identify causes of defects.

The system is interactive, requiring the welding supervisor to answer specific questions about observations made at the site of the weld, the condition of the materials and the environment, and specifics about the welding procedure employed. The system uses a backward-chaining mechanism to reason about probable causes of the defects. It presents the end-user with a ranked list of factors that probably lead to the defect, and suggests methods for improving on the welding operation.

For example, for the following set of inputs (obtained interactively from the user), the system would present the results shown:

Observed defect is POROSITY
Welding process is Gas Tungston Arc Welding (GTAW)
Base material is not galvanized
It is not known whether or not oil was present on the base material
The parts to be welded required matching
Base material was not painted
Base material was not rusty
Base material was not wet
Weld preps. were ground, power wire brushed, etc.
No special moisture prevention precautions were taken prior to welding
Weld finish is ground smooth
Starting the arc is no problem
Stability condition of the arc is not known
Appearance of the weld is clean
Gas cup distance to the work is not known
Gas cup or nozzle is clean
Gas system was not tested
Flow meters are presumed to be tight and in good working order
Gas hoses are presumed to be not leaking
Welding took place inside with drafts

The conclusions presented, listed from most probable to least probable cause, are:

1. It appears that incomplete gas coverage may be the problem. Check the shielding gas system for leaks and provide shields around the weld to prevent gusts of wind or drafts from blowing the shielding gas away from the arc.
2. Welding over foreign material appears to be a problem. Ensure that all

foreign material (including oil, grease, moisture, rust, paint, etc.) is removed prior to welding.

If random defects continue to be a problem after all of the above actions have been taken, then the individual welder(s) should be requalified and reacquainted with the fundamental good workmanship practices.

Implementation of these systems results in an improvement in the overall construction process. By distributing expertise through these microcomputer-based expert systems, a higher level of performance can be achieved, and more consistent standards of quality can be ensured in construction.

7.3.2 Applications in operations and maintenance

In the operation of plants and facilities, the process of maintaining mechanical equipment can be a critical function. When these components fail or malfunction, the consequences can be extremely serious. As part of the process of maintenance of such machinery, many techniques are used to ascertain the operating performance of each component, and evaluations are made as to their health. Many factors are taken into account in this determination, including measurements of process variables (pressure, temperature, flow rates, etc.), vibration measurements, and other relevant information. The process of interpreting the meaning of the data requires expertise. In many cases, the required expertise is only available through the consulting services of senior personnel, while maintenance personnel in the plant are often not experienced enough to interpret the symptoms of problems, in order to determine a remedial course of action. Expert systems have been developed to help these less experienced people solve problems with malfunctioning or failed equipment, that they were previously unable to solve (Finn *et al.*, 1986).

(a) *Centrifugal pump diagnosis*

There are large numbers of pumps in operation at most power and process facilities, the majority of these being centrifugal pumps. In order to help maintenance personnel solve problems with centrifugal pumps, an expert system, called PumpPro™, was developed (Fritsch, 1986). The intent of the program is to allow mechanics, technicians, and millwrights to avail themselves of expert knowledge without having to call in consultants. PumpPro™ was developed by a mechanical equipment specialist, with over 25 years' experience in the industry. The shell that was used was a rule-based system, called Micro-Computer Artificial Intelligence Diagnostic Service (MAID Service) developed at Stone & Webster. The expert system has been distributed to over 400 installations, and is in use for both diagnostic and training purposes.

The operation of the system is separated into four major phases: (i) identification of the symptoms through an interactive consultation with the user; (ii) identification of possible causes through a processing of symptom–cause rules; (iii) provision of tutorials in the cases where the user is unfamiliar with concepts or terminology; these tutorials are invoked at the user's request, so that users who do not need this help may proceed with the session uninterrupted; (iv) remedy suggestion on the basis of possible cause identification.

An example run of the system, with the following inputs, would yield the intermediate conclusions and the final suggestions shown:

The pump capacity is adequate
The discharge pressure is not low
Pump is not losing prime after starting
Pump driver is not overloading
Pump/driver vibration IS excessive
Bearings are not overheating
Bearings are not wearing rapidly
Pump started normally
Power consumption is not excessive
Packing is not leaking excessively
Pump is not overheating
Pump is not excessively noisy
Check valve is not noisy at startup/shutdown
Pipe movement is not excessive at startup/shutdown
Internal gaskets are not leaking
Pump is not seized
Pump history is continually running

After explaining some of the most common causes of excessive vibration, the system concludes that the following causes are possible:

Rotor unbalance
Misalignment
Resonance
Out of range flow rates
Cavitation
Bent shaft

After asking the user to verify certain conditions, the system then determines, in this case, that misalignment is the primary cause of vibration, and explains how the pump and driver should be realigned. In addition, some rules of thumb pertaining to alignment tolerances and running speeds are provided.

The expert system uses 22 symptom classes and a summarized pump history. It allows the entry of multiple symptoms, and takes this information into account when reasoning about possible causes. Approximately 350 rules are used in the cause identification stage, and there are seven major tutorials, with many other minor tutorials. Approximately 70 rules deal with remedial strategies and actions, for a total of more than 460 rules.

(b) *Rotating equipment vibration advisor*

Because vibration measurements are used extensively as a means of obtaining information about rotating equipment, many maintenance personnel have been trained in the use of vibration data acquisition mechanisms. Unfortunately, the process of interpreting all the data and analyses is highly complex, and is usually performed by an expert in the field. An expert system has been built in order to help less experienced personnel interpret these data.

The first task in the design of the Stone & Webster rotating equipment vibration advisor was to define the goals and scope of the project. Because there is a large variety of types of equipment, and because of the potential problems associated with very general scope definitions, it was decided to focus first on one type of machine, and then to expand on this one type as the second phase of the project.

As such, the problem of diagnosing problems with excessively vibrating industrial fans was chosen as the first phase of the project. This component was chosen because of its relative simplicity, and also because the problem of excessive vibrations in fans is relatively common. The software and hardware tools were selected after an investigation into the type and extent of knowledge required, and the type of development and distribution environment desired. A microcomputer-based environment was selected due to its accessibility and ease of use, and, in part, due to the selection of a powerful microcomputer-based shell (which uses a backward-chaining inference procedure).

The system was built by senior personnel from the Acoustics and Vibrations Laboratory at Stone & Webster. The rules were derived from an analysis of existing case histories, and hypothetical cases selected by the experts. The system was built to interactively obtain answers from the user (maintenance technicians with an understanding of the process of acquiring the vibration measurements, but not necessarily an understanding of their meaning), in addition to having the capability to read data files for measurements and analysis results. The session would end when the expert system had reasoned to the extent of its ability, and the user would be presented with a prioritized list of probable causes of the excessive vibration. The final fan vibration advisor can diagnose up to 25 types of problems. This system was made available through a dial-in expert system service (the EXSTRA™ service) in January 1986, to a wide range of construction, process, power, and manufacturing companies. Through the feedback obtained from its users, its knowledge base has grown to include new symptoms and causes. The system has been used to help interpret vibration measurements, and has been successful in identifying causes of problems.

The second phase of the project was to generalize the fan vibration advisor to include other types of rotating equipment. This is possible because of the nature of general rotating equipment and vibration patterns that are common to all types of rotating machinery. Some rules are generic, and apply to almost all types of rotating equipment, while others are specific to certain component types. In addition to the generic rules, the system now includes rules for electric motors, centrifugal pumps, steam turbines, compressors, as well as fans. It has also been successfully used through the EXSTRA™ service, in addition to being installed on site.

7.3.3 Other areas of application

(a) *Scheduling*

In order to investigate the applicability of expert systems technologies as applied to scheduling problems, Stone & Webster developed a prototype system for helping system dispatchers schedule power generation units. The system, known as the unit commitment advisor, combines heuristic rule processing methods with economic/engineering optimization approaches.

In operation, the economic dispatch algorithm computes the optimum production schedule, determining the plants which should generate power on an hour-by-hour basis for a one-week period. This optimum plan may not be practically realizable, because of external, non-economic factors. The expert system analyzes the start-up list, taking into account heuristics relating to all of the practical considerations which the economic algorithm cannot include. Some of the factors that are taken into account include the influence of weather forecasts, take-or-pay fuel commitments, maintenance schedules, and others. The operation of the system is conducted through a question/answer consultation, as well as through the extensive use of advanced interfaces, such as graphics and spreadsheets, to display the breakdown of the hourly generation statistics. An internally-developed forward-chaining inference mechanism was used, in conjunction with existing mathematical algorithms and subroutines.

The operation of the expert system follows a two-phase staged solution. In the first phase, the economic optimization is performed, and those heuristics that apply to individual scheduling steps are used. An initial schedule is thus derived. This schedule, indicating which units should be started up and shut down for every hour of the week, may still be impractical, or non-optimal in some regards. This is due to the fact that some of the heuristics that human dispatching experts use are only applicable when the completed schedule is available. To apply these global scheduling heuristics, a second heuristic analysis is performed in the second phase of the solution, this time with the higher-level rules.

The user then has the capability of questioning the system regarding the availability of units, in order to obtain an explanation of the system's output. This approach to dispatch or scheduling problems is applicable to many similar kinds of scheduling disciplines, and demonstrates that heuristic rules, graphics, and optimization algorithms can be successfully integrated into a microcomputer-based expert system.

(b) *Plant operations*

While many computer simulation systems help plant operators determine the mechanical and physical consequences of operations actions, it is often difficult for operators to obtain advice regarding consequences of actions in the context of regulatory compliance. The process of determining whether any proposed maintenance actions would result in potential violations of operating or environmental regulations can be extremely complicated, and is usually performed by very experienced, specialized personnel. In order to help less experienced operators and maintenance planners/supervisors determine whether or not proposed maintenance would violate regulations, an expert system has been developed. This system, known as the technical specifications advisor, reduces the process of determining regulatory compliance from a complex, time-consuming, often inconsistent procedure, to a simple interactive consultation with the computer. The expert system is designed to interact with a database management system, which keeps track of the status of the components and systems in the plant. Users may examine the status of components, and they may propose to change the status of a set of components. Regulatory consequences of these proposed changes are determined by the inference mechanism, which applies the current state of the plant as the context to the rule base, and the user is immediately informed of the consequences of the proposed actions. The system incorporates the use of graphic displays of systems and components, and allows for close interaction with existing equipment tagging and other maintenance systems.

This system is an effective demonstration of the ability of an expert system to provide useful, timely advice regarding a highly complex problem, in a fashion that allows the user to make better-informed and more consistent decisions.

7.4 CONCLUSIONS

The implementation of expert systems in the construction and engineering workplace results in some significant benefits. Expert systems for advising construction personnel and engineers are in place today, and are being used to effectively solve real-world problems. The availability of expert system building shells has greatly improved the technical development capabilities within the engineering community, and facilitates an ever-increasing effort to implement these programs. Different approaches to the delivery of these systems for construction and engineering applications, including the use of microcomputers and minicomputers allows for a wide range of distribution capabilities, thus broadening their overall effectiveness.

Development of these expert systems requires consideration of development and end-user software and hardware environments, costs of development and commerical tools, and other practical considerations. Because each application is unique in its knowledge requirements and solution method, a determination of appropriate tools should be based on the needs of each application individually.

In the long term, the application and implementation of expert systems for construction and engineering will result in the enhancement of service capabilities, improved productivity in the construction process, and overall improvement in performance in construction and engineering companies.

REFERENCES

Finn, G.A. and Reinschmidt, K.F. (1986) Expert systems in an engineering/construction firm, *Proceedings of the ASCE Symposium on Expert Systems in Civil Engineering, Seattle, Washington.*

Finn, G.A., Reinschmidt, K.F. and Hall, J.R. (1986) Expert systems for dynamic analysis interpretation, *Proceedings of the ASCE 4th Conference on Computing in Civil Engineering, Boston, Massachusetts*, ASCE, New York.

Fritsch, T.J. (1986) PumpPro – a centrifugal pump diagnostic expert system, *Proceedings of the ASME/Texas A and M Pump Symposium, Houston, Texas*, ASME, New York.

Hathaway, W.F. and Finn, G.A. (1986) Microcomputer expert systems for welded construction, *Proceedings of the ASCE 4th Conference on Computing in Civil Engineering, Boston, Massachusetts*, ASCE, New York.

8

Knowledge engineering for a construction scheduling analysis system

C. WILLIAM IBBS and JESUS M. DE LA GARZA

> Computers are revolutionizing a lot of industries. They may revolutionize the construction industry, or they may bury it.
>
> *Ken Reinschmidt*

8.1 INTRODUCTION

Construction scheduling, along with estimating, cost control and quality assurance, is an essential ingredient of effective project control. Schedules, simple and complex, bar charts and PERT diagrams, have found a niche in both design and construction project management. Although industry acceptance of CPM, resource allocation, and time–cost trade-off concepts was slow in coming, the advent of mainframe computers in the 1960s and especially personal computers (PCs) in the 1980s has changed attitudes about quantitative methods of construction management. The time thus seems right for the introduction of knowledge-based expert systems (ES) to a tradition-bound field like construction (Ibbs, 1985, 1986).

In the construction industry, the delivery of a completed facility on time is often more important to a client than cost, especially for revenue-generating projects. Moreover, project cost is to a large degree correlated with time, at least in the case of time-related overhead and staff expenses, interest cost, and lost opportunity costs.

Another concern of the present-day claims-conscious construction industry is the ability to forecast the likelihood of project disputes and analyze their origins to assign liability. Although most claims are a mixture of culpability, any tool that can offer rational and consistent analysis of claims is a meaningful aid to project participants.

For these reasons, the US Army Corps of Engineers is extremely interested in the development of a tool that will better enable Army resident engineers to forecast construction schedule variations, the reasons for those deviations and the party or parties responsible. Under a multi-year research contract, the University of Illinois Construction Engineering Expert Systems Laboratory (CEESL) and the Corps' Construction Engineering Research Laboratory (CERL) have been working to develop a PC-based ES for analysis of construction schedules. That effort, which will be related in this chapter, represents the first half of the research endeavor.

The other significant, and in some ways, vital half of the research program builds upon the work being done with CERL in a more comprehensive and flexible fashion. With the assistance of funding from the US National Science Foundation (NSF) and Inference Corporation, a much more substantial tool is being developed. It will, through object-oriented programming facilities, allow interfaces to cost, schedule, and quality control modules of a broad project control expert system. These other modules are in an earlier stage of development at the University of Illinois.

This chapter describes the current status of a CONstruction Scheduling Analysis System (CONSAS) being developed by the authors. All major issues associated with the development and implementation of CONSAS will be reviewed, from product need and definition, to software development environment, to a point just short of beta-testing. Other parts of the chapter will examine some of the important parallel efforts in project management expert system development.

The emphasis of this discussion will be on the knowledge engineering aspect of this research – the identification and formulation of expertise, the syntactic and semantic interaction, and the construction of a moderately complex knowledge base for a reasonably-sized problem domain. Other chapters in this book and even other books more than adequately describe the computer science aspects of ES. What this chapter can uniquely offer is a review of the slow and difficult steps that these writers passed through to build a fairly sophisticated and useful tool.

8.2 EXPERT SYSTEMS IN CONSTRUCTION

Experience combined with subjective and qualitative judgement provides the essential starting points for a successful project manager. It is of no surprise then to read about the first attempts showing the applicability of expert systems technology in construction to occur in the project management area.

A number of researchers have theorized how expert systems might be structured and usefully applied in the field of construction project management. For example, McGartland and Hendrickson (1985) discussed how this new technology can be conceptually applied to cost control, scheduling and time control, and purchasing and inventory control. They demonstrated, for example, that effective and meaningful relationships can be constructed with basic project data, (e.g. early start, late finish, percentage complete, etc.) to make sound recommendations.

Nay and Logcher (1985) defined an expert system framework for analyzing construction project risks. This framework is based upon the different risk occurrences that can be associated with a work package (e.g. the lowest level of activity definition suitable for progress monitoring). Hitachi Systems Development Laboratory is also developing an expert risk system called the Project Risk Assessment System for large construction projects (Niwa and Okuma, 1982; Niwa and Sasaki, 1983; Niwa *et al.*, 1984). This system focuses on the project execution stage and attempts to identify risks and prevent them in advance. Its goals are accomplished by first identifying risks and risk countermeasures and then mapping these to standard work packages. Others at the University of Texas are also known to be developing a construction risk analysis expert system, and Rehak at Carnegie–Mellon University is reported to be developing an expert system for the automatic creation of construction schedules.

Diekmann and Kruppenbacher (1984) developed a system called the Differing Site Conditions Analysis System (DSCAS) aimed at advising owners, engineers and contractors of the legitimacy of contractor disputes and claims. This system was based on case law on differing site conditions claims in federal jurisdiction for the Corps of Engineers.

Levitt and Kunz (1985) discussed an expert system which included theoretical knowledge of project management and experience-based knowledge of a construction task. The project management knowledge consisted of generic descriptions of activities, resources, risk factors, etc. The risk factors which could impact the duration of planned activities were classified as being favorable or unfavorable. Their effects were then projected on the duration of unfinished activities assuming the risk factors continued to be favorable or unfavorable. Such an expert system exercised project control by generating a meaningful update of the schedule using explicit knowledge about both the particular construction domain and various project management techniques.

The HOWSAFE system (Levitt, 1986) is a PC-based product useful to evaluate the safety of a construction firm. It can be utilized for corporate self-analysis or employed by an owner wishing to prequalify bidders at least partly, on safe working records. This particular discussion is valuable because it focuses on the issues of knowledge representation, reasoning and explanation in the domain of construction safety management.

'What if' scenarios form the basis for exploring, merging and eliminating hypothetical alternatives (Williams, 1985; Clayton, 1985; IntelliCorp, 1985). Along these lines, Kunz *et al.* (1986) discussed the use of these contingent possibilities and time-dependence situations in the design and construction of a construction project. The proposed system represents anticipated contingencies such as different combinations of soil types and labor conditions, and then reasons about the effects of these factors on the cost and duration of the project. The system allows distinction between choices, which are made with certainty by the user, and the implication of choices, where the user generally has incomplete knowledge about which of several possible implications will actually occur. The use of contingent possibilities gives the user the opportunity to identify scenarios of interest and to realize the most favorable contingencies while minimizing the effect of less favorable ones.

O'Connor *et al.* (1986) reported on the progress towards the building of an expert system for the analysis and evaluation of construction scheduling networks from an owner's perspective. This prototype expert system, discussed later in this chapter, relies on the timing of every schedule activity to make sound recommendations. The knowledge base consists of heuristics for the analysis of both initial and in-progress schedules. The system is fully integrated by linking together database, project management, and expert system technology on a single personal computer. This implementation takes advantage of the already available electronic databases generated by project management systems. This integration with an existing project management system is a unique and advantageous feature compared with other systems being developed for this problem domain.

The needs of contractors are more complex and sophisticated in their own way than those of owners. For example, contractors normally schedule to a finer level of detail and separate activities by subcontractors, both conditions which the typical owner can usually ignore. De La Garza and Ibbs (1986) reported on the status of a knowledge engineering effort to extract, formalize, and articulate contractor expertise to develop a useful intelligent assistant in the context of construction schedule analysis.

There are other expert system studies relevant to the field of project management, although not necessarily in construction. For example, Underwood and Summerville (1981) described PROJCON, a prototype project management consultant that advises project managers on software development project problems and their causes. Fox *et al.* (1982) described ISIS-II, a constraint-directed reasoning system for the scheduling of factory job-shops. Goldstein and Roberts (1979) discussed the use of frames in scheduling. Fox *et al.* (1983) described CALLISTO, an intelligent project management system that models, monitors, schedules, and manages large manufacturing projects. Finally, Stabile (1982) described an application of the Frame Representation Language (FRL) to the monitoring of a large computer network. Although the domain of these studies or prototypes is not construction, their domain formalization, approach to knowledge acquisition, awareness of constraints, solution, etc., provided an insight of the possible boundaries for this problem domain.

8.3 SPECIFIC NEEDS OF A SCHEDULING EXPERT SYSTEM

The construction schedule analysis and forecasting problem domain is characterized by the use of expert knowledge, judgement and experience. Typically, project managers use a set of key performance indicators and exception reporting mechanisms to assess the status of the project under development (Egan, 1983; Brown, 1985; McConnell, 1985). Exception reporting is an established variance-based technique (either in percentage terms or absolute numbers) for highlighting those work accounts which have over/underruns exceeding a pre-defined margin. Especially popular in management information reports, the variance may be quantity-, time-, or cost-based. Key indicators are analogous except that they are ratio rather than difference computations. Despite the appearance of precision given by their numeric nature, the use of key indicators during bulk production, for example, is not satisfying (Tatum, 1985). For example, a quantity overrun by a factor of two may or may not be critical depending on the monetary values involved. Bulk production involves a large number of support activities that network-based control systems fail to represent and monitor. Instead heuristic rules are frequently called upon by managers to assess progress status.

Key performance indicators are taken both from the data generated by project management systems (PMS) and from several other relevant, external sources (e.g. the work methods, corporate goals, etc.). These key indicators are formed by combining the relevant project attributes, as reported by PMS, with experimental, judgemental knowledge of the project manager.

PMS are an excellent means to process project information, to find the optimum timing of every milestone, and to summarize project data. In short, they are necessary and even good management tools, particularly for job components that are easily quantifiable and immutable. They do fall short in many regards, though. For example, PMS do not *reason* well about the information they are processing; they do not recognize that 'roofing' should not be scheduled during winter if ambient temperatures are expected to be below specified minimums. PMS do not *complain* when an installation activity is not preceded by a necessary procurement activity. Nor do they assess the causes for lagging construction, an increasingly important issue. Equally serious, the construction knowledge used originally to create the schedule is lost if it is not explicitly transmitted to the project manager and his or her team using the network.

Another preferred feature of an expert scheduling system would be to make use of an existing PMS. PMS are very good for certain tasks; e.g. their computational and scheduling algorithms and report formats are generally quite excellent. It thus is sensible for any new expert system to have direct access to electronic databases containing information generated by PMS. Having to <u>reinput this same attribute information for every activity in a large network</u> defeats the usefulness of any system deployed at the construction site, and is counter to a natural, evolutionary trend.

Also crucial is the capacity to perform both initial and in-progress schedule analyses preferably based on four major categories: (1) general requirements; (2) logic; (3) cost; and (4) time. Initial schedule analysis is defined as the type of verifications owners and contractors perform on the construction schedule submitted during contract award. Project managers need answers to questions like:

1. Are owner's approval activities included?
2. Have major subcontractors participated in the formulation of the plan?
3. What is the overall degree of schedule criticality?
4. Do procurement activities procede special installation tasks?
5. Does the cost estimate comply with the contract documents?

In-progress schedule evaluation provides project managers with answers to questions like:

1. Are winter sensitive activities scheduled during winter?
2. Is the progress payment request reasonable?
3. Should the duration of future activities be modified based on past experience?
4. How can troubled activities be spotted? How might they affect subsequent activities?

As can be deduced, initial and in-progress construction schedule analysis are tedious and cumbersome tasks. It does not take a bad manager to overlook or underestimate the presence of flaws in a schedule. Pro-active rather than reactive management decisions must be based on a careful evaluation of the current schedule.

8.4 BUILDING CONSAES

8.4.1 System parameters

CONSAS is in fact a dual-purpose scheduling system; that is, analysis and recommendations for: (1) initial and (2) in-progress or updated schedules. Figure 8.1 schematically represents the quasi-relational context of the four key subcomponents: general Corps requirements, construction and scheduling logic constraints, time concerns, and cost parameters. The current 'paper' knowledge base is reproduced in Appendix A along with some key rules, and the development of such performance specifications is indicative of one of the earliest steps of ES development.

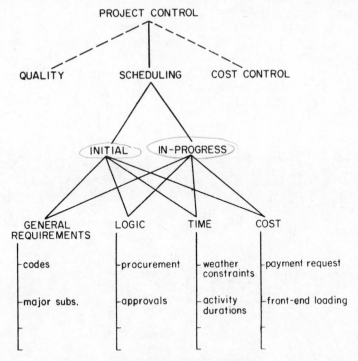

Fig. 8.1 Knowledge structure.

8.4.2 System components

Upon the completion of an extensive review of the pertinent research literature, a research development plan was devised. Remembering that the Corps of Engineers' specifications called for a tool that was PC-compatible, the following hardware–software environment was selected:

(a) *Software*:

- Personal Consultant Plus™
- Primavera Project Planner™
- dBASE III Plus™

(b) *Hardware*:

- IBM PC/XT, AT and compatibles

Personal Consultant™ Plus is a rule-based expert system shell product of Texas Instruments Corp. Important features of the software include external program interface; certainty, help and explanation facilities; frame descriptors

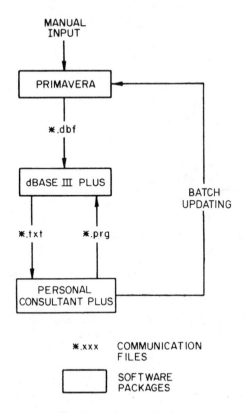

Fig. 8.2 Software interface.

with inheritance traits; and capacity for about 1000 knowledge base elements (rules).

Primavera™ is a commercial software project control package. Its major components are scheduling, resource usage and leveling, and cost control modules. Either precedence or arrow notation may be used to schedule as many as 10 000 activities per project. Up to 96 resources may be tracked for a project. A large variety and number of schedule, resource and cost reports and plots are available from this system.

dBASE III Plus™ is a popular database manager which, with its own programming language, allows interfacing of all the constituent system components.

Figure 8.2 schematically represents the software configuration employed. In this scheme, separate communication files had to be built to effect the interface between the various software packages. The nomenclature used defines these communication files as *.XXX; individually, their purposes are:

*.dbf Output file of the project management system computed information,

such as early start, percentage complete, dollars expended, etc. This is sent to the database manager.

*.prg Command file of system requests from the inference engine.

*.txt Results file generated by the database manager responding to the inference engine information requests.

8.4.3 Knowledge acquisition

To anyone planning to develop an expert system, be prepared to expend an enormous amount of time and effort to accomplish this stage. Knowledge acquisition is crucial to a useful system, and at the same time an ill-structured process. The purpose of this phase is to identify and even define the pertinent knowledge, and somehow to relate all the knowledge elements together.

The first step is to specify a problem domain in as complete and detailed a fashion as possible. Some knowledge engineers recommend that the actual target domain then be sliced in half! Though that may be extreme, the scope of definition will almost certainly be dramatically refined before system completion. A recommended methodology for knowledge acquisition is that of Freiling *et al.* (1985), which was adapted as described below.

The first exploratory step was to determine the breath and depth of the construction schedule analysis domain. This step defined whether the initial and in-progress schedule analyses, as defined in this chapter, are sufficiently narrow and self-contained. The aim was not for a system that is intricately tied to other kinds of knowledge, e.g. automated schedule generation, work package risk identification, assessment of lagging construction, cost control, etc. Rather, the goal was to develop a system that was expert in a limited, yet functional problem domain.

The nature of the construction industry is such that the knowledge about construction schedule control, even for the same type of project (e.g. high-rise reinforced concrete buildings), is not found in a single human expert. Thus, it was important to find and fuse knowledge from multiple experts. The advantages of using a diverse collection of experts, as outlined by Mittal and Dym (1985), more than offset the extra time required to resolve conflicts and contradictions generated by multiple inputs.

The sources of construction schedule expertise can be categorized in three groups: (a) contractors; (b) owners; and (c) in-house. W.E. O'Neil and Pepper Construction companies, large building contractors in Chicago, have been collaborating in this knowledge engineering project by designating one senior project manager who has committed sufficient time to the development of the system. Representatives from CERL articulated an owner's view. Finally, the in-house expertise of several faculty members in the Civil Engineering Department was drawn upon to contribute to the refinement and extension of both contractors' and owner's view.

Each source of expertise used a simple construction schedule to work on. These schedules were representative of vertical building construction: in this case, medium-rise to high-rise reinforced concrete buildings. The advantages of using this type of construction are: (1) it represents a large segment of the building construction market; (2) it is characterized by repetitive operations; and (3) solutions to early diagnosis of problems can be propagated to the rest of the structure. The purpose of these schedules was to develop a prototype. The size of the construction schedule was limited to 150–300 activities so that it would take a human expert 3–5 hours to analyze it.

A 'paper' knowledge base consisting of English sentences, which are representative expressions of the facts, concepts, and rules the CERL experts provided, was produced first. By showing this 'paper' knowledge base to the other experts early in the project, it was possible to obtain a better understanding of the different kinds of expertise prevalent in the domain and which expert practiced which kind(s). In addition, the senior project managers better understood the scope and complexity of this project. In all truthfulness, getting these experts to focus strictly on a narrow, isolated aspect of the problem was not easy.

At this stage of the knowledge acquisition process, a wholesale effort began to acquire knowledge and to identify the kinds of problem-dependent strategies the contractors use. Two main techniques were utilized to extract and formalize the experts' knowledge: (1) experts gave an account of their expertise by describing how they go about evaluating the 'goodness' of a network; and (2) experts exercised their expertise on real problems, and then a model replicating their approach was generated and tested.

The knowledge base was organized according to the diagram in Fig. 8.1. It consisted primarily of scheduling decision rules, general construction knowledge, and project specific knowledge developed or used by the experts when planning a project. Each of these modules is illustrated by means of a simple example:

1. The scheduling decision rules assure that the construction network complies with general requirements, logic, time, and cost constraints imposed by the owner. For example, if the project schedule has been front-end loaded, the knowledge base searches for activities that are either planned near the start of the project and their cost-per-day ratio exceeds the 90th percentile, or activities that are scheduled near the completion date whose cost-per-day ratio is less than the 10th percentile. This analysis may be invoked on activities of a common trade or on activities across all trades.
2. General construction knowledge includes the ability to detect lagging activities belonging to a single trade and to modify the duration of all members of this and related trades whose status is unfinished. Lagging activities are only those experiencing slower than anticipated progress. A

similar approach is followed for activities having a faster that planned progress.

3. At the time the project is planned, special attention is assigned, for example, to the correct timing of winter-sensitive activities. Whenever there is a change in the start or finish of any of these activities, a project manager usually runs a new verification. CONSAS accomplishes this operation by assigning a set of rules that understand weather related constraints to the frames representing these activities. As soon as the start and/or finish value is modified, these rules are fired to assure the new timing is within reasonable limits.

Integrating knowledge from various experts undoubtedly results in conflicts, competing strategies, and personalized 'knowhow'. From the literature review and through the interaction with several research centers, the authors identified those emerging strategies that are being used to address these issues.

8.4.4 Knowledge organization

As the 'paper' knowledge base grew, it began to exhibit some regularity in the sense that expressions of similar form reappeared frequently. Once these regularities were identified, they were captured by building an English-like knowledge acquisition grammar. This grammar allowed expression of facts, rules, and concepts of the construction schedule analysis domain. For example, the syntax for the rule and condition categories might be:

```
⟨rule⟩ ::= IF ⟨condition⟩ THEN ⟨conclusions⟩
⟨condition⟩ ::= ⟨frame⟩ HAS ⟨parameter⟩ OF ⟨value⟩
⟨condition⟩ ::= ⟨frame⟩ IS IN CLASS ⟨frame⟩
```

As a specific example, RULE111 (Look-Ahead Rules)

'Paper' knowledge base format:

Make projections based on what has happened and what was planned.

Knowledge acquisition grammar format:

```
IF ((? some-activity IS IN CLASS activities) AND
    (? some-activity IS IN CLASS concrete) AND
    (? some-activity HAS status OF finished | in-progress) AND
    (? some-activity HAS assessment OF slow-progress) AND
    (concrete HAS lagged OF ( > 5)))
THEN ((? activities IS IN CLASS activities) AND
      (? activities IS IN CLASS concrete) AND
      (? activities HAS status OF unfinished) AND
      (set (? activities HAS new-duration OF (*old delay))))
```

Here, previous job experience with a particular class of work activities is scrutinized for a reliable delay factor. If found, that modifier is then applied to all subsequent unfinished activities in that class to develop a new projected schedule duration. This update is advisory only in nature allowing the system user to see clearly the changes recommended.

8.4.5 Prototype validation

The development of the prototype has demonstrated that this new approach is satisfactory for accelerating many of the brute-force analyses and calculations typical of routine scheduling. However, this methodology cannot be shown to be a sufficient solution through the development of a prototype alone. Thus, subsequent experimentation and analyses are necessary to accomplish this. This validation has established the robustness, scope of applicability, weaknesses, strengths, and boundaries of the knowledge base.

The validity of the expert system has been determined by evaluating the prototype against test cases. The construction schedules tested fell within, on the boundary, and outside the scope of applicability of the system. The results of these evaluations identified the presence of bugs and system bounds, as well as areas for further research.

8.5 FUTURE RESEARCH AND DEVELOPMENT

Complex and ill-structured problems as construction schedule analysis are the domain of artificial intelligence. Thus, the development of a useful system is an evolutionary and exploratory process.

Since formalizing and structuring the knowledge is more valuable than inference strategies, e.g. forward and backward-chaining, a major effort will be devoted to the expansion and refinement of the current knowledge base.

The CEESL long-term research program calls for the development of a series of cohesive knowledge-based expert systems dedicated to: schedule, cost, quality and overhead control, and estimating for vertical general construction. It is unrealistic to believe that one can build the 'complete system' for scheduling control without (a) eventual attachments to other elements of project control, and (b) continued refinement, enhancement and updating. To accomplish this, a more powerful development environment is needed (De La Garza, 1986).

The Automated Reasoning Tool (ART™) has been selected and already acquired as the inference engine to process the knowledge base in this new environment. A large part of construction schedule analysis involves considering and evaluating different possible actions or evaluating a situation that is changing over time. Towards this end, ART provides 'hypothetical worlds' as its most fundamental technique for generating, representing, and evaluating alternatives as well as for representing time-changing states.

The power of CONSAS is derived largely from the knowledge captured within it. Object-oriented programming provides the facilities, e.g. objects, to structure information which describes a physical item, a concept, or an activity. Each object is represented as a frame, containing declarative, procedural, and structural information associated with the object. That is, a frame is a collection of facts that represent an object or class of objects that share certain properties. Object-oriented programming is an extremely advantageous feature of ART, which allows information of common nature to be stored declaratively, in the frames, where it is easily accessible and modifiable.

Since CONSAS deals with a complex domain, it is necessary to impose a structure on the domain. For example, some of the data elements can be organized into related groups, to make them easier to think about, describe and manipulate than hundreds or thousands of unstructured facts.

The ART schema system is a language for classifying data logically as well as for reasoning about data that has been structured. In addition to providing a way to structure all or part of a complex database, the schema system offers a convenient language for indicating that some data items share properties. Schema definitions can be organized into hierarchies in which knowledge about an object can be automatically deduced based on the classes to which it belongs.

During the construction planning phase, a work breakdown structure is defined based on project phases, goals and organization. Milestone descriptions are derived from the work breakdown structure as tasks suitable for

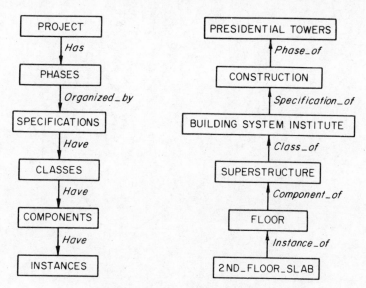

Fig. 8.3 Knowledge base taxonomy.

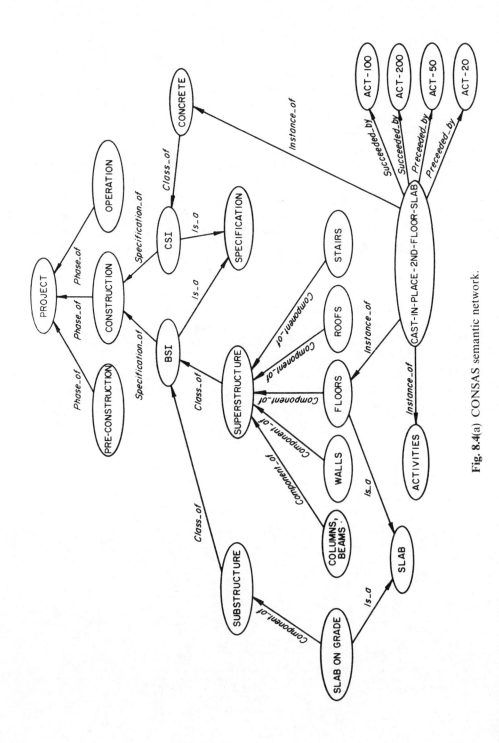

Fig. 8.4(a) CONSAS semantic network.

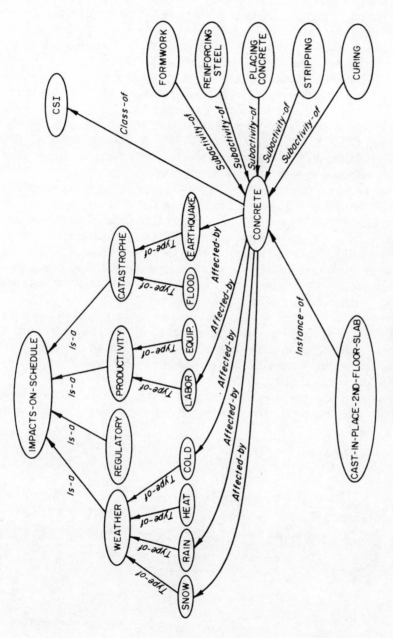

Fig. 8.4(b) CONSAS semantic network.

scheduling and monitoring. Traditionally, milestone descriptions and codes are defined in such a way they convey both a building and a construction process, e.g. 'cast in place 2nd floor slab'. The hierarchical relationship as well as the inheritance path of such a milestone are shown in Fig. 8.3. A relation connects a schema to one or more other schemata. The inclusion of one or more relations in a schema serves to establish that the schema is a node in a hierarchy. In other words, relations are the links that establish a schema hierarchy and permit inheritance of attributes. Note that the arrows shown in the diagram originate with the object that is being defined. They point to each schema that is listed as the value of the relation.

Figure 8.4 depicts a section of the CONSAS semantic network. The primary objective of this representation is to provide a *semantic* interpretation of every milestone in the construction schedule.

When an activity like 'cast in place 2nd floor slab' is found in the schedule, CONSAS immediately deduces a series of facts and implications about it. It will be known that this activity, for example (a) contains all basic schedule parameters, e.g. early start, percentage complete, etc.; (b) represents a slab in the superstructure; (c) is made of cast in place concrete; (d) consists of formwork, reinforcing steel, and concrete placing, curing, and stripping; (e) is sensitive to cold temperatures, snow, rain, labor productivity, etc.; (f) has followers and successors as well; and so forth.

Given the advantages of object-oriented program languages, and the complexity and computational requirements of this research project, microcomputer-based expert system shells, e.g. Personal Consultant Plus, Insight 2, Deciding Factor, etc., were ruled out for not providing the more robust established criteria.

A mapping technique tailored to meet ART's specifications will be defined. This mapping technique will relate the English-like knowledge acquisition

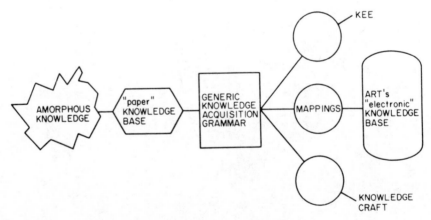

Fig. 8.5 Knowledge metamorphosis.

grammar with ART's knowledge representation language syntax. A different mapping technique would need to be designed for every different inference engine, e.g. ART, KEE, Knowledge Craft (other proprietary, trade-marked systems). However, the results of this research will be useful and available to any interested party working in a system other than ART because this knowledge base will be readily transferable to other environments. Figure 8.5 shows the knowledge metamorphosis proposed.

Future research also includes the creation and refinement of classes from which activities can inherit self creation behavior. These classes will be defined in terms of the necessary activities that must precede and succeed members of such classes. Undoubtedly, this self creation power will enhance the verification capabilities of CONSAS.

ACKNOWLEDGEMENTS

The research described in this chapter has been supported by a number of individuals and institutions, and the authors wish to express their appreciation. Inference Corp. has provided a copy of ART™ as well as consultative support. Texas Instruments donated hardware and software. The US Army Construction Engineering Research Laboratory, and Dr Michael J. O'Connor in particular, have provided personnel support and opened a variety of doors. Of course the construction firms mentioned in the text lent invaluable assistance. Finally, the US National Science Foundation, by way of a Presidential Young Investigator's Award to the senior author, Grant No. MSM-8451561, has been instrumental.

Any opinions, findings and conclusions or recommendations expressed in this publication are those of the authors and do not necessarily reflect the views of the various sponsors.

APPENDIX A — 'PAPER' KNOWLEDGE BASE

At the outset of the system's development, an extensive series of performance specifications were produced by O'Connor *et al.* (1982). The text discusses the reasons for some of them and their specific grouping into four categories. The system requirements for initial and in-progress schedule analyses are presented below. In a few cases, the individual specifications are translated into the IF...THEN format specified by the knowledge acquisition grammar.

Initial analysis

General requirements

1. *I-J numbers.* The user should skip enough numbers to allow revision without disrupting the scheme of ascending numbers.

2. *Description and codes.* Each activity must be coded and include a description of the work involved. Codes and descriptions should match the work breakdown structure specified in the contract.
3. *Activity descriptions.* Each activity must be written so that anyone familiar with the construction work can understand it. Each description should be unique and nonstandard abbreviations should be avoided.
4. *Coding.* The codes must be complete, correct, and reflect the nature of the work. They should be based on the Building System Institute (BSI) or on the Construction Specifications Institute (CSI).

RULE036 (General-Rules)

```
IF ((? some-activity IS IN CLASS activities) AND
    [OR (? some-activity HAS csi OF (> 16| < 1))
        (? some-activity HAS bsi OF (> 16| < 1))])
THEN ((? some-activity HAS code OF bad))
```

5. *Government activities* which affect construction progress should be included in the network. Reasonable durations should be assigned by the contractor and approved by the government. A dollar value must not be placed on these activities.
6. *Participation of major subcontractors.* Any subcontractor performing 10% or more of the total contract work is considered a major subcontractor, and should participate in the contractor's development plan. All major subcontractors may not have been identified at the time the contractor prepares and submits his or her schedule, but those who have should have been involved in its preparation.

Time

1. *Overall completion date.* This date must comply with the contract requirements. The contract specifications define the time period within which the work is to be completed from Notice to Proceed. A schedule consuming more than the specified number of days is not acceptable. However, a schedule showing early completion is acceptable, provided unreasonable time constraints are not placed on governmental activities.
2. *Durations for contractor activities.* These should be reasonable and conform with the limits specified in the contract. Activity duration limits usually range from 1 to 30 calendar days. Generally, very few one-day durations are needed for activities of significant nature. Long-term activities (more than 30 days) of continuous duration should be broken into parts not exceeding 30 days each. Activities with durations of 30 days and above may be acceptable if they do not lend themselves to further

breakdown, or if the dollar value is small enough to allow accurate progress reporting and payment. Durations should also be based on the time of the year the operations are to be executed.

3. *Durations for procurement activities.* These should reflect market conditions. Procurement lead time must be an integral part of the construction schedule.

4. *Float range.* Float should be broad enough to support the premise that it has not been manipulated. Schedules having an inordinate number of critical activities are not acceptable. Zero floating a network defeats its fundamental purpose. One must know which activities are critical and which are not to effectively manage the work. Float is a significant element of the honestly developed network. Float may be used as necessary by the contractor without a change to the contract price. When the Corps wishes to use float to absorb change order work, it must negotiate an equitable price for the amount used. This solution lies in a policy that says, 'float has value to the contractor and must be treated as any other resource when pricing a change order'. However, the price of the float is not constant: (a) overall, it is of more value early in the life of the job than when the job approaches completion, because as the job progresses, the remaining risk factors diminish; and (b) for a given activity, it increases in value inversely to its quality, because uncontrollable events causing small periods of delay are more likely to happen than those producing longer delays.

5. *The critical path.* This usually consists of relatively few activities. If many parallel paths or a large number of critical activities exist, it is likely that some durations have been overstated for the purpose of eliminating float. In addition, managing simultaneous critical paths is harder than managing a single one.

Logic

1. *The scope of work.* It must be reflected in the network. The network must contain all work activities (with clear descriptions) to be performed under the contract.

2. *Submittal activities.* These activities include the contractor's preparation and submittal of shop drawings, catalog cuts, samples, etc., and the Corps' review and approval actions. These time-consuming activities must precede nearly all of the construction-producing activities; thus, all materials and methods requiring prior approval must be represented in the network.

3. *Procurement activities.* These generally occur after the proposed material is approved, but before the construction activity using the material occurs. As with submittal activities, all materials requiring approval should have their procurement lead-time activities represented in the network.

RULE045 (logic-Rules)

```
IF ((? some-activity IS IN CLASS activities) AND
     (? some-activity HAS type OF approval) AND
     (? some-activity HAS csi OF? code) AND
     (? other-activity IS IN CLASS activities) AND
     (? other-activity HAS type OF submittal) AND
     (? other-activity HAS csi OF ? code) AND
     (? some-activity HAS-NOT preceded-by OF ? other-activity))
THEN ((? some-activity HAS logic OF bad) AND
     (EXPLANATION No predecessor of type of SUBMITTAL with the
     same code was found. There can be three reasons that
     explain why a submittal activity was not found:
     (1) There is indeed no such activity;
     (2) There is an immediate predecessor of type SUBMITTAL,
          yet, its code is different from its successor and
          thus, they cannot be related;
     (3) the approval activity includes the submittal phase.
          If this is the case, splitting the activity in two
          is recommended.))
```

4. *Sequencing and interdependencies.* These must be logical. While it is the contractor's responsibility to plan and accomplish the work, many conventions can limit his or her options. For example, foundations will have to be completed before the roof is erected, etc. The Corps reviews the contractor's proposed plan to: (a) confirm it represents a reasonable plan for accomplishing the work; (b) ensure the work is broken down and identified well enough to permit adequate monitoring and reporting progress; and (c) ensure that monetary values are correct for payment purposes.
5. *Constraints.* External constraints should be considered, including site access, work of other contractors, local climate and environmental conditions, working schedules of local suppliers, contract-specific dates, etc. For example, built-up roofing should not be scheduled if expected ambient temperatures are expected to be below specified minimums.

Cost

1. *Total cost.* The monetary value assigned to individual activities must total to the contract amount.
2. *Activity's cost.* The monetary value of each activity should conform to the range stipulated in the contract. The usual range is between 0.1 and 2.5% of the total contract amount. In addition, the monetary value assigned to each activity should represent a reasonable amount for that work. This analysis may be based on the cost of similar work completed recently.
3. *Administrative activities.* The monetary value of administrative activities

should be zero. The cost of preparing submittals is considered part of the overhead the contractor must distribute to other activities. Government activities such as submittal reviews represent no cost to the contractor. A monetary value should not be placed on procurement and delivery activities, since the cost of materials is usually included in the price of the construction activity using them. Payment for on-site materials (when allowed) should be handled outside the network framework.
4. *Front-end loading.* Front-end loading is the practice of placing an excessively high monetary value on activities scheduled for completion early in the project. Since this can result in prohibited over-payments or advance payments, its practice is unlawful.

RULE120 (Cost-Rules)

```
IF ((? some-activity IS IN CLASS activities) AND
    (? some-activity HAS early-start OF 1st-quarter) AND
    (? some-activity HAS cost-per-day OF (> 90th percentile)))
THEN ((? some-activity HAS front-end-evidence OF yes))
```

In-progress revisions

The need for network analysis does not end with approval of the contractor's initial submittal. There are many reasons why the network must be changed during the prosecution of the work. For example, production may fall behind, equipment may unexpectedly break down, material deliveries may not be made on schedule. Such delays do not constitute justification for a time extension. So when a network no longer realistically reflects how the work can be completed on schedule, the remaining work must be rescheduled. When the contractor's network is received, the Corps should evaluate it in the same way as the original schedule submittal, except many of the criteria will no longer be applicable. What follows is a list of relevant concepts that are essential for in-progress analysis.

1. What is the schedule status of the work?
2. What is the actual status of the work?
3. What is the earned status of the work?
4. The contractor should revise the schedule when it no longer accurately represents his or her plan for completing the remaining work, or because actual progress has not kept up with the schedule. Ordinarily, only the durations and the logic of the remaining activities will be changed, with shortened durations implying the assignment of increased resources by the contractor. No increase in contract price or the value of the various activities is permitted, since the need for schedule revision stems from contractor-responsible causes.

5. Use current trends to forecast the degree of success or failure to be expected in meeting future contractual milestones.
6. Identify areas that need remedial action while there is still time for such action to produce a positive effect.
7. Make projections based on what has happened and what was planned.
8. Predict any significant deviations from the official schedule.
9. Make sure that the progress payment request is reasonable.
10. When a progress schedule is approved, it implies the acceptance of a practical way to finish the work on time.
11. It is essential to successful contract administration that the approved planning schedule be current.
12. When a change order occurs, the time factor for the modification can be unilaterally defined by identifying the network activities whose dollar value or duration are affected.
13. Any revised logic or durations may be developed by the contractor and the owner and approved by both parties.
14. To estimate the effect of a change order, the current status of the work and the contractor's approved plan for completing the remaining activities must be known.
15. The change order's time effects can be observed by comparing the current approved plan to the plan generated after the changes to the network have been processed. At this point, it is known whether the change order would delay the completion of the remaining work, and, if so, quantify the delay. This analysis will show those activities both directly and indirectly affected by the change order; the estimate of the dollar amount must take both effects into consideration. The estimate must also consider that time has value, whether or not it is on the critical path.

REFERENCES

Brown, J.W. (1985) *Project Management Journal*, **16**, No. 3, 59–63.
Clayton, B.D. (1985) *ART – Programming Tutorial*, Inference Corporation, Vols 1–3, Los Angles, California.
De La Garza, J.M. and Ibbs, C.W. (1986) *Proceedings 10th Triennial Congress of the International Council for Building Research, Studies and Documentation*, CIB86 Congress – Advancing Building Technology, Washington, DC, Vol. 2, pp. 683–91.
De La Garza, J.M. (1986) *Unpublished PhD Thesis Proposal*, Department of Civil Engineering, University of Illinois at Urbana–Champaign, Urbana, Illinois.
Diekmann, J.E. and Kruppenbacher, T.A. (1984) *Journal of Construction Engineering and Management*, ASCE, **110**, No. 4, 391–408.
Egan, D.S. (1983) *Project Management Journal*, **14**, No. 4, 84–94.
Fox, M.S., Allen, B. and Strohm G. (1982) *Proceedings, National Conference on Artificial Intelligence, Pittsburgh, Pennsylvania, American Association for Artficial Intelligence, Carnegie*–Mellon University, Pittsburgh, Pennsylvania, USA.

Fox, M.S. *et al.* (1983) *CALLISTO: An Intelligent Project Management System*, Intelligent Systems Laboratory, Robotics Institute, Pittsburgh, Pennsylvania, Carnegie–Mellon University.

Freiling, M., Alexander, J., Messick, S., Rehfuss, S. and Shulman, S. (1985) *The Artificial Intelligence Magazine*, **6**, No. 3, 150–64.

Goldstein, I.P. and Roberts, B. (1979) *Artificial Intelligence: An MIT Perspective* (eds. P.H. Winston and R.H. Brown), Cambridge MIT Press, Vol. 1, pp. 257–84.

Ibbs, C.W. (1985) *Proceedings of a Workshop for the Development of New Research Directions in Computerized Applications to Construction Engineering and Management Studies*, University of Illinois, Construction Research Series Technical Report 19.

Ibbs, C.W. (1986) *Journal of Construction Engineering and Management*, ASCE, pp. 326–45.

IntelliCorp (1985) *KEE 3.0 – The Knowledge Engineering Environment Technical Summary*, IntelliCorp, Mountain View, California.

Kunz, J.C., Bonura, T., Levitt, R.E. and Stelzner, M.J. (1986) *First International Conference on Applications of Artificial Intelligence to Engineering Problems, Southampton University, UK*, Vol. 2, CML Publications, Southampton, UK, pp. 707–18.

Levitt, R.E. and Kunz, J.C. (1985) *Project Management Quarterly*, **16**, No. 5, 57–76.

Levitt, R.E. (1986) *Proceedings, First Symposium on Expert Systems in Civil Engineering*, American Society of Civil Engineers Spring Convention, Seattle, Washington, pp. 55–66.

McConnell, D.R. (1985) *Journal of Management in Engineering*, ASCE, **1**, No. 2, 79–94.

McGartland, M.R. and Hendrickson, C.T. (1985) *Journal of Construction Engineering and Management*, ASCE, **111**, No. 3, 293–307.

Mittal, S. and Dym, C.L. (1985) *The Artificial Intelligence Magazine*, **6**, No. 2, 32–6.

Nay, L.B. and Logcher, R.D. (1985) *Technical Report CCRE 85–2*, MIT Department of Civil Engineering.

Niwa, K. and Okuma, M. (1982) *IEEE Transactions on Engineering Management*, EM-**29**, No. 4, 146–53.

Niwa, K. and Sasaki, K. (1983) *Project Management Quarterly*, **14**, No. 1, 65–72.

Niwa, K., Sasaki, K. and Ihara, H. (1984) *The Artificial Intelligence Magazine*, **5**, No. 2, 29–36.

O'Connor, M.J., Colwell, G.E. and Reynolds, R.D. (1982) *Technical Report P-126*, US Army Construction Engineering Research Laboratory.

O'Connor, M.J., De La Garza, J.M. and Ibbs, C.W. (1986) *Proceedings, First Symposium on the Expert Systems in Civil Engineering*, American Society of Civil Engineers Spring Convention, Seattle, Washington, pp. 67–77.

Stabile, L.A. (1982) *Proceedings, National Conference on Artificial Intelligence, Pittsburgh, Pennsylvania*, pp. 327–30.

Tatum, C.B. (1985) *Project Management Journal*, **16**, No. 3, 52–7.

Underwood, W.E. and Summerville, J.P. (1981) *International Conference on Cybernetics and Society*, IEEE, Georgia Institute of Technology, pp. 149–55.

Williams, C. (1985) *ART– The Automated Reasoning Tool: Conceptual Overview*, Inference Corporation, Los Angeles, California.

9

Approximate reasoning in structural damage assessment

T.J. ROSS

9.1 INTRODUCTION

The assessment of damage to a structure from any disturbance, natural or man made, is a difficult process requiring significant human judgement. This process is complicated by the fact that the information needed to make a damage assessment with high confidence is incomplete and involves uncertainty. Evaluation of the situation becomes even more difficult when one realizes that the uncertainties encountered include both random and non-random kinds of data. For instance, in the case of protective structures we lack deep knowledge about explosive effects on an operational facility which is occupied by people, and which contains sensitive, technologically complex equipment. Variability in the ground shock speed through the soil and in material behavior could be classified as random uncertainty. On the other hand, linguistic data, subjective judgement, and imprecise information are typical examples of nonrandom uncertainties for which the sample space is not well defined and the mean and variance are not meaningful.

From the previous discussion, we see that the assessment of damage to any structure, from any extreme disturbance (blast/shock, wind, earthquake, etc.) is a difficult process in which human judgement plays an important role. This is especially true of protective structures. They are usually heavily reinforced and yet may be subjected to very severe if not total failure levels.

Because of a lack of complete understanding of the real problem, in the past, the typical analysis of the damaged structure would simply be assigned to one of two groups – survival or failure. If we take a closer look at the problem, however, we see that it is not a two-class problem, but rather is a continuous one. To illustrate, a damaged element in a protective structure is shown in Fig. 9.1. There is overlap between different damage levels. It is this lack of crispness (or inherent fuzziness) in the problem that causes

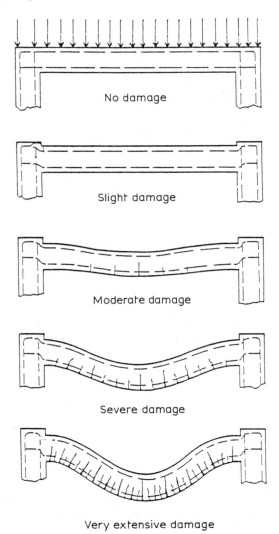

No damage

Slight damage

Moderate damage

Severe damage

Very extensive damage

Fig. 9.1 Linguistic descriptions of damage levels (Savage, 1986).

difficulty, first, in determining the damage level, and second, in deciding on an acceptable level of damage.

The process of damage assessment is a cause and effect situation. The 'cause' usually involves engineering quantities such as pressures and strains, while the 'effect' involves subjective information concerning the functionality and repairability of the structure.

Although there is objective information available to the expert in the form of test data and model simulations, the question of damage assessment is strongly tied to expert judgement. Thus the quality of the assessment process is highly dependent on an expert's knowledge of the actual situation under study.

This chapter will summarize the damage assessment process of protective structures by discussing the kinds of information available to the problem and by discussing the uncertainty in this information. It will also discuss how the information and its associated uncertainty can be used within an expert system which attempts to reach conclusions about damage through an approximate reasoning approach. The chapter will conclude by illustrating a recent case study involving damage to a buried reinforced concrete box-like structure.

9.2 DAMAGE ASSESSMENT PARADIGM

The process of damage assessment can be divided into two subsets: damage descriptors and damage levels. Damage descriptors may be either numerical engineering quantities or subjective linguistic information; in either case, they are used to describe the second subset. Damage levels, on the other hand, are integrally related to three damage criteria: (1) structural integrity, (2) functionality, and (3) repairability. These damage criteria are important for the development of the expert system since their use improves the accuracy of expert opinions.

Structural integrity is the most frequently used criterion to assess damage level since it is related to the stability of the structure or its components. For example, if the stability of an important structural component is disturbed, the structure is assumed damaged. Functionality is related to overall damage of a structure. A damaged structure may not function as originally intended and a structure that is not functioning well can be assumed to be in a damaged condition. Repairability is also related to damage level. In general, a structure or its components needs repair if it is in a damaged condition. On the other hand, a structure that needs repair indicates a certain degree of damage. Hadipriano (1986) gives an excellent review of the three damage criteria as will be discussed below.

9.2.1 Structural integrity

Damage descriptors can be visual but generally are engineering parameters which can be measured. These measured data can be the result of active or passive measurements and can be considered as 'hard' data. The visual images referred to earlier can be considered as 'soft' data in the sense that they carry much information which has not been explicitly quantified and identified before. Finally, information residing in the minds of experts who have experience in assessing damage to structures is valuable but inaccessible

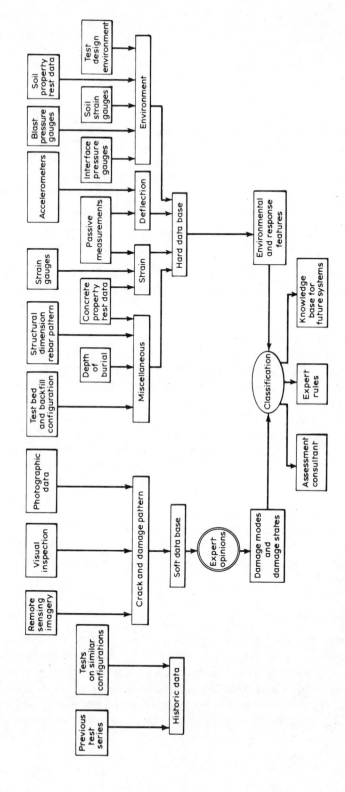

Fig. 9.2 Sources of soft and hard data for use in damage assessment analysis (Ross, *et al.* 1986).

except through laborious and painstaking interviews with the expert. This latter type of information is termed 'historical'. Both the soft and historical data are typically manifested in the form of expert opinion and engineering judgement. These data concepts are shown schematically in Fig. 9.2.

Structural integrity is defined as the stability or capacity of a structure or its components to perform its intended function. Variables affecting the structural integrity are deformation, displacement, and/or separation. A structure experiencing these variables suffers a certain level of degradation to integrity. Deformation includes deflection, bending, and rotation of a structural component relative to other components or to its original shape. The components of a protective structure are the walls and the slabs. A 'very severe' deflection of a roof slab, for example, indicates 'very severe' slab damage.

Displacement is translation of structural components relative to other components or to their original location. Displacement of a component can occur due to the deformation of other components or due to the separation at their connections. As an example, one may relate a 'very severe' displacement of a wall to 'very severe' wall damage. Cracks or material crushings which occur in a structural component can cause separation of the material within the component. A 'severe' crack in a slab, for instance, can represent a 'very severe' damage level of the slab. An example of a production rule for structural integrity is as follows:

IF　(a) deformation of slab is very severe AND
　　(b) displacement of slab is very severe AND
　　(c) cracks in the slab are severe AND
　　(d) deformation of wall is severe AND
　　(e) displacement of wall is severe AND
　　(f) cracks in the wall are moderate
THEN there is suggestive evidence that damage level is very severe.

9.2.2 Structure functionality

Functionality represents the intended use or function of a structure. A protective structure is constructed to protect equipment and its occupants. Destruction of equipment and occupants indicates loss of function of the structure, and hence, represents a certain extent of damage to the structure. Therefore, the type of equipment being protected, equipment damage level, position of occupants (people), and occupant level of injury are the variables that determine the functionality, and subsequently, indicate the damage level of the structure.

An example rule of functionality that produces a severe overall damage level of the structure can be shown as follows:

IF   (a) type of equipment is piping and duct works AND
    (b) equipment damage level is severe AND
    (c) occupants are in standing position AND
    (d) occupant injury level is severe
THEN there is suggestive evidence that the overall damage level of the structure
is severe

Note that the use of functionality alone for assessing a structure's overall
damage level can result in an inaccurate answer. For example, in a 'lucky'
situation where the main component of the structure is damaged considerably
but did not collapse (clearly showing structure losing its protective function),
no equipment is destroyed and none of the occupants is injured. A damage
assessment based only on the amount of equipment destroyed may lead us
to believe that the structure did not lose its protective function, hence, is
undamaged. However, in the absence of the equipment or occupants, an
assessment based on functionality becomes difficult since one has to assume
their existence in order to assess the value of these variables. For the above
reasons, the evaluation of other damage criteria, such as repairability and
structural integrity is essential.

9.2.3 Structure repairability

A damaged protective structure should be repaired in order to restore it to
an original or an acceptable condition. The term 'acceptable' is used here to
indicate that during a 'readiness period' command personnel may only require
that a structure be partially repaired. In this case the structure does not have
to be restored to its original condition. Several variables determine the
repairability of protective structures; they are the amount of repair, repair
time, repair cost, and resource availability.

The amount of repair indicates the degree of difficulty or the efforts required
in order to repair a structure with a certain level of damage. For instance, a
'major' repair may be required to restore a structure with a 'severe' level of
damage. Repair time is the time needed to repair the structure. As an example,
if a period from three to six months is needed to restore the same structure,
the repair time can be assessed as 'long'. The amount of money spent to
restore the structure is the repair cost. If, for the same structure, the cost is
estimated to be about $500 000, then the repair cost can be considered as
'moderate'. Resource availability usually consists of labor, material, and
equipment that are employed for restoration purposes. For a certain
protective structure, for example, one may relate a 'scarce' resource to a
'severe' level of damage. Of course the particular value of each of these
variables and its association with repairability is peculiar to specific classes
of problems, and would change when the situation changes. A rule-based
system can accommodate these changes.

The production rule resulting from the above example may be as follows:

IF   (a) major repair is required AND
      (b) repair time is long AND
      (c) repair cost is moderate AND
      (d) resource availability is scarce
THEN   there is suggestive evidence that the damage level of structure is severe.

9.3 EXPERT REASONING ON STRUCTURAL DAMAGE

9.3.1 General

In many fields of engineering, damage and its interpretation are not precise. This is especially true of protective structures because they are heavily reinforced and, yet, are expected to be loaded into severe damage and even total collapse. Only a limited number of tests can be performed, and the tests are usually done on small-scale structures using simulated loading (Ross *et al.*, 1986).

The evaluation of linguistic damage states such as light, medium, and severe damage can differ from one expert to another. Moreover, the damage ranges naturally overlap, i.e. damage does not change abruptly from light to medium, and from medium to severe upon reaching certain crisp thresholds. Other factors such as scarcity of data and the need to extrapolate the data to realistic loading, full-size prototypes and imperfect structures add much more complexity to the assessment of damage and they highlight the importance of expert opinion in dealing with the complexity.

9.3.2 Soliciting expert opinion

In soliciting and using expert opinion as the basis for the knowledge source of expert systems, several problems are encountered. The experts providing the knowledge have different perspectives, or biases, on the same issue and their opinions can conflict with one another. Moreover, the experience and relevance level of the experts can vary, leading the user to adopt some sort of credibility measure, or weight, to the opinion. These problems have been characterized by Wong, *et. al.* (1986) as a process of solicitation, identification, and aggregation of expert opinion.

The problem of solicitation of expert opinions can be described as follows. Several experts are asked to reason about a single piece of data. If the data are denoted by A and the assessment of the data from expert number 1 is B_1, the assessment from expert number 2 is B_2, and so on, the resulting rule can be expressed as

$$\text{IF } A, \text{ then } B_1, B_2, \ldots.$$

For example in structural damage assessment the data As could be measured strains and deflections, observed crack patterns, and exposed reinforcing steel. Examples of assessment Bs could be damage states, residual strength of structural elements, and the fidelity of laboratory tests.

When there is more than one piece of data to be evaluated, the result of the solicitation is

$$\text{If } A_1, A_2, \ldots, \text{ then } B_1, B_2, \ldots$$

Alternatively, the solicitation process can involve the following. Expert 1 is shown data A_1, and provides assessment B_1. Expert 2 is shown data A_2 and provides reasoning, B_2, and so on. The resulting rules would be

$$\text{If } A_1, \text{ then } B_1, \text{ and}$$

$$\text{If } A_2, \text{ then } B_2, \text{ and so on.}$$

There are different ways to elicit opinions, to weight the experience of the experts, and to include their biases. The precision and form of the assessment is another important factor, as well as the difficult question of how to treat a common database which may have been shared by the experts. The most popular methods involve the notion of expert consensus, but these methods rely on large data populations which usually don't exist for many kinds of structural damage situations. Expert opinions are also seen as nonrandom in nature, especially when weights and bias factors are included.

9.3.3 Identifying/classifying opinion

Wong (1986a) has shown a way to use the theory of fuzzy sets to identify and classify expert opinion. Fuzzy classification is used to separate experts into subgroups according to common attributes and to attach weighting factors to these groups, and fuzzy identification is also used to aggregate the different inferences of members of a subgroup. The aggregation process produces some global inference mechanism which can also summarize the thoughts of the experts.

In the proposition or rule, R: if A, then B, the A is termed the antecedent and B is called the consequent. The proposition of arriving at B given A is a process called inference. The global inference, R, which relates all of the antecedents to all of the consequents, involves the process of identification. This process derives from identifying the inherent relation which provides the best representation of the constituent relations.

The process of expert classification into homogeneous subgroups allows an enhancement of the dependence of opinion within the group while the independence among subgroups is enforced. Working with homogeneous subgoups will also facilitate the evaluation of the importance of their individual contribution and the assignment of weights. By the fact that the boundaries of these groups may be fuzzy and overlap to some extent, the employment of fuzzy classification methods seems most appropriate. Natural grouping criteria might be according to education, experience level and experience type such as research or professional practice. A recent popular and productive scheme for classification is the idea of a fuzzy clustering algorithm as espoused by Bezdek *et al.* (1986). This algorithm allows classes of a problem to have vague boundaries as opposed to the classic clustering schemes which use crisp boundaries to define classes of a problem.

9.3.4 Aggregating opinion

Having obtained the expert opinions, the next step is to combine, or aggregate, them. The assessments B_i can be analyzed and synthesized to arrive at some aggregated or consensus assessment B. However, it should be emphasized that consensus should not be the only goal of aggregation. Contradictory and ambiguous assessments should be justifiably reflected in the aggregated result.

The method of combining expert opinions depends on whether the information is cardinal (numeric) or ordinal (linguistic). Examples of methods used to combine numeric data are max, min, algebraic mean and geometric mean. For a homogeneous subgroup of experts, the opinions of its members should be quite compatible, and all these methods should yield comparable results. However, methods to combine linguistic opinions have produced mixed results as discussed by Wong (1986a). The general problem with some of these linguistic methods is that original data-opinion pairs cannot be reproduced through the optimal inference relations because fuzzy operators, in general, do not have unique inverses. Different variants of these operators involved in the identification algorithm correspond to using different measures and schemes to minimize the optimal inference relation. The differences between the resulting opinions and the original opinions are measured and quantified, however, through the use of any of a variety of similarity methods, as discussed in Wong, *et al.* (1986).

9.4 APPROXIMATE REASONING

9.4.1 General

The terms 'approximate reasoning', 'inexact reasoning', and 'reasoning under uncertainty' are often used synonymously. Several good papers and books (Negoita, 1985; Lecot and Parker, 1986; Blockley, 1980; Ruspini, 1982; Zadeh, 1974) have been written on these subjects and, in fact, the concepts behind these terms are very closely related. The main difference tends to be in the mathematical calculus used to represent the approximate reasoning situation.

For this chapter any reasoning process which is accomplished under uncertainty is termed approximate reasoning.

A lively debate continues in the literature today about which mathematical calculus is best employed in the representation of uncertainty. This turns out to be a difficult task because there is a lack of consensus on the meaning and types of uncertainty. Probabilists would have us believe that all uncertainty is random or can be modeled as a random process. Physicists would have us believe that there is no uncertainty in nature, only varying degrees of ignorance about our understanding of physical phenomena. It is important to remark that many believe that some forms of uncertainty are not amenable to quantifiable description and should be evaluated in their original form as linguistic statements in an expert system. It is perhaps instructive to discuss uncertainty in terms of the mathematical tools which are available to us today. Wong (1986b) has provided an excellent treatise on this subject using a simple interval as the measure of uncertainty.

9.4.2 Representing uncertainty

Different mathematical measures which use the interval model are available to describe uncertainties in a quantifiable form. This chapter will discuss the following interval models, after Wong (1986b), as they are illustrated in Fig. 9.3:

(a) Simple intervals
(b) Possibility measures
(c) Probability measures
(d) Evidence measures
(e) Fuzzy sets

(a) *Simple intervals*

Simple intervals correspond to the minimum information available, as seen in Fig. 9.3(a). The value of a parameter is estimated to be within an interval $[a, b]$, and nothing more is known.

(b) *Possibility measures*

Possibility measures are built upon simple interval uncertainties but with varying degrees of possibilities; hence, they correspond to slightly more information on the value distribution of the parameter, as shown in Fig. 9.3(b) and (c). When the probability of a particular value of the parameter is known (for all possible values of the parameter), we have the probability measure of the uncertainty.

(a) Simple interval uncertainty

$$x \in [a,b]$$

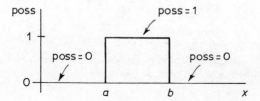

(b) Simple possibility measure involves one interval

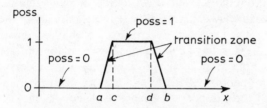

(c) A more intuitive possibility measure involves two or more intervals

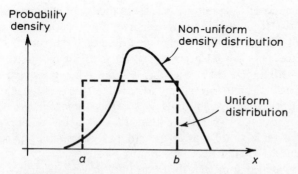

(d) Probability implies knowledge about (random) distribution within the interval

Fig. 9.3 The interval as a basic representation of uncertainty (Wong, 1986b).

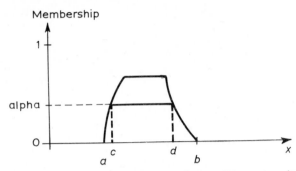

(e) Fuzzy sets can be considered intervals with different degrees of membership

Fig. 9.3 (*contd.*)

(c) *Probability measures*

Probability measure implies exact knowledge of the uncertainty. Although the value of the parameter is uncertain, there is certainty about the character of its randomness; it is described exactly by a probability distribution, as shown in Fig. 9.3(d). This may be unreasonable and inappropriate in certain situations. For example, knowing the probability of event A, denoted by $p(A)$, implies that the probability of the event (not A), denoted by $p(\text{not } A)$, is $1 - p(A)$. In other words, if there is evidence $p(A)$ supporting A, we presume that there is evidence refuting A of the amount $1 - p(A)$.

(d) *Evidence measures*

This stringent presumption of probability theory can be relaxed by introducing the concept of ignorance, as in the theory of evidence advocated by Shafer (1976). His contention is that knowing $p(A)$ should not say anything about $p(\text{not } A)$ unless there is explicit evidence supporting 'not A'. When such evidence is not available, $p(\text{not } A)$ is zero. We are ignorant as to whether there is something against A, and this ignorance is represented by $1 - p(A)$, i.e. everything in the unit interval not assigned to $p(A)$ is assigned to ignorance. When explicit evidence against A exists, then ignorance is computed as $1 - p(A) - p(\text{not } A)$, or everything other than $p(A)$ and $p(\text{not } A)$ in the unit interval. It is understood that $p(A) + p(\text{not } A)$ is less than or equal to one, and ignorance is greater than or equal to zero.

Shafer's evidence approach to uncertainty can be succinctly summarized by describing the uncertainty by two terms, the evidence for $p(A)$ and one minus the evidence against, or $1 - p(\text{not } A)$. The former is called credibility, and the latter plausibility. They form the interval [credibility, plausibility] which contains the actual probability. Physically, the interval means that the probability is at least the credibility since this much supporting evidence is known. On the other hand, it is plausible that the probability can be higher; how much higher is inversely proportional to the known refuting evidence. When there is no known refuting evidence, the probability can be as high as 1, the maximum allowed. When there is known refuting evidence, the ceiling is lowered accordingly. In the limiting case where the refuting evidence is the complement of the supporting evidence, i.e. $p(\text{not } A) = 1 - p(A)$, the plausibility becomes the same as the credibility. The Shafer interval degenerates into a point, and that point is the classical probability. Hence, we see that the classical probability representation of uncertainty is a special case of the Shafer representation.

(e) *Fuzzy sets*

Finally, fuzzy sets can also be represented by intervals using the well-known alpha-cut decomposition, as seen in Fig. 9.3(e). An alpha-cut is the real interval of the fuzzy set which corresponds to a constant membership whose value is alpha (shown in Fig. 9.3(e) as the interval $c - d$). Each interval is associated with a membership value. Set-theoretic operations on fuzzy sets can be translated into operations on the alpha-cut intervals. It can also be shown that Shafer's representation reduces to a normal and convex fuzzy set when the evidences are consonant. To illustrate, suppose we have evidence E_i supporting events A_i. Then by consonant we mean that event A_n is completely contained within the domain of event A_{n-1}, and so on in a recursive manner. A simple description of fuzzy sets follows.

The vagueness or uncertainty as to whether an object belongs to a class or set is a question of membership. In classical set theory, an element is either within the domain of the set, or it is not. Mathematically, this binary notion of set membership is handled with the indicator function. In fuzzy set theory, the degree of memership of an element x in a set A, denoted $\mu_A(x)$, can be any value in the interval $[0, 1]$. For instance, if the membership level is one, then the item or object is definitely a member. If the membership level is zero, then the item is definitely not a member. If the membership value is between 0 and 1, then the value stated indicates the belief that the object is a member of the set.

In fuzzy set theory, the set A can be represented in terms of its membership function as follows.

$$A = \frac{\mu_A(x_1)}{x_1} + \frac{\mu_A(x_2)}{x_2} + \cdots + \frac{\mu_A(x_n)}{x_n} = \sum_{i=1}^{n} \frac{\mu_A(x_i)}{x_i}$$

where each x_i is an element of the set A. When x is a continuous variable, the set A is denoted:

$$A = \int \frac{\mu_A(x)}{x}$$

where the symbol '————' is a delimiter which denotes the association of the membership value $\mu_A(x_i)$ with the element of A, and the symbols '$\int$' and '$+$' denote the union of all elements of the fuzzy subset in the continuous and discrete case, respectively. As an example, suppose the set A represents the universe of discrete concrete strengths:

$$A = [2.0, 3.0, 4.0, 5.0, 6.0, 7.0] \ \text{(ksi)}$$

Then, for this example, the x_i are the discrete values of concrete strength. A moderate strength concrete may be expressed in fuzzy terms as:

$$\text{'Moderate strength'} = \left[\frac{0.0}{2.0} + \frac{0.2}{3.0} + \frac{0.8}{4.0} + \frac{1.0}{5.0} + \frac{0.5}{6.0} + \frac{0.0}{7.0} \right]$$

In other words, this expression means that 5.0 ksi concrete is definitely a member of the set 'moderate strength', 2.0 and 7.0 ksi are definitely not members of the set 'moderate strength', and 3.0, 4.0, and 6.0 ksi concrete are somewhere in between in terms of membership. A classical representation using crisp set theory could be expressed as:

$$\text{'Moderate strength'} = \left[\frac{0}{2.0} + \frac{0}{3.0} + \frac{1}{4.0} + \frac{1}{5.0} + \frac{1}{6.0} + \frac{0}{7.0} \right]$$

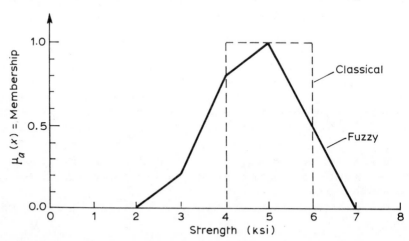

Fig. 9.4 Classical and fuzzy set representations of a 'moderate strength' concrete (Savage, 1986).

The difference between a 'fuzzy' representation and the 'classical' representation of 'moderate strength' is illustrated in Fig. 9.4.

9.4.3 Rule-based inference

Rule-based inference involves the following idea: Uncertainties of the antecedents (the IF portion of a rule) are combined to give the combined antecedent uncertainty. This uncertainty is propagated along a rule and combined with the rule uncertainty to give the uncertainty in the consequent (the THEN portion of a rule), and the various consequent uncertainties are combined.

This 'combination' process is followed regardless of the control process, i.e. whether it is forward-chaining, backward-chaining, or some combination or hybrid of the two.

In principle, uncertainties in the three parts of an inference (among antecedents, along a rule, among consequents) define the inexact reasoning process. In practice, there is no single theory of uncertainty combination which is universally accepted. Currently, Shafer's method enjoys the most support, followed closely by Bayesian probability, but some difficulties still exist. For example, suppose evidence supports the probability of an event A being $p(A) = 0.2$, then in Bayes theory the probability of the complement of A, or *not* A (A'), has to be $p(A') = 0.8$. But there may be no evidence to support such a probability assignment.

A strategy for assessing the uncertainty in the three parts of an inference in an expert system is to use the 'combination' process as follows. The combination process, also described as an *approximate reasoning module*, would possess: (a) uncertainties associated with factual knowledge and (b) uncertainties associated with the inference rules. Most importantly, the module, in conjunction with the expert system, should be able to make decisions with *incomplete* information; it can still solve a problem without knowing all the facts and in the face of uncertainty.

An example of this process should prove helpful. Suppose we have two rules, rule 1 and rule 2, each of which has the same antecedent and different consequents, and suppose further that there is uncertainty attached to each rule. In the combination process the uncertainty in each rule is propagated through to the consequent so that where consequents conflict there is a basis for determining the relative confidence in each consequent. For example, let the rules be:

Rule 1: IF the small fruit is yellow,
        THEN it is a lemon
Rule 2: IF the small fruit is yellow,
        THEN it is a golden delicious apple

Let the rules have the same uncertainty for the antecedent, denoted $E(A)$, and let the uncertainty in each rule be denoted $E(B_1)$ and $E(B_2)$ for rules 1 and 2, respectively. Now suppose we have a very simple product operation to propagate uncertainties and we determine the propagated uncertainty in the consequents C_1 and C_2 as follows:

$$E(C_1) = E(A) \cdot E(B_1)$$
$$E(C_2) = E(A) \cdot E(B_2)$$

Since the uncertainty in the consequents, $E(C_1)$ and $E(C_2)$, will generally be different the combination process will reconcile this difference, depending on the particular calculus chosen. Naturally, for compound rules (rules with multiple antecedents or multiple consequents) these operations become a little more complex in that uncertainties in the antecedents are 'combined' before they are propagated through the inference process.

The purpose of the inexact reasoning module is to combine different kinds of uncertainty including ignorance, into a global uncertainty measure associated with the final assessment. The inference rule results in a propagation of uncertainties for the uncertainties in the antecedents and consequents and for the uncertainty in the inference mechanism itself. The process of aggregating different sources of information is called the combination process. The combination process can be broken down further into two fundamental operations: antecedent combination and consequent combination.

Wong (1986b) suggests that an adequate inexact reasoning module should include the following elements. It should have a structure which defines the uncertainty representation scheme. Although the preferred scheme would use interval theory which involves two values per uncertainty in general, the user should have the option of choosing one value (conventional certainty factor), three-value (true, false, unknown), and multivalue (fuzzy sets) representations. Linguistic representation should also be available. Note that some structures are subsets of others.

The reasoning scheme should have an operation that checks the value of uncertainty prescribed in a selected structure, such as minimum, maximum, and other threshold values. Ignorance and default values could be assigned here. The module should perform antecedent combination which defines the combination operations involving antecedent uncertainties, including at a minimum, conjunction, disjunction and negation. The reasoning module should provide for the propagation of uncertainties along a rule, which is usually called "detachment" in logic. And, the reasoning module should perform consequent combination which defines the combination operations involving consequent uncertainties, including logical as well as arithmetical algorithms such as simple average. An extended Dempster's rule could be included for combining evidences.

9.4.4 Inference control

As in conventional rule-based inference (without uncertainties), an overall control strategy is necessary to perform inexact reasoning. There are two common procedures, forward-chaining and backward-chaining, as outlined again by Wong (1986).

(a) *Forward-chaining*

Approximate reasoning with forward-chaining control consists of the three basic uncertainties mentioned earlier, as illustrated in the previous example in Section 9.4.3. Uncertainties in the antecedents of the rule are combined (using the AND connective) to obtain the uncertainty of the compound antecedent. This uncertainty is combined with the uncertainty in the rule to obtain the uncertainty in the consequent. Finally, the uncertainty in the antecedent is updated with any other uncertainties of the same consequent but deduced from other rules.

Of the three operations the consequent combination is the most difficult to manage. The antecedent combination is easier to manage because a rule statement always includes the specification of all the antecedents to be combined and the connective to be used. Hence, the antecedent combination is explicitly identified. Similarly, the propagation is also well defined since the rule uncertainty is specified as part of the rule statement.

By contrast, the consequent combination is unspecified in the rule statement in the sense that several rules may contribute updates to the estimate of the consequent's uncertainty; these updates must be combined, but one rule has no idea what other rules are being invoked and what operations should be used. In other words, the consequent combination is not specified in any one rule. It is a specification of the knowledge network.

Two other factors make consequent combination even more difficult. First, contributing rules are not fired at the same time. Their contributions come when their respective conditions are satisfied, and the firing order depends on the dynamics of the knowledge base and the inference and is not known a priori. Second, the result of the combination may depend on the order and timing of the uncertainty combination. Some operations such as the weighted average must wait for all data to be in before the operation can be performed. Others such as maximum and minimum are inherently order independent and efficient since they can be performed any time.

This problem can be overcome through explicit control of the rule-firing and by seeking the networking relation prior to inference. For example, backward-chaining control identifies all the rules contributing to a particular node. The correct firing order can also be arranged by arranging the appearance order of the rules in the knowledge base. However, such schemes are artificial and depend on the combination operators to be used. A slight change to the knowledge base, such as addition or deletion of a rule or fact, must be done with care to ensure that the correct firing order remains in effect.

(b) *Backward-chaining*

The implementation described above for forward-chaining appears compatible with backward-chaining control, with one caution. Backward-chaining control currently works with the pre-established knowledge base, i.e. the inference network defined prior to reasoning. This network may be changed as new rules are added and old rules deleted as a result of inference. The backward-chaining control as implemented will not know about these changes.

9.4.5 Comments

Although the approximate reasoning module just described is designed to be a relatively independent unit, the module nevertheless interacts with the system in two important ways. First, there is a close relation between the prescription of uncertainties and the prescription of rules and facts. They restrict each other and the knowledge bases must be represented consistently. This can be handled in a rule-editor where all rules and facts and their associated uncertainties are input to the expert system. Second, to carry out the inference, the required control mechanisms (forward and backward-chaining) must be made available. A complete and satisfactory inference may require several cycles of chaining through the knowledge base, compared with the single cycle (either forward or backward chained) usually encountered in 'exact' expert systems.

9.5 EXPERT SYSTEM APPROACH

The structural framework of an expert system capable of including some form of approximate reasoning is not unlike most in existence today. The system core is an inference mechanism which will allow for both forward-chaining and backward-chaining manipulations of the rule-based knowledge, a knowledge base consisting of expert rules and numeric information, a recorder which acts as an accountant to keep track of all the uncertainties and the rules to which the uncertainties are attached, and a feature which performs approximate reasoning on the rule base. Figure 9.5 shows a schematic of the structure of the expert system. The approach used is described in detail in Ross and Wong (1986) and is based on using fuzzy sets to represent approximate, inexact or vague knowledge. Exact matching is appropriate when the rules are

CODE FEATURES

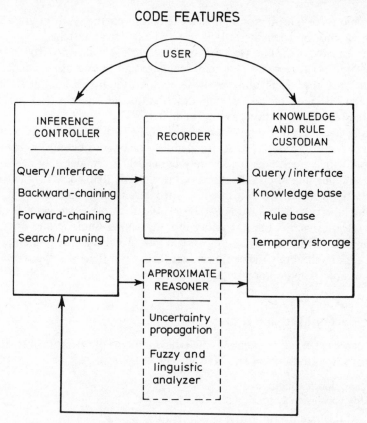

Fig. 9.5 Structure of an expert system. (Ross and Wong, 1986).

crisp. Crisp matching is binary, a characteristic of crisp set theory. Fuzzy matching can be partial, ranging from the exact match to no-match.

9.5.1 Knowledge representation and knowledge uncertainty

The consideration of expert opinions and rules based on these opinions leads to two major issues in expert systems: (1) How can vague knowledge and fuzzy data be represented as rules, and (2) What does matching mean when the rules and facts are approximate and inexact? For these applications, exact matching techniques currently in use are less desirable, and a technique allowing for approximate matching is needed.

In structural damage assessment there is an abundant use of words such as fairly flat, concentrated near, and near vertical. Moreover, different experts use different terms to describe the same deformation mode. For example, pure shear, punching shear, and sliding shear are used to describe the same thing.

For this type of information and rules, language parsing and programming tricks may not be adequate in building a viable expert system.

Because most of the knowledge in an expert system is obtained from human experts and because much of human language and knowledge is vague, it is usually true that facts and rules are neither totally certain nor totally consistent. Because of this, we may describe the reasoning process used by experts in certain situations as approximate.

In any given language, the values of a linguistic variable are words, phrases, or sentences. For example, structural damage can be considered as a linguistic variable with values such as 'severely damaged' or 'moderately damaged'. These are meaningful classifications but not clearly defined. With the use of fuzzy sets, however, we can quantify such terminology and apply it in a meaningful way to help solve a complex problem. An evident advantage of the fuzzy set approach is the possibility of representing numeric and linguistic variables in a uniform way and of using a formalized calculus to manipulate these variables. Simply defined, fuzzy set theory is a theory of the representation of approximate knowledge.

9.5.2 Exact and partial matching

Rule-based expert systems employing exact matching of rules (the overwhelming majority) are built on IF–THEN rules of the form,

> IF condition 1, condition 2,...
> THEN conclusion 1, conclusion 2,...

For example, a rule about structural damage may be:

> Rule 1: IF structure is not usable,
>   THEN damage is severe.

In the forward-chaining mode of inference, a known fact such as 'structure is not usable' is compared with the condition in rule 1. When matching occurs as it does in this case, the conclusion 'damage is severe' is added to the list of known facts about the structure, and the process repeated for other rules in the rule-base and for other facts in the fact-base. However, matching fails for the facts 'structure is usable' or 'structure is not readily usable'. The former fails because 'is' does not match 'is not' and the latter fails because 'readily usable' does not match 'usable'. While the first result is intended, the second is undesirable since a structure which is not readily usable is still is need of repair prior to use and is, hence, still likely to be severely damaged. Backward-chaining inference works in a similar manner starting with the matching of the conclusion clause, and results in similar situations when exact matching is invoked on the chaining process.

In damage assessment, rules obtained from experts almost always contain linguistic as well as fuzzy information. And many of these rules can be combined to form a rule process. Consider a series of rules,

IF x is A_1, THEN y is B_1, or else

IF x is A_2, THEN y is B_2, or else

...

IF x is A_n, THEN y is B_n,

where the rule process, R, can be symbolically denoted as,

$$R = A \times B$$

In the equation above the symbol '$\times$' is a fuzzy cartesian product which uses the operations of minimum and maximum as opposed to the crisp operations of multiplication and addition used in conventional matrix product operations. Now if the information in the antecedents, A_i, is fuzzy, R can represent a fuzzy-rule process. Obviously, when a fact A' matches the antecedent A_1 exactly, the conclusion B_1 will be realized. Similarly, A_2 will yield B_2, A_3 will give B_3, and so on.

When the fact A' does not match A_1 exactly, but only matches it in an approximate or partial sense, the conclusion will be somewhat different from B_1. Call this somewhat different conclusion, B'. If the difference between A and A' is small, the difference between B and B' will also be small. The difference between two fuzzy sets can be measured by a number of techniques. One such measure defines the difference measure as D and a similarity measure as $1 - D$. We say that B' has a membership of $(1 - D_1)$ in B_1, where D_1 is the difference measure of B' and B_1. In other words, A' has triggered the conclusion B_1 to $(1 - D_1)$ degree. Similarly, B_2 and B_3 are triggered to the degrees $(1 - D_2)$ and $(1 - D_3)$, respectively. We see that partial matching is not only possible, but it triggers all relevant rules in the rule-base with the appropriate degrees of membership. Partial matching defined in this context is also consistent with the fuzziness in the rules.

Fuzzy rules can be triggered in cascades in much the same way as crisp rule sets are triggered. Backward-chaining is also possible, although the result is an interval fuzzy set which is analogous to the "or clauses" of a crisp rule. Partial matching in backward-chaining is an arduous process because, unlike crisp matching, the fuzzy logic operations do not have unique inverse operations.

The rules considered above are one-to-one rules consisting of only one antecedent and one consequent, but the methodology is applicable to many-to-many rules. The antecedents and consequents need to be combined using standard fuzzy set operations and the rule will then become a one-to-one rule. In fact, for conventional rule-based inference when the rules contain more than one antecedent such as,

$$\text{IF } A_1, B_1, C_1, \text{ THEN } D_1, \text{ ELSE}$$
$$\text{IF } A_2, B_2, C_2, \text{ THEN } D_2, \text{ ELSE}$$
$$\cdots \quad \cdots$$
$$\text{IF } A_n, B_n, C_n, \text{ THEN } D_n$$

there are n^3 combinations of the antecedents and the inference requires large computational storage. Obviously, the idea of partial matching as presented here is conceptually simple, but because many rules can be triggered in a partial match and these in turn add many facts to the rule-base, this approach can become a computational burden. Future efforts in parallel processing will make partial matching a more plausible approach.

9.6 EXAMPLE CASE STUDY

Savage (1986) has written an expert system to accomplish damage assessment for the single criterion of structural integrity. His system makes use of a commercially available shell, EXSYS, to manipulate rule-based knowledge and to act as a manager for the combination of numeric and symbolic data by calling external programs and using the outputs of these external programs as new facts in the knowledge base. Savage (1986) has used fuzzy sets to assess and combine symbolic knowledge with the knowledge provided from expert opinion. His system inherently accounts for uncertainty by dealing with linguistic information. Some of the specifics of his work are summarized here in this example case study.

9.6.1 Protective structure issues

The response of reinforced concrete slabs under dynamically applied loads is a function of the load magnitude and distribution, slab characteristics, and boundary conditions. Thus, because of the complicated interaction of variables involved in slab behavior under simulated blast overpressures, there is no simple way to predict modes of structural response.

In studying the response of these structures (see Fig. 9.1), it is important to have an idea of whether shear or flexure typically controls response, and how and when shear and flexure each attain their failure levels. The term failure is defined as the point at which the concrete element reaches its ultimate capacity (either in shear or in flexure). It is also important to note that failure in a given mode does not imply complete collapse of the structure.

9.6.2 Numeric information

Numeric data such as digitized waveforms or transducer outputs from a field test is usually thought of as crisp in the sense that the data are quantifiable. The amount of information that can be obtained from digitized waveforms is enormous. From interface pressure data alone, the number of features that can be derived to aid the identification of failure mode is almost endless. Features such as rise time and peak pressure, frequency in terms of the power spectral density, ratios of various impulse values, and decay slope of the pressure record after peak pressure are but a few of the possibilities to be investigated. Whether or not each feature contains information regarding modes of failure is a separate question.

The case study is based on the information from a series of eleven tests conducted in the field on reinforced concrete box-like structures which were subjected to very large blast overpressures. For each of the eleven tests, interface pressures were available at three locations along the roof span. Ross and Krawinkler (1985) pointed out that the pressure decay after initial peak was a good indicator of early time response (less than 1 millisecond) of the roof slab. They noted that pairwise comparison of the three pressure records would indicate whether shear or flexure response dominates at early time.

In the event of flexure controlling failure (case 1), pressure plots are similar for locations 1 and 3, and different from location 2, as shown in Fig. 9.6. Rapid decay of the relatively flexible centerline of the slab indicates movement downward, while readings near the support and over the wall remain higher

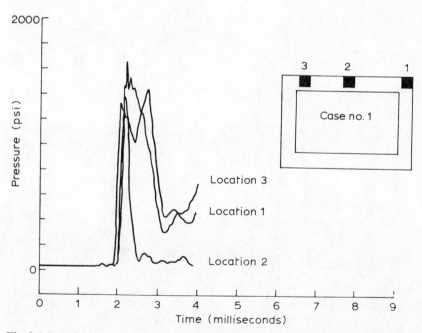

Fig. 9.6 Interface pressure plots of typical flexural failure response (Savage, 1986).

for a longer period of time. These sustained high pressures indicate a rigid boundary condition with these two locations 'seeing' little downward movement.

In the event of shear controlling failure (case 2), pressure plots at locations 2 and 3 are similar in shape and decay much more rapidly than location 1, as shown in Fig. 9.7. Here again, the pressure at location 1 stays higher, longer, indicating a rigid boundary condition. Rapid decay of pressure at location 2 and location 3 indicates downward movement of the entire slab as a rigid body. The only way for this to happen would be for an initial slip to occur at the support.

Experimental data from the eleven tests provide a wealth of information for determining structural modes of response. Obviously, not all data are of equal value, but this information can be used to demonstrate the possibilities that are available for analyzing, combining, and incorporating different types of data into a rule-based damage assessment system.

Another rather simple but effective feature for distinguishing failure characteristics was developed by Savage (1986). This feature is based on deflection profiles of the roof slab and is computed as the integral along the slab width of the deformation profile at 15 milliseconds after the initiation of

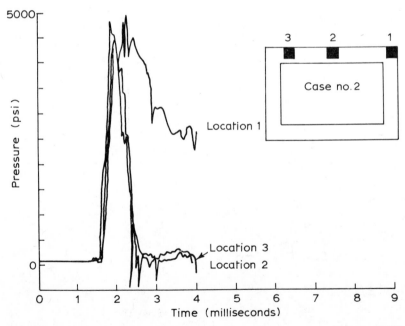

Fig. 9.7 Interface pressure plots of typical shear failure response (Savage, 1986).

the loading. By comparing values calculated for each test with linguistic assessments, a scale (shown below) was created for classifying damage levels.

None	Slight	Moderate	Severe	Very extensive	Collapse

```
|---------+-----------+-----------+------------+-------------+--------->
0.0      0.2         0.4         0.7          1.0           1.3
```

9.6.3 Symbolic information

The assessment of damage to a structure may be a combination of both numeric and symbolic information, as seen in Fig. 9.2. The term symbolic information is meant to describe information that resides in the minds of experts in a particular field who have, over time, accumulated in-depth knowledge in their subject field. Judgement of this type is used often in engineering evaluations, especially to compensate for sparse data and for extrapolation outside a given data range.

For the study conducted by Savage (1986), the engineering judgement was obtained by polling experts in the area of structural damage. A questionnaire concerning the damage to the roof element of the eleven test structures described previously was mailed to 60 structural engineers across the United States (35 responded). The questionnaire contained only post-test photographs of all the test elements.

The purposes of the questionnaire were threefold. First, it was hoped that information obtained from the questionnaire could be used to help determine how experts arrive at their evaluations of conceptually difficult problems. The second purpose was to determine how or why their answers were the same or different. The third purpose was to determine if it is possible to aggregate these assessments into a single database.

The questions asked of these experts were relatively vague in content and were designed as such in order to avoid any built-in bias on the part of the author of the questionnaire. Uncertain wording of the questions allows the experts to interpret the meaning without external constraints forcing their judgement, and allows the maximum information to be derived from a single question. On the other hand, inherent vagueness within a question also increases the possibility of confusion and non-comprehension.

On the topic of damage level, the experts tended to place their reasonings into one of three categories; structural integrity, functionality or use of the structure, and repairability of the structure. Typical responses given for 'slight', 'moderate', and 'severe' damage levels appear in Tables 9.1–9.3. As can be seen from the tables, most experts grouped their reasoning into the category of structural integrity. This is to be expected as they were given no information other than the photographs and, thus, relied heavily on the structural portion of their intuitive knowledge.

Table 9.1 Expert reasoning given for slight damage (Savage, 1986)

Structural integrity
• Minimal permanent deflection
• Damage localized at supports
• No rebar problems and minimal displacement
• Small support rotations
• Still in good shape
• Minimal tensile cracking at centerline and support
• Considerable capacity remains
• No plastic hinge formation
• Small crack lines
• Most structural resistance remains

Functionality
• Still usable
• System remains functional
• Everything inside should have survived
• Can still be used for the purpose for which it was designed
• Reusable

Repairability
• Small permanent deflection can be repaired

Table 9.2 Expert reasoning given for moderate damage (Savage, 1986)

Structural integrity
• End roof still in place even though significant spalling has occurred
• Plastic hinge not fully developed
• Onset of membrane action
• Rebar cage still intact
• Lots of cracking and permanent set
• Some tensile pullout and shear punch on right side

Functionality
• Some unobstructed clear space is provided
• Slight rotation of walls
• Contents probably OK
• Most equipment would survive
• Small debris would fall on contents
• Structure may still be useful for something

Repairability
• Structure serviceable
• Minimum repair needed
• Probably repairable

For modes of failure the experts tended to specify their reasonings depending on the mode of response they believed was involved. Virtually all descriptions were closely related to one of the four major mode groups: shear, diagonal tension, flexure, or tension membrane.

Table 9.3 Expert reasoning given for severe damage (Savage, 1986)

Structural integrity
- Very large permanent deformation
- Severe spalling at joints
- Most of concrete has spalled off roof
- Yielded reinforcing, spalled concrete
- On verge of collapse
- Large support rotations
- No longer able to withstand blast pressures
- Shear hinge at support is fully developed
- End supports nearly broken

Functionality
- Only short term use is possible
- Reasonable chance for survival
- Spalling would have harmed contents
- Contents severely shaken
- Significant debris and pressure ingress
- Associated shock and vibration would have severely damaged contents

Repairability
- Needs a lot of work
- Roof needs replacing
- Could possibly be repaired for temporary use

It was observed that the data could be further subdivided into specific structural attributes or parameters dealing with three unique locations along the span of the roof, i.e. the middle portion of the slab, the slab near the walls, and the wall supports. Tables 9.4 and 9.5 show some of these attributes along with typical descriptions volunteered by the experts for the shear and flexural modes of failure. Interestingly, by reducing or subdividing the expert information into lower levels of knowledge, as seen in Fig. 9.8, attributes or parameters can be defined that describe both modes of failure *and* levels of damage.

9.6.4 Research progress

As discussed in earlier sections of this chapter, the major factors influencing an assessment of the buried box structure included structural integrity, functionality, and repairability. Given sufficient information, it would be possible to determine three separate damage level assessments of the structure, one from each factor. If each of these assessments is then given a weighting or importance value by a decision-maker, a final analysis of the level of damage to the structure can be computed using a variety of methods. The ultimate goal, therefore, is to take the assessment from each of these factors and to combine

Table 9.4 Expert reasoning given for shear damage (Savage, 1986)

Location	Attribute or parameter	Expert description
Main slab (middle 1/3 to 1/2 span)	Curvature	• Relatively flat • Rebar cage appears to be flat • Almost uniform displacement
	Crack pattern	• Not many cracks visible • No yield lines at centerline • No crushing in the compression zone at top centerline
Slab near wall	Displacement	• Clean vertical break • Local vertical deformation • Mostly at supports • Relative displacement at edges • Sharp gradient
	Anchorage	• Sharp bending of bars at support • Broken bars • Apparently yielded reinforcement • Rebar severed at wall • Rebar violently ripped out
	Crack pattern	• Diagonal cracking • Can see diagonal struts
	Spalling/ crushing	• Considerable concrete crushing
Walls	Rotation Spalling/ crushing	• Minimal inward rotation • Wall supports remain intact with little concrete crushing

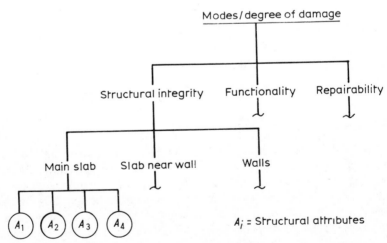

Fig. 9.8 Reducing expert opinion to lower levels of knowledge (Savage, 1986).

Table 9.5 Expert reasoning given for flexure damage (Savage, 1986)

Location	Attribute or parameter	Expert description
Main slab (middle 1/3 to 1/2 span)	Curvature	• Smooth top bar curvature • Moderately curved roof • Interior flexural hinge formation
	Crack pattern	• Cracks indicate 3-hinge mechanism • Most cracks are on the bottom at the centerline • Crack and deformation pattern
	Spalling/ crushing	• Crushed concrete at top centerline • Spalling at centerline
	Displacement	• Large displacement at centerline
Slab near wall	Curvature	• Large rotation near wall
	Anchorage	• Bars pulled out without evidence of yielding
	Displacement	• Lack of vertical offset at wall
	Crack pattern	• Cracks indicate flexural hinge formation • Tensile cracks at top edge • Crack lines at top face
Walls	Rotation	• Minimal inward rotation of walls
	Spalling/ crushing	• Concrete cruched in compression zone of wall face

them into one meaningful assessment. This procedure is represented in Fig. 9.9.

The organizational structure of the system developed by Savage (1986) to accomplish this task is shown in Fig. 9.10. The level of damage from each of the three factors (structural integrity, functionality, and repairability) can be provided using an expert system approach. In this particular case, each of the factors could be developed as a separate module within the expert system architecture. Using an appropriate inference mechanism and knowledge base, assessments for structural integrity, functionality, and repairability can be calculated, and the information shared and stored. With analyses completed, the information in the form of fuzzy sets can be passed to an external program, where a fuzzy-weighted-algorithm (shown in the figure as a fuzzy combination algorithm) is activated to combine the assessments. Details about the use of this algorithm can be found in Savage (1986). At this point only the structural integrity module of Fig. 9.10 has been completed.

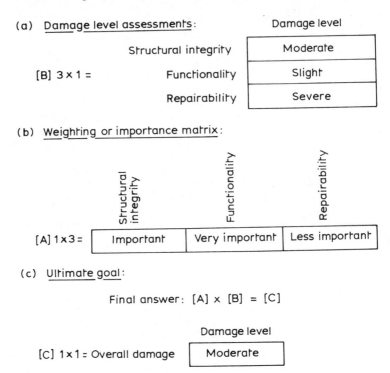

Fig. 9.9 Combining separate damage concepts into an overall damage assessment (Savage, 1986).

9.7 SUMMARY

Structural damage assessment of buried protective structures is a very complex subject which is imbued with a large amount of uncertainty and vagueness. This is due to the fact that much of the information used in the analysis process is derived from expert opinions and uncertain numerical data. Because of this, a new approach for combining this type of information was studied. Of particular interest was the feasibility of incorporating both soft (symbolic) data in the form of expert opinions and hard (numeric) data produced from instrumentation waveforms into a structural damage assessment code capable of approximate reasoning.

The framework developed in the case study is incorporated in a rule-based expert system approach. In an expert system scheme, difficult problems are subdivided into smaller problems, which in turn are represented in antecedent–consequent pairs as rules. These rules are combined with other data and information, to form what is called the knowledge base. The processing and analysis of this information is controlled through an inference mechanism, which retrieves necessary information from the user or the

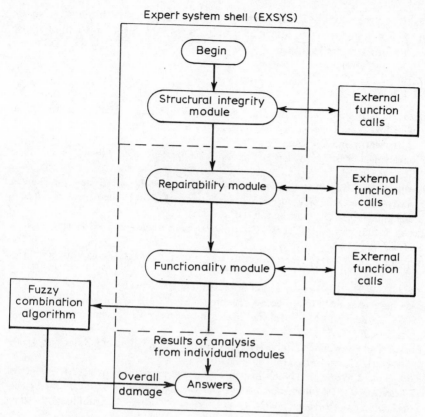

Expert system shell (EXSYS)

Begin

Structural integrity module

External function calls

Repairability module

External function calls

Functionality module

External function calls

Fuzzy combination algorithm

Results of analysis from individual modules

Overall damage

Answers

Fig. 9.10 Organizational structure of damage assessment code (Savage, 1986).

knowledge base using either backward or forward-chaining and reasons about uncertainty in the information using fuzzy logic.

In the case study, an analysis of structural integrity of a buried box element was accomplished. Expert opinions on damage assessment obtained from questionnaires were used as the basis for the subjective information. Because this type of information is vague and uncertain, fuzzy set theory was used to quantify linguistic variables. Also, because of the size and complexity of the problem and the nature of the uncertainty in the information, a numerical method employing fuzzy set theory was used instead of rules to synthesize the subjective data. Objective data, on the other hand, were obtained through the use of external programs which retrieved numerical information from digitized waveforms and placed this information into the rule-base as facts where it was analyzed and interpreted in the inference process.

Several ideas for the implementation of approximate reasoning were explored in this chapter. Some of these ideas, although conceptually simple, result in a tremendous computational burden. However, with the possible use of parallel algorithms and parallel architectures these problems will not pose such a burden in the future.

REFERENCES

Bezdek, J., Grimball, N., Carson, J. and Ross, T. (1986) Structural failure determination with fuzzy sets, *Journal of Civil Engineering Systems*, Volume 3, June, pp. 82–92, Butterworth and Co. Ltd.

Blockley, D. (1980) *The Nature of Structural Design and Safety*, Ellis Harwood, West Sussex, UK.

Hadipriano, F.C. (1986) *Development of a Rule-Based Expert System for Damage Assessment of Air Force Base Structures*, Summer Report to the Air Force Office of Scientific Research, Washington, DC.

Lecot, K. and Parker, D.S. (1986) Control over inexact reasoning. *AI Expert*, Premier Issue, pp. 32–43.

Negoita, C.V. (1985) *Expert Systems and Fuzzy Systems*, Benjamin-Cummings, California.

Ross, T., Wong, F., Savage, S. and Sorensen, H. (1986) DAPS: an expert system for damage assessment to protective structures, *Expert Systems in Civil Engineering* (eds C.N. Kostem and M.L. Maher), American Society of Civil Engineers, New York, pp. 109–20.

Ross, T. and Krawinkler, H. (1985) Impulsive direct shear failure in RC slabs. *Journal of Structural Engineering*, **111**, 1661–77.

Ross, T. and Wong, F. (1986) Structural damage assessment using AI techniques, *Proceedings of 1st International Conference on Applications of Artificial Intelligence to Engineering Problems, Southampton University, UK* (eds D. Sriram and R. Adey), Vol. 2, Springer-Verlag, Berlin, pp. 835–46.

Ruspini, E. (1982) Possibility theory approaches for advanced information systems. *Computer*, **15**, 83–91.

Shafer, G. (1976) *A Mathematical Theory of Evidence*, Princeton University Press, Princeton, New Jersey.

Savage, S. (1986) *Development of a Rule-Based Structural Damage Assessment Code*, MSc thesis, Washington State University, Pullman, Washington.

Wong, F. (1986a) *Modeling and Analysis of Uncertainties in Survivability/Vulnerability Assessment*, Air Force Weapons Laboratory Report, AFWL-TR-85-84, Albuquerque, New Mexico.

Wong, F.S. (1986b) Outline of an Approach to Inexact Reasoning for Rule-Based Survivability and Vulnerability Assessment Systems, *Quarterly Report, Air Force Weapons Laboratory*, F29601-86-C-0213, Albuquerque, New Mexico.

Wong, F., Dong, W., Boissonnade, A. and Ross, T. (1986), Expert opinions and expert systems, *Proceedings of 9th ASCE Conference on Electronic Computing, Birmingham, Alabama*, American Society of Civil Engineers, New York, pp. 43–52.

Zadeh, L.A. (1974) Fuzzy logic and Its Applications to Approximate Reasoning, *Information Processing 74*, Vol. 3, Proc. IFIP Congress, North Holland, Amsterdam, pp. 591–594.

10

Condensation of the knowledge base in expert systems with applications to seismic risk evaluation

WEI-MIN DONG, HARESH C. SHAH and FELIX S. WONG

10.1 INTRODUCTION

The major cause of life loss and injury due to earthquakes is the collapse and failure of vulnerable buildings located in highly hazardous regions. Consequently, for mitigating seismic losses, it is essential that these hazardous regions and vulnerable buildings be identified and ranked in an order so that the limited funds and time can be allocated to achieve maximum reduction of potential losses.

Ranking buildings according to the level of risk they pose is a challenging task because:

1. Risk is not a simple physical measurement but involves many factors. There is no well-formulated model for combining these factors to achieve a consistent, synthetic evaluation.
2. There is a great deal of uncertainty in each factor. The uncertainty is caused by randomness (e.g. where and what size of earthquake would occur), fuzziness (e.g. the complexity of the environment the buildings are exposed to, the way in which the MMI (Modified Mercalli Intensity) scale is defined), and ignorance (e.g. undiscovered fault, soil failure mechanism).
3. The expertise about risk assessment is mostly based upon judgemental knowledge and heuristic rules which have not been explicitly formulated. Such information is not included in conventional approaches to risk assessment.

Hence, the ideal assessment methodology should be capable of synthesizing multi-factors to reach an overall evaluation; it should have a way to process vague information and expert judgement; and it should be flexible enough to handle situations which are slightly different from past experience. Hence, expert system techniques including deductive inference have been brought to bear on this problem.

An important entity in an expert system is the knowledge base. The knowledge base in most expert systems uses IF—THEN rules to extract and represent ill-defined and loosely structured expert knowledge. While this approach is natural in representing the inferential duduction of human thinking, it requires a huge knowledge database. The number of rules can be several hundred or several thousand. A great deal of effort is required to search for the appropriate rule for a specific need. The large storage space and extensive searching effort restrict the use of microcomputers to solve moderately complex engineering problems.

In this chapter, a method for condensing the ill-defined (e.g. linguistic terms) and loosely-structured (e.g. IF—THEN rules) knowledge base used in expert systems is described. The knowledge bases are condensed into a fuzzy system description in which fuzzy, linguistic information can be processed and IF—THEN rules can be combined and then fired without resorting to an extensive search based on exact matching as in the conventional approach. Several options for combining the values of multi-premises to deduce the value of the consequent are described. Fuzzy algorithms for processing ill-defined information are developed. The fuzzy algorithms and combination functions are selected to reproduce consensus opinions from domain experts, obtained by questionnaires. The consensus opinions then constitute the best fit to the knowledge of the diverse pool of experts, and are used as the knowledge base for a microcomputer-based expert system for seismic risk assessment.

The materials in this chapter are organized as follows. A brief description of knowledge representation for seismic risk evaluation is given in Section 10.2. This is followed by a discussion of synthetical evaluation of multi-attributes based on multi-attribute decision theory. Several methods of extracting value information (weights) from experts are presented in Section 10.4. In Section 10.5, interval analysis and fuzzy set theory are introduced to represent and process vague, imprecise information. Section 10.6 is devoted to a description of the decision strategy under uncertain environments. Finally, the seismic risk assessment expert system is described and its application illustrated with an example.

10.2 KNOWLEDGE REPRESENTATION FOR SEISMIC RISK EVALUATION

Seismic risk is defined as the likelihood of loss due to earthquakes and involves four basic components: hazards, exposure, vulnerability, and location. These factors are further defined below.

Hazards or dangerous situations may be classified as:

1. Primary hazards (fault break, ground vibration)
2. Secondary hazards which are potentially dangerous situations triggered by primary hazards. For example, a fault break can cause a tsunami or ground shaking can result in foundation settlement, foundation failure, liquefaction, landslides, etc.
3. Tertiary hazards produced by flooding due to dam break, fire following an earthquake and the like.

All these hazards lead to damage and losses. They may be expressed in terms of severity, frequency and location.

1. Exposure is generally expressed in terms of the inventory of facilities, contents, business, business interruptions, lives, etc., that exists in the seismic region of interest.
2. Vulnerability expresses the quality and type of performance that each of the exposed facilities would experience due to seismic loading.
3. Location is defined as the position of the exposure relative to the hazard.

Losses resulting from seismic hazard are numerous and can be categorized as life and injury, property, business interruption, lost opportunities, contents tax base, and other losses. A seismic risk analysis requires the identification of the losses to be studied as well as the identification of the hazards, exposures, and their locations and vulnerability. For the purpose of this study, life and injury losses resulting from seismic hazard were the major considerations in the evaluation of the risk level.

Parts of the four components considered in the study are organized as shown in Fig. 10.1. Note that not all aspects of the seismic risk evaluation are included. The hierarchy shown in Fig. 10.1 starts with the main idea 'seismic risk'. At the next level are four key ideas: 'seismic hazard', 'building vulnerability', 'building importance', and 'occupancy'. These ideas have additional sub-levels of increasingly specific support.

The 'seismic hazard' idea includes some aspects of the hazards and the location components. Its supporting ideas consist of the primary and secondary hazards. The primary hazard of ground vibration along with the location component was included in the 'ground shaking' supporting idea. A severity parameter (peak ground acceleration, modified Mercalli intensity) is used to measure the ground shaking level. This parameter implicitly includes the location of the exposure relative to the hazard. Two secondary hazards, namely, liquefaction and landslides, are selected for inclusion below 'ground failure potential' along with the primary hazard of fault break. Since landslides tend to occur where the natural grade is relatively steep and where top soil layers are underlain by differing materials or lubricating layers, landslides are further supported by grade steepness and soil geology. The last supporting

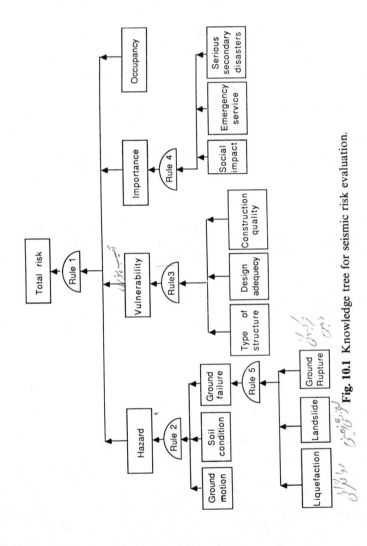

Fig. 10.1 Knowledge tree for seismic risk evaluation.

idea involved is 'soil type' since extreme soil types can affect the seismic hazard level.

The 'building vulnerability' idea reflects the vulnerability component by taking into account the sensitivity of a particular structure to the seismic hazard. Thus, supporting ideas below 'building vulnerability' include structural characteristics such as building type (structural system and type of material used), structural alteration or weakening, quality of construction and seismic areas in the design which may affect the building's seismic performance. This category includes seismic code considerations, vertical stiffness discontinuities, structural system redundancy and architectural configuration factors such as plan and vertical symmetry, significant re-entrant corners, etc.

The 'building importance' idea reflects the utility value that is placed on the structure, where utility is measured in terms of public safety. High importance suggests that damage or destruction of the building due to an earthquake would be detrimental to public safety. Therefore, the supporting ideas are concerned mainly with how building use affects the possible socio-economic loss for the community during and after an earthquake.

The 'occupancy' idea reflects one aspect of the exposure components: the value of human life. Damage of densely occupied buildings will lead to the loss of many human lives and severe psychological impact on the community.

Figure 10.1 represents only a simplified inference network of seismic risk evaluation. As such, there are 12 leaf-nodes (i.e. nodes with no other nodes under them), and information on these nodes must be provided to support the evaluation. Each intermediate node represents an inference rule, an example of which is

IF   seismic hazard is high, and
        building is vulnerable, and
        building is highly occupied, and
        building is for emergency service,
THEN   seismic risk is very high.

Note the evaluation of each node, called the attribute, is usually not binary, i.e. yes or no, but is expressed in linguistic terms such as very high, high and moderate. Hence, to cover all possible combinations of the various attributes will require hundreds of rules in the system knowledge base. Note also that the consequent (THEN portion of the rule) 'risk is very high' is a summary of contributions from all four antecedents (IF portion of the rule). Attributes of other nodes in the network are determined in similar fashion, thus calling for more and more rule combinations.

Hence, it is desirable to have the option to condense some rules obtained from expert judgement into an inference mechanism such that computer storage space can be saved and search efforts reduced. The crucial step in building this option is how to extract an inference mechanism from expert opinions or knowledge, or, in other words, how the experts themselves combine all attributes of the nodes in the network to reach a synthetic evaluation if they were asked to provide the risk level directly. This topic will be discussed in the next two sections.

10.3 SYNTHETIC EVALUATION OF MULTI-NUMERICAL GRADES

In engineering practice, we are often confronted with problems in which several alternatives have to be compared and the 'best' one selected. If all alternatives could be evaluated on a linear scale, say monetary scale, then ranking and decision-making would be relatively simple. However, in practice, this is not the case. Usually, each alternative has several attributes or features. For instance, risk assessment of specific regions is affected by ground motion, vulnerability of structures, importance of buildings, and secondary hazards such as liquefaction, landslide, and ground rupture. If all these factors for one building are worse than those for the others, then the ordering is obvious. This is called Pareto preference. However, 'Pareto preference' does not always lead to ordering of alternatives with multi-attributes. For instance, if some factors for one building are worse than the corresponding factors for another building, but the rest are better, then we will have difficulty in ordering these two buildings based only on the Pareto preference.

Mathematically, Pareto preference is a partial order system, i.e. some objects (or alternatives) are comparable and have order relation, some are not comparable and have no order relation. The problem can be stated as follows.

Suppose that there is a group of n buildings (or objects) $B = \{B_1, B_2, \ldots B_n\}$, and $\geqslant$ stands for order relation, say '$B_1 \geqslant B_2$' implies 'B_1 risk is higher than or equal to B_2'. For each building B_i, we have a score vector for grades of all its attributes $\{x_{i1}, x_{i2}, \ldots, x_{im}\}$. Assume that all scores are normalized to the unit interval $[0, 1]$. Hence, for all n buildings, we obtain a score matrix

$$X = \{x_{ij}\}_{i=1,n; j=1,m}$$

where n is the number of buildings and m is the number of attributes.

For example, suppose there are five buildings ($n = 5$) and three attributes ($m = 3$): (1) A_1 = ground hazard, (2) A_2 = vulnerability, (3) A_3 = importance. Then the score matrix might be given as:

$$X = \begin{matrix} & \begin{matrix} A_1 & A_2 & A_3 \end{matrix} \\ \begin{matrix} B_1 \\ B_2 \\ B_3 \\ B_4 \\ B_5 \end{matrix} & \begin{bmatrix} 0.7 & 0.9 & 0.3 \\ 1.0 & 0.8 & 0.5 \\ 0.6 & 0.4 & 0.4 \\ 0.5 & 0.3 & 0.2 \\ 1.0 & 1.0 & 0.7 \end{bmatrix} \end{matrix}$$

We say $B_i \geqslant B_k$ if and only if $x_{ij} \geqslant x_{kj}$, $j = 1, m$. In our case, we have order relation such as

$$B_5 \geqslant B_2 \geqslant B_3 \geqslant B_4; \ B_5 \geqslant B_1 \geqslant B_4$$

We can construct a graph called the 'Hasse diagram' where two nodes, if connected, have order relation. There is no relation between B_1 and B_2 and between B_1 and B_3 (Fig. 10.2). In order to rank all alternatives, additional preference information is needed to weigh the value for each attribute.

In contrast, with partial order systems, if for a system any two elements B_i and B_j are comparable, i.e. either $B_i \geqslant B_j$ or $B_j \geqslant B_i$, then we call it a total order system or linear order system. In this case, there will be no difficulty in selecting the best or the worst building.

Unfortunately, most decision-making problems involve partial order relations. It is desirable to convert a partial order to a linear scale by some mapping function, that is

$$y = f(X) = f(x_1, x_2, \ldots, x_j, x_m) \tag{10.1}$$

where y is a value on a linear scale and by convention, $y \in [0, 1]$. To be consistent with the partial order relation, all mapping functions have to meet the basic (Pareto preference) requirement:

$$f(\ldots x_j \ldots) \geqslant f(\ldots x_j' \ldots) \text{ if } x_j \geqslant x_j', \quad j = 1, m \tag{10.2}$$

Four mapping functions which exhibit the above properties are presented in

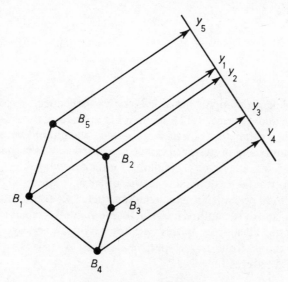

Fig. 10.2 Hasse diagram.

the following. Assume that all scores are normalized to the unit interval, i.e. $0 \leqslant x_i \leqslant 1$.

1. *Type* I:

$$y = f(X) = \sum_{j=1}^{m} w_j x_j, \quad w_j \geqslant 0 \tag{10.3}$$

where w_j are the parameters and $\sum w_j = 1$,

or

$$y = f(X) = \frac{\sum w_j x_j}{\sum w_j}, \quad w_j \geqslant 0 \tag{10.4}$$

2. *Type* II:

$$y = f(X) = (w_1 \wedge x_1) \vee (w_2 \wedge x_2) \ldots (w_m \wedge x_m)$$
$$= \bigvee_{j=1}^{m} (w_j \wedge x_j), \quad 0 \leqslant w_j \leqslant 1 \tag{10.5}$$

where $\vee$ and $\wedge$ stand for maximum and minimum, respectively.

3. *Type* III:

$$y = f(X) = (x_1)^{w_1} \wedge (x_2)^{w_2} \ldots (x_m)^{w_m}$$
$$= \bigwedge_{j=1}^{m} (x_j)^{w_j}, \quad w_j > 0 \tag{10.6}$$

4. *Type* IV:

$$y = f(X) = \min \left\{ \sum_{i=1}^{m} w_j x_j, 1 \right\} \tag{10.7}$$

The selection of a mapping function is context-dependent. Type I is nothing but the weighted average. When all weights are equal, then Equation 10.3 reduces to the arithmetic average. For instance, the ground hazard, vulnerability of structure and importance can be combined by this mapping function to get a total risk grade. Type II is suitable for the case where the highest grade among all attributes is dominant in the ordering. For instance, when we consider the total potential of ground failure, there are several sources, such as liquefaction, landslide, rupture, etc. The total potential is equal to the highest potential among all sources. In this case, the weights w_j are used to constrain the contributions from the respective sources. When $w_j = 1$ for all j, Equation 10.5 reduces to

$$y = \max(x_j), \quad j = 1, m \tag{10.8}$$

Type III makes the total grade equal to the minimum value of all $(x_j)^{w_i}$'s. Since $x_j \leqslant 1$, and $w_j > 0$, the larger the weight w_j, the smaller the value $(x_j)^{w_j}$, and the greater the possibility that the total grade would equal $(x_j)^{w_j}$. When all $w_j = 1$, then Equation 10.6 reduces to

$$y = \min(x_j), \quad j = 1, m \tag{10.9}$$

Type IV relaxes the constraint of $\sum w_j = 1$. However, when $\sum w_j > 1$, it is possible that

$$y = \sum w_j x_j > 1$$

which violates the regulation of $y \in [0, 1]$. Hence Equation 10.7 takes the bound sum with the maximum value of 1.0. This is similar to the case where the ground motion hazard is extremely severe so that other hazards would not matter whether they are present or not.

10.4 EXTRACTION OF WEIGHTS

In order to extract the weights, w_j, from experts, there are two general approaches, direct and indirect, as described in the following.

The direct approach consists of asking the experts to provide the weights for all attributes. Usually, it is easy to do so by pairwise comparison and to get the relative weights, that is, to assign the ratios

$$r_{ij} = w_i/w_j \tag{10.10}$$

to indicate the relative value for the attributes x_i and x_j. Hence we can construct a weight ratio matrix

$$\boldsymbol{R} = \begin{bmatrix} r_{11}, r_{12}, \ldots, r_{1m} \\ r_{21}, r_{22}, \ldots, r_{2m} \\ \cdots \\ r_{m1}, r_{m2}, \ldots, r_{mm} \end{bmatrix}$$

By the definition of Equation 10.10, we have

$$r_{jk} = r_{kj}^{-1} \tag{10.11}$$

$$r_{jl} = r_{jk} r_{kl}, \text{ for all } j, l, k \leqslant m \tag{10.12}$$

The matrix which meets the conditions of Equation 10.12 is called 'consistent'. However, when the experts are asked to assign the relative weights, we usually are not able to obtain a consistent weight ratio matrix. Saaty (1978) suggested that the eigenvector corresponding to the maximum eigenvalue $\lambda_{\max}$ provides a good estimate for the weighting factors. That is, the estimate of the weighting factor, $\hat{\boldsymbol{W}}$, can be obtained by

$$(\boldsymbol{R} - \lambda_{\max} \boldsymbol{I})\hat{\boldsymbol{W}} = \boldsymbol{0} \tag{10.13}$$

where I is the unit diagonal matrix and 0 is a zero column vector. The eigenvalue can be obtained by solving the equation

$$\det |R - \lambda I| = 0 \qquad (10.14)$$

For illustration, three attributes (ground hazard, vulnerability and importance) are considered for which the experts are asked to give their evaluation of relative weight by pairwise comparison. Suppose that the following weight ratio matrix is obtained:

$$R = \begin{bmatrix} 1.0 & 1.1 & 2.0 \\ \dfrac{1}{1.1} & 1.0 & 1.5 \\ \dfrac{1}{2.0} & \dfrac{1}{1.5} & 1.0 \end{bmatrix}$$

From Equation 10.14, we have

$$\det \begin{vmatrix} 1-\lambda & 1.1 & 2 \\ \dfrac{1}{1.1} & 1-\lambda & 1.5 \\ \dfrac{1}{2} & \dfrac{1}{1.5} & 1-\lambda \end{vmatrix} = 0$$

Hence,

$$(1-\lambda)^3 - 3(1-\lambda) + \frac{2}{1.65} + \frac{1.65}{2} = 0$$

From that, the maximum eigenvalue λ_{max} is 3.004. Substituting it into Equation 10.13, we have

$$\begin{bmatrix} -2.004 & 1.1 & 2.0 \\ \dfrac{1}{1.1} & -2.004 & 1.5 \\ \dfrac{1}{2.0} & \dfrac{1}{1.5} & -2.004 \end{bmatrix} \begin{bmatrix} \hat{w}_1 \\ \hat{w}_2 \\ \hat{w}_3 \end{bmatrix} = \begin{bmatrix} 0 \\ 0 \\ 0 \end{bmatrix}$$

Hence, the eigenvector is given by

$$\hat{W} = \{1.000, 0.852, 0.533\}^T$$

The indirect approach is based on available ordering for some of the alternatives from which the weighting factors are extracted. The experts are questioned to give the total evaluation for some typical cases instead of directly providing the weights. Two methods are given here for the Type I and Type II mapping functions.

(a) *The least squares estimate of weighting factors for the Type I mapping function*

For n alternatives, Equation 10.3 can be expanded to a matrix form as follows:

$$\mathbf{Y} = \begin{bmatrix} y_1 \\ y_2 \\ . \\ . \\ . \\ y_n \end{bmatrix} = \begin{bmatrix} x_{1,1}, x_{1,2}, \ldots, x_{1,m} \\ x_{2,1}, x_{2,2}, \ldots, x_{2,m} \\ \cdots \\ \cdots \\ \cdots \\ x_{n,1}, x_{n,2}, \ldots, x_{n,m} \end{bmatrix} \cdot \begin{bmatrix} w_1 \\ w_2 \\ . \\ . \\ . \\ w_m \end{bmatrix} \quad m \leqslant n$$

Suppose that the value vector $\mathbf{Y}$ and score matrix $\mathbf{X}$ are given. The problem is to estimate the weight vector $\hat{\mathbf{W}} = [\hat{w}_1, \hat{w}_2 \cdots \hat{w}_m]$ which will result in the least squares error. Let $\hat{y}_i$ be the estimate of y_i, given the estimate of weighting vector $\hat{\mathbf{W}}$ which is given by

$$\hat{y}_i = x_{i,1}\hat{w}_1 + x_{i,2}\hat{w}_2 + \cdots x_{i,m}\hat{w}_m$$

Then, the error is the difference between y_i and $\hat{y}_i$, that is,

$$y_i - \hat{y}_i = y_i - \left(\sum_{j=1}^{m} x_{i,j}\hat{w}_j \right) \tag{10.15}$$

The error function Q is defined as follows:

$$Q = \sum_{i=1}^{n} (y_i - \hat{y}_i)^2 = \sum_{i=1}^{n} \left[y_i - \sum_{j=1}^{m} x_{i,j}\hat{w}_j \right]^2 \tag{10.16}$$

In order to minimize the error Q, we should select $\hat{\mathbf{W}}$ so that all partial derivatives of Q with respect to $\hat{w}_j$ are zero, i.e.

$$\frac{\partial Q}{\partial \hat{w}_1} = 0,$$

$$\frac{\partial Q}{\partial \hat{w}_2} = 0, \tag{10.17}$$

$$\cdots$$

$$\frac{\partial Q}{\partial \hat{w}_m} = 0$$

From this, we can obtain a set of equations as follows:

$$-\frac{1}{2}\frac{\partial Q}{\partial \hat{w}_1} = \sum_i [y_i - (\hat{w}_1 x_{i,1} + \hat{w}_2 x_{i,2} + \cdots \hat{w}_m x_{i,m})]x_{i,1} = 0$$

$$-\frac{1}{2}\frac{\partial Q}{\partial \hat{w}_2} = \sum_i [y_i - (\hat{w}_1 x_{i,1} + \hat{w}_2 x_{i,2} + \cdots \hat{w}_m x_{i,m})]x_{i,2} = 0$$

$$\cdots$$

$$-\frac{1}{2}\frac{\partial Q}{\partial \hat{w}_m} = \sum_i [y_i - (\hat{w}_1 x_{i,1} + \hat{w}_2 x_{i,2} + \cdots \hat{w}_m x_{i,m})]x_{i,m} = 0$$

Let

$$s_{j,k} = s_{k,j} = \sum_i x_{i,j} x_{i,k} \tag{10.18}$$

and

$$s_{j,y} = \sum_i y_i x_{i,j} \tag{10.19}$$

Then the above set of equations reduces to

$$s_{1,1}\hat{w}_1 + s_{1,2}\hat{w}_2 + \cdots s_{1,m}\hat{w}_m = s_{1,y}$$
$$s_{2,1}\hat{w}_1 + s_{2,2}\hat{w}_2 + \cdots s_{2,m}\hat{w}_m = s_{2,y}$$
$$s_{m,1}\hat{w}_1 + s_{m,2}\hat{w}_2 + \cdots s_{m,m}\hat{w}_m = s_{m,y}$$

or

$$\mathbf{S\hat{W}} = \mathbf{S}_y \tag{10.20}$$

Thus, from this, we can obtain the estimate of the weighting factor $\mathbf{\hat{W}}$

$$\mathbf{\hat{W}} = \mathbf{S}^{-1}\mathbf{S}_y \tag{10.21}$$

As an example, suppose that for the problem of ranking seismic hazard regions with the attributes, the experts have assigned the total scores for five regions as:

$$X = \begin{bmatrix} 0.7 & 0.9 & 0.3 \\ 1.0 & 0.8 & 0.5 \\ 0.6 & 0.4 & 0.4 \\ 0.5 & 0.3 & 0.2 \\ 1.0 & 1.0 & 0.7 \end{bmatrix}$$

and $\mathbf{Y} = \{0.70 \quad 0.81 \quad 0.50 \quad 0.35 \quad 0.92\}^T$. The determination of weighting factors which best fits the experts' overall evaluation is as follows:
From Equations 10.18 and 10.19 we can obtain

$$S = \begin{bmatrix} 3.10 & 2.82 & 1.75 \\ 2.82 & 2.70 & 1.59 \\ 1.75 & 1.59 & 1.03 \end{bmatrix}$$

and

$$\mathbf{S}_y = \{2.695 \quad 2.503 \quad 1.529\}^T$$

Solving Equation 10.20, we can obtain

$$\hat{\mathbf{W}} = \{0.4072 \quad 0.3846 \quad 0.1989\}^T$$

(b) *The modified Newton method (Pedrycz, 1984) for the type II mapping function*

Similarly to Equation 10.16, the error function is defined as follows:

$$Q = \sum_{i=1}^{N} (y_i - \hat{y}_i)^2 = \sum_{i=1}^{n} \left[y_i - \left(\bigvee_j (x_{i,j} \wedge \hat{w}_j) \right) \right]^2 \qquad (10.22)$$

Let $F(\mathbf{W})$ be a column vector as follows:

$$F(\mathbf{W}) = \left\{ \begin{array}{c} \dfrac{\partial Q}{\partial \hat{w}_1} \\[2mm] \dfrac{\partial Q}{\partial \hat{w}_2} \\[2mm] \cdots \\[2mm] \dfrac{\partial Q}{\partial \hat{w}_m} \end{array} \right. \qquad (10.23)$$

where

$$\frac{\partial Q}{\partial \hat{w}_{j'}} = -2 \sum_{i=1}^{n} \left[y_i - \left(\bigvee_j (x_{i,j} \wedge \hat{w}_j) \right) \right] P_{ij'} \qquad (10.24)$$

$$P_{ij'} = \begin{cases} 1, & \text{if } (x_{ij'} \wedge \hat{w}_{j'}) \geqslant \bigvee_{j \neq j'} (x_{i,j} \wedge \hat{w}_j) \text{ and } x_{ij'} \geqslant \hat{w}_{j'} \\ 0, & \text{otherwise} \end{cases} \qquad (10.25)$$

In order to minimize Q, the following iteration scheme to find the approximate solution of $\mathbf{W}$ is used

$$\mathbf{W}^{(k+1)} = \mathbf{W}^{(k)} - [F'(\mathbf{W}^{(k)})]^{-1} F(\mathbf{W}^{(k)}) \qquad (10.26)$$

where superscripts denote the number of iterations and where

$$F'(\mathbf{W}^{(k)}) = \left[\frac{\partial^2 Q}{\partial \hat{w}_i \partial \hat{w}_j} \right]_{i=1,m;\, j=1,m} \qquad (10.27)$$

is an $m \times m$ dimensional Hessian matrix.

A further simplification can be achieved by replacing $[F'(\mathbf{W}^{(k)})]^{-1}$ with a simple scalar multiplier, α_k, which is given by

$$\alpha_k = \frac{1}{(2n + k^\beta)} \tag{10.28}$$

where $\beta \geqslant 0$ is chosen empirically to achieve good convergence and to avoid oscillation in the iteration process. Then, Equation 10.26 reduces to

$$\mathbf{W}^{(K+1)} = \mathbf{W}^{(k)} - \alpha_k F(\mathbf{W}^{(k)}) \tag{10.29}$$

A computer program, called FINDW, has been developed to compute this least squares solution for $\mathbf{W}$. As an example, let us look at a siting problem where four sites are evaluated with respect to liquefaction, landslide, and ground rupture potentials. The score matrix is given by

$$X = \begin{bmatrix} 0.3 & 3.5 & 0.7 \\ 0.4 & 0.8 & 0.5 \\ 0.6 & 0.2 & 0.5 \\ 0.9 & 0.4 & 0.1 \end{bmatrix}$$

and the experts have already assigned the total scores for those four sites as 0.7, 0.6, 0.5 and 0.4, respectively, i.e.

$$\mathbf{Y} = \{0.7, 0.6, 0.5, 0.4\}^T$$

Assuming that the Type II mapping function is suitable to this problem, the modified Newton's iteration method converges to the following solution for the weighting factors

$$\hat{\mathbf{W}} = \{0.4, 0.6, 0.7\}.$$

10.5 SYNTHETIC EVALUATION OF MULTI-LINGUISTIC GRADES

Due to lack of knowledge or data, there is a great deal of uncertainty in estimating the seismic ground motion level, predicting the building performance and appreciating the social impact of the hazard. Instead of point estimate, an interval grade might be more reliable in incorporating the existing uncertainties in the risk evaluation. The interval estimate does not provide any specific confidence to an individual number. It only conveys the information that any number within this interval is possible and any number outside this interval is impossible. Hence, interval estimate can accommodate the ignorance about probability distribution or possibility distribution. A methodology to combine multi-interval grades into a total grade which also would be an interval number is described in the following.

Consider the function

$$y = f(x_1, \ldots, x_m)$$

Suppose that all variables are intervals denoted as $X_j = [a_j, b_j], j = 1, m$. Then the interval, Y, is defined by (Moore, 1979)

$$Y = f(X_1, \ldots, X_m) = \{f(x_1, \ldots, x_m) | x_1 \in X_1, \ldots, x_m \in X_m\} \qquad (10.30)$$

However, the computation of Y is quite difficult, and it is to facilitate this computation that the Vertex Method (Dong and Shah, 1987), summarized in the following, is developed.

For an interval function such as Equation 10.30, all interval variables form an m-dimensional rectangle $X_1 x \ldots X_m$ with 2^m vertices. The ordinates of all vertices are the combination of the m pairs of end points of the interval variables. Let V_i denote the ith combination (or the ith vertex), $i = 1, 2^m$. When $y = f(x_1 \ldots x_m)$ is continuous in the m-dimensional rectangular region and also no extreme point exists in this region, the value of the interval function can be obtained by

$$Y = f(X_1, \ldots, X_m) = \left[\min_i (f(V_i)), \max_i (f(V_i)) \right] \qquad (10.31)$$

When $y = f(x_1, \ldots, x_m)$ have extreme points in the m-dimensional rectangle, using E_k to denote the ordinate of the kth extreme point, then Equation 10.31 can be revised as

$$Y = f(X_1, \ldots, X_m) = \left[\min_{i,k} (f(V_i), f(E_k)), \max_{i,k} (f(V_i), f(E_k)) \right] \qquad (10.32)$$

Consider the following example. Suppose that the interval grades were obtained for four attributes of the total risk with their interval weights as follows:

	Grade	Weight
Ground hazard	[0.4 0.6]	[0.8 1.0]
Importance	[0.7 0.96]	[0.5 0.9]
Vulnerability	[0.1 0.3]	[0.8 1.0]
Occupancy	[0.0 0.2]	[0.5 0.9]

Using the Type I mapping function and the vertex method, there are 2^8 vertices, i.e. $V_i, i = 1, \ldots, 256$. Substituting all coordinates of 256 vertices into Equation 10.31, we obtain the total risk interval as follows:

$$Y = [0.241, 0.561]$$

While interval information incorporates uncertainty and accommodates ignorance, there is an abrupt transition from 'possible' to 'impossible'. Much of the judgemental knowledge is usually linguistic, using words such as 'serious', 'possible', 'importance' and so on. In this case, the uncertainty is embedded in these vague concepts whose denotations are not crisp but fuzzy (Wong and Dong, 1986). In reality, many phenomena are so diverse and complex that it is

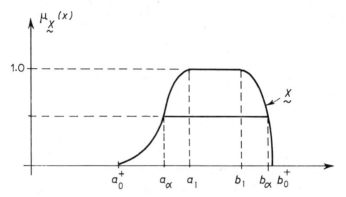

Fig. 10.3 Fuzzy set representation for linguistic grades.

impossible to use crisp quantity or precise statement to describe and summarize them. Rather, vague assertions are more compatible with the range of observed facts. Perhaps that is why the MMI scale for seismic intensity is still being used, even though no numerically precise definition is ever given for this scale.

Vague concepts can be modeled by the fuzzy set theory, originally developed by Professor Zadeh (Zadeh, 1965). For instance, 'high' hazard could be represented by a fuzzy set shown in Fig. 10.3. The representation can be interpreted as:

The most possible grade X_1 is between a_1 and b_1.
The least possible grade X_{0^+} is between a_{0^+} and b_{0^+}.
The grade X_α with possibility α or greater is between a_α and b_α

where

$$X_\alpha = \{ x \mid \mu_{\underset{\sim}{X}}(x) \geqslant \alpha \} \tag{10.33}$$

For instance, with reference to the example on total risk grade mentioned previously, we replace the interval estimates with linguistic grades as follows:

Attribute	Grade	Weight
Ground hazard	'Moderate'	'Very important'
Importance	'Great'	'Rather important'
Vulnerability	'Low'	'Very important'
Occupancy	'Very low'	'Rather important'

For simplicity, we use only two α levels: most possible ($\alpha = 1$) and least possible ($\alpha = 0^+$). The above linguistic grades and weights can be represented by trapezoidal fuzzy sets as shown in Fig. 10.4. Applying the vertex method to these two sets of intervals ($\alpha = 0^+$ and $\alpha = 1$), we obtain

$$Y_{0^+} = [0.145 \quad 0.677]; \qquad Y_1 = [0.298 \quad 0.485]$$

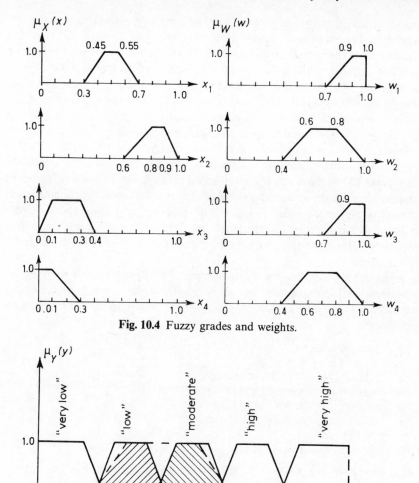

Fig. 10.4 Fuzzy grades and weights.

Fig. 10.5 Fuzzy set representation for linguistic terms.

which represents an approximately trapezoidal fuzzy set for the total grade
(dashed line in Fig. 10.5).

10.6 DECISION-MAKING UNDER A FUZZY
ENVIRONMENT

In the previous sections, we have solved the ordering problem for the multi-
attribute objects (or alternatives). If all the grades are real numbers, a total

grade which is on a linear scale can be obtained. When the grades are represented by fuzzy sets, then by using the method described in Section 10.5, we can obtain the overall grade which is also a fuzzy set. We are then faced with another ranking problem in which the grade is unique but fuzzy with uncertainty. Recall that in statistical decision analysis problems there are several decision-making criteria to rank the alternatives (e.g. the expected value criterion, the pessimistic criterion using the possible maximum risk, the optimistic criterion using the possible minimum risk). Recall also that all the criteria for ordering random variables are designed to define a function to convert the probability distribution to a single value (index) by which the decision could be made based on the largest index value. The same idea can be carried over to the ordering problem of fuzzy variables. There are many criteria to define the index function with different emphases, and no single criterion is satisfactory for all situations. The choice of criteria is context dependent. Hence, we introduce the most popular criteria and leave the choice to the users.

Without loss of generality, we restrict ourselves to continuous membership functions. (All criteria can be easily modified for discrete membership functions.) For convenience of presentation, we shall use the following notation:

A fuzzy number
A_α α-cut of fuzzy number A
a min of A_{0^+} or the left end of supp.(A)
b max of A_{0^+} or the right end of supp.(A)
c min of A_1 or the left end of core(A)
d max of A_1 or the right end of core(A)
a_α the left end of A_α
b_α the right end of A_α

where supp.$(A) = A_{0^+} = [a, b]$, core$(A) = A_1 = [c, d]$, and $A_\alpha = [a_\alpha, b_\alpha]$ (see Fig. 10.6).

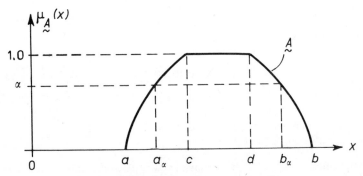

Fig. 10.6 Notation for a fuzzy number $\underset{\sim}{A}$.

10.6.1 The pseudo-expectation criterion

Under this criterion, we define an index function as follows:

$$D_1(A_i) = \int_0^1 x\mu_{A_i}(x)\,\mathrm{d}x \qquad (10.34)$$

where $\mu_{A_i}(x)$ is the membership function for the fuzzy risk A_i.

As an example, suppose that two buildings, A_1 and A_2, have fuzzy risk values as shown in Fig. 10.7. For triangular memberships, Equation 10.34 can be reduced to

$$D_1(A_i) = \frac{(b-a)(a+b+c)}{6} \qquad (10.35)$$

Hence, for building A_1,

$$D_1(A_1) = \frac{(1.0-0.2)(0.2+0.4+1.0)}{6} = 0.213$$

and for building A_2,

$$D_1(A_2) = \frac{(0.8-0.1)(0.1+0.6+0.8)}{6} = 0.175$$

Since $D_1(A_1) > D_1(A_2)$, thus, A_1 is preferred to A_2 (interpreted as A_1 has higher risk than A_2).

Note that the membership functions are not required to be normalized. Hence, $D_1(A_i)$ is not weighted average in the usual sense. The process may lead to a pathological ordering in some cases. For instance, suppose that the two

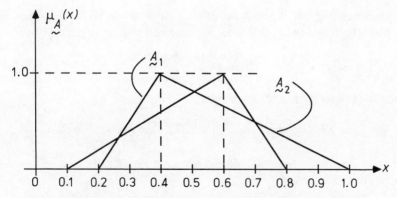

Fig. 10.7 Fuzzy risk values for buildings A_1 and A_2.

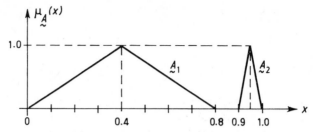

Fig. 10.8 A pathological case for criterion 1.

fuzzy risks, A_1 and A_2, are as shown in Fig. 10.8. Then, we have

$$D_1(A_1) = \frac{(0.8 - 0)(0 + 0.4 + 0.8)}{6} = 0.16$$

$$D_1(A_2) = \frac{(1 - 0.9)(0.9 + 0.95 + 1.0)}{6} = 0.048$$

Since $D_1(A_1) < D_1(A_2)$, then A_1 is preferred to A_2. Needless to say, this decision does not agree with our intuition at all.

10.6.2 The gravity center criterion

Define the following mapping function as index function to order the different alternatives A_i:

$$D_2(A_i) = \frac{\displaystyle\int_0^1 x\mu_{A_i}(x)\,dx}{\displaystyle\int_0^1 \mu_{A_i}(x)\,dx} \tag{10.36}$$

which is nothing but the abscissa of the center of gravity of A_i. When the membership function is triangular, Equation 10.36 can be reduced to

$$D_2(A_i) = \frac{(a + b + c)}{3} \tag{10.37}$$

For the example of Fig. 10.7, we have

$$D_2(A_1) = \frac{0.2 + 0.4 + 1.0}{3} = 0.53$$

$$D_2(A_2) = \frac{0.1 + 0.6 + 0.8}{3} = 0.5$$

Since $D_2(A_1) > D_2(A_2)$, building A_1 is preferred to building A_2, a conclusion which is not different from the previous result. However, for Fig. 10.8, we have

$$D_2(A_1) = 0.4; \; D_2(A_2) = 0.95$$

Under this criterion, since $D_2(A_2) > D_2(A_1)$, we prefer A_2 to A_1 which is an intuitively reasonable ordering. This criterion eliminates the effect of the area under the membership function and is better than criterion 1 in general.

10.6.3 The most possible criterion

This criterion uses the most possible risk as an index to order the alternatives, i.e.

$$D_3(A_i) = x_0 \tag{10.38}$$

where $\mu_{A_i}(x_0) = \max\limits_{x}(\mu_{A_i}(x))$. For triangular membership functions, we have

$$D_3(A_i) = c_i \tag{10.39}$$

and for trapezoidal membership functions, we have

$$D_3(A_i) = \frac{c_i + d_i}{2} \tag{10.40}$$

For the example of Fig. 10.7, the index value for building A_1 is $D_3(A_1) = 0.4$ and the index value for the building A_2 is $D_3(A_2) = 0.6$. Since $D_3(A_2) > D_3(A_1)$, building A_2 is preferred to A_1, which reverses the priority from the previous two criteria. The reason is that this criterion considers only the risk with the maximum membership value.

10.6.4 The pessimistic criterion

Under this criterion, we try to maximize the possible minimum risk, i.e.

$$D_4(A_i) = a_i \tag{10.41}$$

For our example of Fig. 10.7, we have

$$D_4(A_1) = a_1 = 0.2, D_4(A_2) = a_2 = 0.1$$

and $D_4(A_1) > D_4(A_2)$. Hence, building A_1 is preferred to building A_2.

10.6.5 The optimistic criterion

Under this criterion, we attempt to maximize the possible maximum risk, that is, define the index function as follows:

$$D_5(A_i) = b_i \tag{10.42}$$

For the example of Fig. 10.7, the index values of the two buildings are

$$D_5(A_1) = b_1 = 1.0, \; D_5(A_2) = b_2 = 0.8$$

and $D_5(A_1) > D_5(A_2)$. Hence, building A_1 is preferred.

Criteria 4 and 5 use the end values a and b of the support of a fuzzy number as the index values. Note that these values have the smallest membership grade (0^+). It is not reasonable to put so much weight on these end values in decision-making. Thus, a modification is suggested which uses a_α and b_α in place of a and b, and leads to the following two criteria:

10.6.6 The α-pessimistic criterion

Membership value greater than or equal to α is considered. Thus, define

$$D_6(A_i) = a_{i,\alpha} \qquad (10.43)$$

For the example of Fig. 10.7, if we select the threshold level for the membership value $\alpha = 0.8$, then we have

$$D_6(A_1) = a_{1,0.8} = 0.36, \; D_6(A_2) = a_{2,0.8} = 0.5$$

and building A_2 is preferred since $D_6(A_2) > D_6(A_1)$.

10.6.7 The α-optimistic criterion

Under this criterion, we use the possible maximum risk with membership value greater than or equal to α as the index and try to maximize it, i.e.

$$D_7(A_i) = b_{i,\alpha} \qquad (10.44)$$

We have for the example of Fig. 10.7 and $\alpha = 0.8$

$$D_7(a_1) = b_{1,0.8} = 0.52, \; D_7(A_2) = b_{2,0.8} = 0.64$$

which leads us to select building A_2 since $D_7(A_2)$ is larger than $D_7(A_1)$.

Note that criteria 6 and 7 consider single threshold level α only. A more general criterion is suggested which combines different values of threshold level and leads to the following criterion.

10.6.8 The average mean criterion

Define the mean of an α-cut as follows (see Fig. 10.9):

$$m_\alpha = \tfrac{1}{2}(a_\alpha + b_\alpha) \qquad (10.45)$$

then, the average mean value is defined by

$$D_8(A_i) = \int_{0^+}^{1} m_\alpha \, d\alpha \qquad (10.46)$$

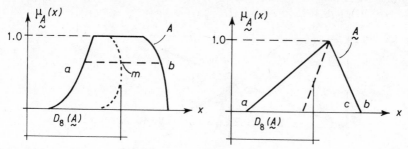

Fig. 10.9 Average mean criterion.

which is used as the index value. For triangular membership functions, Equation 10.46 reduces to

$$D_8(A_i) = \tfrac{1}{4}(a + 2c + b) \qquad (10.47)$$

and for trapezoidal membership functions, we have

$$D_8(A_i) = \tfrac{1}{4}(a + c + d + b) \qquad (10.48)$$

For the example of Fig. 10.7, this criterion will lead to the conclusion that building A_2 is preferable since

$$D_8(A_1) = \tfrac{1}{4}(0.2 + 2 \times 0.4 + 1.0) = 0.5,$$
$$D_8(A_2) = \tfrac{1}{4}(0.1 + 2 \times 0.6 + 0.8) = 0.525 \text{ and } D_8(A_2) > D_8(A_1)$$

So far, all criteria we have described establish an index value on the variable domain (in our example, it is risk) and then compare those indices for various alternatives. Departing from this approach, some researchers have suggested other criteria such as the following.

10.6.9 The nearest to the ideal optimum criterion

Define an ideal optimum alternative (the highest risk) $A_{\max}$ with the membership function as follows:

$$\mu_{A_{\max}}(x) = x^k, \qquad k > 0 \qquad (10.49)$$

and the degree of approaching this optimum for a fuzzy number A_i is given by

$$D_9(A_i) = \bigvee_x (\mu_{A_i}(x) \wedge \mu_{A_{\max}}(x)) = \text{height } (A_i \cap A_{\max}) \qquad (10.50)$$

Hence, $D_9(A_i)$ is not a value of risk, instead it is a degree of approach to the optima of A_i. When we choose that $k = 1$, the membership function for the ideal optimum is a linear function (Fig. 10.10). For our example, we have

$$D_9(A_1) = 0.4, \; D_9(A_2) = 0.6$$

Hence, building A_2 is preferred to building A_1.

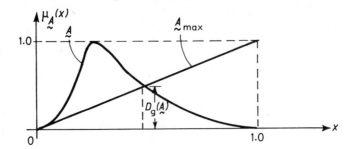

Fig. 10.10 The degree of approach to the optimum.

10.6.10 The dominance criterion

The truth value of a statement that '$a_1 > a_2$' in the context of crisp numbers is binary, that is, either 1 (true) or 0 (false). However, when fuzzy numbers are involved, the truth value of '$A_1 > A_2$' will not be only 1 or 0, except in rare cases. Usually, it may take intermediate values between 0 and 1. Define the dominance degree of A_1 over A_2 as $D_{10}(A_1 > A_2)$ by

$$D_{10}(A_1 > A_2) = \sup_{x_1 < x_2} [\min \mu_{A_1}(x_1), \mu_{A_2}(x_2)] \tag{10.51}$$

For unimodal normal fuzzy numbers, the index $D_{10}(A_1 > A_2)$ is simply given by

$$D_{10}(A_1 > A_2) = \begin{cases} 1, & m_1 > m_2 \\ \text{height } (A_1 \cap A_2), & m_1 \leqslant m_2 \end{cases} \tag{10.52}$$

where m_1 and m_2 are the mean values, i.e. $\mu_{A_i}(m_i) = 1$ (Fig. 10.11).

For our risk example of Fig. 10.7, we have

$$m_1 = 0.4; \quad m_2 = 0.6$$

$$D_{10}(A_1 > A_2) = \text{height}(A_1 \cap A_2) = 0.8 \text{ since } m_1 < m_2$$

On the other hand, the dominance degree of A_2 over A_1 is

$$D_{10}(A_2 > A_1) = 1.0$$

Hence, building A_2 is preferred to building A_1 under this criterion.

This criterion can be extended to determine the dominance degree of A_i over several options $A_j, j = 1, n; j \neq i$. This is, define

$$D_{10}(A_i > A_j, j = 1, n, j \neq i) = \min_{j \neq i} [D_{10}(A_i > A_j)] \tag{10.53}$$

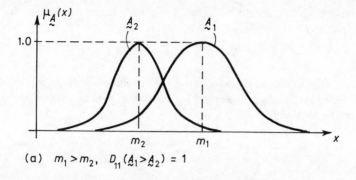

(a) $m_1 > m_2$, $D_{11}(\underset{\sim}{A}_1 > \underset{\sim}{A}_2) = 1$

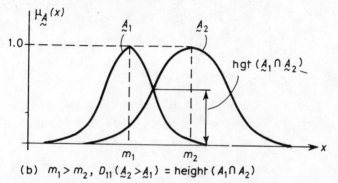

(b) $m_1 > m_2$, $D_{11}(\underset{\sim}{A}_2 > \underset{\sim}{A}_1) = \text{height}(A_1 \cap A_2)$

Fig. 10.11 Truth value of the dominance relation.

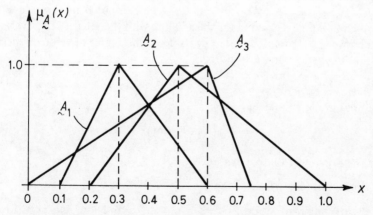

Fig. 10.12 Fuzzy risk values for three buildings A_1, A_2, and A_3.

The best choice would be based upon the maximum dominance degree principal, i.e.

$$D_{10}(A^*) = \max_i [D_{10}(A_i)]$$

As another example, suppose that there are three buildings, A_1, A_2, and A_3, with their fuzzy risks represented by fuzzy numbers as shown in Fig. 10.12. According to Equation 10.52, we have

$$D_{10}(A_1 > A_2) = \text{height } (A_1 \cap A_2) = 0.67$$
$$D_{10}(A_1 > A_3) = \text{height } (A_1 \cap A_3) = 0.67$$
$$D_{10}(A_2 > A_1) = 1$$
$$D_{10}(A_2 > A_3) = \text{height } (A_2 \cap A_3) = 0.91$$
$$D_{10}(A_3 > A_1) = 1$$
$$D_{10}(A_3 > A_2) = 1$$

and from Equation 10.53, we have

$$D_{10}(A_1) = \min [D_{10}(A_1 > A_2), D_{10}(A_1 > A_3)] = 0.67$$
$$D_{10}(A_2) = \min [D_{10}(A_2 > A_1), D_{10}(A_2 > A_3)] = 0.91$$
$$D_{10}(A_3) = \min [D_{10}(A_3 > A_1), D_{10}(A_3 > A_3)] = 1.00$$

Hence, for this example, the preference order would be $A_3 > A_2 > A_1$.

10.6.11 The classification criterion

Set up several templates of ordered fuzzy numbers as representatives of the typical linguistic grades. For example, Fig. 10.5 shows five fuzzy sets for the linguistic grades: 'very low', 'low', 'moderate', 'high', and 'very high', denoted by L_5, L_4, L_3, L_2, L_1. Also in Fig. 10.5, the computed total grade Y for a specified building is given in the dashed line with the area A. The overlapped area between Y and L_i is denoted by A_i. Then the degree of belongingness to a certain linguistic value L is given by

$$D_i = (A_i/A) \tag{10.54}$$

The final grade should be

$$L = L_j \quad \text{if} \quad D_j = \max_i (A_i/A) \tag{10.55}$$

For the previous example, we have

$$D_1 = 0; \; D_2 = 0.177; \; D_3 = 0.577; \; D_4 = 0.6; \; D_5 = 0.146$$

Hence, the linguistic grade is between 'moderate' and 'low' (closer to 'low risk' than 'moderate risk' since $D_4 = \max (A_i/A) = 0.6$, $L = L_4 = $ 'low').

10.6.12 The four point average criterion

For any computed grade of a specific building, we use four end points of two intervals: most possible interval and least possible interval. The average numerical grade is given by

$$G = \tfrac{1}{4}(a_1 + b_1 + a_{0^+} + b_{0^+})\tag{10.56}$$

where a_1, b_1, a_{0^+}, b_{0^+} are shown in Fig. 10.3.

Since G is a real number, its order is well defined. In our example,

$$G = \tfrac{1}{4}(0.145 + 0.298 + 0.485 + 0.677) = 0.4$$

The 12 criteria we have listed so far are by no means exhaustive. There are many other criteria not covered here. Further information is available in Bortolan and Degani (1985). We should point out again that decision-making is a complex process and each individual can have a unique preference structure. The preference can also evolve with time. Thus, it is impossible to establish a universal theory which can fit the behavior of various decision-makers. However, what is important is that the criterion, once identified and established, should be followed throughout the whole process with consistency. In our development of a risk evaluation system, to be described in the next section, we use criterion 12, i.e. the four point average criterion.

10.7 SEISMIC RISK EVALUATION SYSTEM

The Seismic Risk Evaluation System (SRE) is a computer program which provides consultation and risk assessment for existing buildings in seismic regions. The complete knowledge tree for this consultation is shown in Fig. 10.1. The system requires the user to provide answers to 12 questions. The user can give a linguistic answer selected from the menu or give numerical input (single number, interval or fuzzy set). Explanations are built in to assist the user in answering certain questions. The program was first developed in an expert system 'shell'—'Deciding Factor'™ (Miyasato *et al.*, 1986). Later on, FORTRAN 77 was used in order to incorporate fuzzy number operations. The program can be run on an IBMPC XT, AT or equivalent computer with at least 128K of memory.

For clarification, we shall describe the process of building this system in six sequential steps. In the actual development, cyclic repetition of some steps and adjustments is necessary.

Step 1   Constructing the inference tree
Step 2   Questionnaire
Step 3   Checking the consistency
Step 4   Selecting value function for combination
Step 5   Determining the decision criterion
Step 6   Validation

10.7.1 Constructing the inference tree

The inference tree shown in Fig. 10.1 was drawn based on opinions from experts working on a project of risk assessment. The tree shows the interrelationships among the attributes contributing to the total seismic risk. The top node is the total risk which is comprised of four nodes in the lower level. The ground hazard is supported by three nodes: ground motion intensity, soil condition, and ground failure potential. Further, the ground failure potential is based on the potentials of liquefaction, landslide, and fault rupture. The vulnerability of the structure depends on adequacy of design, the construction quality control, and the type of structure. The importance of the structure has three sub-nodes: whether the building is for emergency service, whether damage to the building would cause serious social impact, and whether damage to the building would cause serious secondary disaster. For the pilot study, we restrict the inference tree to this simple form. However, each node in the tree can be expanded to include more detailed considerations.

10.7.2 Questionnaire

To evaluate the total risk, grades of attributes from the sub-nodes must be combined to obtain the grade for the top node. In order to extract the way by which experts make assessments, we give three to five grades for each attribute and list all possible combinations. The purpose of this questionnaire is to try to scope the overall framework of how experts combine different attributes into the total risk. Figure 10.5 shows the grades for all attributes and the explanation.

10.7.3 Checking the consistency

As mentioned in Section 10.3, the multi-attribute decision process is a partial order problem in which some alternatives can be ordered and others cannot be ordered. Therefore, according to the Pareto preference structure, if one alternative y is worse than another alternative z in every aspect, then y should have a higher score than z (note that we use a high score to refer to high risk). However, when experts give their grades for all combinations, it is difficult to maintain consistency. There might be some grades which could reverse the preference. Hence, it is necessary to check and correct them before using them to build the value functions.

A program, CHECK, has been written for this purpose. All inconsistencies can be corrected by reversing the order or making them equal. It can be shown that such correction would not cause any further inconsistency.

10.7.4 Selection of value function for the combination

For each node in the inference tree, the value functions are selected to reproduce the expert's answers most closely. As shown in Fig. 10.1, each node has been numbered from 1 to 5. For the entire tree, three types of mapping functions have been chosen for the best fit to the expert's evaluation. They are Type I, Type II, and Type IV as given in Section 10.4. All scores for the

Table 10.1 Weighting factors for attributes

Attribute	Weight with trapezoidal membership function			
Ground motion	0.6	0.8	1.0	1.0
Soil condition	0.3	0.4	0.6	0.7
Liquefaction	1.0	1.0	1.0	1.0
Landslide	1.0	1.0	1.0	1.0
Rupture	1.0	1.0	1.0	1.0
Secondary disaster	1.0	1.0	1.0	1.0
Emergency service	1.0	1.0	1.0	1.0
Social impact	1.0	1.0	1.0	1.0
Structure type	0.5	0.7	0.9	1.0
Design adequacy	0.2	0.3	0.4	0.5
Construction quality	0.2	0.3	0.4	0.5
Occupancy	0.4	0.6	0.8	0.9
Ground failure	0.1	0.3	0.4	0.5
Ground hazard	0.4	0.6	0.8	0.9
Importance	0.4	0.6	0.8	0.9
Vulnerability	0.6	0.8	1.0	1.0

Table 10.2 Data for seismic evaluation of a tilt-up structure

Idea	Grade				Implication
Ground motion	0.5	0.7	0.8	1.0	Intensity: 9
Soil condition	0.15	0.25	0.45	0.55	Medium to hard
Liquefaction potential	0	0	0.1	0.3	Low
Landslide potential	0.05	0.15	0.25	0.35	Small
Rupture potential	0	0	0.1	0.3	Low
Secondary hazards	0	0	0.1	0.3	None
Emergency services	0	0	0.1	0.3	No
Social impact	0	0	0.1	0.3	None
Type of building	0.7	0.8	0.9	1.0	Tilt-up structure
Design quality	0.4	0.55	0.65	0.85	Seismic considerations not included to a great extent
Construction quality	0.1	0.2	0.3	0.4	Relatively good
Occupancy	0.45	0.55	0.65	0.75	About 100 persons

attributes are represented by fuzzy numbers to fit the linguistic terms. For simplicity, we use trapezoidal fuzzy numbers only. The weights are also fuzzy. They were selected to fit the expert's evaluation. Final weights are listed in Table 10.1. The input for all the attributes is examined as trapezoidal fuzzy numbers. Table 10.2 gives the input data for a tilt-up structure in Palo Alto, California, which is used to illustrate the risk assessment procedure.

10.7.5 Determination of the decision criterion

The final risk attribute value is given in the form of a fuzzy number as shown in Fig. 10.3. We selected the four point average criterion, that is, the index value is determined by the average four point value. The result was 0.52 which falls into the category of moderate risk.

10.7.6 System validation

It is essential that the system be validated by internal and external experts so that the system can perform close to the expert's level. So far, for this pilot system, we have not conducted the necessary validation due to time limitation. Extensive validations and modifications must be performed on the system before it can be distributed.

10.8 SUMMARY

This chapter has presented an overall methodology for evaluating the seismic risk in which the combination of multi-attributes is consistent. Four types of mapping functions are described to provide the flexibility of combining attributes for different situations. By these mapping functions, the number of heuristic rules is greatly reduced and the engineering expertise in the knowledge base is condensed. The Vertex method was introduced to process the vague information so that total risk evaluation can be obtained in complex environments. This methodology has been used to develop a consultation system for seismic risk evaluation – FRA (Fuzzy Risk Analysis) (Dong *et al.*, 1986). It can also be applied to many real problems such as dam safety, siting, etc. which require the combination of multi-linguistic or fuzzy attributes.

ACKNOWLEDGEMENTS

The support of the NSF Grant CEE-8403516 and the advice of Dr C. Astill and Dr S.C. Liu are gratefully acknowledged.

REFERENCES

Bortolan, G. and Degani, R. (1985) A review of some methods for ranking fuzzy subsets. *Journal of Fuzzy Sets and Systems*, **15**, 1–19.

Dong, W. and Shah, H. (1987) Vertex method for computing function of fuzzy variables. *Journal of Fuzzy Sets and Systems*, **24**, 65–78.

Dong, W., Lamarre, M. and Boissonnade, A. (1986) Expert system for seismic risk evaluation, *Proceedings of 8th European Conference on Earthquake Engineering*, Laboratorio Nacional De Engenharia Civil, Lisbon.

Miyasato, G., Dong, W., Levitt, R., Boissonnade, A. and Shah, H. (1986) Seismic risk analysis systems, in *Expert Systems in Civil Engineering* (eds N. Kostem and M. Maher), American Society of Civil Engineers, New York, pp. 121–32.

Moore, R. E. (1979) *Methods and Applications of Interval Analysis*, Society for Industrial and Applied Mathematics, Studies in Applied Mathematics, Philadelphia.

Pedrycz, W. (1984) An identification algorithm in fuzzy relational systems. *Journal of Fuzzy Sets and Systems*, **13**, 153–67.

Saaty, T., (1978) Exploring the interface between hierarchies, multiple objectives and fuzzy sets. *Journal of Fuzzy Sets and Systems*, **1**, 57–68.

Wong, F. and Dong, W. (1986) Fuzzy information processing in engineering analysis, *Proceedings of 1st International Conference on Application of Artificial Intelligence to Engineering Problems, Southampton, UK.* (eds D. Sriram and R. Adey), Computational Mechanics Publications, Springer–Verlag, Berlin, Heidelberg, pp. 247–60.

Zadeh, L.A. (1965) Fuzzy sets. *Information and Control*, **8**, 338–53.

11

Expert systems for condition evaluation of existing structures

X.J. ZHANG and JAMES T.P. YAO

11.1 INTRODUCTION

To build an expert system, it is necessary to know (a) how to represent knowledge (knowledge representation), and (b) how to use the knowledge to solve problems (inference procedure). In general, an expert system consists of a knowledge base and an inference machine. A knowledge base is a storage base in a computer, in which useful knowledge is stored in a stylized form suitable for making the inference. An inference machine is a control process by which an answer may be deduced from a given problem situation by using the stored knowledge. Meanwhile, it is necessary to have a memory for storing available data. In addition, an expert system may include other subprograms such as an explanation machine and a learning machine.

SPERIL (Structural *PERIL*) are expert systems for damage assessment of existing structures, which have been under development since 1980. In SPERIL-1 (Ishizuka *et al.*, 1980–83), an arbitrary damage measure ranging from zero ('no damage') through ten ('total collapse') is used. Separate evidential observations are integrated on the basis of Dempster and Shafer's theory with the use of fuzzy sets. The program portion of SPERIL-1 is written in C. In SPERIL-2 (Ogawa *et al.*, 1983, 1984), the integer exponent n of the order of failure probability 10^{-n} is used as a measure of structural safety. In addition, logic is used to (a) represent rules, facts and available data on the existing structure, as well as (b) control the inference to obtain conclusions. The program of SPERIL-2 is written in PROLOG.

A new version, SPERIL-3, is being developed on the basis of a preliminary version called CES-1 (Civil Engineering System), which consists of the following four parts: inference machine, knowledge base, memory and learning machine (Zhang, 1985). A frame structure is used to represent knowledge in CES-1, and the program is written in LISP.

In this chapter, all three versions of SPERIL are described in some detail. Specifically, knowledge representation, inference procedure, learning process, and practical implementation are explained and discussed.

11.2 KNOWLEDGE REPRESENTATION

11.2.1 General remarks

Knowledge representation in an AI program means choosing a set of conventions for the description of objects, relations and processes in the world (Nilssion, 1980). There are several ways to represent knowledge in AI including production rules, semantic networks, first order logic, and frame (see Chapter 2). SPERIL-1 and 2 are basically rule-based systems with logic representation in SPERIL-2. Frame is used in CES-1 as a knowledge representation. In the following, both production rule and frame are briefly described along with their application in SPERIL systems.

11.2.2 Production (rule-based) systems

In a complex problem, it is efficient to express relevant knowledge as a collection of many small pieces of knowledge. The problem reduction method (Nilssion, 1980) can be used to resolve a problem into simpler subproblems, which may be further resolved into even simpler sub-subproblems. Hence the whole problem can be described hierarchically, and it has its own final goal to be achieved. Similarly, each subproblem has its own subgoal to be achieved from the available information.

Useful information for the assessment of structural damage may come from such sources as (a) visual inspection at various portions of the structure, (b) accelerometer records during an earthquake, (c) documentation of personal observations and (d) other laboratory and field testing data. In Fig. 11.1, observations from visual inspection and accelerometer records are considered as inputs to an inference network of SPERIL-1. The interpretation of these data is influenced to a large extent by the particular kind of structure under study as specified by material, structural type, story height, etc.

In the production system, a piece of knowledge is written as a production rule in the following basic form with a certainty measure, C,

Rule: If X,
THEN H, with C.

For more details, readers should refer to Chapter 2.

As an illustrative example of rules as applied in SPERIL-1, suppose that X_0 indicates damage as indicated by changes in stiffness and H_0 represents the

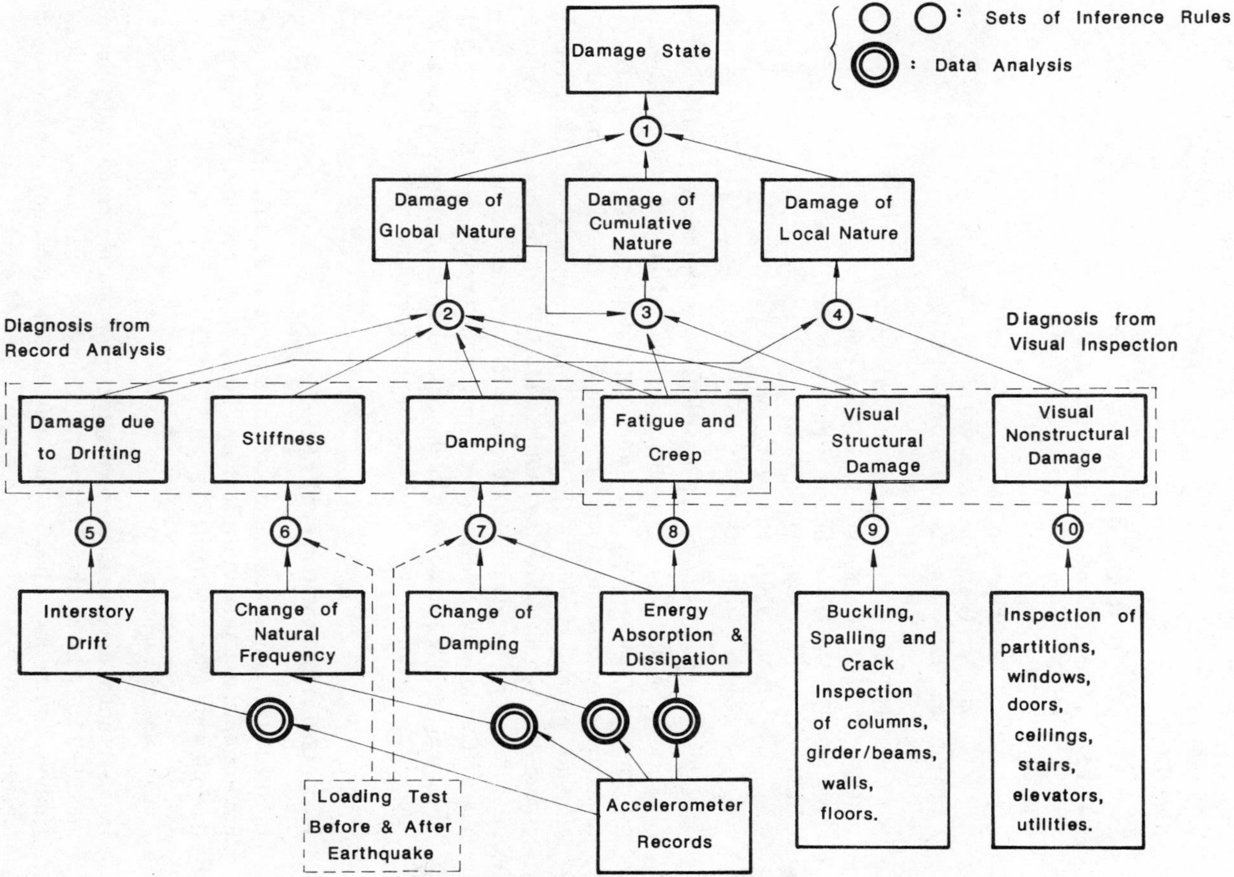

Fig. 11.1 Inference network of SPERIL-1.

hypothesis of global damage. Rule 0202 gives the relationship between these two finite universe sets X_0 and H_0.

Rule 0202

	IF:	Material is steel
THEN	IF:	Change in stiffness is more than 50%,
	THEN:	Global damage is destructive with 0.8.
ELSE	IF:	Change in stiffness is less than 50% and more than 20%,
	THEN:	Global damage is severe with 0.8.
ELSE	IF:	Change in stiffness is less than 20% and more than 5%,
	THEN:	Global damage is moderate with 0.8.
ELSE	IF:	Change in stiffness is less than 5%,
	THEN:	Global damage is slight with 0.8.
ELSE	IF:	Change in stiffness is negligible,
	THEN:	Global damage is nil with 0.8.
	ELSE:	Global damage is unknown

In this way, useful knowledge in SPERIL-1 is represented as IF–THEN rules. In SPERIL-1 and -2, inference for the 'AND' and 'OR' relation is performed by using 'min' and 'max' operators on certainty measures, respectively. Meanwhile, Dempster and Shafer's theory is adopted as a reference method dealing with the COMB relation. Once the inference procedure is established for the COMB and AND/OR relations, the certainty measure can propagate through the hierarchical inference network. Eventually, we can obtain the degree of certainty of the hypothesis in the final goal, which will provide a reasonable guidance for decision-making purposes. The inference procedure will be presented in more detail in the next section.

11.2.3 Logic representation in SPERIL-2

In SPERIL-2, statements are expressed in terms of the first order predicate. For example, to represent the sentence 'Element 3 is a column.' we might use the following atomic formula:

ako (element3, column).

In this formula, 'ako' is called a predicate symbol and 'element 3' and 'column' are called constant symbols. In general, atomic formulas consist of predicate symbols and terms. These terms may include constants, variables and functions.

In SPERIL-2, there are descriptive and logical statements. A descriptive statement is expressed by means of an atomic formula, and a logical statement is formed by using logical connectives such as 'and', 'or', and 'not', among descriptive statements. In this way, a fact can be represented in the form of

data ($\langle$ descriptive-statement $\rangle$ {, $\langle$ certainty-factor $\rangle$ }),

where { } means an option. If the certainty factor is not given, it is assumed to be 1.

Meanwhile, a rule in SPERIL-2 is expressed as:

$\langle$ rule $\rangle$ ::= $\langle$ group-name $\rangle$($\langle$ consequence $\rangle$, $\langle$ premise $\rangle$,
                          $\langle$ certainty-factor $\rangle$)
$\langle$ consequent $\rangle$ ::= $\langle$ descriptive-statement $\rangle$
$\langle$ premise $\rangle$ ::= [{$\langle$ statement $\rangle$} +]|$\langle$ statement $\rangle$
$\langle$ statement $\rangle$ ::= $\langle$ logical-statement $\rangle$|$\langle$ descriptive-statement $\rangle$
$\langle$ logical-statement $\rangle$ ::= and ({$\langle$ statement $\rangle$} +)| or ({$\langle$ statement $\rangle$} +)|
                          not ($\langle$ statement $\rangle$)

The brackets denote a sequence for representing the order of these statements. The value of the certainty factor is a number ranging from 0 to 1: where '0' implies that the rule is not reliable, and '1' implies that the consequence is true if the premise is true. An example of such a rule is given as follows:

estlocal (estimate(A, F),
            and (has (A, [K, in-bearing-region-of, L]),
                cause (K, shrinkage, M),
                is-transform-to (M, F)),
        0.5).

This means that the estimated damage F of structural Element A is obtained with certainty (0.5). Such an estimation is based on inspection data K of Element A on the bearing region of Element L. Shrinkage is the cause of such damage with degree is M, which is transformed to fuzzy set F.

11.2.4 Frame

In recent years, frame-like structures are used as the knowledge representation method in many expert systems (e.g. Aikins, 1983). It was found that the frame-like structure (Minsky, 1975) has advantages in representing sequences of events (Yao and Fu, 1985) and for knowledge acquisition and modification. Consequently, a frame structure is used to represent knowledge in CES-1.

Suppose we want to represent the following fact: 'A severe horizontal crack is observed at the end B of Beam No. 12.'. We may use a semantic network as shown in Fig. 11.2. In AI systems, such a construction as 'location: end' is called a 'slot'. The first expression, 'location', is called the 'slot name', and the second expression, 'end', is called the 'slot value'. One slot has only one name and may have several values. A slot value can be a constant, a variable or a

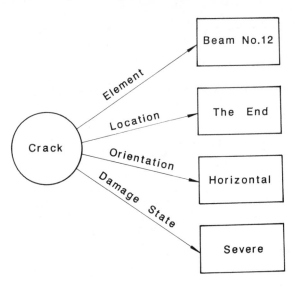

Fig. 11.2 A fact about a crack is represented by using a semantic network.

function. In the frame-like structure, each slot can also be described with another frame. For example, the Beam No. 12 may be described by another frame. The relevant information about this beam, such as length, height, shape, width and material may be contained in corresponding slots. In this manner, complex knowledge may be represented by using a series of frames.

Usually it is convenient to use such slots as ISA ('is a') and AKO ('a kind of'), making class membership and subclass relations explicit, and facilitating the movement of knowledge from one level to another. Meanwhile, for representing knowledge in the domain of damage assessment, it is useful to establish two kinds of slots called CAUSE and REASON for linking events. For example, a sentence: 'The crack i is the result of torsional stresses and causes local damage of Beam No. 12.' may be represented by using both 'REASON' and 'CAUSE' slots. Sometimes, two slots of 'REASON' and 'CAUSE' may consist of an inverse pair, e.g. 'the reason for the crack i is torsional stresses' and 'torsional stresses cause crack i' express the same facts from different views. Both 'CAUSE' and 'REASON' slots may contain several values separately.

From these links, it is possible to obtain a reasonable and efficient damage assessment procedure. It is important to recognize that certain information from inspection results may indicate a particular damage state. For example, a big crack in a reinforced concrete member may cause the corrosion of certain reinforcing steel bars. Therefore, from information on crack i and the link of cause, the machine may be programmed to ask for information about the corrosion of bars.

11.3 INFERENCE PROCEDURE

11.3.1 General remarks

In the first part of this section, control strategies are discussed, which deal with when and how to use both knowledge and information and how to obtain necessary information. As with most complex decision-making problems, most information in the domain of damage assessment is represented linguistically. A linguistic assessment method is, therefore, briefly described and the basic concepts of fuzzy sets theory are introduced in the second part of the section. In the last two parts of this section, we discuss methods for the combination of evidence from different knowledge sources. Moreover, problems with uncertainties are also considered here.

11.3.2 Control strategy

A forward-chaining procedure is used in SPERIL-1 for its inference. Rules are classified according to the subgoals. The sets of rule are indicated by the first digit of a 4-digit rule number, which corresponds to the node numbers as shown in Fig. 11.1. If a relating rule is found in the rule-base, it is processed. When the premise is examined and the associated short-term memory is found to be unwritten or unanswered, a question is issued to obtain additional data. The questions are generated referring to a question file. To avoid unnecessary questions, 'skip/pass' is provided for the case where there is no possibility for action statements to be taken. After one rule is processed, the resultant content of buffer memory is used to update the short-term memory. In SPERIL-1, the short-term memories are classified into the following four types: type 1 for certainty measures of fuzzy subsets; type 2 for linguistic data; type 3 for numerical data; and type 4 for yes–no data. After necessary questions are asked, the final decision can be made according to Dempster and Shafer's lower probabilities of the fuzzy subsets in the final goal (FIN) which is a damage state.

One of the difficulties in a production system is in the representation of knowledge on control strategies. The introduction of metarules (Davis, 1980) may provide a convenient means of representing control information. In SPERIL-2, metarules are employed to control the selection of rule group and suitable inference method. The representation of metarules is similar to the rule form. There are four built-in reasoning methods applied in SPERIL-2 as follows:

bwc: Find one solution path in a depth-first backward reasoning to satisfy the given goal.

bwca: Find all the solutions matching the given goal in a backward reasoning.

bwcatrace: Find all the solutions matching the given goal in a backward reasoning, and display the instances of premise and consequence.

fwca: Store all possible results of the forward reasoning using the given rule group.

Examples of metarules are shown as follows:

1. smj (local_dmg, [cause, damage_to_element], 1).
2. smj (cause,
    [material (concrete),
     datalist(L),
     do_each (L, M, (getcause(M), a_list (precause_con)))],
    1).
3. smj (cause,
    [material(steel),
     datalist(L),
     do_each (L, M (getcause(M), a_list (precause_st)))],
    1).
4. smj (damage_to_element,
    and (material (concrete),
      fwca (estlocal_con)),
    1).
5. smj (damage_to_element,
    and (material (steel),
      fwca (estlocal_st)),
    1).

These metarules are in group smj for the evaluation of damage to elements of the structure with the following explanation:

(a) In metarule 1, subgoal cause should be achieved followed by subgoal 'damage_to_element' to obtain local damageabilities.
(b) In metarules 2 and 3, predicates 'datalist' and 'do_each' are the 'built_in' predicates. Predicate 'datalist(L)' means that L is a list of names of inspection data. Predicate 'do_each (A, B, C)' means that subgoal C is achieved for every element B of list A.
(c) There are two ways to achieve a cause. Metarule 2 is used when the structure material is concrete, and 3 is used for steel. The sequence of 'datalist' and 'do_each' means that damage causes are diagnosed on the basis of inspection data using the rule group suitable to the material. Question for symptoms may be concentrated for each inspection data, and the users can easily understand the questions and answer them.
(d) Metarules 4 and 5 mean that rule groups 'estlocal_con' and 'estlocal_st' are used to estimate the damages of elements in forward reasoning corresponding to materials concrete and steel, respectively.

As described earlier in frame representation, such slots as AKO, ISA, CAUSE, REASON provide an effective way to facilitate the movement of knowledge from one level to another and link events. Effective control procedures can be performed by employing such slots.

11.3.3 Linguistic assessment

In real-world problems, most complex decisions are made in terms of experts' intuition and judgement, and expressed linguistically. Therefore, to model the experts' decision-making process with linguistical expressions is an important task in building an expert system. The values of a linguistic variable are words, phrases, or sentences in a given language. For example, structural damage can be considered as a linguistic variable with values such as 'severely damaged', 'moderately damaged', which are meaningful classifications but not clearly defined. The theory of fuzzy sets (Zadeh, 1965; Brown and Leonard, 1971; Blockley, 1975; Brown, 1979; Yao, 1980) can be used to interpret terms with membership functions, which can be manipulated in a logical manner to obtain an answer to the original and complex problem.

A fuzzy set A in a given sample Ω is a set of ordered pairs $\{\mu_A(x)|x\}$ for each $x \in \Omega$, where $\mu_x(x)$ is called the membership function and Ω denotes the sample space. If the membership set consists of only two elements, say 0 and 1, then A is said to be an ordinary (or nonfuzzy, or crisp) set. For fuzzy sets, the value of the membership is in the interval from 0 to 1. As an example, let N be the set of natural numbers, i.e. $N = \{0, 1, 2, \ldots ,\}$. Consider the fuzzy set A of 'small' natural numbers as follows:

$$A = \{(1|0), (0.8|1), (0.6|2), (0.3|3), (0|4)\}$$

In words, we say that the number '0' has a nonfuzzy membership, '1' has a 'strong' membership, '2' has a 'fairly strong' membership, '3' has a 'weak' membership, '4' and higher numbers have nonmemberships of the fuzzy set A of 'small' natural numbers.

In SPERIL systems, linguistic variables are expressed with fuzzy grade. For example, the degree of damage is expressed as: no, slight, moderate, severe, destructive, unknown. The membership functions of these fuzzy subsets as used in SPERIL-1 are defined accordingly. In SPERIL-2, the integer exponent n of failure probability 10^{-n} is used as a measure of structural safety. For example, a narrow crack is represented in fuzzy set $\{(0.3|6), (1|7), (0.3|8)\}$, which means that the structural element has a probability of failure of 10^{-6} with membership 0.3, 10^{-7} with membership 1 and 10^{-8} with membership 0.3. The membership functions of fuzzy damage grades corresponding to failure probabilities were developed and used in SPERIL-2. In addition, satisfactory–questionable–unsatisfactory classifications are used in SPERIL-2 according to the estimated failure probability as well as the importance of each structure.

The theory of fuzzy sets has been applied as a method for damage assessment and safety evaluation for existing structures in SPERIL systems. Meanwhile, research work has been carried out on the linguistic assessment of structural damage (Hinkle *et al.*, 1986; Watada *et al.*, 1984). The procedure of a linguistic damage assessment includes the following four steps:

1. Assessment of variables in linguistic terms
2. Translations of linguistic terms into fuzzy sets
3. Inference of the fuzzy damage state, and
4. Translation of the fuzzy damaged state into linguistic terms.

In this manner, a complex structural system may be assessed by combining various linguistic and/or numerical sets of information.

As mentioned previously, a problem can be described by an AND/OR/COMB graph with certainty factors. In SPERIL the max (min) of the certainty factors is calculated in an AND(OR) relation. Dempster and Shafer's theory (Dempster, 1967; Shafer, 1967) is adopted as a reference method dealing with the COMB relation. Details of Dempster and Shafer's theory and its application in SPERIL systems are described elsewhere (Ishizuka *et al.*, 1983a; Toussi and Yao, 1982/1983).

11.3.4 Normalized index method

Bresler and Hanson (1982) suggested an index method for evaluating the damageability of existing structures. This method is based on establishing values for response demand, damage threshold and ultimate damage capacity for individual elements, and has been extended to both linguistic and numerical expressions and applied to an expert system CES-1 as a combining model (Zhang, 1985). Although many practical problems are extremely complex, it is possible to find the admissible lower limit y^l ⟨threshold⟩ and the upper limit y^u for certain problems. A normalized coordinate may be defined as follows:

$$x = F(y^l, y^u, y), \qquad x = [0, 1] \tag{11.1}$$

In the normalized coordinate system, a relationship between numerical values and physically meaningful expressions may be defined. For an example, x may be considered as a degree of damage state as five linguistic expressions, i.e. 'no' = 0.0, 'slight' = 0.25, 'moderate' = 0.5, 'severe' = 0.75 and 'destructive' = 1.0. Furthermore, a fuzzy membership function may be incorporated in this normalized coordinate system.

Information as obtained from n knowledge sources may be combined as follows:

$$x = \frac{\sum w_i x_i}{\sum w_i} \tag{11.2}$$

where w_i is called a weighting coefficient for element i, which may be considered as a measure of both importance and belief of the ith element (event).

If a membership function of a fuzzy set is defined on a normalized coordinate, we call this fuzzy set a normalized fuzzy set. When the weighting function as shown in Equation 11.2 is used with fuzzy sets, the concept of α-lever cut may be used for such a calculation. For instance, if the weighting coefficient w_i is assumed to be a nonfuzzy number and x_i is defined as a fuzzy set, then the lower and upper α-level values of the resulting combined fuzzy set c can be expressed as:

$$\underline{x}_c^\alpha = \frac{\sum w_i \underline{x}_i^\alpha}{\sum w_i} \tag{11.3a}$$

$$\bar{x}_c^\alpha = \frac{\sum w_i \bar{x}_i^\alpha}{\sum w_i} \tag{11.3b}$$

where $\underline{x}_c^\alpha$ and $\bar{x}_c^\alpha$ are the lower and upper α-level values of the ith fuzzy subset $(i = 1, 2, \ldots, n)$.

11.3.5 Heuristic procedure

In an assessment process, the more reliable information we have, the more confident we are in making the decision. However, it is neither realistic nor economically feasible to obtain 'complete' information. Therefore, heuristic procedures for making decisions are very important not only for problem solving but also for practical and economical reasons. Yao *et al.* (1984) suggested that a solution may be possible using an iterative procedure. As engineers obtain relevant information and test data, analysis and evaluation are performed. If and when results are sufficient for determining the structural condition, the process is complete. Otherwise, more inspection information and test data must be collected for further analysis and evaluation. The process is repeated until the structural condition is assessed with some degree of confidence.

Available information in CES-1 is classified into several categories such as general information, inspection information, loading condition, and accelerometer records. The order of these questions is ranked according to the degree of difficulty in obtaining such information. At the beginning, CES-1 asks for general information which is useful for consultation purposes. For example, a question about the purpose of assessment is asked. If the answer is 'damage assessment after an earthquake', the slot of earthquake information is filled. Therefore the frames corresponding to earthquake are taken and questions about the particular earthquake will be asked. Otherwise, no question about earthquake records will be asked. In this manner, only relevant questions will be asked. This makes the assessment procedure more reasonable and closer to the experts' way of thinking. Meanwhile, at the beginning of asking each category of questions, the machine may first ask the following question: 'Could you give me some information about '∗∗∗' category of questions?' If the user answers YES, the machine will then ask this kind of question. Otherwise, the machine will ask if the user can give any other information about the next category. Meanwhile, the machine puts the '∗∗∗' category of questions at the tail end of the catalogue of questions. If the results are still not sufficient for determining the structural condition after having asked all categories of questions, the machine may suggest that the user should collect more information concerning the unanswered categories of questions. In this manner, the questions to be asked are reasonable by adjustment through man–machine dialogue.

In the real world, many decisions are usually made on the basis of incomplete and insufficient information. Usually analysis and judgement are required for the engineer to decide which types of information are relevant and necessary. If and when results are sufficient for making a decision, the process is completed. Otherwise, more information may be demanded for further analysis and consideration. The process is repeated until a decision can be made with an acceptable degree of confidence. In contrast, if it is difficult or unreasonable to obtain more information, a rough decision may also be made according to the limited information available. Meanwhile the decision-makers may indicate the roughness of the decision in some cases, by using expressions such as optimistic and pessimistic estimations.

Based on CES-1, the consultant process of SPERIL-3 is designed in a hierarchical fashion. Following Bresler (1985), two phases of consultants are used in SPERIL-3 in order to obtain a good assessment of the structural damage and to keep the cost of the assessment low. In phase I, questions asked include general information, design quality, construction quality and feelings resulting from the visual inspection. On the basis of each type of information, suggestions may be made such as 'no action is needed', 'laboratory tests are required', 'loading tests are required'. In phase II, more detailed information is to be requested and a decision is made according to the information from both phases.

In SPERIL-3, decision-making on the basis of incomplete and insufficient information is considered. A measurement called degree of discrimination of a fuzzy subset is suggested, which is equal to one minus the area enclosed by the membership function. If the degree of discrimination of a fuzzy subset A equals 1, then A is said to be a crisp set. This case corresponds to a nonfuzzy number x which may be considered as a degenerative fuzzy set. On the other hand, if the degree of discrimination of a fuzzy subset A equals zero, then A is said to be completely vague.

During decision-making, it is desirable to combine several separate sets of evidence which may support one hypothesis. If information for a certain set of evidence is available, the membership function of this evidence may be defined. On the other hand, if no information for a particular set of evidence is available, this evidence can be defined as an unknown fuzzy set. In this manner, each set of evidence will have its own membership function. By using Equation 11.3, a resulting fuzzy set can be found. If the degree of discrimination of a resulting fuzzy set is less than a critical value, a decision may be made. Otherwise, more information should be requested. In different phases of the decision-making process, various degrees of confidence may be required. Therefore, different critical values of degree of discrimination can be assigned.

11.4 THE LEARNING PROCESS

11.4.1 General remarks

Learning is one of the most fundamental attributes of human intelligence, which may be classified into the following two basic forms: knowledge acquisition and skill refinement. The former means learning new symbolic information and the ability to apply this information effectively. The latter is the gradual improvement of motor and cognitive skill through practice (Minsky, 1975). As defined by Simon, "learning denotes changes in the system that are adaptive in the sense that they enable the system to do the same tasks drawn from the same population more efficiently and more effectively next time" (Simon, 1983).

In the development of expert systems, a major difficulty in knowledge acquisition lies in establishing effective communication between knowledge engineers and domain experts. Usually a complex problem in an expert system is divided into a series of simple questions. In the computer program, several features are combined to determine the global damage of the structure. In designing such a program, it is difficult to know a priori how much weight should be attached to each feature being used. Furthermore, some elements of the knowledge may be associated with great uncertainty and/or may even be completely wrong. In such cases, a learning machine may be used to (a) automatically acquire new knowledge from domain experts, and (b) verify and modify the knowledge base. It is desirable to incorporate a learning machine into a practical expert system.

Several learning programs have been developed for use in expert systems. For example, by incorporating TEIRESCAS (Davis, 1977), MYCIN (Shortliffe, 1976) (see Section 1.8.2) can be used to acquire knowledge from experts interactively. A parameter adjustment method has been used for learning purposes in a program for playing checkers (Samuel, 1963). In the program for playing the checkers game, each factor (e.g. distance to the goal state and cost) is assigned an initial weight by the programmer. The learning process is accomplished by changing the weights.

An analytical comparison of certain rule-learning programs is given by Bundy *et al.* (1985). Two learning tasks, namely concept-learning and rule-learning are classified. A concept-learning program can be used to learn single concepts by forming a symbolic description of the target concept from examples and non-examples. It is then used for prediction (e.g. Winston, 1975; Young *et al.*, 1977). On the other hand, a rule-learning program is used to modify a set of rules (e.g. Mitchell *et al.*, 1981 and 1983).

SPERIL-3 is being developed on the bases of a preliminary version called CES-1. The system CES-1 has been programmed and is currently accessible on the engineering computer network at Purdue University. The learning machine is used here mainly to accomplish the following three tasks: (a) to learn new knowledge, (b) to verify the existing knowledge base, and (c) to modify the knowledge base. Further investigation is needed and currently underway to improve this system for practical applications.

11.4.2 Automatic knowledge acquisition

In the domain of the safety evaluation of existing structures, the behavior of structures can be so complex that certain damage phenomena have not yet been completely understood. For instance, after each major earthquake, there is often new knowledge to be gained on the behavior of damaged structures. Furthermore, the unique design of most structures makes the structural behavior design dependent. Moreover, there exists a barrier to effective communication between knowledge engineers and domain experts. Therefore, it is desirable to attempt the incorporation of a learning machine in expert systems for acquiring new knowledge from experts and users alike. The learning machine is designed to facilitate communication with experts and users in English concerning domain knowledge.

As mentioned earlier, the knowledge in SPERIL-3 is classified into several different categories and is represented by using frame-like structures. In the frame structure, information is represented explicitly. A frame consists of a set of slots that specify the expected objects and events and each slot has its own name and values. Each slot can also be defined by using another frame. In this way, complex knowledge may be represented by using a series of frames. In the frame structure, it is easy to add, delete, and modify slots. The learning procedure can be implemented by adding, deleting and/or modifying slots and corresponding values of prototypes in the knowledge base.

For example, during each application of damage assessment for a building, the machine may ask several questions for any new damage phenomena. If they are not already included in the knowledge base, the machine will put new knowledge into the knowledge base. When a new phenomenon is told, a new concept is introduced to the machine and a new subset is created in the knowledge base of the system. The learning machine asks the expert user about the relationship between the new subset and existing subsets. For example, the machine may ask the user/expert to determine which category the subset belongs to by using such links as AKO (a kind of) and ISA (is a) to connect them. The machine may also ask the possible reasons and causes of this damage phenomenon by using such links as REASON and CAUSES. If the node of this new phenomenon is not a primitive one in the inference network, its subsets will also be created. In this manner, this new phenomenon and the relationship between it and others may be defined. Meanwhile, the machine may ask for the importance of this damage phenomenon in its subcategory of damage or in global damage by estimating its weighting coefficient. Although the new knowledge as written by the machine may be rather rough, it can be improved continuously through the learning process.

Using this learning machine, it is possible for domain experts to build certain parts of an expert system by themselves even if they are not specialists in expert systems. For instance, the expert may ask the machine what categories of knowledge have been classified in SPERIL-3, and may ask the machine to describe the contents of each category. If the expert feels that it is necessary to add new knowledge to the knowledge base, he or she can introduce a new concept and put it into the machine by communicating with the learning machine using the computer terminal. After the expert introduces the new concept, the machine may ask questions for establishing relationships between the new concept and existing knowledge as described above. In any event, it is necessary for the expert to constantly monitor and evaluate the additional knowledge in order to decide that such modifications represent an improvement of the system as intended.

11.4.3 Knowledge verification and modification

There are two kinds of memory in SPERIL-3, namely short-term memory and long-term memory. The former is a working memory, in which information for current assessment is stored. The latter is used for storing historical records, which consist of two parts: historical records for each structure and historical records for the work of the expert system machine. The former will be used as a file for each structure. The latter is specially designed for the purpose of learning.

Through calibration between experts' and machine's assessments, each item in the knowledge base may be verified and modified. Two coefficients D_{si} and D_{vi} are defined as the degree of dispersity and degree of deviation respectively. The degree of dispersity D_{si} may be considered as a measure of the accuracy for the knowledge applied to the ith knowledge source, and the degree of deviation D_{vi} as a measure of the certainty factor for the ith knowledge source.

Knowledge modification is included in two aspects in this study. One is the revision of wrong knowledge and the other is to modify the weighting coefficients of corresponding knowledge sources. Those that appear to be good predictors of overall success (when both D_s and D_v are small) will have their weights increased. On the other hand, for the cases where D_s are found to be greater than some critical values, their weights will be decreased. Meanwhile, when the degrees of deviation D_v in certain parts of the knowledge sources are found to be greater than critical values, the knowledge of corresponding parts should be modified accordingly.

The experience of using a learning procedure in CES-1 shows that, when we deal with qualitative problems, the weight of each event depends not only on the knowledge source but also on the degree of quality. In real-world problems, it is reasonable to consider continuous-valued logic. In general, it is clear that if the rule $A \rightarrow B$ holds, it does not necessarily imply that the rule $\bar{A} \rightarrow \bar{B}$ also holds. As an example, foundation failure is a good predictor for structural failure. Thus, a large weight may be assigned in structural damage assessment when the foundation appears to be damaged. On the other hand, it is not easy to predict structural damage if little or no damage is found in the foundation. Consequently, it may be assigned a very small weight on such an assessment. As a result, different degrees of damage in the foundation may have different weight in the assessment of structural damage. Generally speaking, it is reasonable for the learning machine to use variable weighting functions rather than to use constant weighting factors. On the basis of this observation, a more reasonable and effective learning model with variable weighting functions is introduced in SPERIL-3.

Another way for verifying and modifying the knowledge in SPERIL-3 is through its explanation machine. The explanation machine performs the following tasks: (1) explains the reasons for each conclusion, (2) explains the reason for requesting additional information, (3) requests experts' explanations in order to modify its knowledge base. During each practical application of the expert system for damage assessment and safety evaluation, the expert may ask the machine to explain the need for this kind of information or its usage. The expert may also ask the machine to explain the solution or the reason for showing this result. To answer these questions, the explanation machine needs only to enumerate corresponding information which has been used in the previous step or will be used in the next step. For instance, if corresponding information is represented in rules, to answer 'How to get the result?' only needs moving one step backward. On the other hand, to answer 'Why?' needs moving one step forward. Similarly, in the frame structure moving from one slot (or frame) to another through the corresponding link will give the explanation. In fact, the explanation procedure is an enumeration of the corresponding part of the knowledge base and its inference procedure.

Through the checking of the explanation by experts, the knowledge base may be verified as well as modified by experts.

11.5 PRACTICAL IMPLEMENTATION

11.5.1 Identification of experts

To develop an expert system, it is necessary to perform the following tasks. First, the problem must be defined and identified. Second, the domain knowledge needs to be analyzed and the key concepts in the domain and the relationship between them need to be defined. In this manner, the knowledge may be organized and the problem may be formulated. More detailed tasks such as knowledge representation and inference making, choice of software and other tools may then follow. An initial implementation of an expert system may be developed on the basis of the above-mentioned tasks. In a large domain, such as the damage assessment of existing structures, knowledge is not well codified. Therefore, it is to be expected that the initial implementation of an expert system will be a rough approximation. Such a large knowledge base must be developed gradually and incrementally. The system needs much testing, extending and improving on a continuous basis. The refinement of a knowledge base plays a very important role in the development of a large expert system.

The procedure in the development of an expert system is essentially a process of transferring the domain experts' knowledge into the system. The most important goal of the development of an expert system is to obtain the high level of performance that a human expert achieves in performing the same task. Therefore, the identification of experts is the key to the successful development of a practical expert system. In fact, it is difficult to identify experts and their tasks in the domain of damage assessment and safety evaluation of existing structures. Different experts may use different methodologies, some even use different definitions and concepts. Especially in decision-making, they may use completely different strategies and apply different methods and rules. It may be extremely difficult to reach a consensus at times. The main difficulty lies in the fact that no unique answer exists in the case of a high-level expert task. Sometimes, only one assessment is made and the result is accepted without question or comparison. However, when several engineering experts or firms are involved, possibly because of allegation of liability and/or obligations to their respective clients, the resulting assessments are often conflicting (Leonards, 1982).

Consequently, the integration or combination of knowledge from different experts remains a challenge in the development of expert systems. To date, most expert systems incorporate knowledge from one expert. Some systems may incorporate knowledge from one major expert, then ask other experts to refine the knowledge base afterwards.

In practice, when a complex decision-making problem is involved, it is often reasonable and more reliable to ask different experts, in order to obtain different opinions. According to the different suggestions of the experts, one of them or a combination of them may be chosen for decision-making. Therefore, it is also desirable to take knowledge from different experts and put it into several separate parts in the knowledge base. Each may focus on one aspect of the problem or each deal with the same problem independently, such that the expert system may give different suggestions and explanations. The users who are capable of making their own decisions may use the system for consultation purposes and choose one according to their own experience and intuition. Meanwhile, the memory of the system may keep some historical records of different experts' decisions. With feedback comments and comparison results the identification of experts' knowledge may be performed.

11.5.2 Communication with experts

As mentioned earlier, a major difficulty lies in establishing effective communication between knowledge engineers and domain experts. Knowledge acquisition has been a bottleneck in the development of any practical expert system, which is not only time consuming but also difficult in establishing communication with experts.

It should be recognized that subjective knowledge and the experience of an expert imply a higher level of intellectual organization. To transfer this kind of knowledge into an expert system is a higher level of intellectual task, which is not a mechanical copy but a process of learning and comprehension of domain knowledge. Therefore, it is important to emphasize (a) the learning of the overall organization of knowledge, and (b) the acquisition of control knowledge about when and how to use certain facts.

Moreover, it should be recognized that most complex decisions are made in terms of experts' intuition and judgement. Knowledge in the damage assessment domain may be imprecise, incomplete and ill defined. It is often difficult for the domain expert to describe knowledge in terms that are precise and complete, and contain sufficient information for use in a computer program. Especially in the development stage of initial implementation of an expert system, the initial formalization of knowledge is usually too general for experts to criticize it. It may be easier for experts to suggest changes during a case study, especially when they find certain conclusions or explanations that are different from theirs. Therefore, it seems to be feasible for knowledge engineers to communicate with experts by incorporating a learning machine.

It is desirable to have both (1) knowledge engineers who have a basic background of domain knowledge and are willing to study the domain knowledge in some detail, and (2) domain experts who will find time to learn the fundamentals of knowledge engineering. Only with the collaboration of these two groups of experts may the required knowledge be acquired for the construction of practical expert systems.

11.5.3 Restriction of users

Although it is desirable to develop an expert system to perform the same high level of tasks as human experts, most current expert systems are developed to function as assistance or consultants to human experts. As mentioned earlier, in many real-world problems such as damage assessment, the decision is made in terms of experts' intuition, experience and judgement. It is still difficult to transfer this kind of knowledge into a computer program. In fact, the state of the art of computer technology for dealing with intuition remains to be further developed.

Consequently, some questions as asked by machine can be answered only by human specialists in the domain. As a result, it is reasonable and necessary to restrict users for different purposes of applications.

11.6 DISCUSSION AND CONCLUDING REMARKS

The development of SPERIL systems for damage assessment and safety evaluation of existing structures has been summarized and discussed in this chapter. Knowledge representation methods in expert systems and their application in SPERIL systems are discussed. It seems that the appropriateness of representation depends on the character of the knowledge and the specific application.

Several inference procedures as applied in SPERIL systems have been described. A linguistic assessment method and the basic concepts of fuzzy sets theory are introduced and briefly described. The decision-making method with uncertain and insufficient information is also discussed. More research work is needed to better understand the decision-making process with uncertain, imprecise, and insufficient information. There remains a bottleneck in knowledge acquisition for the development of a practical system, which is not only time consuming but also difficult in establishing communication with experts. A learning machine can be developed for automatic knowledge acquisition. Meanwhile, domain experts may interact with the knowledge bases and try to teach the computer system directly. Therefore, the system can be continually improved by learning important knowledge directly from both experts and its own 'experience'.

It must be recognized, however, that currently available learning systems work in a fixed manner as developed by the designer. In fact, such systems learn automatically only parts of knowledge. Although some low levels of learning have been incorporated in expert systems, the machine is not capable of learning in the same way as the human being. There are many difficult problems for both human and machine-learning to understand and to incorporate in practical systems. Much research work has been focused on understanding human learning and developing machine learning to date, and remains to be further developed. Machine learning will play a very important role in the development of large expert systems, which contain great amounts of knowledge. Therefore, it would be desirable to see a breakthrough in machine learning in the near future.

Due to space limitation, readers who are interested in obtaining a more detailed description of these systems are referred to the two technical reports by Zhang and Yao (1986a, 1986b). These reports will be available through the National Technical Information Service, 5285 Port Royal Road, Springfield, VA 22161.

ACKNOWLEDGEMENT

This investigation is supported in part by the National Science Foundation through Grant No. CEE 8412569.

REFERENCES

Aikins, J.S. (1983) Prototypical knowledge for expert systems. *Artificial Intelligence*, **20**, No. 2, 163–210.

Blockley, D.I. (1975) Predicting the likelihood of structural accidents. *Proceedings of the Institution of Civil Engineers*, London, UK Part 2, **59**.

Bresler, B. and Hanson, J.M. (1982) Damageability and reliability of existing structures, *Proceedings 9th US National Congress of Applied Mechanics, Cornell University.*

Bresler, B. (1985) State-of-the-art assessment, presented at *ABE Workshop on Earthquake Safety of Existing Hazardous Non-Federal Buildings.*

Brown, C.B. and Leonard, R.S. (1971) Subjective uncertainty analysis, presented at the *ASCE National Structural Engineering Meeting, Baltimore, Maryland*, Preprint 1388, pp. 19–23.

Brown, C.B. (1979) A fuzzy safety measure. *Journal of the Engineering Mechanics Division*, ASCE, 105, (EM5), 855–72.

Bundy, A., Silver, B. and Plummer, D. (1985) An analytical comparison of some rule-learning programs. *Artificial Intelligence*, **27**, 137–81.

Davis, R. (1977) Interactive transfer of expertise acquisition of new inference rules. *IJCAI*, **5**, 321–8.

Davis, R. (1980) Meta-rules: reasoning about control. *Artificial Intelligence*, **15**, 179–222.

Dempster, A.P. (1967) Upper and lower probabilities induced by a multivalued mapping. *Annals of Mathematical Statistics*, **38**, 325–9.

Hinkle, A., Watada, J. and Yao, J.T.P. (1986) Linguistic assessment of fatigue damage of welded structures, *Proceedings, 1986 Conference of the North American Fuzzy Information Processing Society, New Orleans,* Louisiana, pp. 200–24, June 2–4.

Ishizuka, M., Fu, K.S. and Yao, J.T.P. (1980) Inference method for damage assessment system of existing structures. *Report CE-STR-80-17*, School of Civil Engineering, Purdue University, Indiana, USA.

Ishizuka, M., Fu, K.S. and Yao, J.T.P. (1981) Inexact inference for rule-base damage assessment of existing structures, *Proceedings of 7th International Joint Conference on Artificial Intelligence*, pp. 837–42.

Ishizuka, M., Fu, K.S. and Yao, J.T.P. (1982a) Computer-based system for the assessment of structural damage, Invited Paper, *Proceedings IABSE Colloquium on Information in Structural Engineering, Bergamo, Italy*, pp. 89–98.

Ishizuka, M., Fu, K.S. and Yao, J.T.P. (1982b) An expert system for assessment of existing structures, Presented at *6th International Conference on Pattern Recognition, Munich, F.R. Germany*.

Ishizuka, M., Fu, K.S. and Yao, J.T.P. (1983a) Inference procedure under uncertainty for the problem-reduced method. *Information Science*, **28**, No. 3.

Ishizuka, M., Fu, K.S. and Yao, J.T.P. (1983b) Rule-base damage assessment system for existing structures. *Solid Mechanics Archives*, **8**, 99–118.

Leonards, G.A. (1982) Investigation of Failures, *Journal of the Geotechnical Division*, ASCE, **108**, No. GT2, 187–246.

Minsky, M.L. (1975) A framework for representing knowledge, in *The Psychology of Computer Vision* (ed. P.H. Winston), McGraw-Hill, New York pp. 4510–9.

Michell, T.M., Utgoff, P.E., Nudel, B. and Banerji, R. (1981) Learning problem-solving heuristics through practice, in *Proceedings of 7th International Joint Conference on Artificial Intelligence, University of British Columbia, Vancouver, BC*, pp. 127–34.

Michell, T.M., Utgoff, P.E. and Banerji, R. (1983) Learning by experimentation: acquiring and modifying problem-solving heuristics, in *Machine Learning* (eds R.S. Michalski, J.G. Garbonell and T.M. Mitchell) Tioga, Palo Alto, California, pp. 163–90.

Nilssion, N.J. (1980) *Principles of Artificial Intelligence*, Tioga, Palo Alto, California.

Ogawa, H., Fu, K.S. and Yao, J.T.P. (1983) *An Expert System for Structural Damage Assessment*, Technical Report CE-STR-83-33, School of Civil Engineering, Purdue University.

Ogawa, H., Fu, K.S. and Yao, J.T.P. (1984) *SPERIL*-II: *An Expert System for Structural Damage Assessment of Existing Structures*, Technical Report CE-STR-84-11, School of Civil Engineering, Purdue University.

Shafer, G. (1976) *A Mathematical Theory of Evidence*, Princeton University Press.

Shortliffe, E.H. (1976) *Computer-Based Medical Consultations: MYCIN*, American Elsevier.

Samuel, A.L. (1963) Some Studies in Machine Learning Using the Game of Checkers, in *Computer and Thought* (eds E.A. Feigenbaum and J. Feldman), McGraw-Hill, New York, pp. 229–47.

Simon, H.A. (1983) Why should machines learn?, in *Machine Learning* (Eds R.S. Michalski, J.G. Garbonell, and T.M. Mitchell), Chap. 2, Tioga, Palo Alto, California.

Toussi, S. and Yao, J.T.P. (1982/1983) Assessment of structural damage using the theory of evidence. *Structural Safety*, No. 1, 107–21.

Watada, J., Fu, K.S. and Yao, J.T.P. (1984) Linguistic Assessment of Fuzzy structure damage, *Report CE-STR-84-30*, School of Civil Engineering, Purdue University, Indiana, USA.

Winston, P.H. (1975) Learning structural descriptions from examples, in *The Psychology of Computer Vision* (ed. P.H. Winston), McGraw-Hill, New York.

Winston, P.H. (1984) *Artificial Intelligence*, Addison-Wesley, Reading, Massachusetts.

Yao, J.T.P. (1980) Damage assessment of existing structures. *Journal of the Engineering Mechanics Division*, ASCE, **106**, (EM4), 785–99.

Yao, J.T.P., Bresler, B. and Hanson, J.M. (1984) Condition evaluation and interpretation for existing concrete buildings, presentation at ACI 348/437 *Symposium on Evaluation of Existing Concrete Buildings, Phoenix, Arizona*, American Concrete Institute, Detroit, Michigan, USA.

Yao, J.T.P. and Fu, K.S. (1985) Civil Engineering applications of expert systems, *Proceedings of the 4th International Offshore Mechanics and Arctic Engineering Symposium Vol. II, ASME*, New York.

Young, R.M. Plotkin, G.D. and Linz, R.F. (1977) Analysis of extended concept-learning task, in *Proceedings 5th International Joint Conference on Artificial Intelligence, Cambridge*, Massachusetts, p. 285.

Zadeh, L.A. (1965) Fuzzy sets. *Information and Control,* **8**, pp. 338–53.

Zhang, X.J. (1985) Expert system for damage assessment of existing structures, in *Some Prototype Examples for Expert Systems* (ed. K.S. Fu), School of Electrical Engineering, Purdue University, Vol. 3, Chap. 14.

Zhang, X.J. and Yao, J.T.P. (1986a) *Methodologies for Safety Evaluation of Existing Structures – Literature Review*, Technical Report CE-STR-86-28, School of Civil Engineering, Purdue University.

Zhang, X.J. and Yao, J.T.P. (1986b) *The Development of SPERIL Expert Systems for Damage Assessment*, Technical Report CE-STR-86-29, School of Civil Engineering, Purdue University.

12

An expert system for earthquake intensity evaluation

XIHUI LIU and PEIZHUANG WANG

12.1 INTRODUCTION

One of the most important and common tasks in the domain of earthquake engineering and engineering seismology is earthquake intensity evaluation. Earthquake intensity is a yardstick for measuring the integrated effect and intensity of ground motion during an earthquake. After the occurrence of a strong earthquake, the first procedure to be carried out by seismologists in the field survey is to draw a picture of the intensity distribution in the affected region. A so-called earthquake intensity isoseismal map is made covering the area surrounding the epicentre of the event. Thus the evaluation of earthquake intensity at different districts must be carried out soon after the event occurs. These isoseismal maps are very useful in many respects. For example, they may show the damage grades to buildings and other engineering structures. They can also be used to study the mechanism of seismic origins, the attenuation rules of the ground motion effect, and so on. To delineate the isoseismals, it is necessary to carry out earthquake intensity evaluation from place to place in the affected areas.

Generally, earthquake intensity as a yardstick for measuring the effect of strong ground motion is expressed in the form of earthquake intensity scales. In these scales, the earthquake intensity is divided into several grades or degrees, for instance, 12 degrees in China. Due to the complex nature of ground motion and its effect, it is very difficult to give a clear manifestation to the effect of the attack by some physical parameters of ground motion. Up to the present, almost all the earthquake intensity scales in the world are expressed mainly by linguistic statements about the damage situation to buildings and other man-made engineering projects, the phenomenon of ground failure, and human reaction. Although some specific physical para-meters are given in certain earthquake intensity scales in relation to every degree, these parameters can only be used as secondary criteria for earthquake intensity evaluation. It is precisely for the above-mentioned reason that carrying out earthquake intensity evaluation is dependent on experts' experience and subjective judgement to a great extent. It is so important to incorporate specialists' expertise that a correct isoseismal map could not be given without it. Some methods have been developed for dealing with the fuzziness involved, including quantification of fuzzy concepts and fuzzy comprehensive evaluation. Perhaps the methodology and technique most applicable to the problem in hand is the knowledge-based expert system (KBES). This is the very reason why we chose earthquake intensity evaluation as the first item for creating an ES in the domain of earthquake engineering and engineering seismology.

In this chapter, the ES for earthquake intensity evaluation – EIE – is presented. The general framework of the system is constructed by employing the falling-shadow theory developed in recent years. The falling-shadow theory was used by authors for earthquake-induced damage forecasting in urban regions, and successfully applied to practical application for urban earthquake disaster mitigation planning of several cities in China. This time it is used as a powerful tool for comprehensive evaluation. The approximate reasoning approach is also incorporated in the system so as to handle the fuzziness involved. Since the earthquake intensity scale is described by the phenomena of several factors, EIE is divided into several modules. The knowledge base is written in four modules, one of which is related to a factor. Another module is for comprehensive evaluation. The modular structure of the ES makes the modifying of the rules in the knowledge base very easy.

In the following sections, the earthquake intensity scale of China is first introduced. Some methods for earthquake intensity evaluation are then reviewed in order to compare these procedures with that presented in this chapter. There follows a brief introduction to the falling-shadow theory. How to use it as a tool for comprehensive evaluation is also described. Finally, the detail of our EIE system is described, including a description of the treatment of uncertainties.

List of symbols

$\in$	Belonging to
μ	Membership function and falling shadow
η	Random set
ξ	Random set
α	Confidence of a rule
$\wedge$	Minimum
$\vee$	Maximum
Ω	Basic space

∋   Covering
σ   σ-field
ω   Element in Ω
⊂   Containment

12.2 EARTHQUAKE INTENSITY SCALE OF CHINA

There are two generations of earthquake intensity scale in China. The first is named the New China Earthquake Intensity Scale, and it was compiled in 1956 (Xie, 1957). It is one of the so-called macroscopic scales, characterized by expressions for damage to buildings and other engineering structures such as chimneys and earth dams, and the phenomenon of ground surface failure and human response. It does not have any quantitative parameters of ground motion. The second generation of earthquake intensity scale in China is named the China Earthquake Intensity Scale (1980), and it was compiled in 1980 by researchers of the Institute of Engineering Mechanics attached to the State Bureau of Seismology of China (IEM, 1980). Similarly to the first generation scale, it has twelve degrees. The principal difference between the two is that the latter gives two kinds of quantities in addition to macroscopic phenomena to depict every degree of intensity. One is the average damage index. Another is physical parameters of ground motion. The damage index is the quantification of damage grades of buildings, and the average damage index is the average value of those indices of buildings within a specified area (Survey Group for Tonghai Earthquake, 1977). The latter shows the general level of building damage during an earthquake. Zero is assigned to perfectly intact, while 1 is assigned to totally destroyed to the ground. The values between 0 and 1 may be given to intermediate grades of damage to buildings. Since the linguistic description of damage grades is vague and ambiguous, the authors have converted to fuzzy quantification by employing fuzzy numbers (Liu and Wang, 1984b). The physical parameters chosen to attach to every degree are acceleration and velocity of ground motion. However, ground motion records can rarely be obtained everywhere in the affected area, so those physical values given in the scale are mainly used for determining the design parameter values other than the earthquake intensity. However, it also constitutes one of the factors used for earthquake intensity evaluation.

According to the Chinese 1980 scale, a definition of earthquake intensity may be given as follows. Earthquake intensity is a measure of the intensity of ground motion at a specific spot during an earthquake; it shows the average level of ground motion intensity in a district. Attached to every degree are four indications. They include human response, building damage (as well as the average damage index), other phenomena (mainly ground surface failure), and physical parameters of ground motion (maximum acceleration and maximum velocity). All the macroscopic factors are described by linguistic statements, except physical parameters given a concrete value. Since people are concerned about those degrees which may cause disaster, the ES EIE is compiled to be used for degrees VI to XI. The following is an extract from the Chinese 1980 scale.

Human response

VI	panic-striken, escape in panic
VII	majority escape in panic
VIII	shaken, hard to walk
IX	unsteady sitting and standing, perhaps fall while moving
X	fall down from bike, thrown away to a meter while in unsteady condition
XI	(no description given)

Damage to buildings

VI	very slight damage, few with falling bricks and tiles, tiny crack on wall
VII	slight damage, damage to part, possible to live in
VIII	moderate damage, damage to load-bearing structure, repair needed
IX	severe damage, many cracks on wall, partial collapse, difficult to repair
X	collapse, majority destroyed, no means to repair
XI	devastating

Physical parameters (maximum acceleration is adapted here only)

VI	45–89 cm/sec^2
VII	90–177 cm/sec^2
VIII	178–353 cm/sec^2
IX	354–707 cm/sec^2
X	708–1414 cm/sec^2
XI	(not given)

In practice, seismologists and engineers make their evaluation of earthquake intensity not only according to so simple a scale, but also according to certain empirical rules. We have collected more than eighty samples of earthquake intensity evaluation made over the past decades for strong events that occurred in the mainland of China (Liu *et al.*, 1983). All the samples show that the rules, taking the damage situation as an example, embody not only a single level but also several levels of damage to buildings for the evaluation of a certain intensity. For example, an VIII degree district was delineated according to building damage by an empirical rule as follows: "none intact, only very few slightly damaged, a great many damaged to moderate or even severe level, a few collapsed or partially collapsed". The empirical rules for human response and ground surface failure phenomena are similar. Therefore the best way to carry out earthquake intensity evaluation incorporating most experts' experience in a consistent manner is to write down rules with respect to several factors and make an evaluation by approximate reasoning. In other words, an ES is most suitable for the problem. We will present a detailed discussion in the following section.

12.3 SOME APPROACHES TO EARTHQUAKE INTENSITY EVALUATION

In order to make earthquake intensity evaluation more logical and consistent, a number of approaches have been suggested. An overview of them is necessary, since the ES EIE is developed on the basis of these approaches.

The first approach to be mentioned is that proposed by the field survey group for the inspection of the Tonghai earthquake in 1970 (Survey Group for Tonghai Earthquake, 1977). The damage index $ind \in [0, 1]$ was first suggested by the researchers in that group. A few words on the damage index were given in the preceding section. For the purpose of carrying out an evaluation of earthquake intensity, samples of buildings within a specific region are collected and then to every sample a damage index in the interval $[0, 1]$ is assigned according to the damage level of that building. The average value of the damage index is then calculated and an evaluation is made according to this average value. The following ranges for the average damage index are used as a measure for intensity evaluation.

VI	0–0.1
VII	0.11–0.3
VIII	0.31–0.5
IX	0.51–0.7
X	0.71–0.9
XI	0.91–1.0

The shortcoming is obvious: a difference of 0.01 in the damage index can cause a difference of one degree in the earthquake intensity. For example, an average damage index equal to 0.5 means that the intensity is VIII; however, 0.51 belongs to IX. As shown in the preceding section, the acceleration value for structure design will be doubled when the intensity increases one degree. This means that a 1% increase in the damage index reflects a much stronger shaking with double acceleration. Obviously, this is not rational, and is unacceptable. The shortcoming is caused by the fact that we are dealing with fuzzy concepts by employing a crisp and distinct quantified method.

The fuzzy set theory first advanced by Professor L.A. Zadeh (Zadeh, 1965) was introduced by the authors to present the fuzzy earthquake intensity concept (Liu *et al.*, 1983). We have made a fuzzy quantification for damage grades of buildings. Analysis of more than 500 samples led to a series of fuzzy sets on the interval ind $\in [0, 1]$ for various damage grades, i.e. intact, slight damage, moderate damage, severe damage, partial collapse, and collapse (Liu and Wang, 1984b).

$$A = \text{(intact)}$$
$$= 1/0 + 0.91/0.05 + 0.7/0.1 + 0.42/0.15 + 0.2/0.2$$
$$A = \text{(slight damage)}$$
$$= 0.3/0 + 0.7/0.1 + 1/0.2 + 0.7/0.3 + 0.2/0.4$$
$$A = \text{(moderate damage)}$$
$$= 0.2/0.2 + 0.7/0.5 + 1/0.4 + 0.7/0.5 + 0.2/0.6 \quad\quad (12.1)$$
$$A = \text{(severe damage)}$$
$$= 0.2/0.4 + 0.7/0.5 + 1/0.6 + 0.7/0.7 + 0.2/0.8$$
$$A = \text{(partial collapse)}$$
$$= 0.2/0.6 + 0.7/0.7 + 1/0.8 + 0.7/0.9 + 0.2/1.0$$
$$A = \text{(collapse)}$$
$$= 0.1/0.8 + 0.42/0.85 + 0.7/0.9 + 0.91/0.95 + 1/1$$

The sign '+' stands for union, the numerator of each term stands for the membership function, and the denominator for the base variable index. On the basis of such an analysis, the fuzzy earthquake intensity concept was first put foward. By definition, earthquake intensity is a measure showing how strong the ground motion is. The measurement is made through the effect or consequence imposed on buildings and the ground surface by the ground shaking. All the effects and consequences are described by linguistic expressions. Thus fuzziness and ambiguity are caused by these noncrisp expressions. A more rational way of depicting earthquake intensity by the damage index is to give a fuzzy set taking ind $\in [0, 1]$ as the base variable, other than a crisp interval, for every intensity from VI to XI (Liu *et al.*, 1984c). The analysis of some 80 samples led to the results shown in Table 12.1.

The first step in evaluating earthquake intensity is to calculate $\hat{I}$ from the following equation:

$$\hat{I} = \sum_{i=1}^{6} m_i A_i \quad\quad (12.2)$$

where m_i is the percentage of buildings classified into the ith damage grade. The second step is to compare $\hat{I}$ with I shown in Table 12.1 and make an evaluation. A practical method for intensity evaluation, either by filling in some forms or by computer calculation, was presented in Liu *et al.* (1984a).

Regarding ground motion, taking PGA (peak of ground acceleration) as the base variable, for intensity degrees VI to X the fuzzy sets were also given in the model for urban planning (Liu *et al.*, 1984c). It reads as in Table 12.2: $\mu_I(a)$ is

Table 12.1 Fuzzy intensity (taking ind as base variable)

Intensity	ind $\mu_{\tilde{i}}$ 0	0.05	0.1	0.15	0.2	0.25	0.3	0.35	0.4	0.45	0.5	0.55	0.6	0.65	0.7	0.75	0.8	0.85	0.9	0.95	1.0
VI	0.55	0.86	1	0.86	0.55	0.26	0.09														
VII		0.09	0.26	0.55	0.86	1	0.86	0.55	0.26	0.09											
VIII					0.09	0.26	0.55	0.86	1	0.86	0.55	0.26	0.09								
IX									0.09	0.26	0.55	0.86	1	0.86	0.55	0.26	0.09				
X												0.09	0.26	0.55	0.86	1	0.86	0.55	0.26	0.09	
XI															0.09	0.26	0.55	0.86	1	0.86	0.55

Table 12.2 Fuzzy intensity (taking PGA as base variable)

VI		VII		VIII		IX		X		XI	
$\bar{x}$	c	$\bar{x}$	c	$\bar{x}$	c	$\bar{x}$	c	$\bar{x}$	c	$\bar{x}$	c
60	40	130	60	240	100	450	180	850	340	—	—

Note: The membership degree is calculated by

$$\mu_{\underline{l}}(a) = \exp(-(\bar{x} - a)^2/c^2)$$

the membership function of PGA($= a$), while $\bar{x}$ and c are two coefficients for calculating $\mu_l(a)$.

On the one hand, we use the earthquake intensity as a linguistic variable, and grades I, II, III,..., XII as its values, which are quantified terms standing for the expression of disaster such as catastrophic, devastating,..., strong,..., and fuzzy sets of damage index ind and PGA as shown in Tables 12.1 and 12.2 as its word meaning defined by fuzzy set theory. On the other hand, a determined value of damage index refers to several degrees of intensity with different membership function, that is, a fuzzy set of intensity degree. We can also construct a fuzzy set similar to this for a determinate value of PGA. For the purpose of engineering use, the universe of discourse is the set $Z = \{$VI, VII, VIII, IX, X, XI$\}$. A fuzzy set of intensity degree reads as

$$\underline{I} = \sum_{j=\text{VI}}^{\text{XI}} \mu_{\underline{l}}(I_j)/I_j \tag{12.3}$$

where $\mu_{\underline{l}}(I_j)$ is the membership function of intensity I_j. This is the very point which lays the foundation of our system.

Professor Wang (1984) has presented an alternative approach for earthquake intensity evaluation. This approach is based on multiple-stage comprehensive evaluation, which was first developed by the second author of this chapter.

Suppose the evaluation of earthquake intensity is determined by the factors $U = \{u_1, u_2, u_3, ..., u_m\}$, which can be clustered into several categories. For instance, for $U = \{U_1, U_2, U_3, U_4\}$, U_1 may involve those values of average damage indices calculated from collected samples of buildings, chimneys, and other engineering structures, U_2 may involve the peak values of horizontal and vertical components of acceleration, velocity and other ground motion parameters, U_3 may involve magnitude, distance to epicentre and other geophysical parameters, and U_4 may involve human response, ground surface failure and other phenomena. The first stage of fuzzy comprehensive evaluation leads to the results $\underline{B}_k$, $k = 1, ..., 4$.

$$\underline{B}_k = \underline{A}_k \circ \underline{R}_k \tag{12.4}$$

$\underset{\sim}{R}_k$ is the fuzzy relation matrix, every element of which is determined by given rules.

$$\underset{\sim}{R}_k = \begin{bmatrix} r_{k1}^1 & r_{k2}^1 & \cdots & r_{k6}^1 \\ \vdots & \vdots & \ddots & \vdots \\ r_{k1}^s & r_{k2}^s & \cdots & r_{k6}^s \end{bmatrix} \tag{12.5}$$

s is the total number in the factor group U_k. The number 6 stands for the total number of degrees concerned, VI to XI. r_{ki}^j represents the membership function of the factor u_k^j which expresses to what degree the earthquake intensity under judgement belongs to degree i from the point of view of factor $u_k^j \cdot \underset{\sim}{A}_k$ is called the factor fuzzy vector, which may be given by considering what an important role the factor plays in the evaluation process. The sign $\circ$ represents the algorithm selected. It may be adopted as $(\wedge, \vee)$, $(\cdot, \vee)$, $(\cdot, +)$, etc., where $\wedge = \min$, $\vee = \max$, $\cdot = $ arithmetic multiplication, $+ = $ arithmetic addition. The second stage of evaluation is then carried out as

$$\underset{\sim}{B} = \underset{\sim}{A} \circ \underset{\sim}{R} = \underset{\sim}{A} \circ \begin{bmatrix} \underset{\sim}{A}_1 \circ \underset{\sim}{R}_1 \\ \underset{\sim}{A}_2 \circ \underset{\sim}{R}_2 \\ \underset{\sim}{A}_3 \circ \underset{\sim}{R}_3 \\ \underset{\sim}{A}_4 \circ \underset{\sim}{R}_4 \end{bmatrix} \tag{12.6}$$

According to Equation 12.4 every row $\underset{\sim}{B}_k$ means a fuzzy set on universe Z. Now the fuzzy factor vector $\underset{\sim}{A}$ is given from the viewpoint of what an important role the kth factor group plays in the evaluation process.

The falling-shadow theory (Wang, 1986) also provides an effective method for comprehensive evaluation, especially for synthesizing experts' opinions on certain problems. A detailed discussion will be given in the following section.

12.4 FALLING-SHADOW THEORY AS A TOOL FOR COMPREHENSIVE EVALUATION

The falling-shadow theory provides one method to construct the membership function by set-valued statistical experiments, especially those including psychological factors. The authors have used it for urban earthquake-induced disaster forecasting (Liu *et al.*, 1985).

The falling-shadow theory is now being employed for the creation of expert systems by our colleagues for the diagnosis of trouble in aircraft engines (Zhuang and Zhuang, 1986). We use it here as a tool for conducting fuzzy comprehensive evaluation.

In classical statistics, each trial yields a precise point in the phase space (the set of possible results of observations). If each trial yields a crisp or fuzzy set in the phase space, we call it set-valued statistics. On the basis of a duality relationship between classical statistics and set-valued statistics, the falling-shadow theory was established.

In classical statistics, an event A is a fixed subset in the basic space Ω, while any experiment has an outcome ω that varies randomly in Ω. The probability of A, $P(A)$, is the frequency of ω falling in A. In set-valued statistics, the result of an experiment is a crisp (or not) set A^* in the universe of discourse U. Now, given a fixed point u_0 in U, the falling shadow of u_0 is the frequency of random set A^* covering u_0. The duality relationship between classical and set-valued statistics is shown in Fig. 12.1. In the case of classical statistics (Fig. 12.1(a)), event A is fixed while element ω is moving. In the case of set-valued statistics (Fig. 12.1(b)), element u_0 is fixed, while random set A^* is moving. If we define

$$\dot{u} = \{A^* \subset \mathscr{P}(U) \,|\, A^* \ni u\}, \quad (u \in U) \tag{12.7}$$

and

$$\dot{U} = \{\dot{u} \,|\, u \in U\} \tag{12.8}$$

where $\mathscr{P}(U)$ is the power set of U, $\ni$ means 'contain' and $\in$ 'belong to', so obviously $\dot{u}$ is a set of sets A^* on U, which contains u. Taking $\mathscr{P}(U)$ as the universe of discourse, then A^* becomes a point in $\mathscr{P}(U)$. Given a specific point u_0 in U, then $\dot{u}_0$ corresponds to a cycle in $\mathscr{P}(U)$. In the case of set-valued statistics, the random set A^*, now a randomly moving point, either falls in the cycle $\dot{u}_0$ or not. The frequency of set A^* covering u_0 is now transformed into the frequency of a point falling in cycle $\dot{u}_0$. So a set-valued statistical model on U can be transformed into a classical statistical model on $\mathscr{P}(U)$.

Given a σ-field $\mathscr{\check{B}}$ containing $\dot{U}$ on $\mathscr{P}(U)((\mathscr{P}(U), \mathscr{\check{B}})$ is a measurable space), then the measurable mapping from a probability field $(\Omega, \mathscr{F}, P)$ to $(\mathscr{P}(U), \mathscr{\check{B}})$

$$\xi : \Omega \rightsquigarrow \mathscr{P}(U) \tag{12.9}$$

is a random variable in the case of set-valued statistics. Obviously, ξ is a random set on U.

Let

$$\mu_\xi(u) = P(\{\omega \,|\, \xi(\omega) \in \dot{u}\})$$
$$= P(\{\omega \,|\, \xi(\omega) \ni u\}) \quad (u \in U) \tag{12.10}$$

$\mu_\xi(u)$ is called the falling shadow of ξ.

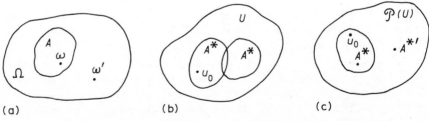

Fig. 12.1 Duality relationship between classical and set-valued statistics.

Suppose that two random sets $\xi:\Omega \rightsquigarrow \mathscr{P}(X)$ and $\eta:\Omega \rightsquigarrow \mathscr{P}(Y)$ are given, then

$$\mu_{(\xi,\eta)}(x, y) = P(\{\omega \mid \xi(\omega)\ni x, \eta(\omega)\ni y\}) \tag{12.11}$$

is called the joint falling shadow. Suppose that $\mu_\xi > 0$, then

$$\mu_{(\eta|\xi)}(y\,|\,x) = P(\eta(\omega)\ni y \,|\, \xi(\omega)\ni x) \tag{12.12}$$

is called the conditional falling shadow of η given $\xi \ni x$.

Let

$$\bar{m}(\xi) = \int_X \mu_\xi(x)m(\mathrm{d}x) \tag{12.13}$$

where m is a positive measure on the measurable space $(X, \mathscr{B})$. The meaning of $\bar{m}(\eta\,|\,\xi\ni x)$ is similar.

The formula for the marginal falling shadow

$$\mu_\eta(y) = \int_X \mu_{(\xi,\eta)}(x, y)m(\mathrm{d}x)/\bar{m}(\xi\,|\,\eta\ni y) \tag{12.14}$$

always holds, if every term exists. And the total falling-shadow formula

$$\mu_\eta(y) = \int_X \mu_\xi(x)\mu_{(\eta|\xi)}(y\,|\,x)m(\mathrm{d}x)/\bar{m}(\xi\,|\,\eta\ni y) \tag{12.15}$$

also always holds, if every term exists. Now let us move to employing these formulae for earthquake intensity evaluation. As shown in Fig. 12.2, on axis x are factors selected to be used to carry out the evaluation, while on axis y are earthquake intensity degrees. To every inspected district during the field survey after a strong attack each expert may assign a crisp (i.e. an interval) or

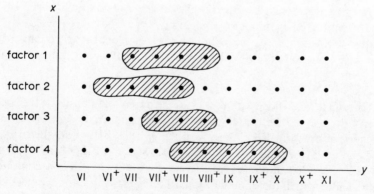

Fig. 12.2 Example of intensity evaluation.

fuzzy set for earthquake intensity from every influential factor. In this case, every set covers only a factor, so it may be viewed as a conditional falling shadow $\mu_{(\eta|\xi)}(y|\xi \ni x)$. The marginal falling shadow $\mu_\xi(x)$ may now be viewed as a weight factor to synthesize the conditional falling shadow to yield the total falling shadow $\mu_\eta(y)$. Thus the problem of earthquake intensity evaluation is threefold. First, we construct the conditional falling shadow $\mu_{\eta|\xi}(y|\xi \ni x)$, which is a fuzzy set similar to that shown in Equation 12.1. It is an evaluation result from each factor. Second, comprehensive evaluation is implemented by integrating as shown in Equation 12.15. And third, determinate evaluation is conducted according to the given criterion. For example, we might take the degree with the maximum membership function as the finally determined result.

12.5 AN ES FOR EARTHQUAKE INTENSITY EVALUATION (EIE)

ES development is one of the most practical branches of Artificial Intelligence (AI). Although development of ES has a relatively short history, its applications to some fields have shown its power capacity and great potential for problem-solving. But the application of ES to engineering seismology and earthquake engineering is only at its initial stage (Furuta *et al.*, 1985). The Expert System for Earthquake Intensity Evaluation (EIE) is written in PROLOG. In order to make it useful at different levels of organization, EIE has developed on an IBM PC/XT or AT. Thus the language used is a version of micro-PROLOG suitable for personal computers.

The knowledge representation form used in developing EIE is the production system. The knowledge is encoded in a series of rules of the general form:

IF (antecedent) THEN (consequence)

The antecedent may also be called the situation or condition, which is several propositions linked by the logic conjunction AND. The consequence may also be called the action; any proposition in the antecedent may perhaps be the consequence of another part of the rule. So all the rules constitute a reasoning tree.

The system EIE uses a goal-driven (backward-chaining) inference mechanism. Users first raise the question: what is the degree of intensity at the specific district? Because of the simple nature of our problem, a depth-first search strategy is adopted in EIE. As shown in Fig. 12.3, EIE is organized in five modules, four factor conditional falling-shadow modules (FM) and a synthetic total falling-shadow module (JM). Every FM module yields a conditional falling shadow, then all the conditional falling shadows are synthesized in module JM, and a judgement is made to give a final answer to the question –

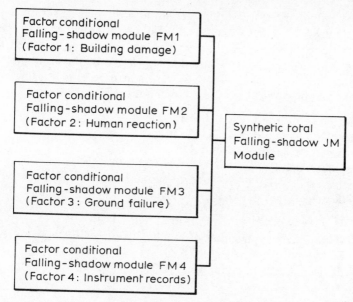

Fig. 12.3 Framework of EIE.

what is the degree of intensity? Four factors are adopted for the evaluation. They are the situation of the building (included in module FM1), human reaction (included in module FM2), ground surface phenomena (included in module FM3), and instrument records (included in module FM4). The factor conditional falling-shadow module for buildings situation FM1 will be described in more detail. The principle for writing other FM modules is the same.

The elements concerning the buildings situation are (1) the type of buildings classified from the point of view of their earthquake resistance capacity, (2) the damage grades and (3) the percentages of buildings damaged in each grade.

The intensity of ground motion can be reflected through the damage situation of engineering facilities, especially that of buildings. The damage level of a building is affected by many factors. It is not only the intensity of ground motion that plays an important role, but also the frequency content, duration, area covered by principal pulses, etc. have an influence on the damage level of buildings. However, in implementing earthquake intensity evaluation, only the overall and synthetic effect is taken into consideration. Thus the damage situation of buildings in a specified area may be taken as a yardstick for indicating the overall and synthetic effect of ground motion. However, it should be pointed out that the earthquake resistance capacity of buildings cannot be ruled out. In the description of compilation of the China Earthquake Intensity Scale (1980) the expression given for the word 'building' is – 'all buildings in the scale are those without earthquake resistant construction measures'. Nowadays, almost all buildings in seismic activity areas are designed according to an earthquake resistant design code or strengthened according to some criterion. Thus buildings should be classified into several categories in accordance with their earthquake resistance capacity. For example, buildings may be classified as follows:

1. Earthquake resistant designed (VII)
2. Earthquake resistant designed (VIII)
3. Earthquake resistant designed (IX)
4. Strengthened (VII)
5. Strengthened (VIII)
6. Strengthened (IX)
7. Others

The seventh category includes all buildings without earthquake resistant design and without strengthening.

The damage grades of buildings are often divided into:

1. Intact
2. Slight damage
3. Moderate damage
4. Severe damage
5. Partial collapse
6. Collapse

Sometimes, grade 5 – 'partial collapse' – and grade 6 – 'collapse' – are merged into one – 'collapse' only. In EIE, six grades are adopted.

The number of buildings damaged to various levels is given by linguistic expression. A large number of documents on field surveys after strong earthquakes have been summarized. The linguistic expressions most frequently used are:

1. Almost total
2. The overwhelming majority
3. A great number
4. Nearly half
5. A part
6. A small number
7. A few
8. None

For the purpose of practical use, the universe of discourse is taken as:

$$U = \{VI, VI^+, VII, VII^+, VIII, VIII^+, IX, IX^+, X, X^+, XI\} \quad (12.16)$$

We can now write down a series of rules relating to earthquake intensity evaluation from the point of view of damage to buildings according to experts' experience. A few examples are given here:

"A small number of buildings not designed according to earthquake resistant code and not strengthened collapsed, a part of them severely damaged or even partly collapsed, nearly half of these buildings damaged to moderate level, only a few intact or slightly damaged; the earthquake intensity is then most possibly to be VIII, but also possibly to be VIII^+ or VII^+, even sometimes to be considered as VII or IX."
"Buildings not strengthened and designed earthquake-resistant, a great number intact, a small number slightly damaged, only a few damaged to moderate level; the earthquake intensity is then most possibly VI, but sometimes may be considered VI^+, or even VII."

PROLOG has only three kinds of statements which read thus:

$$p_0 \leftarrow p_1, p_2, \ldots, p_m$$
$$p_0 \leftarrow$$
$$? - p_1, p_2, \ldots, p_t$$

The first statement is a formal expression of the rule 'IF p_1 and p_2 and $p_3 \ldots$ and p_m THEN p_0', p_j stands for a proposition. All rules given by linguistic expressions such as the examples shown above may be transformed into the form of a first statement. The second statement represents a known fact which may be an input datum or already stored in the program. The third statement is a question, the answer to which will prove whether the propositions p_1, $p_2, \ldots, p_t$ are true.

All rules given in a linguistic manner such as these examples may be translated into a statement $p_0 \leftarrow p_1, p_2, \ldots, p_m$. But the uncertainty about facts and rules should be discussed here before we give concrete examples. One kind of uncertainty is raised by an incomplete matching between propositions in the rule and input fact. For example, one of the damage grades of buildings in a district may not be classified for certain into the grade 'severe damage' or 'partial collapse'. Perhaps it is more rational to attach a certain membership function to it when a classification is made. A similarity may be found in those cases where building kind and building quantity are being matched. It is possible that some buildings in a specified district are strengthened to the so-called degree VII of intensity. It means that the capacity of these buildings to resist earthquake attack is so strong that they will be damaged only to a slight extent during an earthquake registered as degree VII. However, the quality of construction often varies to a great extent. In this case, it is perhaps more rational to classify them into a category 'strengthened (VII)' with a certain membership function and also into a category 'not strengthened' with another membership function as well.

Another kind of uncertainty is caused by the confidence that a rule possesses. For example, the rules presented previously expressed the fact that the experience of experts also possesses ambiguity. The collected facts cannot determine a degree of intensity with full confidence, but to a certain degree of confidence only.

Hence the rule in the form

$$p_0 \leftarrow p_1, p_2, \dots, p_m \qquad (12.17)$$

should be written in the form

$$p_0(b) \overset{\alpha}{\leftarrow} p_1(a_1), p_2(a_2), \dots, p_m(a_m) \qquad (12.18)$$

$a_1, a_2, \dots, a_m \in [0, 1]$ are membership functions of the proposition p_j when matching is made with the input fact, α is a real number in the interval $[0, 1]$, which stands for the confidence attached to this rule. The value of b is determined by a given function of $\alpha, a_1, \dots, a_m$, that is

$$b = f(\alpha, a_1, a_2, \dots, a_m) \qquad (12.19)$$

The function f is given according to the rules for different facts, but all the functions given result in a value of $b \in [0, 1]$. What does the value b mean? If p is a proposition 'intensity is $(x, b)'$, $x = $ VI, VI$^+, \dots,$ IX$^+$, X, X$^+$, XI, then b is the value of the falling shadow (here the conditional falling shadow resulting from a specified factor) over the base variable. All the rules in a module FM yield a conditional falling shadow from only one factor of that module. Finally, four conditional falling shadows are obtained by FM1, FM2, FM3, and FM4.

fs1 (A11, A12, A13, A14, A15, A16,
      A17, A18, A19, A110, A111)
fs2 (A21, A22, A23, A24, A25, A26,
      A27, A28, A29, A210, A211)
fs3 (A31, A32, A33, A34, A35, A36,
      A37, A38, A39, A310, A311)
fs4 (A41, A42, A43, A44, A45, A46,
      A47, A48, A49, A410, A411)

Some examples of input are shown as follows:

i intact $(X, A) \leftarrow$ print (intact: please input the quantity:), read (X),
          print (please give the membership degree:) read (A), replace $(i$, intact
          $(X, A) \leftarrow)$
i   collapse $(X, A) \leftarrow$ print (collapse: please input the quantity:), read (X), print
          (please give the membership degree:), read (A), replace $(i$, collapse
          $(X, A) \leftarrow)$
i   building-kind $(X, A) \leftarrow$ print (please input the building kind:), read (X), print
          (please give the membership degree:), read (A), replace $(i$, building
          kind $(X, A) \leftarrow)$

where i is the number of that statement in that module. If the input for the first statement is 'nearly half' (quantity) and 0.92 (confidence), then after being executed, the statement will be changed as

intact (nearly half, 0.92) ←

And if the input for the second statement is 'a few' and '0.84', then it will be changed as

collapse (a few, 0.84) ←

The synthetic total falling-shadow module will then make the last evaluation from Equation 12.15.

$$
\begin{aligned}
&m(A01, A02, A03, A04, A05, A06, A07, A08, \\
&\quad A09, A010, A011) \leftarrow \text{fs1}\ (A11, A12, A13, \\
&\quad A14, A15, A16, A17, A18, A19, A110, A111), \\
&\quad \text{fs2}\ (A21, A22, A23, A24, A25, A26, A27, A28, \\
&\quad A29, A210, A211),\ \text{fs3}\ (A31, A32, A33, A34, \\
&\quad A35, A36, A37, A38, A39, A310, A311),\ \text{fs4} \\
&\quad (A41, A42, A43, A44, A45, A46, A47, A48, A49, \\
&\quad A410, A411),\ \text{sum}\ (A11, (A21, A31, A41), \\
&\quad A01),\ \text{sum}\ (A12, (A22, A32, A42), A02), \ldots \\
&\quad \ldots, \text{sum}\ (A110, (A210, A310, A410), A010), \\
&\quad \text{sum}\ (A111, (A211, A311, A411), A011)
\end{aligned}
$$

m is the total falling shadow calculated from fs1, fs2, fs3, fs4,. For the sake of simplicity, we use an equally distributed margin falling shadow. Then we can find the $A0$ with maximum membership function from the following statement.

$$
\begin{aligned}
&b(Z) \leftarrow m(A01, A02, A03, A04, A05, A06, A07, \\
&\quad A08, A09, A010, A011),\ \text{mg}\ (A01, (A02, A03, \\
&\quad A04, A05, A06, A07, A08, A09, A010, A011), Z)
\end{aligned}
$$

Finally, the evaluation is made by some such statement as:

$$
\begin{aligned}
&w(X) \leftarrow b(Z), m(A01, A02, A03, A04, A05, A06, \\
&\quad A07, A08, A09, A010, A011),\ \text{eq}\ (Z, A02),\ \text{let} \\
&\quad (\text{intensity} - \text{VI}^+, X)
\end{aligned}
$$

To run the program, the user may input the question as:

$$? \leftarrow w(X),\ \text{print (the earthquake intensity} = X)$$

where 'let' is an interior predicate which means 'giving value to', and 'eq' means 'equal to'. 'sum' is a defined external predicate which sums all the elements.

$$\text{sum}(X), (Y|Z), \ T) \leftarrow \text{add}(X, Y, X1),$$
$$\text{sum}(X1, Z, T)$$
$$\text{sum}(X, (\ ), X) \leftarrow$$

'add' is an interior predicate which makes the sum of two variables. 'mg' is also an exterior predicate which finds the maximum of a group of numbers.

$$\text{mg}(X, (Y|Z), X1) \leftarrow \text{ge}(X, Y), \text{mg}(X, Z, X1)$$
$$\text{mg}(X, (Y|Z), X1) \leftarrow \text{mg}(Y, Z, X1)$$
$$\text{mg}(X, (\ ), X) \leftarrow$$

'ge' means 'equal to or greater than'.

At present, the program is written by PROLOG using English predicates, but we plan to develop a new version using PROLOG with Chinese characters.

12.6 CONCLUSION

The Expert System Earthquake Intensity Evaluation is an attempt to introduce ES techniques into the field of earthquake engineering seismology. There are many problems in this domain which need experts' experience for their solution. Among these may be listed the following: the determination of seismic origin areas for seismic hazard analysis according to seismogeological evidence in the vicinity surrounding the construction site, judgement on the possibility of the liquefaction of saturated sandy site-soil for seismic micro-zonation, preliminary design of earthquake-resistant structures, appraisal of the seismic environment for a city's development planning, and so on. It may be expected that some expert systems for practical use will emerge. The ES EIE presents a general framework for expert system compilation by using fuzzy set theory. It is only a prototype at this stage. Some problems, such as the treatment of uncertainty, and the dependent relationship between the influence of factors, need more investigation. Efforts will focus on approximate reasoning in our future work.

REFERENCES

Furuta, H., Fu, K.S. and Yao, J.T.P. (1985) Structural engineering applications of expert systems. *Journal of Computer-aided Design*, **17**, No. 9, 410–19.

IEM Report (1980) Earthquake Intensity Scale (in Chinese), Institute of Engineering Mechanics, State Bureau of Seismology, Harbin.

Liu, X.H., Wang, M.M. and Wang, P.Z. (1983) Fuzzy earthquake intensity (in Chinese). *Journal of Earthquake Engineering and Engineering Vibration*, **3**, No. 3, 62–75.

Liu, X.H. and Wang, M.M. (1984a) Practical method for evaluation of fuzzy earthquake intensity (in Chinese). *Journal of Seismological Research*, **7**, No. 3, 335–49.

Liu, X.H. and Wang, M.M (1984b) Fuzzy quantification of earthquake-caused structure damage grades (in Chinese). *Journal of North China Earthquake Sciences*, **2**, No. 3, 9–16.

Liu, X.H., Wang, M.M., Dong, J.C. and Liu, J.W. (1984c) A tentative application of fuzzy set theory to damage prediction, *Proceedings of 8th World Conference on Earthquake Engineering, San Francisco*, Vol. 1, pp. 329–36.

Liu, X.H., Chen Y.P., Zhang, W.D. and Wang, P.Z. (1985) Quantity estimation of damaged buildings by employing falling-shadow Bayesian principle (in Chinese). *Journal of Earthquake Engineering and Engineering Vibration*, **5**, No. 1, 1–12.

Survey Group for Tonghai Earthquake (1977) Intensity Distribution and Site Influence of Tonghai Earthquake (in Chinese), *Reports on Earthquake Engineering*, Publishing House of Sciences.

Wang, G.Y. (1984a) Two-stage comprehensive evaluation of earthquake intensity (in Chinese). *Journal of Earthquake Engineering and Engineering Vibration*, **4**, No. 1, 12–19.

Wang, P.Z. (1984b) *Fussy Set Theory and Its Application* (in Chinese), Publishing House of Shanghai Technology and Sciences.

Wang, P.Z. (1986) *Fuzzy Sets and Falling-Shadow of Random Sets* (in Chinese), Publishing House of Beijing Normal University.

Xie, Y.S. (1957) New China Earthquake Intensity Scale. *Journal of Geophysics*, 1.

Zadeh, L.A. (1965) Fuzzy sets. *Journal of Information and Control*, **8**, 338–53.

Zhuang, H.M. and Zhuang, F.M. (1986) Private communication.

13

A knowledge-based approach to engineering information retrieval and management

WILLIAM J. RASDORF and BRUCE R. WATSON

13.1 INTRODUCTION

The operation of a computer-aided engineering environment often depends on an organization's underlying databases which act as its information sources. Such databases routinely undergo dynamic change. Changes in a database schema commonly result from the evolution of a design, from changes in the design process itself, and from changes in other subsequent downstream processes. Such continuing changes must be reflected in the database schemas and they subsequently require that application programs be updated and that online users be educated on a continuing basis.

This chapter describes a knowledge-based database interface designed to help alleviate these problems. The interface attempts to capture the knowledge that experienced human users incorporate in their search for data in a database, i.e. it seeks to identify and use the generic knowledge needed to operate a database management system (DBMS) to retrieve data (Rasdorf and Watson, 1986). This knowledge is used by the interface to enable both the online users and the application programs to request data without knowing the data's exact location or precisely how to ask for it. Further, the interface makes use of optional SYNONYM relations that allow the user to request data without knowing the exact name by which it is stored in the database.

13.1.1 Scenario

The use of computers in civil engineering is commonplace and computer applications continue to grow in number. The use of integrated computer-aided design systems which incorporate knowledge-based expert systems (ESs), database management systems (DBMSs), and traditional numerical analysis tools is more recently emerging in response to the need to control information flow and to facilitate information management (Rasdorf and Salley, 1985). These systems can support a host of applications and users as Fig. 13.1 shows.

In an integrated environment, many users, both individuals and application programs, must have access to one or more of the organization's databases to provide, use, or modify data. A typical example is a design engineer who, working at a computer-aided design (CAD) workstation, must continually access and use data. In initial design stages, for example, he or she must establish structural configuration, geometry, and loading conditions. This information can then be used to analyze the structure to determine its forces, moments, and deflections. Simultaneously, project managers, mechanical engineers, electrical engineers and others are making design decisions, running application programs, and drawing upon the other resources they have in hand to complete the design process.

A similar scenario exists in a parallel and, in many ways, comparable design/construction environment – manufacturing. Suppose that a mechanical engineer has specifications for a new part to be designed. He or she must first check a design database to determine whether or not a similar part already exists. The materials database must then be checked to determine

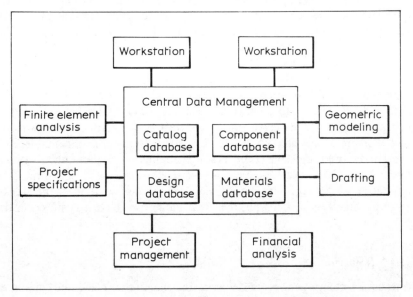

Fig. 13.1 General computer-aided engineering environment.

what materials are in stock that may be used to build the part. When the part is designed, it is added to the design database by inserting a new record describing the part into one or more of the database's relations. If the part being designed is the first of a new class of parts, a new relations will need to be added to the design database schema to represent the new class of parts.

These two examples illustrate the similarities between the processes of construction, manufacturing, and assembly. The ideas presented in this chapter, therefore, are as applicable to industrial, mechanical, and aerospace engineering as they are to civil and structural engineering.

13.1.2 Problem definition

One of the major problems facing engineering organizations is how to train personnel to use the proliferating number of computers and programs that are available for engineering computing. On a more limited scale, just teaching users how to use the various DBMSs that exists is a challenge since each has its own data definition language (DDL), data query language (DQL), and data manipulation language (DML). Many DBMSs even have a separate interface for application programs called the application program interface (API) which enables conventional programming languages to access the database. Because there are many databases that can be present in an engineering environment, it is a difficult task for an administrator to be familiar with the operation of all of them.

In addition to the difficulties associated with using database management systems, there are difficulties that are associated with structuring the information stored in databases. In design, for example, database schemas are often dynamic in nature; new structures, components, materials, catalogs, etc. must be incorporated as correctly and efficiently into the database as they are into the as-built structure. Users must be continuously informed of changes, application programs must be maintained, and the database administrator (DBA) must modify the various database schemas.

The problem to be addressed in this chapter is that it is difficult for designers and application programs to get the data that they need, when they need it, from the multiple heterogeneous DBMSs that have evolved in design and construction organizations. The diversity and dispersion of the participants in the building industry hinders a full integration of the knowledge embodied in the building process.

13.1.3 Problem solution

One solution to the problem of efficient, accurate data retrieval is to build a general interface between users and the many sources of data available to them (Lafue, 1983). This in itself is not a new suggestion; many researchers have addressed parts of this problem. In general, the interfaces that they have developed to date are best suited to environments where the structure of the database is static and does not change over time (Maher and Howard, 1985). What this chapter proposes that is different from existing work is an interface which handles the dynamic nature of design databases, enabling a designer to obtain the most accurate and up-to-date information as the structure and content of the underlying databases change. The designer should be able to simply specify his or her data needs and the interface should be able to interpret and satisfy those needs. To do so requires a knowledge-based approach (Parker, 1985). The structure of an ES designed to deal flexibly with engineering information needs is discussed in the following sections (Rasdorf and Parks, 1986).

13.2 BACKGROUND

As stated earlier, a number of researchers have addressed the problem of locating data that is stored in multiple heterogeneous databases. This section reviews some of the more prominent user–application–DBMS interface projects. Presented are a brief overview of KADBASE, Multibase, Mermaid, Serius-Delta, DAVID, IMDAS, FRED, and IISS. Similarities and differences between these systems are also discussed.

13.2.1 KADBASE

The KADBASE project (Howard and Rehak, 1985; Rehak and Howard, 1985; Rehak *et al.*, 1983 and 1984) at Carnegie–Mellon University is a recent investigation into the problem of interfacing users, application programs, and expert systems to a number of databases. The KADBASE architecture consists of three basic parts. The first part is the Knowledge-Based System Interface (KBSI). A KBSI module is attached to each process (where a process is an identifiable computing entity, such as a user terminal session or an application program) that wishes to access data that is stored somewhere in the system. The job of a KBSI module is to take the user's queries, process them into an intermediate internal query language, and send the reformulated queries to the Network Data Access Manager (NDAM), the second component of the KADBASE architecture. NDAM is the actual interface. NDAM receives queries from the requesting KBSI, uses a global schema to locate where in the system the data is stored, issues a local query to the Knowledge-Based Database Interface (KBDBI) in question to get the data, and coordinates the transfer of data back to the requesting process. The KBDBI is the third part of KADBASE. A KBDBI is attached to each DBMS in the system and acts as a front-end processor which takes queries from NDAM and reformulates them to meet the specific requirements of the DQL of the DBMS to which it is attached. Quite simply, it is a query translator.

In summary, KADBASE utilizes knowledge-based back-ends for the applications (KBSI), knowledge-based front-ends for the DBMSs (KBDBI), and a knowledge-based interface between applications and DBMSs (NDAM) that locates data using a global schema and an intermediate internal query language. Each front-end application can use its own query language as can each back-end DBMS. Translations, or mappings, are therefore made on both sides of the interface.

13.2.2 Multibase

The Computer Corporation of America has undertaken research on a project named Multibase (Smith *et al.*, 1981). There are two main components in the Multibase architecture, a schema design aid and a run-time query processing system.

The schema design aid is a tool used by one who is integrating a collection of databases into a common data source (this is typically a DBA function). The purpose of the schema design aid is to help the DBA build a global schema and to help him or her define the mappings between the local database schemas and the global schema.

The run-time query processing system takes user queries (called global queries) and maps them across the global schema to the local schemas. It decides how to access the data and it issues to the local DBMS, through the local DBMS's API, the commands for obtaining the data. Query optimization and resolution of database inconsistencies (such as data stored in more than one database or in different forms) is also performed by the run-time query processing system.

Multibase is designed primarily for network model databases. Multibase does not require front-end interfaces for the local DBMSs, nor does it require back-end interfaces for the processes. Unlike KADBASE, which uses a sequence (translator, interface, translator) of separate modules, Multibase does all of its translations and processing in a single module. It does, however, require that the local schemas be duplicated in the global schema and that users use a single, standard global query language known as DAPLEX.

13.2.3 Mermaid

The Mermaid project at System Development Corporation (Brill and Templeton, 1984) is another attempt to allow a user to access multiple heterogeneous databases. Mermaid is 'a front-end to relational DBMSs'. It utilizes a 'split architecture' in its implementation that is similar to the Multibase and the Serius-Delta architectures in that it is composed of a common user interface and a distributed back-end to handle the interface to the individual databases.

As with KADBASE and Multibase, Mermaid makes use of a global schema which replicates the local database schemas. This global schema is used by the Mermaid interface to map a global query to a particular local schema of an underlying database. Like Multibase, Mermaid makes use of a single input language for users called Ariel. It translates this user interface language into an intermediate language called DIL which is then translated into the local DBMS's DQL. One of the primary thrusts of Mermaid is the efficient implementation of queries across multiple heterogeneous DBMSs (where the DBMSs themselves may be capable of handling data distributed across multiple computers). Mermaid is designed to interface with the DBMSs even if they reside on different computers with different operating systems.

13.2.4 Serius-Delta

Serius-Delta (Esculier, 1984) is a project being conducted at INRIA in France. It permits data access via the use of a variety of query languages which are translated into an intermediate internal query language called PETAL. Serius-Delta also uses a global schema to map from a global PETAL query to a local query on an underlying DBMS. The Serius-Delta project is similar to the Mermaid project in that it acts as a front-end to multiple underlying DBMSs. Serius-Delta, however, does not place as much emphasis on query optimization as the Mermaid project, but it does permit multiple external query languages as KADBASE does and as the remainder of the survey projects discussed below do not.

13.2.5 DAVID

The Distributed Access View Integrated Database (DAVID) is a project under development at the National Aeronautics and Space Administration (NASA) (Jacobs, 1985). The DAVID project's intent is to provide an easy-to-use system through which one can uniformly access multiple distributed and/or heterogeneous databases. DAVID can be viewed as a DBMS of views which is built on top of already existing DBMSs. It therefore contains a global schema that is thought to be similar in nature to those discussed previously. Communication with the individual databases is through a common DQL system that is referred to as 'database logic'. DAVID's job is to perform the external-to-conceptual mappings and the query translations so that the user does not need to know where the data is located or how to physically access it.

13.2.6 IMDAS

The National Bureau of Standards (NBS) in Gaithersburg, MD and the University of Florida are developing the Integrated Manufacturing Database Administration System (IMDAS) (Barkmeyer *et al.*, 1986). IMDAS is a distributed interface which allows users to access distributed and/or heterogeneous databases. The interface itself is distributed over computer systems and is organized in a hierarchical structure. It is therefore neither fully distributed nor is it centrally controlled. NBS refers to it as a hybrid architecture.

IMDAS is designed to be used in Computer-Integrated Manufacturing (CIM) systems. In particular, it will be used in NBS's Automated Manufacturing Research Facility (AMRF). NBS chose a hybrid approach to facilitate a hierarchical architecture that is able to respond to the time-critical data requirements of the manufacturing processes while maintaining system-wide reliability. Its hierarchical distributed nature makes it an ideal candidate testbed for investigating computer-aided building design applications.

As with many of the other projects, IMDAS uses a global DQL. It also uses a global schema to help it find data in the distributed systems. A unique feature of the NBS approach is that the global schema is automatically generated during system startup. The local schemas are integrated into the next higher layer of the IMDAS hierarchy as the individual computers and programs which make up IMDAS (including the back-end databases) come on line. When all of the components which make up IMDAS are online, IMDAS has an integrated global schema similar to the global schemas used by the previously mentioned projects.

The distributed, hierarchical architecture of IMDAS enables it to run (in a degraded mode) while individual components are offline, thus maintaining IMDAS availability. A prominent feature of IMDAS is its ability to handle queries at as low a level as possible, i.e. to provide as direct a path to the data as possible. If a query is issued that requires access to a DBMS which resides on a local computer, IMDAS is able to obtain the required data from the local DBMS without passing the query up through the hierarchical control structure. This helps reduce network traffic and increase system reliability.

13.2.7 FRED

GTE Laboratories' Knowledge-Based Systems Department is developing a FRontEnd for Databases (FRED) (Jacobson *et al.*, 1986). A major thrust of the program is to create an Intelligent Database Assistant (IDA) that features a natural-language user interface.

FRED is implemented on a Xerox 1108 AI workstation and resides between the user and GTE Terminet medical information databases. The DBMSs that FRED is currently being interfaced with include Oracle, Focus, and ADR Dataquery. FRED consists of five major components: a Communication Monitor (CM), a Natural Language Processor (NLP), a Query Planner (QP), a Database Processor (DP), and the Domain Specific Knowledge Base (DSKB).

The CM is the component that controls the intermodule interactions and the user/FRED interactions. The NLP is responsible for parsing the user's input query into a form usable by FRED. The results of this step comprise the input to the QP which plans a virtual query. This virtual query (in a special language called V/DELPHI) is based on a universal relation view of the various databases that make up the entire system. This requires that FRED have access to a unified global representation of the various database schemas. Next, the virtual query produced by the QP is input into the DP. The DP is a translator that is responsible for generating a query in the target DBMS's own DQL. The last component of the FRED system is the DSKB. All of the knowledge used by the intelligent modules discussed above is located here.

13.2.8 IISS

The Integrated Information Support System (IISS) (Judson, 1986) is a US Air Force project that was begun in 1978. It is intended to be a generic system that deals with the problems of multiple heterogeneous computers with multiple heterogeneous DBMSs operating within the scope of a single business. IISS provides users with access to the multiple machines and DBMSs and attempts to make all of the machines and data appear to the user as a single machine containing all of the data in a single, uniform format. IISS is implemented with four major subsystems. These are the Common Data Model (CDM), the Network Transaction Manager (NTM), Communications (COMM), and the User Interface (UI).

The CDM and its processors are responsible for making the data residing on the distributed machines and DBMSs look as if the data were in a single database. This is accomplished with the aid of a 'conceptual schema' which is a composite of the local database schemas. The NTM is the message-passing coordinator of the IISS system. It is responsible for controlling the interactions and information flow between the IISS subsystems. COMM is the subsystem that allows the different machines in the IISS network to communicate. It uses an NBS/OSI architecture and supports both Manufacturing Automation Protocol (MAP) and Technical and Office Protocol (TOP). The UI is the subsystem that provides users with access to data anywhere it may reside in the system. It provides a virtual terminal facility and other utilities that aid the user in obtaining information from the various data management systems.

13.2.9 Summary and Comparison

The above descriptions present the similarities and differences between some of the recently developed DBMS interface systems. All but two of these efforts (KADBASE and Serius-Delta) require that the user learn and use a special-purpose global query language to communicate with the interfaces. Most of them perform a translation from the global query format into an internal query format to facilitate the mapping from a global schema to the local database schemas. Some even require a translation from application-dependent query formats to the global query format. Finally, each project depends on incorporating each local database schema into a single, common global schema which, unfortunately, results in schema duplication and its attendant consistency problems. The global schema is then used by the interface program to locate the data that the user has requested.

The primary difference between these systems and the Adaptive Database Interface (ADI) is that ADI is an attempt to capture the knowledge of an experienced DBMS user and apply that knowledge to find and retrieve the engineering data that the requester is seeking (Rasdorf and Watson, 1986). The goal of this investigation was to first determine what knowledge is required for a human user to operate a DBMS, and then to build a knowledge-based interface that emulates the human user. To do this, ADI must acknowledge the inherently dynamic nature of a database's schema and be able to respond to it. As such, ADI does not use a global schema and, therefore, it does not inherit the consistency problems that are just as inherent in duplicating a local schema as they are in duplicating data.

13.3 ADI OVERVIEW

The Adaptive Database Interface (ADI) is a knowledge-based database interface which attempts to satisfy engineering information needs in much the same way that a human expert would. A human expert at using databases understands how to access, interpret, and manipulate a database's schema and data. In particular, the expert knows how to use the schema to determine whether or not the required data exists in the database. Furthermore, the expert is able to make judgements about the naming conventions that the DBA has used in defining a database schema, enabling him or her to understand, for example that *beam* and *girder* are equivalent entities. A human expert will also be able to satisfy a user's query in a reasonably short period of time; this is one of the qualities that makes him or her an expert.

The key objective of the ADI research effort is to identify, formalize, and encode the knowledge that an expert uses to operate one or more DBMSs. However, the design of ADI has other goals as well as the capture of human knowledge. From a practical point of view, it is felt that ADI should acknowledge the dynamic nature of the local design database schemas. This precludes the use of a permanent global schema as a tool to locate entities in various local databases. If the local schema is dynamic, the duplication of schemas caused by use of a permanent global schema can result in system-wide inconsistency when a local schema is changed but the global schema is not correspondingly modified in a timely fashion. Maintaining system consistency in support of schema duplication places a very large workload on the DBA. ADI was therefore designed to eliminate the need for a permanent global schema.

ADI is layered software system that can grow in ability with successive enhancements. The first stage of the development of the system consisted of implementing the basic capabilities of query translation and naming convention hiding. The next stage of development will incorporate the more advanced capabilities of natural language processing, context sensitivity, and query abstraction.

13.3.1 Basic capabilities

The most basic capabilities that ADI must possess are the ability to translate and build queries and the ability to work properly without forcing users to know the naming conventions of the target database. With these functions in place, ADI is 'usable', and demonstrates the concepts on which it is built. These capabilities serve as a base on which the advanced capabilities can be built.

The query translation problem is twofold. First, ADI must be able to translate a user's query into its own internal format. Second, ADI must be able to translate a query from its internal format into the format of the target database's DBMS. ADI should have the ability to handle more than one target DBMS.

Hiding the database's naming conventions from the users is desirable because it frees them from having to contend with the exact names as they appear in the database. It allows the users to use names with which they are familiar rather than names that may have been arbitrarily selected by the DBA. ADI accomplishes this by using an optional SYNONYM relation in each database. If a SYNONYM relation exists for a given database, then ADI can consult it to define attributes from a user's query in terms of the actual names as they appear in the target database.

13.3.2 Advanced capabilities

In order for ADI to plan the order of search of the various databases that are available to satisfy a user's data request, it must possess a knowledge of semantic interpretation. This requires ADI to have natural-language processing abilities, the ability to solve queries in the context of the current query session, and the ability to break abstract queries into multiple, simpler queries.

Understanding natural language requires both syntactic and semantic knowledge of the language of choice and general world knowledge of the topic of interest (Rich, 1983). A natural-language understanding capability will enable ADI to decide where the required data resides: first by translating a user's English query to the relational algebra format of ADI, then by using the content of the translated query to interpret the request. In doing so, ADI will be able to determine that a user is asking for information about material properties, for instance, and will therefore look in the materials and design databases rather than look in the finance and personnel databases. A syntactic translation, therefore, proceeds a simple semantic interpretation. In this case it is assumed that there is a one-to-one correspondence between the items in the English query and the items in the relational algebra query.

Language can be said to be efficient. By efficient it is meant that the same expressions may be used over and over again by different people in different situations and at different times to mean different things (Barwise and Perry, 1983). This property may be referred to as the context of an expression. The ability to use the context of the current query session will allow ADI to further narrow its database search paths and to dynamically improve its own performance by filling in gaps in a user's query with information from his or her previous queries. For example, if the user's previous queries have been about material properties in the materials database, ADI might assume that the current query is about materials and use that assumption to complete a partially specified query. This will allow ADI to process incomplete queries in much the same was as a human expert rather than rejecting the queries or asking the user for more information.

Finally, ADI should have the ability to handle multiple levels of query abstraction (Vossen and Brosda, 1985). This will allow ADI to interpret the meaning of high-level queries such as:

What is the size of the pipe?

For queries such as this, ADI should be able to combine conceptual decomposition with context sensitivity to determine, for example, whether the user wants the physical length, the outside diameter, the weight, or some combination of these attributes that describe size. To do so requires that ADI first interpret the meaning of the query and then translate it into one or more relational algebra format queries that will enable it to satisfy the original query. A semantic interpretation must therefore be made before the correct syntactic translations can be generated. In this case the correspondence between the items in the English and relational algebra queries is a one-to-many rather than a one-to-one mapping.

13.3.3 Assumptions

A number of assumptions were considered and fundamental design decisions were made when developing the implementation plan for ADI. The most significant of these, relative to engineering data-management needs, are listed below.

- Commercially available DBMSs are to be used with no alterations or additions permitted.
- The introduction of ADI into a computing environment must not *require* the modification of previously existing application programs which access one or more of the DBMSs. In practice, products which require modification of existing programs meet with very low acceptance.
- Similarly, no interference with the actions of experienced users of the DBMSs is permitted. While ADI supplies users with a single common DQL, users who already know the DQL of an existing DBMS may prefer to continue to use the local DBMS directly. New users may prefer to use the single, common DQL supplied by ADI. In either case, the user's freedom of choice and the continuity of existing operations must be maintained.
- ADI must enable both new and experienced users to find and retrieve data without having to know where the data is stored locally or what its specific naming conventions are.
- Finally, ADI must have a minimal impact on the host organization's DBA. In particular, ADI should not introduce system-wide inconsistencies that the DBA will have to resolve on a continuing basis.

13.4 IMPLEMENTATION

The actual implementation of ADI is described in this section. Included are discussions of the computer system environment in which ADI currently operates, the relational DBMS model on which it is based, a portion of the database used to test ADI, the structure of the ADI interface between users and the computing environment, ADI's theory of operation, the methods ADI employs to build a variety of queries, and the current status of ADI.

13.4.1 Computer system environment

The target computer environment for which ADI is being developed consists of a Digital Equipment Corporation (DEC) VAXstation-II running the VMS operating system. ADI is written in three languages: FORTRAN, C, and OPS83 (Forgy, 1985). The initial target DBMS is Boeing Computer Service's Relational Information Manager (RIM) version 5.0 (Erickson *et al.*, 1981).

13.4.2 Relational Database Management System

The RIM DBMS is based on the relational data model (Date, 1981). Associated with the data model are a set of operators that perform the insertion, deletion, modification, and retrieval functions. These concepts are discussed briefly in the following sections.

(a) *The relational database model*

A data model defines the overall logical structure of a database (Ullman, 1980). It provides a structural framework into which the data is placed. A relational data model is a collection of interrelated relations represented in two-dimensional tabular form (Date, 1981) as shown in Table 13.1.

Table 13.1 is the TUBES relation from a structural engineering PIPING database. This table illustrates the structure of a relation. The rows of a relation are called tuples and its columns are called attributes. The domain of an attribute is the set of allowable values the attribute may possess. The values for attribute X_dim in Table 13.1 are drawn from the domain consisting of the set of positive real numbers. Each tuple represents an individual component and contains a value for each attribute. All tuples are distinct; duplicates are not permitted (Date, 1981). Tuples and domains have no order; they may be arbitrarily interchanged without changing the data content or the meaning of the relation. Tuples are accessed by means of a key which may be a single attribute or a combination of attributes that uniquely identifies a tuple.

A standard shorthand notation to represent relations is as follows:

RELATIONname (ATTRIBUTEname1, ATTRIBUTEname2,...)

with the TUBES relation of Table 13.1 being represented as:

TUBES (Size, X_dim, Y_dim, Wall_thk, Weight, Area, Ix, Iy),

The name of the relation is listed first followed in parentheses by the names of all of its attributes. The underlined attribute of a relation is the key.

The overall logical structure of a database is called its schema. When all relations have been defined and their attributes and associated properties specified the schema is completely defined. An introduction to relational databases using structural engineering examples was presented in Schaefer *et al.* (1984). Discussions of their role and incorporation into structural design systems are given in Fenves and Rasdorf (1982 and 1985).

Table 13.1 TUBES relation from the PIPING database

Size	X_dim	Y_dim	Wall_thk	Weight	Area	Ix	Iy
3 × 2	3.00	2.00	0.1875	5.59	1.64	1.86	0.98
4 × 2	4.00	2.00	0.1875	6.86	2.02	3.87	1.29
4 × 3	4.00	3.00	0.2500	10.50	3.09	6.45	4.10

Table 13.2 TEMP relation resulting from join operation

Pipe	Size	Length	Total_Force	Next_Pipe	X_left	X_right	Y_left	Y_right
P1	4	10.0	200.0	P2	0.0	10.0	0.0	0.0
P2	4	5.0	500.0	P3	10.0	10.0	0.0	5.0
P3	2	15.0	150.0	P4	10.0	25.0	5.0	5.0
P4	$\frac{1}{2}$	25.0	50.0	none	25.0	40.0	5.0	25.0

(b) *Relational DBMS operations*

The data insertion, deletion, and modification operations are part of the Data Manipulation Language (DML). These database manipulation functions have not yet been built into ADI. ADI uses the RIM Data Query Language (DQL) operators of Select and Join (Erickson, *et al.*, 1981).

The Select operator is used to selectively display data from a single relation that meets the selection criteria. The criteria are represented in the Select command by boolean predicates in a where clause. All tuples in the relation for which the where clause evaluates to true are retrieved. As an example, suppose that the TUBES relation from the structural engineering database of Table 13.3 is to be queried. The designer wants to know which tubes have a wall thickness that is less than 0.20 inch. The RIM query:

SELECT SIZE, WALL_THK FROM TUBES WHERE WALL_THK LT.20

will display the SIZE and WALL_THK attributes of the subset of tuples from the TUBES relation that have wall thicknesses up to 0.20 inch.

The Join operator is used to create a new relation in the database by merging two existing relations. The joining is controlled by naming a common attribute in each of the relations to be joined and by specifying a boolean relationship between these attributes. The result of a join is a new relation in the database that contains all of the attributes and data from both of the original relations. Using the structural engineering database of Table 13.3, assume that the user wants to know the sequence of pipes, and the length of each pipe. To obtain this information the following queries are issued:

JOIN SCHEDULE USING PIPE WITH ARRANGEMENT USING PIPE
    FORMING TEMP WHERE EQ
SELECT ALL FROM TEMP

This results in the creation of a new relation (TEMP) and displays all of its attributes and tuples as shown in Table 13.2.

13.4.3 Example database

The examples used in the remainder of this section are based on a small structural engineering database of piping information (extracted from the

American Institute of Steel Construction Manual for the Design, Fabrication, and Erection of Structural Steel for Buildings (AISC, 1980), which includes the following relations (Rasdorf *et al.*, 1986)

SCHEDULE (Pipe, Size, Length, Total_force),
PIPES (Size, Outside_dia, Inside_dia, Wall_thk, Weight, Area, I),
TUBES (Size, X_dim, Y_dim, Wall_thk, Weight, Area, Ix, Iy),
LOADS (Pipe, Load_type, Force), and
ARRANGEMENT (Pipe, Next_pipe, X_left, X_right, Y_left, Y_right).

The attributes are defined as follows:

Pipe	unique pipe identification number
Size	nominal pipe diameter in inches
Length	pipe length in feet
Total_force	total tensile force applied to pipe in pounds
Outside_dia	outside diameter of the pipe in inches
Inside_dia	inside diameter of the pipe in inches
X_dim	width of the tube in the X direction in inches
Y_dim	height of the tube in the Y direction in inches
Wall_thk	thickness of the pipe wall in inches
Weight	pipe weight in pounds per linear foot
Area	cross-sectional area of the pipe in square inches
Ix	moment of inertia of the tube in X direction in inches$**4$
Iy	moment of inertia of the tube in Y direction in inches$**4$
I	moment of inertia of the pipe in inches$**4$
Load_type	type of loading applied (e.g. dead load, wind load, etc.)
Force	magnitude of the applied tensile load in pounds
Next_pipe	pipe to the right of a given pipe
X_left	X coordinate of the left end of the pipe
X_right	X coordinate of the right end of the pipe
Y_left	Y coordinate of the left end of the pipe
Y_right	Y coordinate of the right end of the pipe

The SCHEDULE relation contains the schedule of pipes used on a specific project. Pipe indicates the label of each pipe, Size and Length specify its dimensions, and Total_force indicates the sum of the axial loads applied to it. The relation LOADS specifies the type of each individual load applied to a pipe (there may be more than one) and its magnitude.

The PIPES and TUBES relations describe the physical characteristics of various stock members including their wall thickness, weight, area, and moment of inertia. Additionally, for pipes, the inside and outside diameters are specified, and for tubes the *X* and *Y* outside dimensions are given. The relation ARRANGEMENT describes the plan layout of the piping configurations. Connectivity between pipe sections is given as well as end point coordinate locations. The data contained in the example piping database is shown in Table 13.3. This database adequately demonstrates the functionality of ADI.

Table 13.3 Example structural engineering PIPING databse

Schedule

Pipe	Size	Length	Total_force
P1	4	10.0	200.0
P2	4	5.0	500.0
P3	2	15.0	150.0
P4	$\frac{1}{2}$	25.0	50.0

Pipes

Size	Outside_dia	Inside_dia	Wall_thk	Weight	Area	I
$\frac{1}{2}$	0.840	0.622	0.109	0.85	0.25	0.017
2	2.375	2.067	0.154	3.65	1.07	0.666
4	4.500	4.026	0.237	10.79	3.17	7.230

Tubes

Size	X_dim	Y_dim	Wall_thk	Weight	Area	Ix	Iy
3×2	3.00	2.00	0.1875	5.59	1.64	1.86	0.98
4×2	4.00	2.00	0.1875	6.86	2.02	3.87	1.29
4×3	4.00	3.00	0.2500	10.50	3.09	6.45	4.10

Loads

Pipe	Load_type	Force
P1	Live load	200.0
P2	Dead load	200.0
P2	Live load	300.0
P3	Dead load	150.0
P4	Dead load	50.0

Arrangement

Pipe	Next_pipe	X_left	X_right	Y_left	Y_right
P1	P2	0.00	10.00	0.00	0.00
P2	P3	10.00	10.00	0.00	5.00
P3	P4	10.00	25.00	5.00	5.00
P4	none	25.00	40.00	5.00	25.00

13.4.4 Interface structure

Figure 13.2 shows ADI's relationship to the other components of an engineering information system. ADI is intended to be used by both designers at terminals and by application programs. As the figure shows, ADI's position within an organization's computer system is between its users and its databases. ADI communicates with the DBMSs through the DBMS's API and its DQL.

In the initial application, ADI uses RIM as the target DBMS. ADI is viewed simply as another application program using the RIM API (Erickson *et al.*, 1981). It neither alters RIM, nor does it interfere with existing application programs that might use the RIM API. In this manner ADI expands an organization's data retrieval capabilities without disrupting any of its ongoing operations.

ADI uses a query language based on relational algebra rather than a formal language such as SQL (Date, 1981) because of its simplicity, generic nature, its wide acceptance in the field of database research, and the ongoing effort to establish it as a standard. For an example of the use of the query language, consider the structural engineering PIPING database discussed above. To use ADI to determine the nominal size, area, and moment of inertia of

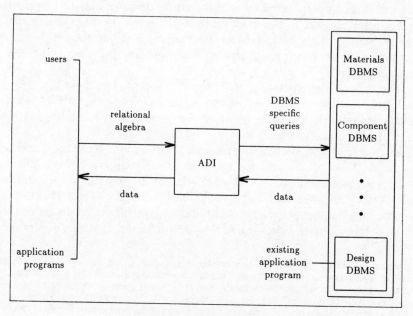

Fig. 13.2 ADI environment.

```
type attribute = element
{
      name:       symbol;
      relation:   symbol;
      database:   symbol;
      DBMS:       symbol;
}
```

Fig. 13.3 Definition of ADI schema representation.

available pipe sections that have a diameter less than 3.00 inches, a user or application program would issue the following relational algebra style query:

select size, area, inertia where od < 3.0

One of the key features of ADI is its ability to directly access a database's schema. This feature enables ADI to quickly locate data when presented with a query such as that given above. To insure that the names and locations of the attributes are known while respecting the dynamic nature of the databases' schemas, ADI reads the database schemas directly into ADI working memory and creates a time stamp, also in working memory, that identifies the name of the database, the name of the DBMS, and the date and time that the schema was read in. Note that there is *no global schema*; the local database schema is read, interpreted, and used at the time that an initial query is made. Subsequent accesses to the same local database can use the same internal representation of the local schema, provided that it has been in working memory for less than a predetermined length of time.* System consistency is thus assured.

The internal representation of each attribute in the database is a unique identity, as shown in Fig. 13.3. Attributes are identified by attribute name, relation name, the database in which they reside, and the DBMS which operates on that database.

In the event that an attribute name that is given in a user's query cannot be found directly by examining the internal representation of the schema, ADI reads in an optional SYNONYMS relation, if it exists, from the database (see Table 13.4). The information contained in the SYNONYMS relation equates any number of synonyms with the actual attributes of an underlying local database thereby allowing ADI to determine, for example, if attributes

---

*By accessing the working memory representation of the schema, load time is reduced; however, after a specified period of time the working memory representation of the schema must be discarded. The next access to that database causes the rebuilding of the working memory representation of the local schema. This is more reasonable than reading the local schema into working memory each time the database is to be accessed, yet it insures periodic reinitialization so that working memory remains current.

Table 13.4 Selected synonyms from the PIPING database

Synonym	Actual
girder	beam
pipe_number	pipe
pipe_name	pipe
inertia	i
od	outside_dia
id	inside_dia

girder and *beam* are equivalent within the context of that particular database. A SYNONYMS relation provides one means of hiding naming conventions from database users. If the SYNONYMS relation does not exist, ADI must ask the user for definitions of unknown attributes.

13.4.5 Theory of operation

In ADI the knowledge that a human uses to locate database relations to satisfy queries is stored in rules in a knowledge base. In OPS83 and other expert system frameworks, these rules are cast in the standard 'if... then...' form of production rules (See Section 2.2.3). ADI uses the knowledge embedded in this framework to determine which relations to query to obtain the data from the underlying databases. The knowledge base also contains knowledge about how to create joins and projections to assemble the requested collection of data.

Figure 13.4 shows an example OPS83 rule from the ADI knowledge base.

```
rule adi_va_2
--
--   Make the whereclause attribute a query attribute.  This is
--   done to insure that we use all the information that is
--   available to us in the search for relation(s) to query.
--
{
    &1 (goal  action = verify_attributes;  status = active);
    &2 (wclause);
     ~ (attrib  name = &2.watt);
    -->
    make (attrib  name = &2.watt;  set_by = |ADI|);
};
```

Fig. 13.4 A rule from the ADI knowledge base.

This rule is used to break a query into separate elements in ADI's working memory so that they can be interpreted prior to searching the database. For every attribute in a query, ADI creates an *attrib* in working memory. ADI uses all of the attributes available from a user's query, including the attributes in the where clause. Since an attribute may appear in a user's query more than once, ADI must avoid making duplicate *attribs* in working memory. The rule in Fig. 13.4 is used to determine if the attribute in the where clause of the user's query can be used as an *attrib* in working memory. In particular, this rule keeps ADI from making duplicate *attribs* in working memory; human experts do the same thing. In a human expert this knowledge is not given much thought. It is, nonetheless, an important part of the process of searching through the database schema to find the requested data. For a complete listing of the ADI knowledge base, see Watson and Rasdorf (1986).

The rule consists of the conditions necessary to invoke the rule, and the actions to be taken if the conditions are met. The conditions state that in order for this rule to be fired, the working memory must contain a *goal* element of active status whose action is to verify attributes. There must also exist an element known as a *wclause*, and there must not be an *attrib* element whose name is the same as the name of the *wclause* element. If the above conditions are met, then ADI can create an *attrib* in working memory that has the same name as the *wclause*.

The first step in interpreting a user's query is to accept the input, check it for form and completeness, and parse it into ADI's internal representation. ADI's internal representation consists of *attribs* and *wclauses*. The example query from the previous section (select size, area, i, where od < 3.00) would be parsed by ADI into three *attribs* (SIZE, AREA, and INERTIA) and a single *wclause* (OD LT 3.00).

```
attrib
   name      = OD

synonym
   syn       = OD
   actual    = OUTSIDE_DIA

attribute
   name      = OUTSIDE_DIA
   relation  = PIPES
   database  = PIPING
   DBMS      = RIM
```

Fig. 13.5 ADI working memory before synonym match.

```
attrib
   name       = OUTSIDE_DIA

synonym
   syn        = OD
   actual     = OUTSIDE_DIA

attribute
   name       = OUTSIDE_DIA
   relation   = PIPES
   database   = PIPING
   DBMS       = RIM
```

Fig. 13.6 ADI working memory after synonym match.

Once the parser has interpreted the query, the *attrib*s must be matched against the actual names used in the database. ADI does this by first reading the database's schema into working memory as described above. Next, it tries to find a match between the *attrib* and a schema attribute name. If a match is not found, ADI tries to match the *attrib* against a schema relation name. If neither of these attempts is successful, ADI looks for the SYNONYMS relation in the database. If it is found, the relation is read into working memory just as the schema was read. ADI then tries to match the *attrib* to a synonym in the SYNONYMS relation. If a match is found, the *attrib* is replaced by the actual attribute name. For example, suppose that ADI working memory contains the elements shown in Fig. 13.5. The *attrib* OD does not match against any schema attribute name. It does, however, match against a synonym element. When ADI finds this match, it modifies the *attrib* name from OD to OUTSIDE_DIA which is the actual attribute name in the database. The result of the modification is shown in Fig. 13.6.

If ADI is not able to verify that the *attrib* name is an actual attribute name, a relation name, or a synonym, it must ask the user for a definition of the *attrib*. If the user cannot define the *attrib*, ADI must fail the query.

13.4.6 Query building

Once ADI has parsed the user's query and verified the *attrib*s, it can decide how to get the requested information from the system. There are, of course, many cases to consider and many ways to solve the problem. ADI solves the problem using a sequential method similar to human problem-solving methods. ADI handles three major classes of queries: single-relation queries, queries which require joins between relations, and random queries.

(a) *Single-relation queries*

The simplest user query is one containing the key word *select* followed by a relation name (or a synonym for a relation name). One such query might be:

   select pipes

ADI recognizes this single-relation class of query rapidly, notes that the user wishes to retrieve all of the attributes in the relation, and generates commands using the local DBMS's DQL to retrieve the data. ADI would generate the following commands for the RIM DBMS and PIPING database to satisfy this data request:

   OPEN PIPING
   SELECT ALL FROM PIPES

A slightly more complex case arises when the user's query specifies the names of attributes from a relation in addition to the relation name. Such a query might be:

   select size, pipes, od, id

ADI cannot tell from the context whether the user is interested in only the named attributes *size, od* and *id*, or is in fact interested in the contents of the entire PIPES relation which is also specified. ADI makes conservative assumptions and judgements, so it will generate a request for the entire content of the relation:

   OPEN PIPING
   SELECT ALL FROM PIPES

Another case of a single-relation query is one in which only the names of attributes are specified. To satisfy this type of query ADI must find the single, unique relation which contains all of the *attrib*s. For example, the user query given previously:

   select size, area, i, where od < 3.00

will result in the ADI generated commands:

   OPEN PIPING
   SELECT SIZE, AREA, I FROM PIPES WHERE OUTSIDE_DIA LT 3.0

This is the case of a single-relation projection.

In all of the single-relation queries, ADI tries to find a unique relation in the database from which it can extract the required design data. If it cannot find a unique relation, it will try to form a join of two relations as discussed below.

(b) *Joins*

Joins are a more interesting and complicated class of query. A join is necessary when a user's query requires information from more than one relation. A join is accomplished by combining the relations over an attribute which is common to all of the participating relations. The result of the join is a new, temporary relation. The required data is then projected from this temporary relation. After the data has been extracted, the temporary relation is deleted from the database.

As an example of a query that requires a join on two relations, consider the following:

```
select pipe_number, length, next_pipe
```

As discussed previously, ADI will parse the query and verify the *attribs*. ADI will then try to find a single relation to satisfy the request as discussed in the previous section. When it is unable to find a single relation, ADI will try to find relations that contain at least two of the requested *attribs*. In this case, the attributes PIPE and LENGTH occur in relation SCHEDULE and the attributes PIPE and NEXT_PIPE occur in relation ARRANGEMENT.

Because two distinct relations have been found, ADI will generate the following RIM commands to join them and satisfy the user's data request:

```
OPEN PIPING
JOIN SCHEDULE USING PIPE WITH ARRANGEMENT USING PIPE
    FORMING ADITMP1
SELECT PIPE LENGTH NEXT_PIPE FROM ADITMP1
REMOVE ADITMP1
```

The data to be returned will tell the requester all of the pipe numbers, their associated lengths, and the next pipe to which they connect.

(c) *Random queries*

A random query is one for which ADI cannot find any relationships between its attributes and cannot, therefore, satisfy the user's data request. Using the RIM DBMS and the PIPING database as examples again, such a query might be:

```
select od, width
```

ADI will parse this query, read in the PIPING schema and the SYNONYMS relation, and find that the *attribs* OUTSIDE_DIA and X_DIM are indeed attribute names in the PIPING database. These attributes do not occur together in any of the same relations, however. Since the attributes exhibit no relationship to one another, ADI is unable to create any commands to

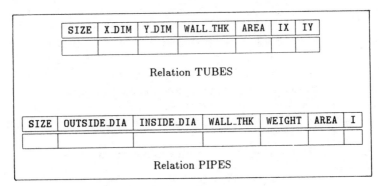

SIZE	X_DIM	Y_DIM	WALL_THK	AREA	IX	IY

Relation TUBES

SIZE	OUTSIDE_DIA	INSIDE_DIA	WALL_THK	WEIGHT	AREA	I

Relation PIPES

Fig. 13.7 Schema of two relations from the PIPING database.

retrieve meaningful data using this combination of attributes. The query fails and a message is issued to the user explaining the lack of known relationships.

Closer examination of the example will show why the query must fail. While there is no relation in the database that contains both OUTSIDE_DIA and X_DIM, there are two relations that contain one of them. These are PIPES and TUBES, the schemas of which are shown in Fig. 13.7. For these relations, *most* of the attributes are common to both relations.

Given that the user has requested OUTSIDE_DIA and X_DIM, how can ADI generate commands to retrieve meaningful data? If ADI were to join these two relations on the key (in this case SIZE, which acts as a pipe identification number), no matches will take place during the join because pipes and tubes have different identification numbers. The result is an empty join. If ADI should join on AREA, the result of the join would be information about pipes and tubes which have the same area. If ADI should join on WALL_THK, the result of the join would be information about pipes and tubes which have the same wall thickness. Clearly, ADI has no way to determine which join will result in information that first, is meaningful to the user, and second, is what he or she wants. The query must fail because the two requested attributes have no meaningful relationship to each other.

To clarify an ambiguous random query such as this, the user must specify a third attribute – one common to both relations. As explained in the previous section on joins, a user's query must give ADI at least this amount of information so that it can decide how to perform a join between relations.

13.4.7 Current status

An initial prototype of ADI was completed using the expert system framework M.1 (Watson, 1986). The prototype was a demonstration effort that established a proof of concept upon which the current OPS83 ADI program is based. At the present time the OPS83 prototype includes a forward chaining inference engine that fires the production rules, the interfaces to RIM and to the human user at the keyboard, and debugging tools that allow the knowledge engineer to examine the OPS83 conflict set and working memory.

The inference engine incorporates a means of determining the 'cost' of firing a rule which enables, during the conflict-resolution procedure, those rules with the lowest cost to be fired before those with a higher cost. This method of controlling when rules within a conflict set (those that match a given goal) are fired eliminates, to some extent, the requirement for rules in the knowledge base whose sole function is to direct the flow of control of the problem-solving process (Balaban and Nelson, 1985).

The ADI user interface (called the parser) has been completed. The parser is used by ADI to gather input from the user. It accepts the user's query and the answer to questions that ADI may ask. The parser incorporates some aspects of a 'user friendly' environment in that it accepts a variety of word separators (usually punctuation such as commas, but extended to cover most nonalphanumeric characters). The parser is of the free-format variety and places no restrictions on the use of interword spacing. It also checks queries to determine their conformance to the relational algebra style and converts the user's query into the internal representation used by ADI.

ADI incorporates an interface to the API library of RIM (Erickson *et al.*, 1981). This interface is used by ADI when it reads the schema or the SYNONYMS relation from a database. The interface consists of algorithmic subroutines which call the subroutines contained in the RIM API.

The ADI knowledge base contains a portion of the knowledge that a human user uses to locate, access and retrieve design data from an engineering database (Watson, 1986). ADI can now solve all forms of the single-relation query, it can solve problems involving random queries, and it can handle two-relation joins. ADI's output consists of the correct sequence of commands to retrieve data from a database. At present, ADI does not invoke the RIM DQL directly but rather, utilizes its programming language interface.

13.5 SYSTEM EVOLUTION

Before ADI is completed its functionality must be increased. ADI must, for example, be able to use the schema manipulation operations *join* and *project* in support of performing a complete set of multirelation data accesses. These database schema manipulation capabilities and others are being added to ADI on a continuing basis.

In addition to query capabilities, ADI must also be able to handle database *insert*, *delete*, and *update* operations. Additional levels must be added to the knowledge base to achieve this functionality. These data manipulation operations are required of a complete database interface and constitute the

DML. At the present time, ADI handles only DQL operations. Future development should extend its capabilities to include DML operations.

To be fully functional, the ADI system must be able to create and communicate with subprocesses. In order for ADI to access the PIPING database using the RIM DBMS, for example, ADI must create a subprocess for RIM and communicate with RIM through the RIM DQL. This is necessary since the RIM API does not support a *join* operator. Other DBMSs that do offer a full set of operators through the API will not require a subprocess.

Since there are normally several DBMSs in an engineering environment, ADI should be extended to allow access to several commercial DBMSs. These DBMSs should be representative of the different commonly available models (relational, network, and hierarchical) as well.

When a fully functional system is developed, performance studies will be run. Of interest is the performance of ADI versus other expert systems, DBMS interfaces, and human experts for satisfying engineering information needs.

13.6 OBSERVATIONS

Work to date with ADI has yielded some interesting results and a few observations. First, a very important and often overlooked characteristic of an expert is the speed with which the expert can accomplish a task or solve a problem. The OPS83 version of ADI is a compiled expert system. The compiler takes great advantage of pointers and stores and accesses knowledge in somewhat the same way that a DBMS stores and accesses data. Although ADI cannot be as fast as a DBMS's own DQL, it does seem to be considerably faster than other expert systems (Forgy *et al.*, 1984). In addition, the enhanced performance of OPS83 may offset the speed lost by copying the local database schema into working memory on the first query to a database.

Writing device drivers that connect ADI to the underlying DBMS is a task of varying difficulty. Nearly all widely available commercial DBMSs support interfaces to applications written in a variety of programming languages. The difficulty of interfacing to the DBMS is related to the complexity of the local DBMS's API. In many cases, it may be more straightforward to run the DBMS as a subprocess to ADI and communicate with it through the DBMS's own DQL rather than through the API. The choice of whether to use the API or the DQL is mostly one of implementation. The decision must be made on an individual basis when considering the use of various DBMSs. There is nothing inherent in ADI which is partial to either approach.

The ADI system does *not* use a global schema to create a global picture of the available data resource. ADI, therefore, avoids schema redundancy and inconsistency. By avoiding the need for a global schema, ADI decreases the workload on the DBA. The DBA does not have to continuously update the global schema to reflect changes that have been made to the local schemas. ADI picks up these changes automatically from the local schemas themselves.

ADI has presently satisfied most of the design goals that were established for the prototype. It accomplishes data hiding by the use of synonyms. It permits the addition of new DBMSs with little impact on users or current applications programs. Finally, it does more than simple query translation. ADI contains a portion of the knowledge necessary to *operate* a DBMS.

13.7 SUMMARY

Building design, construction, operation, maintenance, and control are all processes that have achieved various levels of computer use. Although the degree of computerization varies significantly, one common aspect of the computing needs of each process is an abundance of data in the form of tables, standards, project definition information, catalogs, etc. In most cases this data is stored in files which are independently used for input to stand-alone single-process application programs, such as a structural analysis application. The utility of these independent files is limited.

As concepts of integration of engineering applications evolved, the use of databases and DBMSs increased. Two issues of significant concern emerged. First, there is a need to retrieve data from many independent, possibly widely distributed databases. Second, there is a need for a uniform means of doing so. This chapter described a knowledge-based expert system that provides access to and integration of the many underlying databases needed to support the building design/construction process. The unique aspect of the expert system presented in this chapter is its capture of the knowledge that a human possesses for operating large computer programs. In doing so it formalized the levels of complexity of that knowledge and pointed out the multi-disciplined applications of the research results.

REFERENCES

AISC, (1980) *Specification for the Design, Fabrication, and Erection of Structural Steel for Buildings*, 8th edn, American Institute of Steel Construction, Chicago, Illinois.

Balaban, D. and Nelson, D. (1985) Flat is not necessarily good. *Processings of Computers in Engineering Conference 1985*, **3**. American Society of Mechanical Engineers Boston, USA, pp. 361–4.

Barkmeyer, E., Mitchell, M., Mikkilineni, K., Su, S. and Lam, H. (1986) *An Architecture for Distributed Data Management in Computer Integrated Manufacturing*, National Bureau of Standards, Gaithersburg, Maryland United States Department of Commerce Report NBSIR 86-3312.

Barwise, J. and Perry, J. (1983) *Situations and Attitudes*, The MIT Press, Cambridge, Massachusetts.

Brill, D. and Templeton, M. (1984) Distributed query processing strategies in MERMAID a frontend to data management systems, *Proceedings of International Conference on Data Engineering 1984*. The Institute of Electrical and Electronics Engineers, Los Angeles, USA, pp. 211–18.

Date, C.J. (1981) *An Introduction to Database Systems*, 3rd edn, Addison-Wesley Reading, Massachusetts.

Erickson, W.J., Gray, F.P. and Limbach, G (1981) *Relational Information Management System*, User Guide Version 5.0, Boeing Commercial Airplane Co., Seattle, Washington.

Esculier, C.L. (1984) The SIRIUS-DELTA Architecture: A Framework for Co-Operating Database Systems, *Computer Networks*, **8**, 43–8.

Fenves, S. J., and Rasdorf, W. J. (1985) Treatment of Engineering Design Constraints in a Relational Database, *Engineering with Computers*, **1**, No. 1, 27–37.

Fenves, S.J. and Rasdorf, W.J. (1982) Role of database management systems in structural engineering, *Proceedings of the IABSE Colloquium on Informatics in Structural Engineering*, International Association of Bridge and Structural Engineers (IABSE), Bergamo, Italy, pp. 229–42.

Forgy, C.L. (1985) *OPS83 User's Manual and Report*, Production Systems Technologies, Pittsburg, Pennsylvania.

Forgy, C.L., Gupta, A., Newell, A. and Wedig, R. (1984) Initial assessment of architectures for production systems, *Proceedings of the National Conference on Artificial Intelligence*, American Association for Artificial Intelligence, pp. 116–20.

Howard, C. and Rehak, D. (1985) Knowledge-based database management for expert systems. *SIGART Newsletter*, No. 92, pp. 95–7.

Jacobs, B.E. (1985) *Applied Database Logic I*, Prentice Hall, Englewood Cliffs, New Jersey.

Jacobson, G., Lafond, C., Nyberg, E. and Shapiro, G. (1986) An Intelligent Database Assistant, *IEEE Expert*, pp. 65–78.

Judson, D.L. (1986) Integrated information support systems, *CIM Technology*, pp. 23–30.

Lafue, G.M.E. (1983) Basic decisions about linking an expert system with a DBMS: a case study, *Database Engineering*, **6**, No. 4, 56–64.

Maher, M., and Howard, C. (1985) Accessing design databases from expert systems, *SIGART Newsletter*, No. 92, 99–100.

Parker, D. (1985) Knowledge-based management systems simplify engineering and design, *Systems and Software*, pp. 109–14.

Rasdorf, W. and Parks, L. (1986) Expert Systems and Engineering Design Knowledge, *Proceedings of 9th Conference on Electronic Computation*, American Society of Civil Engineers, Birmingham, Alabama, pp. 28–42.

Rasdorf, W. and Salley, G. (1985) Generative engineering databases – toward expert systems, *Computers and Structures*, Pergamon Press, **20**, Nos 1–3, 11–15.

Rasdorf, W., Ulberg, K. and Baugh, J. (1986) A structure-based model of semantic integrity constraints for relational databases. *Engineering with Computers*, Springer Verlag, **2**, No. 1.

Rasdorf, W. and Watson, B. (1986) ADI: an adaptive database interface for dynamic databases, *Proceedings of the 1986 ASME Symposium on Knowledge-Based Expert Systems for Manufacturing*, American Society of Mechanical Engineers, Production Engineering Division, Anaheim, California.

Rehak, D. and Howard, C. (1985) Interfacing expert systems with design databases in integrated CAD systems, *Computer-Aided Design*, **17**, No. 9, 443–54.

Rehak, D., Howard, C. and Sriram, D. (1984) Architecture of an integrated knowledge based environment for structural engineering applications. *Knowledge Engineering in Computer-Aided Design*, Budapest, Hungary.

Rehak, D., Howard, C. and Sriram, D. (1983) *An Integrated Knowledge Based Structural Engineering Environment.* Unpublished project report, Department of Civil Engineering, Carnegie–Mellon University, Pittsburgh, Pennsylvania.

Rich, E. (1983) *Artificial Intelligence*, McGraw-Hill, New York.

Schaefer, M.J., Rehak, D.R. and Fenves, S.J. (1984) Introduction to relational databases using structural engineering examples. *Journal of Technical Topics in Civil Engineering*, **110**, No. 1, 1–18.

Smith, J.M., Bernstein, P.A., Dayal, U., Goodman, N., Landers, T., Lin, K.W.T. and Wong, E. (1981) Multibase – integrating heterogeneous distributed database systems. *American Federation of Information Processing Societies National Computer Conference Proceedings*, **50**, 487–99.

Ullman, J.D. (1980) *Principles of Database Systems*, Computer Science Press, Potomac, Maryland.

Vossen, G. and Brosda, V. (1985) A high-level user interface for update and retrieval in relational databases – language aspects (ed. S. Navathe), *Proceedings of ACM-SIGMOD 1985*, The Association for Computing Machinery, Austin, Texas, USA, pp. 343–53.

Watson, B.R. and Rasdorf, W.J. (1986) *Adaptive Database Interface: A Knowledge-Based Data Retrieval System*, User Guide version 2.0, Integrated Manufacturing Systems Engineering Institute, North Carolina State University, Raleigh, North Carolina.

Watson, B.R. (1986) *ADI: An Adaptive Database Interface for Dynamic Databases*, Final Project Report, Integrated Manufacturing Systems Engineering Institute, North Carolina State University, Raleigh, North Carolina.

14

Knowledge acquisition for expert systems in construction

GEOFFREY TRIMBLE

14.1 INTRODUCTION

The following points must be borne in mind in reading what follows:

1. The problems of knowledge acquisition for expert systems in construction are probably indistinguishable from those of knowledge acquisition in most other domains. The problems depend on the situation rather than the domain. By situation we mean such things as, the extent to which the knowledge is held in specific or intuitive (unconscious) form; the availability of the domain expert and his or her motivation; whether any of the information can be obtained from published material.
2. No formal methodologies have crystallized. Virtually all new expert systems are assembled *ad hoc* with few if any guidelines as to the methods that will prove most fruitful.
3. The number of working expert systems in the 'real world' of construction can probably be numbered on one hand, or at most two. By a 'real world' system we mean a system that has been commissioned by a client who has specified what the system should do and knows why he or she wants it and why it should be of the form specified.

Although this chapter is entitled 'knowledge acquisition for expert systems in construction' comment is also included, particularly in Section 14.2 on the selection of appropriate domains.

The contents of this chapter draw extensively on the experience of the author and his colleagues. This includes

- The development of CONPLANT, a demonstration system to select appropriate materials handling equipment on site.
- The development of BREDAMP, a system to diagnose the cause of dampness in buildings.

BREDAMP was commissioned by the (British) Building Research Establishment. Work on it reinforced our view that only 'real world' systems can provide useful guidance on knowledge acquisition. This observation has influenced the group in its later development of CRANES, a tightly focused system to select appropriate cranes for multistorey construction and to assess the appropriateness of pumping concrete. In this application the host contractor has agreed to act as though he were our client and is ensuring that the final system will be of real practical value. In particular he is insisting that buildings must be treated as irregular three-dimensional solids. The system therefore incorporates an interactive graphics module in addition to modules dealing with the more general aspects and the calculation of the required crane hours.

14.2 INITIAL OBSERVATIONS

Within construction a variety of domains can be identified, for example

1. Codifying topics that have hitherto been largely undefined (e.g. selecting appropriate construction plant).
2. Ensuring that nothing gets overlooked (e.g. the check points in a building design).
3. Providing positive guidance in interpreting regulations (e.g. Fire Regulations).
4. Providing pointers to strategic design (e.g. the type of heating system as amplified in the text).

An early step in creating an expert system is to decide whether the proposed domain is suitable. It is clear that certain types of domain are very much more suitable than others. In particular, if the system comprises a set of defined goals with rules that lead to these goals, then it is likely to prove successful. Thus systems to diagnose faults or to select from a set of pre-defined pieces of advice are particularly suitable. Claims about expert systems that 'design' should be examined critically. On examination they usually turn out to be one of two forms. The first is an hierarchical selection process, the second is a process whereby the user generates trial solutions and the system analyses these solutions and offers comment. As an example of an hierarchical approach we could cite the design of a heating system. The first stage might select waterborne heating as the appropriate type; the second might select from a range of possible radiator or convector types and so on. In each case all the possibilities will have been pre-defined. Design is clearly a knowledge-based process and in due course it can be confidently predicted that successful and practical expert system approaches to design will be developed. This is an area for careful research and not for current application.

The identification of the goals of the system is a crucial part of the preparation of the system. The following list of types of application defines, in each case, the goals that such a system would incorporate. It is included to help readers to assess whether their own possible applications can be represented in a suitable format.

- In a system to advise on the appropriate scheduling and control method the goals may include 'Direct preparation of a bar chart'; 'Network analysis'; 'Line of balance'; 'Resource-oriented scheduling with parallel strategy'.
- A system to diagnose faults in a diesel engine would include goals such as 'The fault lies in the circulating pump'. The other goals would represent faults in other components.
- A system to advise on the staffing of contracts would have as its goals the names of the possible key personnel.

In some cases the goals will be found and given some probability rating. Two more examples follow.

- A system to diagnose the cause of dampness in buildings would have goals that correspond to the pre-defined possible causes such as 'rising damp'; 'rain penetration'; 'condensation'. This system would probably search for all the causes (now defined as goals) and attach a probability to each one that it has not specifically eliminated.
- A system to advise a design construct contractor on whether or not to bid would have only one goal. This would be evaluated by some numbered scale which can be selected to suit the user. Some of the questions may be posed in the form 'Rate the technical sophistication in the range -5 to $+5$'. The user would be expected to interpret -5 as very simple and $+5$ as very sophisticated. If this rating scale has been used extensively during the dialogue the user may feel comfortable with a recommendation that also uses the -5 to $+5$ scale.

14.3 SITUATIONS THAT AFFECT THE ACQUISITION PROCESS

It is clear that the nature of the situation within which the knowledge is acquired will have a major influence on the method(s) to be selected. The categories so far identified are

1. The knowledge is held in largely intuitive undefined format.
2. As category 1 but some closely similar domains have been examined.
3. Cases can be defined that reflect a body of decision-making within the domain.
4. There is published material about the domain.
5. The domain expert has sufficient knowledge about expert systems to enable

him or her to define the knowledge (or at least to play a significant role in its definition).

Superimposed on this list of categories are other dimensions such as

1. The 'depth' of knowledge to be represented, i.e. does it represent fundamental knowledge such as that relating to molecular structure or 'heuristic' knowledge which includes a substantial amount of personal opinion.
2. The extent to which a consensus among experts can be found.

The foregoing categories are now elaborated.

14.3.1 Intuitive knowledge

Some knowledge engineers favour a method which requires the development of a prototype system based very often on the prior knowledge of the knowledge engineer. The prototype is demonstrated to the domain expert who suggests modifications and amplification. The changes are made and the revised system demonstrated again. The iterations of this process continue until the domain expert is satisfied and the model is acceptable. If a good initial model is produced this method can be very productive. However, it can have the effect of prejudicing the responses of the expert and thus diverting him or her from some of the subtle, more intuitive knowledge, that might be of crucial importance to the operation of the system. An alternative is to start with a blank sheet of paper and ask the domain expert to tell you what he or she knows. A fairly extensive set of knowledge is then assembled before the initial system is coded. This approach is fundamentally better but its success is critically dependent on the time that the domain expert can devote to the process.

14.3.2 Intuitive knowledge with precedents

Where systems have been produced for very similar domains it is usually safe to introduce a short-cut in the form of structured interviews based on the content of the previous systems. The danger of prejudicing responses must always be borne in mind.

14.3.3 Defined cases

There are several computer programs that will induce rules from sets of cases. Of these EXPERT-EASE (see Section 4.4.1) is probably the simplest and best known. At first sight this approach has much to recommend it. However, extensive trials of the early programs have revealed some disconcerting problems. One of these is that the natural sequence of questioning that is inherent in a domain is not respected. For example a pair of questions might be

- Is the pipe a drain?
- Have you performed a drain-test?

If the sequence of these questions is reversed as it often is in rule-induction the confidence of the user will quickly evaporate. Another problem is that, like regression analysis, rule-induction works on cases irrespective of any causal connections.

It is not, of course, imperative to use the rule-induction program. Manual inspection of sets of cases will often indicate relationships that can be coded on an ad hoc basis.

14.3.4 Published material

There is a lot of interest in the use of expert systems to guide users in the interpretation of regulations and codes of practice. Clearly, in this situation, there should be no problem of human interaction as the views of the human expert should be fully recorded in the published text. As an aside it should be noted that attempts to 'computerize' regulations were made before the recent surge of interest in expert sytems. These attempts often revealed inconsistency and vagueness which made full 'computerization' difficult. Some investigators have suggested that this should be anticipated as differences between the views of the members of the drafting committee eventually have to be resolved by compromise.

14.3.5 Coding by the expert

When domain experts are also reasonably competent users of computers it is often possible for them to produce their own expert system without the use of an intermediary. They may or may not be inclined to use an expert system shell to assist them (and constrain them) in their endeavours.

14.4 SELECTING THE METHOD

The previous section identifies the following methods of knowledge acquisition

- Unstructured interviews.
- Structured interviews.
- Prototype system evolved iteratively.
- Rule induction.

To this list should be added

- Observational.

In this additional method the knowledge engineer observes the domain experts as they perform tasks which require them to draw on their expertise.

Our studies started with the view that we should be able to isolate situations (or combinations of factors) that would point to the selection of a single method. Our experience has not borne out this view and for example in one of our applications four different methods were used at different stages. Thus our current advice is to acquire a feel for the alternative methods and to use them flexibly as the position unfolds. The following comments augment those in the preceding section.

Unstructured interviewing has the great merit of not prejudicing the responses of the domain expert. Thus less obvious points emerge that can be very important. The method however is time consuming and requires patience on the part of the expert.

Structured interviewing achieves results quickly and is appropriate when the knowledge engineer is fairly confident of his or her understanding of the domain. This understanding may result from prior knowledge or from the results of earlier acquisition methods.

Prototyping has much to recommend it particularly as each iteration can provide cues to prompt experts in their thoughts about their intuitive knowledge. As with structured interviewing there is a danger that less obvious points may get overlooked.

The author has little experience of the observational method. However, it must be a beneficial approach in providing at least the initial evidence that the knowledge engineer will require in structuring the problem.

Rule induction appears to be satisfactory for simple well-defined applications. However, for applications even of quite modest levels of complexity we have found that rules prepared by induction are unsatisfactory for direct incorporation in the system. Despite these shortcomings we have found that attempts to apply rule induction to limited modules of a total application can force the expert into considering factors that are not revealed by other methods. This must improve the validity of the knowledge base even though the induced rules are themselves discarded.

14.5 SOME OF THE FINDINGS TO DATE

So far the great variety of domains that have been attempted and the approaches adopted have made generalized analysis virtually impossible. However, one conclusion is inescapable, namely that there are at least two distinct kinds of situation, i.e.

1. A client has identified his or her own need for an expert system and engaged an employee or contractor to deliver a system to the client's requirements.
2. An enthusiast, typically an academic, has defined an interesting application and has persuaded host organizations to provide relevant knowledge.

Our main finding to date is that the nature of the relationship between the client (or host organization) and the knowledge engineer is of crucial importance. Where a client has defined his or her own needs it is likely that the experts will be readily available and that they will be uninhibited by company policy and commercial confidentiality. They may still be inhibited by their own motivations. At one extreme they may be eager to impart the knowledge in order that the expert system will eventually relieve them of routine tasks which have degenerated into boring chores. At the other extreme they may fear that revealing their knowledge will undermine their own security and generate a situation where they become redundant. Where an application is undertaken by an enthusiast who has defined his or her own objectives the experts will be less readily available and may be strongly inhibited by commercial consider-ations. This type of situation however may be more fruitful in revealing deeper, intuitive knowledge, provided that the knowledge engineer can encourage the experts to join him or her in the research objective, i.e. that of revealing hitherto uncharted relationships.

14.6 SOME OF THE PRACTICAL ISSUES

Some domains lend themselves to a definitive approach in which questions are given specific answers and recommendations are given by the system without equivocation. Others require the use of some form of probability. The PROSPECTOR system (see Section 1.8.3) generates a number of derivatives and all depend on Bayes theorem. An example will illustrate this and show another facet of knowledge acquisition.

BREDAMP is an expert system commissioned by the (British) Building Research Establishment and assembled by the author in association with Roger Allwood. Its purpose is to diagnose the cause of dampness in buildings. It was coded using the shell SAVOIR which permits the use of conditions, fuzzy logic, and probability and to do so in combination. For example, there are several conditions that will totally rule out 'rising damp' as the cause of dampness. These conditions can be tested first and if this cause has not been eliminated its probability will then be calculated using Bayes theorem to combine the effects of several factors.

The domain expert was almost certainly unrepresentative of domain experts in that he had defined knowledge in very explicit terms. He had himself tried to capture it in some form of computer program but had not had access to an expert system shell. Despite this background there remained a communication problem as the use of Bayes theorem requires the assessment of the negative and affirmative factors that it processes. It would have been impractical to get Bayes factors from the expert directly. The method adopted was first to identify all the goals (i.e. the causes of dampness which were to become the basis of diagnosis) and then to discuss with the expert the factors that he would associate with each. Having discussed a cause and the associated factors the author was able to draw up a table of representative situations, e.g.

Factor	Suggested values	
Evidence	A stain	A stain
Height	9 inches	15 inches
Age of building	8 years	9 years
Component wetter inside than out	Yes	Don't know
Positive salts test	Don't know	Yes
Probability of rising damp	?	?

These tables were put to the expert who was able to assess the probability in each case on the basis of the experience he has accumulated over 20 years. The use of regression analysis then enabled Bayes factors to be calculated where appropriate. The conditional relationships were identified, by normal interview techniques.

This case illustrates two further points, namely confidence limits and knowledge base verification. At present BREDAMP offers only a set of probabilities for each of the defined causes of dampness. For example

Rising damp	90%
Rain penetration	27%
Others	less than 5%

The rising damp figure may in fact mean that the probability is in the range 89–91% or it may mean that it is in the range 80–100%. Users would react differently if they had these ranges available. With a narrow range they are likely to conclude that they have gone as far as the system will allow and they may then decide to take remedial measures to cure the problem on the assumption that the cause is in fact rising damp. If the wider range (80–100) is shown they will probably undertake additional, quite cheap, tests to improve the reliability of their diagnosis. This extension of the information provided by a system has been mentioned in several contexts, but no actual implementation has so far been identified by the author.

The second point revealed by BREDAMP, and indeed any medium to large system, is that verifying a knowledge base is a much bigger problem than verifying a computer program. An algorithmic program usually has a quite limited number of alternative computational paths but the alternatives through a medium-sized knowledge base are prodigious. A possible testing procedure, not so far implemented, would be to use the prototype expert system as part of a simulator. Thus, a range of answers could be specified for each question and automatically processed by the system. The results could be recorded and graphed, so providing succinct records of the system behavior.

Domain experts can reasonably be expected to comment on output summarized graphically where it would be impractical to have them examine tabulations of all the possible results.

14.7 HUMAN FACTORS

Knowledge acquisition for expert systems is a human process and several of the human aspects have already been mentioned. The purpose of this section is to itemize the human problems that arise so that readers can be aware of them. This is not to suggest that we can yet offer solutions; the process is likely to remain largely *ad hoc* for some time. Before proceeding it is worth reminding ourselves what the process of knowledge acquisition is, namely the transfer and transformation of knowledge from some source (usually human) to a computer program.

14.7.1 Resistance

Domain experts may fear that, by giving up their knowledge, they will weaken their position within their organization. Unless some incentive can be engineered such experts are unlikely to provide the basis for a useful system. Organizational resistance may also arise and has been observed in the Community Clubs established in Britain by the Alvey Directorate. For example, one club member may provide an expert but then realize that commercially valuable skills could be transmitted via the system to a competitor. It should be noted, on the other hand, that positive motivation may be encountered when an expert is bored with providing personal advice in one subject and would welcome the chance to have this process automated.

14.7.2 Accessibility and prejudicing responses

Experts may have the necessary knowledge and motivation but may have other duties that prevent their spending an adequate amount of time with the knowledge engineer. We have already mentioned the dangers of prejudicing responses by over-structuring interviews and by offering detailed prototypes. However, the methods that prejudice responses are usually quicker so some compromise will often be necessary.

14.7.3 Cues and examples

Experts are often better at doing things than explaining what they are doing and why. So one method of obtaining knowledge is to watch experts at work and then ask why they did what they did. The problem is that experts often cannot recall from their subconscious the rules and relationships that have become intuitive. A method that also deals with this problem is to generate artificial examples as cues and to ask the experts what they would do in these circumstances. Our experience in obtaining the Bayes factors for BREDAMP is an illustration of this method.

14.7.4 Rapport and roles

It does not need a psychologist to identify the fact that the knowledge acquisition process will proceed more smoothly and effectively when a rapport is established between the knowledge engineer and the domain expert. As a corollary to this, it is usually better to separate the tasks of knowledge acquisition from those of coding the information for the computer. This enables the knowledge engineer to concentrate on the knowledge as perceived by the expert and on establishing a good human relationship with him or her.

14.8 CONCLUSIONS

The following are offered as reminders of the key points in this chapter.

1. Knowledge acquisition methods depend much more on situation than on domain.
2. Formal methodologies have not yet crystallized.
3. Very few real world systems exist for construction domains.
4. The system is more likely to succeed if it is goal oriented i.e. leading to a pre-defined piece of advice or diagnosis.
5. Using a computer program to induce rules from cases may provide some enlightenment but is unlikely to provide working rules except perhaps for simple systems.
6. Regulations often contain logical inconsistencies.
7. An ideal situation in which to produce an expert system is one in which there is a clearly defined 'client' who knows what kind of system he or she wants and how he or she will use it.
8. Even with a very responsive expert, ascertaining Bayes factors is best done by examples.
9. We should be looking for more sophisticated systems that attach a form of reliability measure to their answers.
10. Verifying a knowledge base carries special problems and the use of the system as a simulator may provide a partial solution.
11. Human beings and organizations may have strong motivation against (or sometimes for) providing knowledge.
12. Offered solutions can prejudice responses but may be necessary when time is at a premium.
13. Cues and examples can help in recalling intuitively held knowledge.

14. There are many arguments in favour of separating the roles of knowledge acquisition from that of computer coding. Amongst these arguments is that the separation of roles leaves the knowledge engineer free to establish effective rapport with the domain expert.

REFERENCES

Welbank, M. (1983) *A Review of Knowledge Acquisition Techniques for Expert Systems*, British Telecom Research Laboratories, UK.

Gotts, N.M. (1984) *Knowledge Acquisition for Medical Expert Systems – a Review*, Artificial Intelligence in Medicine Group, University of Sussex, UK.

Buchanan, B.G. (1985) *Some Approaches to Knowledge Acquisition*, Department of Computer Science, Stanford University, UK.

15

Codes and rules and their roles as constraints in expert systems for structural design

SHUICHI FUKUDA

15.1 DESIGN: WHY IS IT DIFFICULT?

Expert systems can be classified roughly as analysis (or diagnostic) type and synthesis (or design) type. What makes the development of a design type expert system difficult is that the goal is not uniquely determined.

Let us consider a jigsaw puzzle for example. If we are trying to assemble one jigsaw puzzle into shape, then it is relatively easy, since as we go on, the number of pieces needed for pattern matching decreases. But let us imagine another game where several different jigsaw puzzles are disassembled and we would like to assemble one of them into shape. In this case, the number of pieces needed for pattern matching does not decrease as we proceed. What makes this game complicated is that the goal is not uniquely known at the outset. Which goal will be reached or which jigsaw puzzle will be completed is determined by which pieces have been used. In other words, we have not only many routes but also many goals.

Let us consider another example. Suppose we wish to support some load on the wall (Fig. 15.1). If we try to support it with a cantilever, the cantilever itself and the fixed end must be very strong. But suppose we add an oblique member such as that shown in Fig. 15.1 as broken lines; the cantilever member could be substituted with a less strong one. What should be stressed here is that if we focus our attention only on securing the strength of a cantilever beam there is a possibility that we will be unable to obtain the solution if the load is too heavy or if we do not have an appropriate size member. But if we look at the problem from different viewpoints and try to support the load with two members instead of one, then the strength or part of the fabrication problem such as attaching the member to the wall could be greatly reduced. This kind of change of viewpoint is quite difficult to deal with in conventional programming.

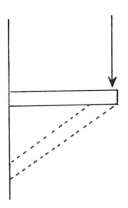

Fig. 15.1 Design model.

Apart from the discussion of changes of viewpoint, design is an inverse process in problem-solving procedures even from a fixed viewpoint. Conventional programming has been trying to solve the problem under given conditions, i.e. for example, we try to find the stress or strain of a structural member with a given geometry. But design is fundamentally the other way around. We have our goals, i.e. desired stress or strain, for example, and what we try to do in design is to find the geometry or to set up appropriate connectivities of structural members to realize such a stress or strain. In this sense, design is an inverse analysis. What makes inverse analyses difficult is again that unlike regular analyses solutions are not uniquely determined.

15.2 STRUCTURAL DESIGN: THE ROLE OF CODES, STANDARDS, AND REGULATIONS

What should be stressed about structural design is that structures are designed based on codes, standards, and regulations. Structural design could, therefore, be described as a process of demonstrating and justifying that the design models and their changes comply with the requirements of the codes, standards, and regulations.

The primary role of codes, standards, and regulations is to set constraints in the lines of reasoning. We have a wide variety of design models to choose from and if there are no constraints, we at once come across the problem of combinatorial explosion as can easily be imagined from the above example of a jigsaw puzzle. Thus, one of their important roles is initially to set the search space within reasonable limits. These intial conditions are so to speak inputs in the conventional programming. The search space they set up will be narrowed later during the TSS (Time Sharing System) session, but it will not be broadened.

So they are sometimes called 'hard' constraints. Thus the fundamental role of 'hard' constraints is to reduce the number of candidates or design models.

Another role of codes, standards, and regulations is to provide negotiable constraints or 'soft' constraints. This type of constraint will be changed if necessary during the TSS session. Its primary role is to guide us through the proper routes or lines of reasoning. What is important in this latter role is that the constraints may be relaxed if necessary while in the former role they are fixed until the end of the analysis. Therefore, the 'hard' constraints reduce the number of alternatives while the 'soft' ones select the better alternatives through negotiation.

Most of the numerical analyses up to now are the 'regular' type so that their initial or boundary conditions are 'hard' constraints. If the analysis is inverse, the problem is solved by trial and error. Therefore, soft constraints constitute a characteristic feature of an expert system.

Past structural analyses place great emphasis on the aspect of numerical processing, but symbolic processing takes a great portion of structural design as can easily be understood from the above discussion. Therefore, it is of the utmost importance to know how to re-interpret design codes, standards, and regulations as constraints in an expert system for structural design, since the design goal is reached by constraint-driven applications of procedures.

15.3 DESIGN CODES, STANDARDS AND REGULATIONS: PAST AND PRESENT

Past laws and regulations are 'closed' within themselves so that the final solution can be obtained by using them alone. Or, in other words, most of the laws are 'hard' constraints. Those of the present day, on the other hand, are becoming more and more 'open' and they leave many matters to the decision of the designer. Thus designers have a much wider choice than previously. For example, they can use either empirical formulae or finite element methods or some other numerical analyses or experimental results if they so desire. What is important is that this is not merely a matter of choosing the right tool, i.e. if they choose a certain tool at a certain stage of reasoning, then the constraints propagated will change. Thus, the more open the rules become, the more there are spaces for negotiation so that the number of possible combinations increases. In short, modern rules leave as much space for negotiation as possible and expect that designers will justify the procedures they take. Therefore, an expert system is expected to serve a great deal for this purpose and thus the management of constraints is a vital part of the system.

In the following sections, we will first describe the outline of our system DEST and then discuss how design codes, rules or regulations may be represented as constraints with the practical example of an oil storage tank, based on our experience of developing DEST (a prototype of *D*esign Support

*E*xpert System for Oil *S*torage *T*anks) (Fukuda, 1985; Fukuda and Moto-oka, 1985; Fukuda, 1986).

15.4 OUTLINE OF DEST

15.4.1 Purpose of development

DEST was developed in an attempt to establish a generic methodology for the preliminary design support of a structure which is produced to order or in small quantities. The design procedures for these kinds of structure are repeated individually from structure to structure and there are, therefore, more trials and errors in decision-making. Thus, the burden on the design engineer is very heavy.

The aim of our system is to aid the designer in making a preliminary design or in determining the rough size and geometry for a more detailed design. We already have such versatile and useful tools as finite element analysis, etc., but what seems to be more needed now to alleviate the burden of designers of a structure of this kind is to provide them with more exact knowledge of the boundary conditions in which they are working. However, the boundary conditions are not fixed at all from the beginning. In the case of a mass-produced product, it is not difficult to recognize what the boundary conditions are. But in the case of structures produced only in small quantities, the design conditions differ appreciably from case to case so that preliminary designs become more important.

Codes, standards, and regulations are our wisdom to lighten the burden of the designer. They are aggregations of pieces of past experience and collections of available engineering and technological knowledge. In the past designers were properly guided toward their goal by referring to these codes, standards, and regulations. But today codes and standards are becoming more and more open than before and leave many matters to the decision of the designer as was described in the previous section. And even if they are closed, they are becoming more and more complicated so that expertise is required to know how to apply them reasonably. Past structural analysis placed great emphasis on the aspect of numerical processing, but the part of the design procedures that consists mostly of symbolic processing and is carried out by trial and error is not computerized so much as other parts where numerical processing is involved. What we are trying to pursue here is to computerize the 'design' portion because the 'analysis' portion has already been computerized to a large extent.

However, numerical processing plays quite an important role in structural design. Although the great majority of past expert systems are more oriented toward developing better inference mechanisms and put more emphasis on symbolic processing, numerical data and their processing are no less or rather more important than symbolic processing as far as structural design is concerned. Thus, what differentiates an expert system for structural design from those for other fields is that the coupling of numerical and symbolic processing is most important. Therefore, what we are attempting here is to provide a basic methodology for developing a preprocessor for detailed design of a structure.

15.4.2 Motivation: why did we choose an oil storage tank?

As may be understood from the description of the previous section, it is not our aim to develop a system for very limited applications. Although we would like our system to be practical, we would like it to be versatile at the same time.

We chose an oil storage tank because although the structure is very simple, there are still many problems pressing for solution such as corrosion and earthquake. As corrosion and earthquake conditions differ very widely from structure to structure and from location to location, the problem must be examined individually for each case and further the growing variations of contents and increasing capacities calls for modification of present day design codes, standards, and regulations to correspond to rapidly changing design conditions.

Thus, the situation being what it is, the codes, standards and regulations must be updated more quickly than ever before, at least for an oil storage tank. The situations are similar for other structures, too. These structures, however, are more complicated and their design codes are too voluminous. It is our understanding that basic methodologies will be the same for any kind of structure. Thus we chose an oil storage tank as a good example.

15.4.3 Why is an expert system used?

As has been described previously, the symbolic processing portion of design procedures plays a fundamental role in setting the design subgoals and the final goal. The decision-making is performed at this stage and is carried out by trial and error. Therefore, to computerize this portion, the system must be flexible enough to cope with an extensive variation of problems and must be capable of rapid updating. The conventional programming method of decribing design procedures in an algorithmic manner is thus not adequate for the present purpose.

Further, expertise and/or experience play quite an important role in decision-making and in facilitating its accomplishment. It is more often the case that some members have already been checked and proven to comply with the requirements of the codes, standards, and regulations, and all we have to do is to demonstrate that other newly designed members comply. If we know which members are already checked in the past design and proven to be structurally sound by past operations, then we can utilize the results without repeating the procedure and analyzing it again, thus greatly reducing the amount of labor.

In preliminary structural design, it is not always the case that all relevant information is supplied beforehand. In some of the procedures we have to use, default values are generated through past design and operation experience.

Thus, the design goal and subgoals are pursued by the constraint-driven application of procedures. The solution to this kind of problem we have today is an expert system.

15.4.4 The hardware and programming environment

DEST was implemented on HITAC M280H using PROLOG/KR and FORTRAN. The program size is approximately 1 MB. Frames are fundamentally used for knowledge representation and are described in PROLOG. Procedural attachment and meta-knowledge as to when to call a necessary frame are described using PROLOG/KR's LISP function. Although this UTILISP permits floating point numerical calculations, the size of numerical computation is very much greater. Therefore FORTRAN was used for complicated and large-scaled numerical calculations, because it processes them much faster and a large number of FORTRAN packages include graphic primitives.

As too many numerical data are generated in such structural analysis as the finite element method (FEM), files are used to transfer numerical data between PROLOG and FORTRAN. Simple calculations such as thickness calculations based on primary membrane stress or checking of buckling strength for shell plates are carried out using LISP, since UTILISP supports floating point calculations. The reason we used files is that we often have to abandon PROLOG and return to the OS (Operating System) level to carry out large numerical processing, and sometimes because the numerical calculation itself is too large to be carried out in a TSS environment due to the limitation of computer resources so that it is much more conveniently processed in a batch mode. For example, soil–structure interaction is a problem of this kind. The use of files has another advantage. As PROLOG/KR is implemented only at the University of Tokyo as far as universities are concerned, this system was developed at the University of Tokyo on one occasion and on other occasions through the university network system N-1 in Japan. But this network system does not support graphic data transmission so that we can transmit only characters. If we utilize files, then we can use another FORTRAN graphic package at Osaka University. Thus we can reduce machine dependence to a considerable degree.

15.4.5 Knowledge base

Our knowledge base was constructed primarily on the basis of HPI (1978, 1979 and 1980), JIS (1976) and Shiroko (1981). These are the documents on laws, standards, and regulations on the design and related problems of an oil storage tank. The knowledge is at present restricted to the design of a main tank. We hope to extend it in the future to include attachments or accessory members. It is expected that far better interaction between the design of the tank itself and the design of the attachments or accessories could then be secured, thus greatly reducing the often observed failures due to a mismatch between them.

DEST performs the following:

1. Determination of the basic geometric form of a tank based on codes, standards, and regulations. Many heuristic rules are stored and utilized as necessary such as the relations between diameter and capacity, between capacity and diameter/total height and anticipated loadings, etc.
2. Selection of materials for shell, annular and base plates. Material selection appreciably affects the basic geometric form of a tank.
3. Determination of shell plate thickness considering circumferential stress (primary membrane stress) due to liquid pressure and the minimum thickness limitation set by the law which takes the corrosion margin into account. This value is checked against buckling strength during an earthquake and is modified if necessary.
4. Determination of the base plate thickness. This calls for a large numerical calculation such as FEM. Simplified versions such as beam theory calculations could be substituted if so desired.
5. Structural stability is checked against wind and/or earthquake.

A sample of a CRT screen is shown in Fig. 15.2. Thus, DEST carries out the preliminary design and part of the detailed design of a tank itself. We are now attempting to expand it to more detailed design which would require more practical knowledge of fabrication such as plate arrangement, selection of welded joint type, etc. As this portion of design is not on the whole legally codified yet and many choices are left to the designer, a better man–machine interface must be provided, and it is interesting to know that there are many AI-oriented problems such as the solution of geometrical interference, the combination of design and fabrication, etc. A difficulty is expected, however, regarding the means of acquiring knowledge, since this portion of structural design is at present carried out purely on an industrial and commercial basis and there is little public documentation available.

In the next section, we discuss how codes and standards are represented as constraints and how they are managed in order to guide us toward our goal.

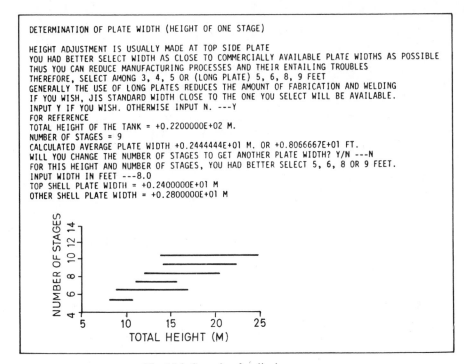

```
DETERMINATION OF PLATE WIDTH (HEIGHT OF ONE STAGE)

HEIGHT ADJUSTMENT IS USUALLY MADE AT TOP SIDE PLATE
YOU HAD BETTER SELECT WIDTH AS CLOSE TO COMMERCIALLY AVAILABLE PLATE WIDTHS AS POSSIBLE
THUS YOU CAN REDUCE MANUFACTURING PROCESSES AND THEIR ENTAILING TROUBLES
THEREFORE, SELECT AMONG 3, 4, 5 OR (LONG PLATE) 5, 6, 8, 9 FEET
GENERALLY THE USE OF LONG PLATES REDUCES THE AMOUNT OF FABRICATION AND WELDING
IF YOU WISH, JIS STANDARD WIDTH CLOSE TO THE ONE YOU SELECT WILL BE AVAILABLE.
INPUT Y IF YOU WISH. OTHERWISE INPUT N. ---Y
FOR REFERENCE
TOTAL HEIGHT OF THE TANK = +0.2200000E+02 M.
NUMBER OF STAGES = 9
CALCULATED AVERAGE PLATE WIDTH +0.2444444E+01 M. OR +0.8066667E+01 FT.
WILL YOU CHANGE THE NUMBER OF STAGES TO GET ANOTHER PLATE WIDTH? Y/N ---N
FOR THIS HEIGHT AND NUMBER OF STAGES, YOU HAD BETTER SELECT 5, 6, 8 OR 9 FEET.
INPUT WIDTH IN FEET ---8.0
TOP SHELL PLATE WIDTH = +0.2400000E+01 M
OTHER SHELL PLATE WIDTH = +0.2800000E+01 M
```

Fig. 15.2 Sample of a display screen.

15.5 CONSTRAINT MANAGEMENT

Laws and regulations thus specify not only physical boundary conditions but also logical networks. Our system DEST contains rules in the form of frames which are written in PROLOG/KR (Nakashima, 1983). PROLOG/KR is written in UTILISP (Chikayama, 1981).

PROLOG/KR (KR stands for knowledge representation) was developed to deal with both declarative and procedural types of knowledge. In structural design, both of these types appear; we use tables or databases for selecting material which is typically declarative type knowledge and most of the design codes are procedural. PROLOG/KR can be used either as PROLOG or as LISP according to the type of knowledge although primarily it is, of course, PROLOG. We can utilize, therefore, the strong pattern-matching function of PROLOG and we can also add a complicated inference control mechanism in the same manner as in LISP. PROLOG is indeed useful for utilizing tabular knowledge because we can retrieve information forward and backward due to PROLOG's unification.

Design is a succession of goal-oriented procedures and PROLOG is very convenient in specifying what goal will be next, but how to reach that goal is more easily described in LISP. In PROLOG/KR, programs and data are completely identical in form, i.e. they are expressed as lists. Thus, a program is just a special case of data so that meta-level descriptions such as the predicates for control become as easy as in LISP.

PROLOG/KR also provides reasonable arithmetic and can manipulate floating-point data. Complicated arithmetic can be processed by calling LISP functions. As numeric information plays an important role in structural design, the capability of manipulation of floating-point data is a prerequisite for the programming environment. To facilitate the processing, we used some other method as well to represent numeric data. That is, we calculate beforehand, put the numerical results into tabular form and either by interpolating or by extrapolating obtain the numeric data. If we utilize this kind of method, PROLOG's backtracking and unification functions can be used very effectively.

There are two kinds of inference control mechanism in our system. One is the utilization of PROLOG/KR's world mechanism shown in Fig. 15.3, which provides priorities for the application of laws and regulations and thus determines which logical network to take.

The other is a constraint control mechanism which features our system. As PROLOG essentially does not have global variables and each variable is only valid for each assertion, it is sometimes very incovenient in terms of constraint propagation, because in the case of hard constraints, such values of variables as relate to specifications, for example, will be propagated without change until the end. And it is often the case that we have to temporarily preserve constraint status until later, to the point where we have to relax some of the constraints and come back to the related node again.

To propagate such constraints appropriately and to find adequate back-tracking points for the revision of search space, it is necessary to develop some control mechanism because PROLOG's embedded control strategy is too simple, i.e. to backtrack to the last node immediately before. To cope with such constraint propagation, it is necessary to discriminate values which are to be preserved from those which are not, and to determine when to rewrite them.

The mechanism we developed is based on the utilization of the specially prepared predicate DEFINED-RANGE for defining ranges for variables and their values. Constraints are propagated through these defined ranges and we can trace upward or downward hierarchically so that the present constraint values can be easily known and we can also find an appropriate backtracking

Fig. 15.3 Law hierarchy.

point by referring to these defined ranges. Thus, these defined ranges also serve as a controller for preventing a combinatorial explosion.

Each variable is classified either as numerical or as choice (symbolic). Numerical is for the numerics and sets the upper and lower bound. If the numerical value obtained falls outside these bounds, then the prescribed diagnostic action will be taken; that is, backtracking within the node or backtracking to the previous node, or backtracking to the specified node takes place. Choice is for selecting discrete symbolic values such as material HT60 (high (60 kg/mm^2) tensile strength steel), and multiple choice is also permitted. As the reasoning goes on, the number of elements in the CHOICE list decreases. Thus, the upper and lower bounds in the numerical type variables and the CHOICE lists in the symbolic type variables determine the search space.

Although these DEFINED-RANGE definitions primarily provide bases for controlling, the CONSTRAINT-CONTROL frame is prepared for overall

```
----------------------------------------------------------------------
FRAME:INITIAL
 CONTENT:CRUDE-OIL
 CAPACITY:100000
 DIAMETER:80

     .

     .

 LOCATION: TOWN-A
  demon: "set next frame to check-law applicable to
          town A"
NEXT-FRAME:CHECK-LAW
----------------------------------------------------------------------
----------------------------------------------------------------------
FRAME:CHECK-LAW
 TOWN:A
 PREFECTURE: D
 CONTENT:
  demon: "check content proc"

   .

   .

 MATERIAL:
  demon: "fill in the slot according to the law proc"

   .

 NEXT-FRAME:INITIAL-CONSTRAINT
----------------------------------------------------------------------
```

Fig. 15.4 Constraint management (to continue).

```
--------------------------------------------------------------
FRAME: INITIAL CONSTRAINT
  CONTENT: CRUDE-OIL

    .
    .
  MATERIAL: [SS41, SM41A, ......]
    .
    .
  BOTTOM-SHELL-PLATE-THICKNESS:[10, 50]
    .
  NEXT-FRAME:
   demon: "select appropriate next-frame proc"
--------------------------------------------------------------


--------------------------------------------------------------
FRAME: CONSTRAINT-CONTROL
  CONTENT: CRUDE-OIL
   STATUS: FIXED
    .
    .
  MATERIAL: [SS41, SM41A]
   STATUS: FIXED
    .
  BOTTOM-SHELL-PLATE-THICKNESS: 15
   STATUS: NEGOTIABLE
    .
    .
--------------------------------------------------------------
```

Fig. 15.4 Constraint management.

control strategy. By referring to this frame, we can backtrack to an appropriate node and reset the search space.

As the TSS session begins and a user specifies initial conditions, such as in which part of the country the tank is going to be installed, the preprocessing constraint mechanism selects the appropriate logical network and sends the corresponding default values to the frames for constraint control (Fig. 15.4). Regarding the constraints which do not receive any message from the constraint preprocessor (laws and regulations), they are filled in with 'common sense' values. Therefore, the values of all variables of a global nature have defined ranges.

15.6 CONSTRAINT REPRESENTATION

Constraints are fundamentally classified here as either of the two types described before: hard or soft. There are two types of hard constraint to be exact; one is as given by the constraint preprocessors (laws and regulations). They provide so to speak 'the initial or boundary conditions of the problem'. The other type of hard constraint is as determined at that node alone or as either satisfied or violated at that node in the TSS session. If we come across this type of node, we have to make our decisions there and we cannot postpone them later to subsequent nodes.

For example, a town law such as 'The total height of a tank must be less than 22 m' provides the hard constraint of the first type and a rule such as 'If mild steel is used for the bottom shell plate, SM41C (Japanese industrial standard mild steel) must be used for the annular plates' is the second type, because the first limitation determines the specification itself or the initial condition and the second statement has to be satisfied if such a condition was derived during the TSS session. If we cannot satisfy this rule at this node (MATERIAL-SELECTION-FOR-ANNULAR-PLATE) and if there are 'soft' constraint nodes prior to this node, we backtrack to one of these 'soft' constraint nodes again and take a different rule, thus following another different logical link. And we may not visit this node again. In this case, we might change the side shell plate thickness to that required where the tank is without annular plates.

Generally those statements in laws or regulations that contain the words 'should' or 'must' provide hard constraints. It must be noted, however, that if there are choices or the values cannot be determined as a single value, then they are 'soft' constraints. Such a rule as 'If the thickness of the bottom shell plates exceeds 15 mm, then the material must be SM41C or SM50C' provides 'soft' constraints, because we can choose either SM41C or SM50C and take a different logical link, i.e. we might have to come back to this node again when we have to reset the search space in order to find a proper solution. But we must be careful if the choice is multiple, i.e. if we take as the material the list (SM41C, SM50C), it then becomes 'hard' because the list transferred to the next node is unique. In short, if the rule is invoked once, then it is 'hard' and if it has the possibility of being invoked more than once, then it is 'soft'. Thus, the evaluation of a number usually gives a 'hard' constraint but the calculations themselves do not.

Such a rule as 'The instalment of annular plates is desirable' is a 'soft' constraint because if we first start out to go without annular plates and it turns out later in the TSS session that we cannot secure the strength without annular plates, we come back to this node again and restart tracing the different logical links of tank construction with annular plates.

Preferences or styles of a designer are 'soft' constraints. Skilled designers have their own style and they turn 'soft' constraints into 'hard' ones

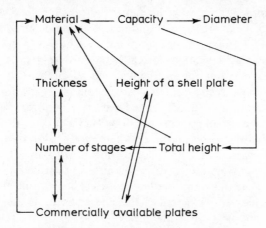

Fig. 15.5 Style of a designer: an example.

according to their style, thereby narrowing the search space for more effective problem-solving (Fig. 15.5). Such preferences or styles are satified in our system by providing special predicates. These predicates consist of a chain of goals, thus skilled designers can specify the goal orders and where to turn 'soft' constraints into 'hard' ones.

It must also be mentioned that there are cases where a solution cannot be found within the search space specified by a user. The user may possibly be a novice but even if very skilled, there are such cases. In such a case our system takes the most commitment action and invokes the constraint control mechanism to properly reset the search space. To cope with this situation, the predicate PREFER is prepared and heuristic rules are invoked and the old constraints are superseded by the new constraints. These new constraints are hard ones so that it may be that we start all over again from the beginning with different boundary conditions.

For example, if we have difficulty in determining the thickness of a base plate for the construction of a tank without annular plates, then such rules as the instalment of annular plates and the corresponding range of thicknesses of base plates are activated by the computer based on stored heuristic rules.

The principle of our system is to maintain the least commitment policy so that lazy evaluation is adopted. That is, suppose we have OR-parallelism in our goals; $A_1 \nabla A_2 \nabla \cdots \nabla A_n$. If the backtracking is shallow, i.e. the failure occurs at such a shallow level of A_1, A_2, then we do not have much trouble. The real problem occurs when the backtracking is deep, i.e., A_{n-1} or A_n fails. In the real computation, each A_i consists of a chain of goals so that the enormous amount of time and memory space will be exhausted. If we could satisfy ourselves only with possible solutions for $A_1 \nabla A_2 \ldots \nabla A_n$, or with the solution of a set of all possible solutions, then all shallow backtrackings are terminated when the set is obtained. Thus we can reduce the number of possible deep backtrackings, searching goal by goal for the next candidate. But conversely, unless this OR-parallelism part is terminated, we cannot move on further in the computation where deep backtracking might be called for. To solve this problem, we adopted the lazy evaluation technique which computes the above set successively when called by need, instead of computing it all at once.

In practical terms, we define a range for every global variable, so that we start out with a wide set of possible solutions. As we go on with the reasoning, we visit a node in the logical network where many rules (they are recast as frames to be exact) are stored and they constitute OR-parallelism. Unless we prepare a range for every global variable and take the rule for satisfied if the rule does not violate this range, we have to select a right rule at this node. In other words, we have to evaluate the value related to this node with accuracy. Otherwise, we cannot go on to the next node.

In our system, on the other hand, we can choose any rule at this node as long as it does not violate the defined ranges and go on to the next node. And as we go on, there is a possibility that we cannot go any further unless we choose another more appropriate rule at this node. At this point, the precise evaluation at this node is called for and we backtrack to this node for the final selection of the appropriate rule.

This kind of inference control mechanism was contrived because **PROLOG** is provided with a built-in control mechanism of backtracking, and we have to develop a control mechanism compatible with this one. But this mechanism has a great advantage. As the evaluation is done in 'lazy' mode, we can take our time and wait and see what other constraints would be, and then finally make a decision. In short, we do not have to make decisions on the spot. We are allowed to make them in broader perspective.

15.7 SUMMARY

We briefly described our expert system DEST for the support of the preliminary structural design of an oil storage tank, and discussed how codes and regulations can be reinterpreted as constraints for an expert system for structural design.

What we should like to emphasize here is that structural design, especially the preliminary design, is nothing more than a process of demonstrating compliance with the requirements of the codes, standards, and regulations and of justifying the design and its changes. Codes, standards, and regulations are our natural language way of expressing constraints. Thus, although past structural analysis placed great emphasis on the aspect of numerical processing, symbolic processing plays a large part in structural design. Decision-making in design is carried out more or less by trial and error, so that the algorithmic representation of design procedures is not adequate. An expert system approach, however, permits the constraint-driven application of rules, which therefore represent our designing processes more appropriately. Thus, the reinterpretation of codes, standards, and regulations for computer processing is a fundamental issue of the greatest importance for structural design.

REFERENCES

Chikayama, T. (1981) *Utilisp Manual*, Computer Centre, University of Tokyo.

Fukuda, S. (1985) Development of a computer based consultation system for preventing structural failures using Prolog, *Structural Safety and Reliability: Proceedings of 4th International Conference*, Vol. 1, Kobe, Japan, pp. 27–36.

Fukuda, S. and Moto-oka, T. (1985) Development of a design support system DEST-1 for oil storage tanks. *Computers in Engineering 1985*, **3**, ASME, 441–4.

Fukuda, S. (1986) Development of an expert system for the design support of an oil storage tank, *Applications of Artificial Intelligence in Engineering Problems: Proceedings of 1st International Conference*, Vol. 2, Southampton University, UK, pp. 791–6.

HPI (1978, 1979) *Engineering Standards and Safety of Oil Storage Tanks*, Japan High Pressure Institute, Tokyo (in Japanese).

HPI (1980) *Non-destructive Inspection and Reliability of Oil Storage Tanks*, Japan High Pressure Institute, Tokyo (in Japanese).

JIS (Japanese Industrial Standard) (1976) Welded steel tanks for oil storage, *JIS B8501*, Japanese Standards Association, Tokyo (in Japanese).

Nakashima, H. (1983) *Prolog/KR User's Manual*, Computer Centre, University of Tokyo.

Shiroko, T. (1981) *Design and Safety Management of Oil Storage Tanks*, Shisaku-Kenkyu-Center, Tokyo (in Japanese).

Index